OTHER BOOKS BY G. W. CHOUDHURY

Pakistan's External Relations (with Hasan Parvez), 1958

Constitutional Developments in Pakistan, 1959; revised edition 1968

Democracy in Pakistan, 1963

Documents and Speeches of the Constitution of Pakistan, 1967

G. W. CHOUDHURY

Pakistan's Relations with India

1947-1966

FREDERICK A. PRAEGER, *Publishers*

New York · Washington

BOOKS THAT MATTER

Published in the United States of America in 1968
by Frederick A. Praeger, Inc., Publishers
111 Fourth Avenue, New York, N.Y. 10003

© 1968, in London, England, by G. W. Choudhury

Library of Congress Catalog Card Number: 68-25336

Printed in Great Britain

To Pappu and Saad

CONTENTS

PREFACE

In 1957, I was requested by the Pakistan Institute of International Affairs to write a paper on Pakistan's External Relations. While writing the booklet for the Institute, I decided to work on a full and comprehensive account of the most important and dominating aspect of Pakistan's foreign policy: her relations with India. I could not turn then to the work, however, because of my preoccupation with two other books. Subsequently, in the 1960s, I was selected by the government of Pakistan to be a member of the Pakistan delegation to the United Nations General Assembly on several occasions. This gave me an opportunity to study Pakistan's external relations at closer quarters, and from 1964 I applied myself fully to the work on the present volume.

In the meantime, I received an invitation from the Association of Commonwealth Universities to go as a Commonwealth Visiting Fellow to the University of Cambridge, and St John's College was kind enough to offer its hospitality to me. This opportunity of coming to Cambridge has helped me greatly in my work. I am grateful to the members of the Faculty Board of History, and particularly to Professor Mansergh, for their kind initiative in offering me this visiting fellowship, which enabled me to complete my task.

I should also like to acknowledge here my debt to my wife, Dilara, for her encouragement and help during the period when I was writing the book, and for assistance, including the typing of the completed text, in putting the book into shape.

Although Pakistan's relations with India are the most important factor in her external relations, no work has yet been published on the subject giving a full account of Pakistan's unhappy and strained relations with her biggest neighbour. There have been several volumes from India dealing with her relations with Pakistan. The result has been that Pakistan's legitimate grievances and viewpoints have not been properly projected or appreciated. The object of this volume has been to review and analyse Pakistan's problems and her anxieties and fears in her relations with India, and how these factors have affected her foreign policy.

In matters where one's own country is involved in serious dispute with another, one's impartiality may be questioned. But there are, after all, facts and they may speak for themselves. I have made extensive references to and quotations from non-Pakistani scholarly sources, including documents and periodicals, together with the world press, to substantiate those facts. I sincerely hope that this volume will be of use to those who wish to understand Pakistan's perils and anxieties and her constant search for security in defence of her freedom.

G. W. CHOUDHURY

Pakistan's Relations with India, 1947–1966

INTRODUCTION

THE gravest discord between any two members of the Commonwealth of Nations is found between Pakistan and India. There exists
between them a state of tension at once weakening the economy of
both and threatening to pass from a state of cold war to actual conflict,
as has happened twice between 1947 and 1965. It is most tragic that
India and Pakistan have looked upon one another as enemies since
their independence, and that their relations with each other are charged
with an envenomed load of bigotry, prejudice, religious and national-
istic hostility. This is a bitter disappointment, not only to the people
of the two countries, but also to their friends and well-wishers all over
the world. Instead of the peace and progress which the people of both
countries expected, the years since independence have brought warfare, vituperation, frustration and fear.[1] Instead of devoting all their
resources to economic development, both countries have spent millions
of rupees on defence against each other. The subcontinent was split
by mutual consent, but the mistrust, antagonism and fear between the
two successor states of the British *Raj* persisted. The brave aims of both
countries to uplift their people's pitiably low standard of living have
been greatly hampered by their corrosive quarrels and conflicts. There
has been lack of co-operation between these two new Asian countries
in political, economic and financial matters; and not only lack of
co-operation: in many instances their policies have tended to aggravate
mutual difficulties. Indeed, Asia's ugliest unsolved problem has been
the constant bad relations between India and Pakistan. As a foreign
scholar has observed: 'The relations between India and Pakistan since
the partition of 1947 have been characterised by extreme tensions

much of the time, tension almost all of the time, economic blockade on one occasion . . . periodic threats of war and continuous ideological and political warfare which have produced, to put it mildly, a shambles in the relationship between these two countries.'[2]

Yet geography, defence, economic development and the welfare of the people of the two countries demand that they should live as good and friendly neighbours. Why is there mutual distrust and enmity? Why could not India and Pakistan live on friendly terms as do Norway and Sweden, whose union was dissolved with by no means unmitigated good will?

The roots of the trouble lie far back in history. Present day Indo-Pakistan tension is a prolongation of the Hindu-Muslim feelings that characterised India long before independence and partition. A full and comprehensive account of Indo-Pakistan relations cannot be made without going into the historical background of the Hindu-Muslim problem of undivided India. Was this problem merely a question of 'religious differences', as that phrase is understood in the West? Or were the basic differences fundamental which created maladjustment between the two peoples in almost every situation of their lives? To try to answer these questions, we give in chapter 1 a résumé of the Hindu-Muslim antagonism in India, particularly after the British government introduced the policy of 'progressive realisation' of responsible government in India. The experiments of representative institutions under the 'colonial democracy', rather than bringing the two communities nearer, served to widen the gulf.

When the British government in 1892 introduced, in a rudimentary way, the principle of election and representative institutions, the Muslims expressed their apprehension of being dominated by a majority with whom they differed in every sphere of life. The Muslim leader of this period, Sir Syed Ahmed, warned the Muslims against the dangers of majority-rule in India contending that 'the larger community would totally over-ride the interests of the smaller community'. This fear of domination by the Hindus governed the Muslim policies and actions; the Muslim minority in undivided India considered itself to be in perpetual danger of domination by an intolerant majority.

There were a number of attempts to bring a rapprochement between the two communities. The Lucknow Pact of 1916 is an example in point. In 1928, the Muslims of India under the leadership of Jinnah, the founder of Pakistan, made sincere attempts to solve the Hindu-Muslim problem. Their demands were modest: a true federal form of government with autonomy for the provinces so that the Muslims could govern their affairs in those areas where they were in a majority. The Congress leaders failed to appreciate the honest aims of Jinnah who was known, at that time, as the ambassador of Hindu-Muslim unity, and his efforts to solve India's constitutional problems by an honourable agreement between the two major communities came to a sad end.

Then, in 1937, came the opportunity for constructive co-operation between the two communities, when responsible government was introduced in the Indian provinces under the Government of India Act, 1935. Unhappily, the Muslims' offer of coalition government was turned down by the Congress, which then seemed to be intoxicated with power as a result of its victory in the elections. The result—the total exclusion of the Muslims under the first experiment of parliamentary democracy, with its principle of majority-rule—was disastrous. The Congress rule in the provinces from 1937 to 1939 was a real threat to the Muslims' political and economic interests and to their culture and cherished way of life. The Congress rule was marked by such systematic attacks on Muslim rights and their culture that the Muslims observed a 'Day of Deliverance' when that rule came to an end with the outbreak of the Second World War.

From this bitter experience of majority-rule in undivided India, the Muslims were driven to one alternative: a separate Muslim state. The vision of a separate state had already been expressed by the poet-philosopher Allama Iqbal in 1930, but it remained a 'poet's vision' until the implications of majority-rule in India were made clear to the Muslims by the Congress rule in the provinces.

The demand was formally proclaimed on March 23, 1940, and Jinnah declared that Hindus and Muslims were two nations by any definition or test of a nation. Pakistan was claimed as a homeland for Indian Muslims on the principle of the right of self-determination. But the idea of a separate Muslim state was totally abhorrent and repugnant to the Congress leaders, for whom the unity of India was an article of faith. Thus began the bitterest quarrel between the two communities. For the Muslims it was a struggle for survival; for the Hindus it was to avoid 'vivisection of the motherland'. When the British government finally decided to grant self-rule to India in 1946, the two communities were engaged in a bitter struggle involving violence and communal riots on a vast scale.

Finally, the partition of India was accepted and a 'truncated' and 'moth-eaten' Pakistan was carved out. Did the Indian leaders accept partition without mental reservations? This is the vital question which agitates the minds of Pakistanis to the present day.

The tragic events immediately before and after independence made good relations between the two countries almost impossible. The communal murder and mass migration gave them the worst possible start. As soon as the effects of these calamities were overcome, fresh sources of political and economic friction appeared. Quarrel followed quarrel. The most alarming development was India's resort to arms to settle the dispute over the accession of three princely states: Junagadh, Hyderabad and Kashmir. In less than five months after the attainment of independence, the two countries were on the verge of war over this issue, and in less than a year the armed forces of the two Commonwealth countries were in combat over the mountains in Kashmir.

What are the basic issues and facts in the Kashmir dispute, a dispute that led to a limited war in 1948 and to a fuller war in 1965—one involving the biggest tank battle since the Second World War? The trouble in Kashmir began in August 1947, when the Hindu maharaja wanted to accede to India against the wishes of the overwhelming majority of its population. India did not allow the rulers of Junagadh and Hyderabad to exercise the option of choosing one or the other dominion or to remain independent because it was alleged that the action contemplated or taken by these rulers seemed to be contrary to the wishes of the majority people of these states; but India sent her troops, tanks and aeroplanes to uphold the cause of an autocratic ruler who was engaged in killing and suppressing the people who rose against his tyrannical rule. Since India's military intervention in Kashmir in October 1948, the Kashmir dispute has kept Pakistan and India divided. The festering sore of this dispute has infected the relations of the two countries so seriously that it is responsible for their failure to reach agreement on any major issues. Until this dispute is settled, the threat of war in the subcontinent is bound to persist. Any effort to improve Indo-Pakistan relations, as was made at the Tashkent Conference in January 1966, is likely to come to grief over this dispute.

The Kashmir question was brought before the Security Council in January 1948. It has been before the Security Council ever since. The failure to reach an agreement lies clearly at the door of India. Nehru consistently made conditions for a plebiscite that would make a farce of it, and rejected every constructive proposal for a solution. India wanted a plebiscite in Kashmir but only if an Indian-installed government were functioning and the Indian army in control. Then, in 1953, India declared that her promise to hold a plebiscite was invalidated by Pakistan's changes in foreign policy, as if the right of self-determination for the people of Kashmir were dependent on Pakistan's following a particular foreign policy which must be approved in New Delhi. India's latest argument for refusing an internationally supervised vote in Kashmir is that, if the Muslims of Kashmir opt for Pakistan, the lives of India's 50 million Muslims would be endangered and her 'secularism' would be destroyed. Kashmir is needed as a showpiece for India's 'secularism'.

Whatever the Indian arguments might be, Pakistanis can never be expected to forget this problem because, to them, it looks like a matter of life and death. For ethnological, economic and strategic reasons, Pakistan cannot possibly allow a hostile or potentially hostile country to hold Kashmir.

There were other disputes; in fact, the history of Pakistan-India relations is chequered with disputes. The two countries were engaged in bitter trade and economic warfare in 1949, when India refused to accept Pakistan's decision not to devalue her currency following the devaluation of sterling and of the Indian rupee. This economic warfare caused hardship to the people of the two countries and added more bitterness to the political disputes. Economic tensions between India and Pakistan became a political matter. The economic war of attrition brought the trade between them to a complete standstill. Newspapers on both sides were clamouring for reprisals. The impact of the 'battle of the rupees' on the trade patterns of both countries has been profound and far-reaching. Since the trade war of 1949–50, Indo-Pakistan trade has never regained its former dimensions. The two countries, in their mutual distrust and conflict, tried to be independent of supplies from each other. The complementary character of the subcontinental economy was shattered for good.

In the 1950s, the two countries were 'on the edge of a precipice' in two successive years (1950 and 1951). A major crisis arose between them over resurgence of communal troubles in the two Bengals in early 1950. Nehru threatened Pakistan with 'other methods' and concentrated troops on her borders. Similarly, in 1951, when the so-called constituent assembly of Kashmir was summoned, Nehru made a demonstration of strength by massing practically the whole of India's armour on the borders of Pakistan. What an extraordinary freak of history it was that Nehru, the apostle of peaceful coexistence, should have pursued the old-fashioned policy of making troop demonstrations!

Pakistan and India, if they would have acted together, could have made a very valuable contribution to the maintaining of international peace. But, because of their perennial disputes, they have been pushed into an antagonism that threatens the peace and prosperity of the whole of South Asia and in its turn constitutes a grave menace to international peace and security. The feeling of mistrust between the two countries is perhaps nowhere more prominent than in the conduct of their foreign affairs. Mutual fear and distrust have warped the whole international outlook of the two nations, and the foreign policy of both countries has been perverted by their quarrels. While antipathy to Pakistan has been the pivot of India's foreign policy, the main aim of Pakistan's has been to obtain a shield against a possible attack from India, and to maintain her territorial integrity, repeatedly threatened by India.

As a foreign scholar puts it, the position is that India considers Pakistan a hostile state and Pakistan considers India a 'proven aggressor'; while another impartial interpreter says that, whatever might be the outward semblance, 'a cardinal underlying purpose of Indian policy was to keep her smaller neighbour weak and isolated, for eventual reabsorption'.[3] Indian foreign policy 'amounts to little more than the containment of Pakistan'.[4] No amount of Pandit Nehru's idealist oratory about *Panch Shila* or a 'third area of peace in Asia' or the 'Bandung Principles' could obscure India's unfriendly, if not hostile, policies and actions towards Pakistan. Even Nehru's policy of non-alignment was converted into anti-Pakistan attitudes.

The result has been a fundamental divergence of outlook in the foreign policies of the two countries. When, in the 1950s Pakistan turned to the West, it was not so much due to the contemporary 'fashionable' fear of international communism as to her fear of Indian aggression. When Pakistan joined the West, India turned to the USSR. The Soviet Union appeared to have perceived that antipathy to Pakistan was the pivot of Indian foreign policy. There was a sudden upsurge of Soviet-Indian friendship in 1954–55. Khrushchev during his visit to India in December 1955 attacked the partition of India in 1947 as the product of the British policy of 'divide and rule' and upheld India's stand on Kashmir.

Nehru seemed to be sensitive to anything in South Asia of which he was not the architect. India wants to establish a 'sphere of influence' in South Asia. Pakistan, however, reacts almost violently to any suggestion of Indian leadership in South Asia. This is natural in view of her experiences since independence; this attitude also has deep roots far back in history.

In the 1960s, India's friendship with China—*Hindi-Chini Bhai-Bhai* —was coming to an end. To the West, India's importance to the policy of 'containment' against China became more and more evident, while the needs of military alliances were no longer so important, and hence friendship with Pakistan was not so much appreciated. The Soviet Union, on the other hand, seemed to have second thoughts on her partisan attitude towards Indo-Pakistan disputes. The global interests of the big powers made great changes in the alignment of the two countries. Pakistan raised a protest against massive Western military aid to India following Sino-Indian border conflicts in 1962. She insisted that aid to India should not be of such magnitude as to upset seriously the balance between India and Pakistan. When the Western 'allies' did not listen to Pakistan's appeal or appreciate her anxieties, Pakistan became a disgruntled and grudging 'ally' of the West, and sought to normalise her relations with the Soviet Union and also with China, with whom a new friendship seemed to be growing.

An analysis of the course of Indo-Pakistan relations reveals that causes of the recurrent crises between them fall into two main categories. First, there are specific quarrels, such as Kashmir, border incidents, eviction of the Muslims from Assam and Tripura, the problems of the religious minorities in the two countries, and the conflicting aims and purposes of their foreign policies. Serious disputes also arise from the upheaval of partition, such as the division of assets of the formally undivided Indian government, and the sharing of the Indus Valley waters. Secondly, there are the different outlooks of the two countries, which shape the mental image that each has formed of the other and serve greatly to complicate their relations.[5] Behind the political and economic quarrels lie the more dangerous tensions based on prejudices, myths and age-old hatreds. India seems to regard Pakistan as the effective challenge to her ideal of a united India which the Congress leaders still continue to cherish and foster; Pakistan is regarded as the 'embodiment of all the principles that India denies'. Pakistan is also regarded as an intolerant theocratic state where the Hindu minorities 'may at best live on sufferance as helots'.

Many Indians seem to regard the creation of Pakistan as a tragic mistake which might still be corrected. Many Pakistanis have real fears about India's ultimate aim of reuniting the subcontinent. The fundamental cause of the animosity between India and Pakistan, many Pakistanis feel, is basically India's unwillingness to respect Pakistan as a sovereign state, to accept the reality of her existence. In their public statements, Indian leaders frequently made insufficient allowance for Pakistan's susceptibilities. They have indicated on many occasions that 'partition is merely a temporary division'; and hopes have often been expressed in India that 'seceding areas' would beg for reunion. Pakistanis believe that India regards their country as an ephemeral and unnatural product doomed to early collapse—which the Indian government appears, in the eyes of many Pakistanis, to be hastening by all measures.

The real problem is mistrust. The outstanding disputes may be solved, but the prospects for an abiding 'good neighbour' relationship are vitiated by the depth of the mistrust and prejudice. 'Pakistan does feel', says Professor Quincey Wright, 'that India has its eye out for reannexation of Pakistan.'[6] This fear and mistrust have been greatly contributed to by the utterances of the Indian leaders; they have

continued to preach the goal of the unity of India to the present day,
sometimes in threatening language, sometimes in platonic fashion. The
ideal of united India still seems to dominate a powerful section of
Indian opinion. 'As late as 1963', states Professor Trager, 'Nehru
regarded Pakistan as an area which should be reincorporated into an
Indian dominated confederation.'[7]

In the following pages we shall examine in greater detail the
problems of Pakistan's relations with India that have been outlined
here: her perils and anxieties; her constant search for security to protect
her territorial integrity and freedom. 'India' has been the most dominating aspect of her external relations. Pakistanis admit this fact frankly.
Since her inception, Pakistan's policy has been directed to securing an
adequate protection against possible aggression from her fellow
member of the Commonwealth. Fear and anxiety have sometimes
driven her to desperate situations and dangerous frustration. Expression
to these feelings was given in 1957 by Pakistan's prime minister, Mr
Suhrawardy: 'A situation might develop in which a country might
think it necessary to give up its life in a sweep, rather than be throttled
inch by inch; rather than wait for progressive annihilation.'[8]

I

HISTORICAL BACKGROUND

A COMPREHENSIVE ACCOUNT of Indo-Pakistan relations cannot be
made without going into the historical background of Hindu-Muslim
problems in British India. The present-day unhappy relations between
Pakistan and India are, in a sense, a continuation of age-old Hindu-
Muslim antagonism, now transformed into an international problem
between two sovereign states. Just as the Muslim minority in undivided
India considered itself to be in perpetual fear of domination by an
intolerant majority, so the smaller Pakistan today considers herself
beset with perilous anxieties in her relations with her bigger neighbour.

What led the Muslims to demand a separate state? Why could they
not be fused into a single nation with the Hindus with whom they
had lived for centuries? Like the creation of any other national state,
Pakistan's birth was conditioned by many factors—political, economic,
sociological, psychological—operating at a particular time and juncture.
It would perhaps be oversimplifying things to look for a single factor
or cause. Yet the fact remains that the raison d'être of the emergence
of Pakistan as an entity independent of the rest of India has been the
recognition of the distinctions in the rights, interests, and culture of
Hindus and Muslims considered as distinct nations.[1] *Quaid-i-Azam*
Mohammed Ali Jinnah, the founder of Pakistan, declared in 1944
that Muslims and Hindus were two major nations by any definition
or test of a nation. Pakistan was claimed as a homeland for Indian
Muslims on the principle of the right of self-determination.

This fact has not yet been fully appreciated. It has been misconstrued
variously as religious intolerance, as a return to medievalism, and so on.
Religion is no longer stressed as an essential attribute of nationality.

Most modern nationalities flourish without insisting on uniformity of religious belief. Hindu-Muslim differences in India were not merely a question of religious differences, as the phrase is generally understood in the Western world. The differences were more pervasive and created maladjustment between its two peoples in almost every station of their daily lives.

Nor is it correct, as sometimes alleged, that the British policy of 'divide and rule' was responsible for the partitioning of India. The British may have utilised Hindu-Muslim differences at certain stages of their rule, but it would be unfair and inadequate to explain these differences in undivided India in terms of British policy. The real causes of those fundamental differences had existed long before the British rule was established; they were neither furnished by the British nor encouraged by them. Anyone who studies the works of British authors and statesmen on the Muslim demand for Pakistan will find how opposed they were to the idea of partitioning India. Regarding the unity of the subcontinent as the greatest achievement of their rule, the British genuinely wanted to leave India united. The British Cabinet Mission that visited India in 1946, entrusted with the task of transferring power to the Indians, denounced the idea of partition in unqualified terms.[2] At the time of transfer of power in 1947, *The Economist* observed: 'In spite of the Congress contention that the Pakistan agitation has never been anything but a device of wicked British imperialists for keeping control of India, the British government has in fact been very unwilling to give up the idea of a united India.'[3]

The creation of Pakistan can be explained adequately only in terms of fundamental differences between Muslims and Hindus in undivided India. Jinnah said:

Differences in India between the two major nations, the Hindus and Muslims, are a thousand times greater when compared with the continent of Europe. . . . India is not a national state, India is not a country but a subcontinent composed of nationalities, the two major nations being the Hindus and the Muslims whose culture and civilisations, language and literature, art and architecture, name and nomenclature, sense of value and proportion, laws and jurisprudence, social and moral codes, customs and calendar, history and traditions, aptitudes and ambitions, outlook on life and of life are fundamentally different, nay, in many respects antagonistic.[4]

The Muslim intelligentsia pinpointed repeatedly the fallacious assumption that Muslims of the subcontinent had everything in common with the Hindus except their religion. 'The situation in fact', says Professor I. H. Qureshi, 'was that the two peoples had little in common. Islam and Hinduism built two entirely different kinds of society. But it was not only social structure that was different: the variance ran through in all the details.'[5] Professor Ahmad Ali observes:

> No two societies could be more divergent. In their attitude both towards the universal and the particular, God as well as man, the Hindus and Muslims remained at opposite poles of thought. These divergences of belief were so fundamental that, though the Muslims have been living side by side with the Hindus for over a thousand years, their cultures have remained separate. This fact has not been fully realised by America and the West; it is this which lay at the root of the creation of Pakistan, for though living in one country the Hindus and Muslims have remained two separate nations.[6]

When the Indian Statutory Commission came to the Indian subcontinent in 1930 to examine the problems and prospects of representative institutions in India, it stated: 'It would be an utter misapprehension to suppose that Hindu-Muslim antagonism is analogous to the separation between religious denominations in contemporary Europe. Differences of race, a different system of law, and the absence of inter-marriage constitute a far more effective barrier. It is a basic opposition manifesting itself at every turn in social custom and economic competition as well as in religious antipathy.'[7] A British author in the 1930s observed that France and Germany were to Europeans 'the standard example of enemy nations', and yet a young Frenchman might go to Germany for business or study; he might take his residence with a German family, share their meals and go with them to the same place of worship; eventually he might marry the daughter of the house and nobody would find this a matter for scandal or surprise. 'No Muslim', he concluded, 'can live on such terms within a Hindu family.'[8] The Muslims in undivided India found themselves in every social and economic sphere total aliens with the Hindus; and in the political sphere there was sharp and fundamental antagonism. The problem of India, said Allama Iqbal (who is regarded as the poet-philosopher of Pakistan), was international and not national. The Indian Muslims were afraid that their separate culture, way of life, economic and political interests would suffer greatly in an undivided India where the Hindus could exercise the power of a numerical majority and the Muslims would be a permanent and stagnant minority. This realisation led them to demand an independent Muslim state consisting of those areas of undivided India where they constituted a majority.

A fuller history of the Hindu-Muslim differences and the movement for Pakistan is outside the scope of this volume. We shall only give a résumé of the Hindu-Muslim struggle for political power in the recent period, particularly after the British government's introduction of the policy of 'progressive realisation of responsible government'. The experiments of responsible government under the 'colonial democracy' did not bring the two communities nearer; rather, they widened the gap. As the prospect of transfer of power from the British came closer, the Hindus and Muslims engaged in a bitter struggle for power. The impact of this struggle for political power upon the corrosive quarrels between India and Pakistan since their independence in 1947 has been great. So long as the authority was firmly established in British hands (the Indian Statutory Commission observed), and self-government was not thought of, Hindu-Muslim rivalry was confined within a narrower field. This was not merely because the presence of a neutral bureaucracy discouraged strife. A further reason, the Commission added, was that, before the reforms of the late nineteenth century, there was little for members of one community to fear from the predominance of the other. But the coming of the reforms and anticipation of what might follow them, it continued, had given new point to Hindu-Muslim competition. One of the big problems and dilemmas facing the British government in introducing representative institutions in India was the conflicting claims and interests of the two major communities.

The process of introducing representative institutions began in India after the great political upheaval and revolution of 1857 which resulted in the transfer of direct political control from the East India Company to the British Parliament, acting through the Secretary of State for India. The Indian Council Acts of 1861 and 1892, followed by the Morley-Minto reforms of 1909, were the rudimentary steps towards the realisation of representative institutions in India. Then came the 'most momentous utterance ever made in India's chequered history' by the Secretary of State for India, Edwin Montagu on August 20, 1917, in the House of Commons. The British government adopted the policy of 'progressive realisation of responsible government in India'. The result was the Act of 1919, under which partial responsible government was introduced in the Provinces. The partial responsible government was popularly known as 'Dyarchy', by which certain subjects at provincial level were transferred to the control of ministers who were responsible to the members of the provincial legislature. The Dyarchy was an unique experiment in the constitutional development of India, and it was given a trial in the Provinces for a period of sixteen years (1920–37). The authors of the reforms of 1919 expected that the introduction of responsible government might bring the two great communities, Hindus and Muslims, closer; but, as Professor Coupland remarked, 'more serious on long view than the failure of the Act of 1919 to make a reality of responsible government was its failure to overcome the barriers of caste and creed'.[9] In fact, the biggest hurdle in the path of representative government in India was Hindu-Muslim differences. Democracy requires for its success agreement on fundamentals, mutual toleration and understanding, and these were utterly lacking in undivided India. Muslim and Hindu ministers in the same government often canvassed against each other, as happened in the Bengal Council over the Calcutta Municipal Bills. The Hindus and the Muslims belonged, as Jinnah declared in subsequent years, to two different civilisations which were based on conflicting ideas and conceptions. The authors of the reforms of 1919 looked to the goal of 'Indian nationhood', not only as an end in itself, but as a means of overcoming the dissensions which obstructed the path of political advance. But the goal was not brought nearer by the reforms. By 1928, the gulf was wider than it had been in 1918.[10] The Muslims' numerical position in the Central Legislature and in most of the provincial councils made them realise the implication of majority-rule in India. Its fullest implication for them was to become apparent with the passing of the Government of India Act of 1935, when full responsible government was introduced in the Provinces.

The introduction of parliamentary government in the Provinces in 1937 under the Act of 1935 ushered in a new era of Hindu-Muslim relations in undivided India. It was an era of parting, in which political developments were moving nearer and nearer toward the partition of the subcontinent. Already by 1930, Allama Iqbal was proclaiming that the future of the Muslims, with their distinct cultural and spiritual characteristics, lay in a separate state. For a time, Iqbal's ideal remained a 'poet's vision', but their sad experiences of majority-rule under the Act of 1935 eventually led the Muslims, under the leadership of Jinnah, to transform the poet-philosopher's vision into a living force and an international reality.

The Congress captured most of the Hindu seats in the provincial elections held in 1937 under the Act of 1935. The Muslim League was not then properly equipped to face an election; the Muslim seats were, therefore, divided among a number of organisations. In Bengal, the Muslim seats were shared by the Muslim League and the Krishak Proja party of Fazlul Huq; while, in the Punjab, the majority of such seats went to the Unionist party of Sir Fazli Hussain. Subsequently, members of the Krishak Proja party in Bengal and of the Unionist party in Punjab joined the Muslim League under Jinnah's leadership. Out of 1,771 seats throughout India, the Congress won 706—less than half. The Congress's claim, as made by Gandhi at the Round Table Conference of 1930-32, that it was the sole representative body in India was disproved by the results of the 1937 election, which also disposed of its assertion that it effectively represented the Muslims. The Congress gained only 5 per cent of the Muslim seats—which seats, moreover, were confined to one area only, the North-West Frontier Province, where (thanks to a temporary alliance with the leader of the Red Shirts movement, Khan Abdul Ghaffer Khan) it won about 38 per cent of the seats, including non-Muslim seats. The Congress gained a clear command in five Hindu-majority Provinces— Madras, United Province, Central Province, Bihar and Orissa— and in Bombay also it was in a position to form a government with the help of some pro-Congress groups.

The Congress demanded an assurance that the provincial governors would not exercise their special responsibilities before it agreed to accept ministerial offices. One of the special responsibilities assigned to the governors was the 'safeguarding of all the legitimate interests of minorities'. The Muslims viewed the Congress's demand with concern and anxiety. The Secretary of State for India declared in the House of Lords that the governors could not be expected to give up their special responsibilities or 'safeguards'. On June 21, 1937, the Viceroy issued a statement which softened the Congress's attitude. Although this statement did not meet the Congress leaders' demand to scrap the 'safeguards', it assured them that the governors would 'leave nothing undone to avoid and to resolve all conflicts with their ministers'.[11] There were suspicions among the Muslims that a secret understanding had been reached between the Viceroy and the Congress. Whatever might be the case, the Congress agreed to accept offices as a result of the statement of June 21, forming ministries in eight out of eleven Provinces, and Congress rule in these eight states continued from July 1937 to October 1939.

This period of rule by the Congress had a tremendous impact on Hindu-Muslim relations and, more than anything else, it hastened the partition of India and the setting up of two separate states. The Congress rule was marked by such systematic attacks on the culture and way of life of the Muslims, that, in Jinnah's words, it 'killed every hope of Hindu-Muslim settlement in the right royal fashion of Fascism'.[12] The Congress leaders refused to have any representatives from the Muslim League or any other group in their ministries. 'In due course of the discussion from which the Act of 1935 was evolved', Coupland wrote, 'it was generally agreed that the main minority communities, particularly the Muslims, ought to be and in fact would be represented in the provincial ministries.'[13] In affirming the Muslim League's willingness to form coalitions with the Congress, Jinnah said: 'The constitution and policy of the League do not prevent us from co-operation with others. On the contrary, it is part and parcel of our basic principle that we are free and ready to co-operate with any group or party from the very conception, outside or inside the legislature, if the basic principles are determined by common consent.'[14] A prominent figure from the Congress side, Abul Kalam Azad, has stated: 'Choudhury Khaliquzzaman and Nawab Ismail Khan were then the leaders of the Muslim League in the UP [United Provinces]. When I came to Lucknow to form the government, I spoke to both of them;

they assured me that not only would they co-operate with the Congress, but would fully support the Congress programme.'[15]

The Congress's response to the League's offer of co-operation was to demand that the League group in the United Provinces legislature cease to function as a separate group; that the existing members of the Muslim League party become part of the Congress party; that the League's parliamentary board be dissolved and that no League candidates thereafter be put forward at any by-election.[16] The Congress demand, to quote the words of Jinnah, was 'abjure your party and forswear your policy and programme and liquidate the Muslim League'.[17] No political party with an iota of self-respect, as Qureshi puts it, could possibly accept these demands.

The fatal mistake of the Congress in rejecting the idea of coalition with the Muslims in Provinces where the former had gained a majority destroyed a great opportunity for uniting the two communities in a constructive effort of self-government in India. This deliberate spurning of the Muslim offer of co-operation, which was to have far-reaching consequences, was inspired by the 'intoxication of victory' among the Congress leaders. 'They took their triumph at the polls as the signal not for a policy of compromise and conciliation but for a bold attack . . . to come to terms with the Muslim League in the first place was a negation of totalitarian doctrine which had now taken so firm a hold in Congress minds.'[18] After the creation of Pakistan, Abul Kalam Azad lamented: 'If the UP League offer of co-operation had been accepted, the Muslim League Party would, for all practical purposes, have merged in the Congress. Jawaharlal's action gave the Muslim League in the UP a new lease of life. All students of Indian politics know that it was from the UP that the League was reorganised. Jinnah took full advantage of the situation and started an offensive which ultimately led to Pakistan.'[19]

The effects of the Muslim League's exclusion from the Congress ministries were soon to appear. In every Hindu-majority Province, the Muslims complained of unfair treatment. They did not get their due share of promotion in government service; they were deprived of local and municipal offices wherever possible; and in every way they suffered administrative discrimination. 'The Congress . . . used its strength unwisely.'[20] 'Muslims can expect neither justice nor fair play under a Congress government', Jinnah declared.[21] On March 20, 1938, the council of the All-India Muslim League passed a resolution on the complaints reaching the League office of the 'hardships, ill-treatment and injustice that is meted out to the Muslims in various Congress government Provinces and particularly to those who are the workers and members of the Muslim League.'[22] A committee of eight members was set up to investigate the Muslim sufferings and grievances under the Congress rule. The committee submitted its report, popularly known as the Pirpur Report, on November 15, 1938. Its findings were supplemented by two other reports: the Shareef Report, published in March 1939, and *Muslim Suffering under Congress Rule*, by Fazlul Huq, the Chief Minister of Bengal, in December 1939. These reports gave balanced and well-documented accounts of the suppression and oppression of the Muslims by the Congress rule in India under the first experiment in majority-rule of the parliamentary system of government. Their experiences of this period indicated clearly to the Muslims what their fate would be in a Hindu-dominated free India and, as mentioned earlier, their bitter resentment against Congress rule had considerable impact on their demand for a separate state. 'This bitterness', writes Sir Percival Griffiths, 'had its inevitable reaction on Muslim constitutional thought. Up to now the Muslims had been prepared to depend for their protection on "weightage" or "safeguards". By 1939, they were convinced that, whatever safeguards might be designed, an Indian federation in which the centre retained substantial power would in fact mean Hindu domination.'[23]

In examining the Muslim allegations against the Congress rule, the Pirpur Report included a summary account of events in all the Congress-governed Provinces (except the North-West Frontier Province), based on personal enquiries made by the committee. The report stated:

> The Congress has failed to inspire confidence in the minorities and has failed to carry them with it in spite of its oft-repeated resolution guaranteeing religious and cultural liberty to the various communities because its actions are not in conformity with its words. . . . The Indian National Congress conception of nationalism is based on the establishment of a national state of the majority community

in which other nationalities and communities have only secondary rights. The Muslims think that no tyranny can be as great as the tyranny of the majority.[24]

It is not only a question of their religion and cultural freedom . . . they must obtain their due share in the government of the country. The Congress has denied them this—it has tried, indeed, to break the political power of the Muslims by the old device of 'divide and rule'. . . . The flag, the anthem, the reverence paid to Mr Gandhi, the emphasis laid by Mahatma himself on 'cow protection'—all these are evidence of a deliberate and far-reaching attack on the civic and cultural rights of the Muslim community.[25]

The Shareef Report confined its enquiry to Bihar; 'it depicted the reign of terror let loose upon the Muslims of the province'.[26]

Fazlul Huq began his account by analysing the Congress policy. This policy, he wrote, had set the stage 'for the blatant arrogance of the militant Hindus to burst the bounds of restraint which non-partisan governments had hitherto imposed . . . they set about to impose their will on the Muslim minorities . . . the religion of Muslims must be humbled because was not this the land of the Hindus?'[27] Then followed a description of seventy-two incidents in Bihar, thirty-three in the United Provinces, and a more summary account of similar events in the Central Provinces.

The Muslim intelligentsia were seriously concerned over the threats to the Muslim culture and education under the Congress rule. The All-India Muslim Educational Conference, at its 52nd session in Calcutta in 1938, appointed a committee to investigate the plight of the Muslim education in the Congress-governed Provinces. The Congress had already formulated a plan, known as the *Vidya Mandirs* 'scheme', which was a part of a bigger plan, known as 'Wardha scheme', under which the Hindu culture and way of life were to be imposed on the Muslims. The ideas behind these schemes, Coupland has pointed out, 'were certainly coloured by Hindu rather than by Muslim thought'.[28] The report of a subcommittee of the Muslim Educational Conference, published in 1942, drew a sombre picture of the position of Muslim education. 'That Muslim school children should be obliged to honour the Congress flag, to join with "folded hands" in singing *Banda*

Mataram, to wear Gandhi caps and homespun clothes—all that was bad enough, but its significance might seem primarily political. Could the same be said of the children not merely celebrating Mr Gandhi's birthday but doing *Puja*—a ceremonial act of reverence or worship—before the Mahatma's portrait?'[29]

Such were the experiences of Muslims under the Congress rule. 'For the Muslims of the Hindu-majority Provinces', Qureshi declares, 'the rule of the Congress ministries from July 1937 to October 1939 was nothing short of a nightmare.'[30] The Muslim League raised its voice vigorously against the Muslim suffering under the Congress *raj*. It condemned the majority party's policy of 'foisting *Banda Mataram* as the national anthem upon the country in callous disregard of the feelings of Muslims'. It criticised the provincial governors 'for their failure to enforce the special powers entrusted to them for the safeguard of the interests of the Musalmans and other important minorities'. It 'viewed with alarm' the large number of communal riots in Hindu-majority Provinces and censured the Congress ministries for their failure 'to discharge their primary duty of protecting [the Muslims in] the Muslim-majority Provinces'.[31] The League pointed out that the Wardha scheme would destroy Muslim culture and that it sought to superimpose upon education the ideology of the Hindu community; that it aimed at indoctrinating the Muslim students with the ideals of the Congress. Jinnah spoke bitterly of the aims of the Congress rule: '*Hindi* [is] to be the national language of all India and . . *Banda Mataram* is to be the national song and is to be forced upon all. The Congress flag is to be obeyed and revered by all and sundry. On the very threshold of what little power and responsibility is given, the majority have clearly shown their hand that Hindustan is for the Hindus.'[32]

These Muslim grievances were brushed aside by the Congress and its press 'with more or less contempt or ridicule'.[33] They challenged the allegation of maltreatment and unfair dealing as brought out in the various reports. Jinnah later stated: 'Our complaints were dismissed as false, frivolous and vexatious, and even Mr Gandhi, before whom I placed our charges as far back as May 1938, sidetracked the question. . . .'[34] Jinnah demanded the appointment of a Royal Commission to enquire into the oppression and suppression of the Muslims, but this

B

offer of an impartial commission was turned down. The tendency to refuse to settle any dispute with the help of an impartial or international body is continued to the present-day by India's rejection of proposals for submitting or settling major Indo-Pakistan disputes through the United Nations or any other impartial organisation. India's record on Kashmir is the best illustration of this tendency.

When the Congress rule came to an end in 1939, the Muslims all over India observed a 'Day of Deliverance' on December 22, 1939, 'as a mark of relief that the Congress regime has at last ceased to function' (Jinnah). Resolutions were passed at Muslim meetings denouncing the Congress leaders who 'have done their best to flout the Muslim opinion, to destroy Muslim culture and have interfered with their religious and social life and trampled upon their economic and political rights'.[35] It demonstrated the widening gulf between the two communities as a result of the Congress policy and actions between 1937 and 1939. The Muslims observance of the 'Day of Deliverance' led Nehru to write to Jinnah: 'Our sense of values and objectives in life and politics differ so very greatly.'[36]

The inevitable result of this widening gap was the Muslim demand for a separate state. 'The Muslims no longer wanted an Indian federation. No longer was it a question of merely voting in favour of or against a certain (or even any) federal scheme . . . the Indian political situation had undergone a fundamental, basic, vital change. Never again was it to be the same.'[37] On August 13, 1939, the council of the Muslim League declared that the federal scheme as embodied in the Government of India Act, 1935 was totally unacceptable to the Muslims because it allowed 'a permanent hostile community to trample upon our religious, political, social and economic rights'.[38]

On March 23, 1940, came the historic proclamation from the Muslim League that

> . . . no constitutional plan would be workable in this country or acceptable to the Muslims unless it is designed on the following basic principles, viz., that geographical contiguous units are demarcated into regions which should be constituted with such territorial readjustment as may be necessary that the areas in which Muslims are numerically in a majority, as in the North–western and eastern

zones of India, should be grouped to constitute 'independent states' in which the constituent units shall be autonomous and sovereign.[39]

Jinnah, explaining the Muslim League resolution of March 23, 1940, said:

> The problem in India is not of an intercommunal character but manifestly of an international one and it must be treated as such. So long as this basic and fundamental truth is not realised, any constitution that may be built will result in disaster and will prove destructive . . . the only course open to us is to allow the major nations separate homelands by dividing India into 'autonomous national states' . . . it is a dream that the Hindus and Muslims can ever evolve a common nationality and this misconception of one Indian nation has gone far beyond the limits and is the cause of the most of your [India's] troubles and will lead India to destruction if we fail to revise our notions in time. . . . Muslim India could not accept a constitution which must necessarily result in a Hindu majority government.

Hindus and Muslims, brought together under a democratic system, Jinnah pointed out, 'would only mean Hindu *raj*'. He concluded: 'We have had ample experience of the working of the provincial constitution during the last two and a half years, and any repetition of such a government must lead to civil war . . . .'[40]

With this proclamation of their political destiny and goal, the Muslims were gathered in an unique way under the dynamic leadership of Jinnah, who gave new significance and shape to their quest for liberty. They began to acquire new hope and confidence in their destiny. Once Jinnah became convinced that there was no other solution of India's constitutional problem, he threw himself heart and soul into the effort to convert the British government and Indian opinion to his point of view; and throughout all the years of negotiation and agreement that preceded the grant of self-rule to the people of India, he stuck with a single-minded devotion to his ideal of a free Muslim state of Pakistan. In the plebiscitary elections of 1946, the Muslims demonstrated their solid support of the demand for Pakistan. *The Economist* wrote on March 22, 1947:

The adoption of territorial separation as a policy by the Muslim League and the sweeping success of the League in getting the mass of support of Moslems were direct consequences of the attitude and behaviour of the Congress after the elections of 1937. In the provinces where Congress governments were formed, there were various forms of discrimination against the Muslim community . . . and the fear that Congress ascendency at the centre would produce similar results for India as a whole led to a rapid spread of belief that the interest of Muslims would only be safe if they had a territory of their own of which they would be the masters without interference.

The Australian statesman R. G. Casey, who became the Governor of Bengal in 1944, tried to probe into 'the present state of mind of the Muslims' and the factors that led them to demand a separate state. Writing in 1947, Casey traced it to two principal factors: 'the memory of past humiliations, and the lack of present economic opportunity'. Elaborating these two factors, he observed: 'A great many Muslims who are now of middle age have bitter recollections of the humiliations that they suffered at the hands of the caste Hindus in their early days.' Turning to 'the lack of present economic opportunity', he remarked that 'it is not too much to say, as regards employment in the great majority of Hindu-controlled business, that "no Muslim need apply"'.[41] Pakistan's first Prime Minister, Liaquat Ali Khan, during his visit to North America in 1950 explained why the Muslims desired a separate state:

> As the day of freedom for these four hundred million people drew near, it became increasingly obvious that at the end of the British rule, the one hundred million Muslims would have to live their new life as a perpetual political minority. Long experience and the history of several countries had taught them that under a dominating majority of three to one, freedom from British rule would mean to the Muslims not freedom but merely a change of masters.[42]

When a special mission of the British cabinet—consisting of Lord Pethick-Lawrence (the Secretary of State for India), Sir Stafford Cripps (President of the Board of Trade) and A. V. Alexander (First

Lord of the Admiralty)—came to India with the task of transferring power from the British to the Indians, the biggest issue was whether India should remain united or the Muslim demand for a separate state conceded. United India was an article of faith for the Hindu-dominated Congress. The Muslims, on the other hand, were now deeply attached to the vision of Pakistan as a separate Muslim homeland.[43] To ignore the Muslim demand, which by 1946 had become very powerful, would be to consign India to near-civil war with all its attendant suffering and possible international consequences. The Muslims were unwilling to take part in a single constituent assembly for the whole of India because they were afraid of being outvoted by the Hindus. They were not prepared to give up, in any circumstances, their demand for Pakistan and the partitioning of India. On the other hand, the Congress declared that it was not going to agree to the Muslim demand for Pakistan under any circumstances whatever, even if the British government agreed to it. 'Nothing on earth', declared Nehru, 'not even UNO is going to bring about Pakistan which Jinnah wants';[44] while Sardar Patel, the Congress strongman, told Muslims that they could have Pakistan only at the cost of civil war between Muslims and Hindus.[45] Such was the deadlock and distrust between the two parties when the British Cabinet Mission began the historic negotiations in 1946 for the transfer of power.

Yet the Cabinet Mission applied itself vigorously in search of formulas to save the unity of India. Its members seemed to be strongly averse to the idea of the partitioning of India in any form or shape. After their preliminary exchanges of ideas with the leaders of various groups, a tripartite conference (the Mission and the Viceroy, and the representatives of the Congress and the Muslim League) was held in Simla on May 5, 1946. The basis of discussion at the conference was suggested by the Mission. It envisaged that a Union government would deal with foreign affairs, defence and communication. There would be a grouping of Provinces, dealing with other subjects which the Provinces in the respective groups desired to be dealt with in common. The provincial governments would deal with all other subjects and would have all the residuary rights. The Mission could not, however, bring the Congress and the League to any agreement. The Congress insisted on a strong and all-powerful centre, and wanted the Union to deal not only with the three subjects as suggested by the Mission, but also with currency, customs and planning, 'as well as such other subjects as on closer scrutiny may be found to be intimately allied to them'. The Union should be able to raise such revenue as it required and to take action in the case of a breakdown of the constitution or other emergencies. The Congress ideal of a strong centre, as expressed by the Nehru Committee of 1928, seemed to be still cherished. The Muslim League, on the other hand, wanted to build up strong Muslim groups, which would amount in practice to the realisation of Pakistan, and to reduce to a minimum the powers of the Union. There was, in addition, the question of parity between the Hindu and Muslim provinces in the Union legislature and executive; this the League insisted on but the Congress opposed it.[46]

The failure of the Simla conference made the Cabinet Mission realise that it would be futile to expect the Congress and the Muslim League to arrive at a compromise over the constitutional problems. The Mission was now left with the choice of making its own recommendations regarding the transfer of power; hence, the famous Cabinet Mission Plan, announced on May 16, 1946.[47] The British ministers examined the Muslim demand for Pakistan and concluded that neither a larger nor a smaller sovereign state of Pakistan would provide an acceptable solution for the communal problem. They referred to what they termed as 'weighty administrative, economic and military considerations' against the idea of partitioning India and setting up two sovereign states. Indeed, the Cabinet Mission denounced the Muslim demand for Pakistan in unqualified terms. This alone should serve to demonstrate the hollowness of the popular idea that the British policy of 'divide and rule' was responsible for the partitioning of India.* 'The unwillingness of the Mission', says Sir Percival Griffiths, 'to recommend partition was understandable and indeed honourable, for partition meant the destruction of that unity

---

* Even so, from this time and up to the present, Indian leaders have continued to aver that partition was the result of the British policy of 'divide and rule'. Propaganda of this kind has been vigorously deployed by them in the Arab world, where the word 'partition', ever since the creation of Israel, has powerful overtones. Nehru and his colleagues also secured Khrushchev's endorsement of the 'divide and rule' argument against Pakistan during his visit to India in 1955.

which had perhaps been Britain's greatest contribution to India. In a sense, to advise partition would have been to admit Britain's failure, and His Majesty's Government was therefore most reluctant to take any step in that direction.' Even so, the Cabinet Mission Plan could not but acknowledge, 'the real Muslim apprehensions that their culture and political and social life might become submerged in a purely unitary India in which the Hindus with their greatly superior numbers must be a dominating element'.[48]

To produce 'a stable and practicable form of constitution', such as would safeguard the essential claims of all parties, the Cabinet Mission recommended that the future constitution of 'All India' should take the following basic forms. 1. There should be a Union of India, embracing both British India and the Indian princely states, and dealing with foreign affairs, defence and communications. It should also have the powers necessary to raise the finances required for these departments of state. 2. The Union should have an executive and a legislature constituted of British India and states 'representatives'. Any question involving a major communal issue in the legislature should require for its decision a majority of the representatives present and voting of each of the two major communities as well as a majority of all members present and voting. 3. All subjects other than the Union subjects and all residuary subjects should vest in the Provinces. 4. The princely states should retain all subjects and powers other than those ceded to the Union. 5. Provinces should be free to form groups, with executive and legislature, and each group should be able to determine the provincial subjects to be taken in common. 6. The constitutions of the Union and of the groups of Provinces should contain a provision whereby any Province could, by a majority vote of its legislative assembly, call for a reconsideration of the terms of the constitution after an initial period of ten years and at ten years' intervals thereafter.

The Cabinet Mission then outlined the procedure for setting up a constituent assembly, to be elected by the members of the provincial assemblies. After a preliminary meeting to settle the order of business and to elect officers, the provincial representatives would divide into three sections: Section A, to consist of the Provinces not claimed for Pakistan; Section B, to consist of the Punjab, the North-West Frontier

Province, Sind and British Baluchistan; and Section C, to consist of Bengal and Assam. Each section would then settle the provincial constitutions for the Provinces included in it, and would also decide whether there should be a group constitution and, if so, with what subjects it should deal. Finally, the whole assembly would come together again to draw up the Union constitution.

The Cabinet Mission Plan also stressed the importance of the immediate establishment of an interim government having the support of the major political parties, so that the urgent and difficult tasks confronting the country could be tackled by a government based on popular support. The statement ended with an appeal to the leaders and the people of India to accept the proposals in a spirit of accommodation and good will, bearing in mind that the alternative was a grave danger of violence, chaos and even civil war.

Whatever the criticisms or shortcomings of the plan might be, it was, no doubt, a sincere and bold attempt to maintain the unity of India and avoid partitioning of the country. If the Congress leaders had responded to the appeals of the Cabinet Mission, or if they had appreciated the strength of the Muslims' feelings and their fear of domination by the majority community, the unity of India could have been maintained under this plan. This was the last and most comprehensive bid to save the unity of the subcontinent.

The initial reaction of the Congress to the Cabinet Mission plan was favourable. Gandhi welcomed it as containing 'a seed to convert this land of sorrow into one without sorrow and suffering'.[49] The Hindu press was jubilant to find the Mission rejecting the demand for Pakistan in such unqualified terms; in fact, the preamble to the British ministers' statement set forth the kind of arguments against the creation of Pakistan that had been urged repeatedly by the Hindu press. The *National Herald*, Nehru's daily, wrote triumphantly of the plan: 'Pakistan, the Pakistan of Mr Jinnah's conception, receives a state burial in the document submitted by the Cabinet Mission. And lest there should be any doubt about its demise or any fear of the possibility of its resurrection, it is emphatically announced that the Cabinet Mission's sentence of death on Mr Jinnah's Pakistan has already obtained the approval of the British government.'[50] A Bengali-language daily newspaper of Calcutta asserted that Jinnah's Pakistan had been torpedeod in the Bay of Bengal by the Cabinet Mission Plan.

The Muslims, on the other hand, were greatly disappointed by the rejection of the demand for Pakistan. Their sullen and resentful mood was in marked contrast to that of the Hindus, who felt that they had secured a 'victory', while speeches of Congress leaders exuberantly assumed that 'the victory' could be taken for granted. Jinnah said in a statement on May 22: 'It is all the more regrettable that the Mission had thought fit to advance commonplace and exploded arguments against Pakistan and resorted to a special pleading couched in a deplorable language which is calculated to hurt the feelings of Muslim India.' This was done, he declared, 'to appease and placate the Congress'.[51]

But the Cabinet Mission's policy of 'appeasement' of the Hindu majority had the disastrous effect of destroying any chance of a tolerant attitude from the Congress, which seemed to have concluded that it was now in a position to dictate the terms of compromise with the Muslims. The Congress began to emphasise that the constituent assembly would be a sovereign body, unhampered by any external authority, and that it would be able to vary in any way it liked the recommendations and procedure suggested by the Mission. In particular, the Congress leaders levelled an attack on the principle of grouping, a vital part of the plan from the Muslim viewpoint. The Mission had to tell them that the provision in its statement relating to the groups was most important as it sought to maintain the unity of India by meeting, to some extent, the Muslim demands for self-rule in those areas where they constituted a majority. V. P. Menon relates Gandhi's opinion of the role of the constituent assembly: 'It was open to the constituent assembly to abolish the distinctions of Muslims and non-Muslims which the Mission felt forced to recognise.'[52] The Congress still seemed to be unable or unwilling to realise the importance and significance of the Hindu-Muslim problem in India.

The Council of the Muslim League, meeting on June 6, 1946, termed the arguments of the Cabinet Mission as 'unwarranted, unjustified and unconvincing'. Nevertheless, the League agreed to co-operate in the scheme outlined by the Cabinet Mission. Jinnah risked his popularity among the Muslims by accepting this compromise, yet it was highly commendable, and refuted the allegations of those critics who said that he invariably negatived every proposal which fell short of his vision of an independent and sovereign Pakistan.

Unfortunately, this initial acceptance by the Muslim League of the Mission's proposals was taken as a sign of weakness rather than as evidence of a spirit of co-operation. 'As in 1942, when the belief that British power was about to crumble before the Japanese advance had encouraged Congress in its intransigence towards the Cripps offer, so now its under-estimate of the strength of Muslim feeling led it to suppose that its supremacy was unassailable and so to make the tragic error of over-playing its hand.'[53] On June 26, the Congress decided that it would join the proposed constituent assembly with a view to framing the constitution of a 'free united and democratic India'. Its president, Azad, made it clear that the leaders would work out the plan according to their 'own interpretation' and with a view to achieving 'our objective'. Thus, the Congress's acceptance of the plan was accompanied by a claim to interpret the plan in such a way as repudiated the Mission's basic principles. This destroyed the basis of the compromise which the British ministers had been at such pains to devise.

On July 8, 1946, Pandit Nehru, who had by then become the Congress president, declared: 'We are not bound by a single thing except that we have decided for the moment to go to the constituent assembly.' On grouping he said: 'There will be no grouping.' He went on to prophesy the inevitable enlargement of the powers of the Union. Defence and communications would embrace the large numbers of industries necessary for their support, foreign affairs must include foreign trade. Finally, he asserted that the centre must obviously control currency and credit and it must deal with interprovincial disputes or economic breakdown.[54] Pandit Nehru's statement left nobody in doubt about the real intentions and plans of the Congress. Its leaders had planned to enter the constituent assembly with the intention of torpedoing those vital aspects of the plan which the Mission had devised to allay the Muslim fears of domination by the majority community and to protect their legitimate interests and rights. The formation of 'groups' and the strict limitation of the powers of the centre, which were the most important features of the plan, were not acceptable to the Congress. Nehru's statement was described by his colleague, Abul Kalam Azad, 'as one of those unfortunate events which changed the course of history'.[55] The British author, Leonard Mosley, wrote: '[Nehru] was telling the world that once in power, Congress would use its strength at the centre to alter the Cabinet Mission Plan as it thought fit. . . . Nehru's remarks were a direct act of sabotage.'[56] His statement dismayed the authors of the plan. Lord Pethick-Lawrence complained: 'Having agreed to the statement of 16 May and the constituent assembly elected in accordance with that statement, [the Congress leaders] cannot, of course, go outside the terms of what has been agreed. To do so would not be fair to other parties. . . .' Sir Stafford Cripps declared in the House of Commons that 'it would be a clear breach of the basic understanding of the scheme'.[57]

The declarations, the professions and the actions of the Congress ultimately led the Muslim members to boycott the session of the constituent assembly, and thus was lost the last and the most sincere attempt to maintain the unity of India. On July 29, 1946, the Muslim League Council decided to withdraw its acceptance of the Cabinet Mission Plan and 'to resort to direct action to achieve Pakistan'. Jinnah, in the course of his speech in the Council, observed that the Muslims had been willing to sacrifice the full sovereignty of Pakistan and to have an all-India Union in their anxiety to come to a peaceful settlement with the Congress party, but this gesture of peace had been treated with defiance and contempt. 'Today we bid goodbye to constitutional methods.'[58] The Muslims decided to observe 'Direct Action Day' on August 16, 1946. The Muslim League thus gave up constitutional methods for the first time in its career. The importance and implications of this were great.

The Congress Working Committee, in its resolution of August 10, expressed regret at the decision of the Muslim League not to participate in the constituent assembly and requested its co-operation. But, even in this resolution, the Congress made it clear that it would use the constituent assembly to achieve 'free and united India' without any interference from any authority. So it failed to win the confidence of the Muslims.

In the meantime, the Viceroy, Lord Wavell, asked Nehru to form an interim government, thereby disregarding the promises and pledges given to the Muslims by the British government. The result of the formation of a Hindu government in India, at a time when communal feelings were running high, was disastrous. It led to communal riots and bloodshed on an unparalleled scale. Winston Churchill, in a debate of the House of Commons in December 1946, condemned the 'cardinal error of the British government' in calling one single party to form the interim government, pointing out that it had led to strife and massacre over a wide region, unparalleled in India since the 'Indian Mutiny' of 1857. 'Indeed,' he said, 'it is certain that more people have lost their lives or been wounded in India by violence since the Nehru government was installed in office four months ago than in the previous ninety years.'[59]

The serious situation in India led the British government to convene a new conference in London. The constituent assembly was to meet on December 9, 1946. The British government invited Lord Wavell, two Congress and two League representatives, and one Sikh representative to London to discuss the basis of a common understanding between the Congress and the League. The Congress at first declined the British invitation, but this decision was revoked at the personal request of the British Prime Minister, Clement Attlee. Nehru alone went to London to represent the Congress, while Jinnah and Liaquat Ali Khan represented the League. After the conference ended on December 6, the British government issued a statement explaining the Cabinet Mission's scheme of May 16. After summarising the points of dispute, this December statement announced that the British had taken legal advice which confirmed the Mission's interpretation of the disputed point. This interpretation 'must therefore be considered an essential part of the scheme of May 16, for enabling the Indian people to formulate a constitution which His Majesty's Government would be prepared to submit to Parliament. It should, therefore, be accepted by all parties in the constituent assembly.'[60] The statement urged the Congress to accept the view of the Cabinet Mission in order that a way might be opened for the Muslim League to participate in the constituent assembly. It concluded:

There has never been any prospect of success for the constituent assembly, except upon the basis of an agreed procedure. Should a constitution come to be framed by a constituent assembly in which a large section of the Indian population had not been represented, His Majesty's Government could not of course contemplate—as the Congress have stated they would not contemplate—forcing such a constitution upon any unwilling parts of the country.[61]

The Muslim League greatly welcomed the new statement of the British government as it endorsed its interpretation of the Cabinet Mission Plan. But a more important triumph for the Muslims was the recognition by the British that the Cabinet Mission Plan of May 16 might have to be abandoned, and that the demand for a sovereign Pakistan in some form might be conceded. In the House of Commons, Sir Stafford Cripps put the position even more bluntly by saying that, if the Muslim League could not be persuaded to come into the constituent assembly, then the parts of the country where they were in a majority could not be held to be bound by the assembly's decisions. This was the beginning of the abandonment of the idea of one constituent assembly for India as a whole, in favour of two assemblies, one for India and another for Pakistan.

The British government statement of December 6, 1946, changed the political atmosphere radically, and the partition of India was now regarded as inevitable. There was little hope that the last attempt for the maintenance of the unity of India under the Cabinet Mission Plan would be successful. Jinnah, however, indicated that, if the Congress unequivocally accepted the Cabinet Mission's constitutional proposal, he might still call a meeting of the Muslim League Council to reconsider its decision to boycott the constituent assembly. But the Congress would not modify its position; the Working Committee on December 22, 1946, termed the statement of the British government of December 6 as 'an addition to the statement of May 16, 1946, which clearly, in several respects, goes beyond the original statement'. The Muslim League resolution on the December statement recorded its satisfaction that its reading of the Cabinet Meeting Plan was vindicated by the British government, and regretted that the Congress, by rejecting the final appeal of the British to accept the correct interpretation of the Cabinet Mission Plan, 'converted the constituent assembly into a body of its own conception, has destroyed all fundamentals of the statement of May 16, and every possibility of compromise on the basis of the Cabinet Mission's Constitutional Plan'.

In the meantime, the constituent assembly met in December without the Muslim members. Dr Rajendra Prasad, who was elected president of the assembly, stressed in his inaugural address the claim that the constituent assembly was a 'self-governing and self-determining independent body . . . whose decisions no one outside can upset, alter or modify'.[62] His speech, once more, confirmed the Muslims' apprehensions that the Congress did not consider itself bound by any agreement relating to constitutional proposals as set out in the Cabinet Mission Plan. Not that more reasonable views were unvoiced. When Nehru moved the 'Objectives Resolution' on December 13, Dr M. R. Jayakar (a former judge of the Federal Court of India) moved an amendment seeking the 'co-operation of the Muslim League and the Indian states'; he urged a postponement of the adoption of the Objectives Resolution to enable the representatives of the Muslims to participate, if they would so choose, in the deliberations of the assembly.[63] But the Congress was not in a mood to listen to any counsel of patience or co-operation; being assured of what Jinnah called 'brute majority' in the assembly, its leaders were determined to ride roughshod.

The Congress's uncompromising attitude and obstinacy were leading the country fast to a civil war; communal riots and massacres continued; the whole atmosphere was charged with tension and hatred. The uncertain situation was brought to an end by the statement of the British government on February 20, 1947, in which Attlee declared:

His Majesty's Government desire to hand over their responsibility to the authorities established by a Constitution approved by all parties in India in accordance with the Cabinet Mission's plan. But unfortunately there is at present no clear prospect that such a constitution and such authorities will emerge. The present state of uncertainty is fraught with danger and cannot be indefinitely prolonged. His Majesty's Government wish to make it clear that it is their definite intention to take necessary steps to effect the transfer of power to Indian hands by a date not later than June 1948. . . . His Majesty's Government will have to consider to whom the powers of the Central Government in British India should be handed over, on due date, whether as a whole to some form of Central Government in British India or in some areas to the existing Provincial Government or in such other way as may seem most reasonable and in the best interests of the Indian people.[64]

It was clear from this statement that, if the Muslim representatives should continue to boycott the constituent assembly, the powers would not be transferred to that body for India as a whole, and the partition of India would be inevitable.

There was a change of Viceroy. Lord Wavell had to go because he had lost the confidence of the Congress, and Lord Mountbatten was appointed the last Viceroy of India. Soon after his arrival, he started a new series of conferences and talks with the Congress and the League. The Cabinet Mission Plan was dead; partition was considered inevitable. Lord Mountbatten began to work out the plan for the partition of the country. We need not go into details of the evolution of Mountbatten's scheme for the transfer of power; this has been narrated in a number of volumes by British authors. Mountbatten claimed that he had worked 'hand in glove' with the Indian leaders at every stage and step of the development of the new plan. But the real story is that the final shape of this plan, which involved not only partition of India but also subdivision of Bengal and Punjab to take away from these two Muslim-majority provinces the Hindu-majority districts, was worked out by his Hindu Constitutional Adviser, V. P. Menon, in consultation and with the approval of the leader of one party, Pandit Nehru of the Congress. The other party, the Muslim League, was not taken into confidence. The story of the final drafting and approval of the Mountbatten Plan of June 3, 1947 is based on the accounts given by E. W. R. Lumby, Leonard Mosley, Lord Ismay and others who had knowledge of the inside story. The result of the Mountbatten Plan was a 'moth-eaten truncated' Pakistan whose viability was seriously doubted in many quarters.

The Mountbatten Plan outlined the procedure to ascertain the wishes of those areas whose majority of representatives boycotted the constituent assembly: whether their constitution should be framed by the existing constituent assembly; in other words, whether they wished to join Pakistan or not. Both the Congress and the Muslim

League accepted the plan. The result was as had been generally expected. The Muslim-majority areas of India decided in favour of Pakistan. By the end of June 1947, the procedure of deciding on the unity or partition of Bengal and Punjab had been worked out; in each case it had resulted in a verdict in favour of partition. That Sind and Baluchistan would vote to join Pakistan was never in doubt. The Sind Assembly registered this decision on June 26, and in Baluchistan the result was a unanimous vote in favour of Pakistan. The referendum in the North–West Frontier Province and in the district of Sylhet similarly resulted in a vote in favour of Pakistan.

The increasing tempo which marked the new plan, as compared with the Cabinet Mission Plan, was further accelerated by the Indian Independence Bill. Within one month the Bill was drafted, referred to the Viceroy, and discussed by him with the Congress and League leaders, so that on July 4 it was introduced in the British Parliament. On July 18, only fourteen days after its introduction, the Bill received the royal assent. On the day after the Indian Independence Act was passed, the legal birth of the new dominions was marked by the splitting of the interim government at New Delhi into two groups, representing the two successor governments: India and Pakistan. A boundary commission was also set up to demarcate the new frontiers of the two states. Lord Mountbatten came to Karachi to inaugurate formally the new state of Pakistan on August 14, 1947.

Why did the Congress accept the partition of India which they had so vehemently opposed, and to which many Indians are still unable to reconcile themselves?

We have shown in our discussion that the Hindu-Muslim problem in undivided India was not merely a religious issue as that phrase is usually understood in the West; it was also a conflict between two major national groups. The minority group was afraid of domination by the majority group, and when the British government initiated representative institutions in India, the Muslims were anxious to protect their interests and rights from the rule of an intolerant and hostile majority. The majority group opposed the legitimate rights and aspirations of the minority. They failed to win the confidence of the latter. In 1928, the Muslims under Jinnah were agreeable to a federal scheme with modest demands, but the Hindu leaders could not accept the Muslim proposals for a federal constitution with autonomy for the Provinces. Then, in 1937, when parliamentary democracry was introduced in the Provinces, the Congress turned down the Muslim League's offer of a coalition government, thus rejecting a valuable opportunity for constructive co-operation between the two major communities. Finally, when the British Cabinet Mission made a sincere bid to maintain the unity of India in 1946 by formulating a three-tier constitutional plan, that too, was rejected by the Congress.

Yet the Congress apparently accepted partition in 1947. Why? We shall try to examine the motives that led Indian leaders to agree to a 'moth-eaten' and 'truncated 'Pakistan. It is essential to understand the Congress's real intentions towards partition, for this will give a clue to the understanding of the unhappy relations between the two successor states of the British *Raj*.

2

INDEPENDENCE: INITIAL
DIFFICULTIES AND PROBLEMS

On August 15, 1947, the Dominions of Pakistan and India assumed their independent—and divided—existence. There was great popular rejoicing and enthusiasm in both the Dominions. For the people of Pakistan it was not only liberation from foreign rule; it also meant freedom from the threat of a majority rule in a caste-ridden social system where they would have been destined to be a permanent and stagnant religious minority.

Mohammad Ali Jinnah, *Quaid-i-Azam* (the Great Leader), who gave expression to the inarticulate desire of the Muslims of the subcontinent to form a distinct and independent political unit, was, perhaps, the happiest man; he was particularly happy to find, after working against heavy odds, the successful conclusion of his movement for a separate Muslim state. Referring to the complete transfer of power from the British government, Jinnah declared that 'such voluntary and absolute transfer of power and rule by one nation over others is unknown in the whole history of the world'. He was also greatly appreciative of the fact that the British ultimately realised that 'the only solution of India's constitutional problems was to divide it into Pakistan and Hindustan'.[1] He was reported to have said to his ADC at Government House in Karachi that he had never expected to see his dreamland, Pakistan, realised in his lifetime. The Muslims were indeed happy to get a homeland where they could preserve and foster their cherished way of life and culture.

After the acceptance of the partition plan, Jinnah expressed to the new India his friendly feelings and desire for full co-operation; he even wished for a joint defence plan. Speaking at Delhi on May 21, he said that Pakistan would be in 'friendly and reciprocal alliance with India'. He advocated friendly relations in the mutual interest of both—'that is why I have been urging that we separate in a friendly way and remain friends thereafter'. Jinnah concluded: 'I do envisage an alliance, pact or treaty between Pakistan and Hindustan (India) in the mutual interest of both and against any aggressive outsider.'[2] On August 15, 1947, as the first Governor-General of Pakistan, he declared: 'We want to live peacefully and maintain cordial relations with our immediate neighbours and with the world at large.'[3] But the joy and enthusiasm were short-lived. Soon Jinnah complained: 'We have been victims of a deeply-laid and well-planned conspiracy executed with utter disregard of the elementary principles of honesty, chivalry and honour',[4] and the Prime Minister, Liaquat Ali Khan, declared that 'Pakistan was surrounded on all sides by forces which were out to destroy her'.[5]

COMMUNAL MURDER AND MASS MIGRATION

The Pakistani leaders were led to view the situation with such gloom and anxiety because of a number of serious developments taking place immediately after independence. Communal murder on a scale unprecedented in the modern history of India began in August 1947. It was not the type of communal rioting that used to occur at regular intervals in major cities of the subcontinent; it was nothing less than a war of extermination against the Muslim minority of East Punjab and in a number of adjoining princely states. These massacres have been described in detail; fair and impartial accounts of the Punjab massacre have been given by British and foreign authors.[6] Yet it is necessary to make some reference to these tragic happenings because they profoundly affected relations between the two countries in the early years of independence.

The communal murders and the mass migration gave the two Dominions the worst possible start. Liaquat Ali Khan declared that 'happenings in East Punjab had deeply cut the heart of every Muslim'.[7] The massacre of Muslims in East Punjab and in the adjoining States was well-planned and organised; it might not be 'genocide' in the formal sense, in that the central government of India was not a party to it, but it was actively organised and executed by the State troops and officials of the princely states, and it had the blessing and support of the civil authorities in East Punjab. Of the many accounts of this gigantic massacre, one of the most reliable is that of *The Times* correspondent, published on August 25, 1947:

> 'A thousand times more horrible than anything we saw during the war' is the universal comment of experienced officers, British and Indian, on the present slaughter in East Punjab. The Sikhs are on the war-path. They are clearing eastern Punjab of Muslims, butchering hundreds daily, forcing thousands to flee westward, burning Muslim villages and homesteads, even in their frenzy burning their own too. This violence has been organized from the highest levels of Sikh leadership and it is being done systematically. Some large towns like Amritsar and Jullahdur are now quieter because there are no Muslims left. Appalling atrocities have been committed; bodies have been mutilated; none has been spared—men, women or children.

In editorials on the 'Sikh Rising', published between August 27 and September 5, 1947, *The Times* spoke of it as 'terrible in its savagery; it spares neither age nor youth, its watchword is total extermination without remorse or pity'; as an 'avalanche of violence' which, 'carefully planned and carried out with the most ruthless ferocity, has driven a pitiful flood of Muslim refugees from East Punjab'.[8]

The Muslims in East Punjab and in the Indian princely states of Kapurthala, Faridkot, Nubha, Jind, Patiala, in Baratpur, Alwar and Gwalior, had been routed by the bullets and bayonets of the forces of law and order. Long-planned and directed from a very high level, the immediate purpose of the massacre was to clear the East Punjab of Muslims; the ultimate purpose was to restore Sikh supremacy in the Punjab.[9] Sir Muhammad Zafrullah Khan, Pakistan's Foreign Minister, made a specific accusation before the Security Council of the United Nations: 'On August 9, the organized campaign of genocide directed at the Muslim population of East Punjab began under the auspices and leadership of His Highness, the Maharaja of Patiala.'[10]

Within a period of six or seven weeks between August 1 and September 20, 1947, nearly half a million Muslims were killed. Then the communal murder spread to Delhi, the capital of free India and the seat of its government. The tragic drama of mass Muslim killing in Delhi—the city which, for centuries, was the nursery of Muslim culture in India—lasted for the whole of September 1947. It was an integral part of a deep-laid conspiracy for the extermination of the Muslims. The *Daily Mail* in London published a vivid description of mass massacre in Delhi under the headline "Police look on as Delhi Mobs slay" on September 9, 1947: and, sixteen years after the event, Ian Stephens wrote:

> It happened almost on the door step of the new independent Indian Government where influential people of all sorts lived and who could see and report what was going on. For the savageries against an outnumbered and terrified Muslim minority, the killing, burning, and looting were not confined to the crowded poverty-stricken areas of the old walled city nor to the nearby villages; they swept at times unchecked along New Delhi's wide tree-lined avenues, past the huge Lutyens-Baker Government buildings of the recently extinct British regime, the arcaded modern shopping quarter, the comfortable bungalows of the officials.[11]

The account of Lord Ismay, the Viceroy's chief of staff, as given to Jinnah, was a balanced and fair one. Ismay wrote: 'Delhi itself was on the verge of chaos. Muslims were systematically hunted down and butchered.' Jinnah asked him: 'How could any civilised government permit such a state of affairs?'[12] Field Marshal Auchinleck reported to the British Prime Minister that 'no Muslim can move about freely without risk to his life'.[13] Even Lord Mountbatten, who is regarded in many quarters as one of the best friends of New India, had to confess that 'whereas in Karachi there have been very few incidents, in Delhi there has been almost complete dislocation'.[14]

It is, however, true that, as a result of the massacre of Muslims in India, there were violent reactions in Pakistan, and communal murders and atrocities, to the great shame and sorrow of the government of Pakistan, occurred on a large scale in West Punjab. There was, however, one big difference between the atrocities in East and West Punjab: in East Punjab, the massacre of the Muslims and the atrocities committed against them were the result of a plan, a conspiracy which was systematically carried out; in West Punjab, there was no preparation for months. As Ian Stephens notes, 'large slaughters by Hindus and Sikhs had been carefully planned, whereas few, if any, of this sort of wickedness can be found on the Muslim side'.[15] This reaction in West Punjab to what had happened in East Punjab was deplorable and to be condemned, and Jinnah himself denounced it in the strongest terms. He urged the Muslims to secure the 'protection of minorities as a sacred undertaking', in accordance with the teaching of Islam.[16]

The result of the Punjab massacre was the flight of millions in both directions. Many refugees suffered indescribable horrors, relatives and friends mercilessly slaughtered, women folk outraged, ancestral homes and property looted and abandoned.

How did this unprecedented massacre in Punjab start? Was the Interim Government of Lord Mountbatten aware of the Sikhs' intentions? If so, did his government take adequate steps to stop this human carnage and suffering? These and similar questions still agitate the minds of many. The enforced mass migration not only brought untold human misery and suffering; it also created deep distrust, mutual hatred and suspicion between the two new Dominions; its legacy is still there to complicate further the strained relations between them. The government of West Punjab published three documents entitled *Note on the Sikh Plan*, RSSS (Rashtriya Swayam Sevak Sangh), the activities of the secret terrorist Hindu organisation in the Punjab, and *The Sikhs in Action*. These documents were based on the reports of the Chief Secretary to the government of the undivided Punjab before independence as well as on reports from the Criminal Investigation Department of the same government. These confidential reports, forwarded to the central government in Karachi, indicated that the preparations which the Sikhs were making for creating large-scale disturbances were known to the authorities in New Delhi; in fact the Sikh leaders made no secret of them. This is also confirmed by Lord Ismay, who had long talks with such Sikh leaders as Master Tara Singh and Giani Kartar Singh. They made quite clear to him and Sir Eric Miéville the plans they were devising. Ismay records that 'we told them if they resorted to violence, they would be roughly handled', but confesses that 'we did not feel that our warnings had the slightest effect'.[17] The Governor of the Punjab, Sir Evan Jenkins, had warned the Viceroy about the Sikh Rising.[18] Field Marshal Auchinleck, the last commander-in-chief of the undivided Indian army, had similar views; he wrote to General Rees: 'The massacres, arson and disorder which started in Amritsar . . . was undoubtedly planned long beforehand.'[19] So overwhelming was the evidence that the Viceroy was compelled to warn the Maharaja of Patiala, Master Tara Singh and other Sikh leaders that stern action would be taken against them. Maulana Abul Kalam Azad, the president of the Indian Congress for many years, records that Lord Mountbatten assured him: 'I shall see to it that there is no bloodshed and riot. I am a soldier not a civilian . . . I will order the Army and the Air Force to act and I will use tanks and aeroplanes to suppress anybody who wants to create trouble.'[20] Similar assurance is recorded by Raja Ghazanfar Ali Khan, who was a minister of Lord Mountbatten's government. Khan relates that, 'before partition I drew Lord Mountbatten's pointed attentions to the preparations which the Sikhs and the RSSS were known to be making for large-scale attacks on Muslims in East Punjab. He told me he had received similar information from other sources. Lord Mountbatten gave definite assurance that if any community started trouble he would take strongest measures.' Yet, 'after a large-scale killing of Muslims in East Punjab had started, I reminded Lord Mountbatten in August of his promise, but found him cold and indifferent'.[21] Not only that; at a meeting in July 1947 between the leaders of the Congress and the Muslim League, including Nehru, Patel, Jinnah, Liaquat and the Viceroy, it was decided to arrest immediately prominent Sikh leaders.[22] But Patel opposed these arrests and they were postponed on one ground or another, and the Sikh plan was allowed to be put into operation. The view that no effective measures were taken beforehand to avert one of the greatest tragedies in modern history is shared by many impartial authors. Ian Stephens writes: 'By mid-June signs of imminent trouble in the central Punjab grew. Yet nothing whatever was done, whether by arrests or troop movements, that in the event proved at all adequate. The ill-fated 60,000 strong Punjab Boundary Force was not brought into being until August 1, four days before the outbreak started and the Sikhs' disciplined rural attacks, stretching over an area about half that of Ireland and much more populous foredoomed its task to failure. . . . By July, reports of Sikh intentions from intelligence sources had become precise.'[23] Another British author writes: 'Step by step, Delhi had been advised of the increasing gravity of the situation in the Punjab. The warnings were there, the Viceroy had, at least, three chances to avert a massacre and each time—from wariness, from lack of foresight, or from aversion to another clash with Jinnah—he looked the other way. The result was disastrous.'[24]

The unwillingness of Lord Mountbatten to take effective measures to avert the Punjab massacre was deeply and widely resented in Pakistan and it is recollected even today, over twenty years later. Ghulam Mohammad, who became the third Governor-General of Pakistan, said: 'When the history of the disorders following partition would be written, almost the whole blame would rest on the shoulders of the man who had been the Viceroy, Lord Mountbatten.' He alleged that Lord Mountbatten knew of 'a deep-laid conspiracy by a militant section of the Sikhs to throttle Pakistan by eliminating the Muslim population but no action was taken to prevent it'.[25]

The Commonwealth Relations Office in London gave a reply to Ghulam Mohammad's allegations against the Viceroy. Its statement pointed out that Lord Mountbatten's action in not arresting the Sikh leaders had the support of the British government and that it was also supported by the Governor of the Punjab. An answer to this was issued by the Ministry of Foreign Affairs and Commonwealth Relations of the government of Pakistan, making charges against the Viceroy.[26] A controversy arose between the Commonwealth Relations Offices of the two governments. We need not go into this unhappy controversy, but it highlighted the deep feelings in Pakistan on this issue: an issue which not only affected relations between Pakistan and India but also between Pakistan and Britain.

It was argued that the total number involved in all these massacres and uprooting from homes did not exceed 3 per cent of India's total population, but it has to be explained that 3 per cent of the population of the Indian subcontinent means more than the total population of Canada and 40 per cent of the total population of Australia.

During these terrible days, the leaders of the two countries were drawn to co-operation and joint efforts to stop the mass-killing. The Prime Ministers of Pakistan and India, Liaquat Ali Khan and Pandit Nehru, undertook joint tours of affected areas; they issued appeals to their countrymen to restore peace and protect the lives of minorities. But co-operation between the two governments, even at this hour of human misery and massacre, was not satisfactory; the mutual suspicions and hostilities continued to embitter the relations between the two countries. The tense situation created as a result of mass-killing constituted a threat to peace and stability in the subcontinent. The divisions were deep and the scars were many. It seemed perilous indeed for the future of peace in the subcontinent. Behind the communal quarrels lay the more dangerous and deeper tensions which created the grave discord between these two Commonwealth countries. Since the Punjab massacre of 1947, India and Pakistan have looked upon each other as enemies. A million people who became victims of violence, rape and arson were not easily going to be forgotten. The 10 million people who crossed the borders brought with them memories of great injustice, suffering and oppression. Asia's ugliest unsolved problem—the strained relations between Pakistan and India—began to manifest itself with the mass-killings and migration of 1947.

Pakistan's Prime Minister, Liaquat Ali Khan, complained on September 14, 1947, that the government of India and that of East Punjab had not honoured and implemented the decisions jointly undertaken by the government of the two countries in Lahore some days before. In the meantime, Pakistan's Foreign Minister said at Lake Success that, unless the government of India took steps to end the slaughter of Muslims, the government of Pakistan would file a formal complaint with the United Nations against the genocide in India. When the matter finally reached the United Nations along with the Kashmir dispute in January 1948, the government of Pakistan complained: 'While this vast scheme of genocide was being put into execution in East Punjab and neighbouring areas, the Pakistan Government made repeated efforts to persuade the Union of India to arrest its course. A number of conferences were held between the two Dominions almost invariably at the instance of the Pakistan Government, but while lip service was paid to the necessity of restoring order, no serious effort was made by the Indian Government to implement their promises.'[27] The tragic outbreaks of communal violence in India and Pakistan had involved the two governments in embittered controversy in which lurked the seeds of open conflict. On September 21, 1947, however, they issued a joint statement which was encouraging and heartening. It said: 'Any conception of a conflict between India and Pakistan is repugnant, not only on moral grounds but because any such conflict will result in disaster for both. The two governments will, therefore, work to the utmost of their capacity to remove the causes of conflict.'[28]

In pursuit of peace as reflected in the joint statement of September 21, the government of Pakistan had asked the government of India to agree to a joint request being made to the UN to fly out immediately twelve international observers to study the conditions in the two Dominions and particularly the refugee camps and movement of refugees. The government of Pakistan felt that the presence of neutral observers in both countries would put all concerned on their best behaviour and so halt the vicious circle of communal disorders. Both governments could take action on findings made by neutral observers. Pakistan also appealed to the governments of Commonwealth countries for help and advice to end the murderous raids on trains and columns of refugees in various parts of India. The request was made through the British government, which immediately passed it on to Canada, Australia, New Zealand and South Africa and to Nehru's government at Delhi. The government of Pakistan gave an analysis of the communal situation prevailing in the Indo-Pakistan subcontinent at that time and then asked the member countries of the Commonwealth to consider ways and means of ensuring safety and peace. Whether Britain and other Commonwealth countries could intervene actively or do anything positive to quell the conflict was doubtful but, like the United Nations, they could, as *The Times* said, 'exercise a restraining influence'.[29]

But the government of India, for all its advocacy of the obligations and responsibilities of the United Nations and of the need for friendly mediation and help, was very resentful of Pakistan's quest for peace through the help of the United Nations or friendly countries of the Commonwealth. India would not tolerate any 'outside interference' in her domestic problems; the Indian press saw sinister motives in Pakistan's moves towards peace. Her approach to the United Nations and Commonwealth countries was dubbed 'shock tactics against India'; it was also described as 'trick to hide guilt', though it was very difficult to understand how a country would 'hide guilt' when it sought neutral observers and outside help and assistance. India's refusal to accept Pakistan's suggestion to seek the help of the United Nations or of the friendly countries in a matter where millions of human lives were at stake revealed an early application of her double standard of international morality. However strong her advocacy of international action against colonialism and aggression overseas, India would not tolerate any UN intervention where her own national interests were involved, whether it was Kashmir, Hyderabad, Goa or the attempt to strangle Pakistan.

In the meantime, the fate of refugees continued to be uncertain and they were subjected to all sorts of brutality and inhuman treatment. The need for neutral help, as Pakistan requested, to escort the helpless refugees was imperative. There could be no denial that when these fugitives, reduced to the last extremity of human misery, painfully made their way by road and rail to the areas where they hoped to find safety, they were often fiercely attacked and sometimes ruthlessly butchered by mobs whose communal passion had blinded them to every impulse except a vindictive lust for blood. When neutral help was sought for these tragic victims of violence, it should have been accepted, on humanitarian grounds alone.

Serious complaints about the atrocities against the refugees continued to be made. Early in November 1947, a special train carrying about 5,000 refugees from Karalia camp in Ambala (East Punjab) arrived at Gojjra (Lyallpur, West Punjab); 2,000 of them were found sick and 85 per cent were suffering from dysentery. About 100 persons had already died on the journey. This aroused suspicion and a sample of *atta* (flour) that had been supplied to the refugees at Karalia camp was sent for chemical analysis; it was found that it contained powdered copper sulphate—an irritant poison. The viscera of some of the dead bodies were chemically examined and copper sulphate was detected in most of the samples. The government of West Punjab protested to the government of East Punjab about the poisonous food supplied to the refugees, and asked for a joint enquiry and investigation—but without any result.[30] Similarly, on December 4, Pakistan protested to India about attacks by Indian troops on Muslim refugee girls travelling in a train which left Delhi for Lahore on November 11. The girls were brutally raped by members of the Indian army escort on the train. These incidents, involving the Indian troops escorting refugee trains, were even worse than the crimes of mobs.[31] Field Marshal

Auchinleck informed the British Prime Minister, Clement Attlee, on September 27, 1947: 'Today there is an organised system of information and control which enables Muslim refugee trains to be attacked with impunity.'[32] A few days before, 1,500 helpless refugees were said to have been massacred in one such train at Amritsar, the escort (including the British officer in command) being killed or wounded.

Continuing to press her demand for an impartial investigation into the massacres of 1947, Pakistan requested the Security Council to investigate the charges of mass destruction of Muslims in the areas now included in the Indian Union, to compile a list of the rulers, officials and other persons guilty of genocide and other crimes against humanity and abetment thereof, and to suggest steps for bringing these persons to trial before an international tribunal. Pakistan also made it clear that she would welcome reciprocal investigation.[33] When the legal committee of the United Nations was considering measures for the prevention of genocide on October 3, 1947, the Pakistan delegate at Lake Success accused India of race murder: 'Thousands and hundreds of thousands were being butchered by one community with the connivance of the police and military authority for no other reason than that they belonged to a different faith.'[34]

Pakistan's plea for impartial investigation and international tribunal was vigorously opposed by India. The United Nations Commission on India and Pakistan (1948) was directed by the Security Council 'to study and report to the Security Council' on the matters raised by Pakistan; but, due to India's opposition and intransigence, no attempt was made to investigate the circumstances in which nearly one million people were butchered and 10 million people uprooted from their homes for good.

While millions of people were thus being subjected to suffering and misery after being uprooted from home, talk of war between the two governments was frequently heard. No less a person than Mahatma Gandhi, the great apostle of non-violence, began to talk about war with Pakistan. At a prayer meeting on September 26, 1947, Gandhi chose to declare that, though he had always opposed all warfare, if there were no other way of securing justice from Pakistan and if Pakistan persistently refused to see its proved error and continue to minimise it, then the Indian government would have to go to war against it. He further said that Indian Muslims whose loyalty was with Pakistan should not stay in India.[35] Indian newspapers published Gandhi's remarks under banner headlines and hinted at immediate war with Pakistan. In a subsequent clarification, Gandhi said that India and Pakistan should settle their differences by mutual consultation and, failing that, arbitration; but he went on to point out that, if consultation and arbitration failed, the 'only way left was that of war'. It is the same Gandhi who, in 1940, preached non-violence to the British government against Nazi Germany, but who, in 1942, when Japan was knocking at the door of India, allowed his followers to indulge in all sorts of violence in his 'Quit India' campaign against the British authority in India which was believed to be militarily weak at that moment. Similarly, in 1947, when Pakistan had hardly any military strength, he thought fit to threaten the weaker neighbour with war for atrocities which had first started in his own country and for mitigation of which Pakistan was prepared to submit herself to the verdict of the United Nations. When Winston Churchill referred to the 'fearful massacres occurring in India' in his speech at Snaresbrook on September 27, 1947, Gandhi chided him and declared that he had rendered 'a disservice to the nation of which he is a great servant'. Gandhi put the blame for the massacres in India on 'builders of Empire'.

His aggressive remarks about Pakistan not only caused concern and anxiety in that country (whose Prime Minister sent a cable to the government of India protesting against the threat of war made by Gandhi); it also evoked strong criticism elsewhere. Leading organs of the press in Britain, in particular, were markedly adverse in their reactions. 'The holy man is now talking truculently about war against Pakistan; somewhat inappropriately he chose a prayer meeting at which to make his first appearance as a war lord.'[36] 'A number of people will be startled by Mr Gandhi's sudden desertion of pacifism. The gloss he offered later upon what may very well have been an impulsive statement did not by any means clear up the matter. The pacifist, under all circumstances, cannot sanction or even accept war.'[37] 'There is now open talk of war in India. Mr Gandhi has unfortunately given an impetus.'[38] Sir Zafrullah Khan, Pakistan's Foreign Minister, in commenting on Gandhi's remarks, observed later in the Security

Council that 'it has always been one of the weaknesses of pacifism that no one could be really sure as to how it would stand up to the strain of real horror, the kind of horror that the Nazis knew how to practise and the kind that is now desolating parts of India.[39]

Pandit Nehru rebuked the foreign press for its handling of reports about communal massacre in India. At a press conference in New Delhi on August 27, 1947, he took the foreign press correspondents to task for what he termed 'an abuse of hospitality'. While it is true, that Nehru (like his counterpart in Pakistan, Liaquat Ali Khan) made a number of conciliatory speeches and appeals to maintain communal peace, yet, like Gandhi, he also thought it fit to talk in terms of war against Pakistan. Addressing a meeting to maintain communal peace in India, he remarked: 'I would have liked the armies of India to march into Pakistan for the protection of the helpless',[40] and regretted that the Indian army, instead of marching into Pakistan, had to engage itself to quell the disorders in India. Field Marshal Auchinleck stated in his report to the British Prime Minister on September 27, 1947: 'There is no doubt that today the communal feeling and tension between the two Dominions of India and Pakistan is so great that there is a real risk of their becoming involved in open war with each other at short notice.'[41]

Gandhi and Nehru won reverence all over the world for their respect for tolerance, peace and justice. Yet Pakistanis cannot forget that even these great Indian leaders threatened their country at a time when it was hardly set up. These and similar utterances by the leaders of their large and powerful neighbour engraved deep distrust and fear on the minds of Pakistanis. 'You cannot escape the impression', wrote the correspondent of the *Observer* in September 1950, 'that Pakistan is eaten by fear, not the fashionable contemporary fear of a country whose border marches with Russia but fear of her neighbouring fellow member of the Commonwealth.'[42]

DISPUTES OVER THE PROCESS OF PARTITION

The communal riots and mass migration, as we have stated, gave the two Dominions the worst possible start. The bad effects of these calamities had hardly been overcome when fresh sources of political and economic friction appeared; quarrel followed quarrel. We now turn to a number of disputes that arose over the process of partition. These disputes, some of which were never solved, gave rise to further bitterness, mistrust and fear. The atmosphere, already poisoned by the Punjab massacre, was further worsened by these disputes.

When Punjab was in flames, the award of the Punjab Boundary Commission was announced on August 17, 1947. As was expected, the award gave full satisfaction to neither of the contending parties, and both were unhappy over the details of the awards. We shall not go into those details here; the Radcliffe award, however, had one important aspect which needs to be discussed because the most serious and fatal dispute between Pakistan and India is, in a sense, the legitimate child of the Radcliffe award: the dispute over Kashmir. This might not have been such a disastrous affair if the Radcliffe award had been true and fair to its terms of reference. As we have noted in the previous chapter, the two Boundary Commissions, in demarcating the eastern and western frontiers between India and Pakistan, were to follow the principle of allotting the Muslim-majority areas to Pakistan and the non-Muslim areas to the Union of India. They were also instructed to take into account 'other factors'. Though these were never clearly defined, the most important guiding factor would clearly need to be the religious affinity of the inhabitants of the areas to be demarcated. Suggestions had been made to seek the help of the United Nations or the International Court of Justice for delimiting the frontiers of the two states, but India opposed such moves and ultimately the two commissions were set up as described in chapter 1, i.e., with two Muslim and two non-Muslim members, under a British chairman. Due to differences between the Muslims and non-Muslims members of the Punjab Boundary Commission, no agreed decisions could be made; ultimately the frontiers of the two states were drawn by the award of the British chairman, Sir Cyril (later Lord) Radcliffe. In most of the cases—in fact, in almost all cases except in one important and vital area—the chairman had followed the 'religious affinity' factor and had awarded the Muslim majority-areas to Pakistan and the non-Muslim majority-areas to India. But in the case of the Gurdaspur district of the Punjab, which was a clear Muslim majority area, Sir Cyril Radcliffe, to the great agony and surprise of the government and people of Pakistan, gave it to India. Loss of the Gurdaspur district was not merely a 'territorial murder of Pakistan', it meant something much more. The Gurdaspur district had a Muslim majority; the district consisted of four *tehsils* (subdistricts): Batala, Shakargarh, Gurdaspur itself and Pathankot. Of the four *tehsils*, three had clear Muslim majorities and only Pathankot had a small Hindu majority. The district as a whole, according to the principle by which the sub-continent was divided, should have gone to Pakistan. At best, the Pathankot *tehsil* might have been separated and given to India. But to assign to India the whole district, with overwhelming Muslim majority-areas in three *tehsils* out of four, was a flagrant violation of the principle the Boundary Commission was committed to observe in demarcating the frontiers of the two states.

What is the significance and importance of Gurdaspur district? 'A glance at the map will show', wrote Lord Birdwood, 'that had this district as a whole been awarded to Pakistan, the position of troops landed by air in Kashmir from India would have been quite untenable.' Even if three Muslim-majority *tehsils* of the district had gone to Pakistan,

> . . . the maintenance of Indian forces within Kashmir would still have presented a grave problem for the Indian commanders for their railhead at Pathankot is fed through the middle of Gurdaspur *tehsil*. It was the Radcliffe award which rendered possible the maintenance of an Indian force at Jammu based on Pathankot as railhead and which enabled India to consolidate her defences southwards all the way from Uri to the Pakistan border. . . . Had the Gurdaspur district not been awarded to India, India could certainly never have fought a war in Kashmir.[43]

Without Gurdaspur, India had no claim whatsoever to Kashmir. Was Sir Cyril Radcliffe influenced and persuaded by Lord Mountbatten in favour of India? This unfortunate but deep-seated query agitates the minds of Pakistanis to the present day. The suspicions and doubts created in Pakistan were supported by a sketch map which Sir Francis Mudie, Governor of West Punjab found in the confidential safe at Government House in Lahore, left there by Sir Evan Jenkins, the last Governor of the undivided Punjab. Sir Evan, who was anxious to avoid communal bloodshed in the Punjab, asked for advance information on the possible boundary line. He telephoned the Viceroy's private Secretary, George Abell, who contacted Sir Cyril Radcliffe. The contents of the Boundary Award so far as it related to the Punjab were passed on to Sir Evan, and the information was put in the form of a sketch map. According to this map, the *tehsil* of Ferozepur and Zira was to be assigned to Pakistan; this was confirmed by Radcliffe himself to Justice M. Munir, who was a member of the Punjab Boundary Commission. Munir says that the Punjab Boundary award was finalised on August 8, 1947; yet there was mysterious delay in disclosing the contents even to the leaders and members of the partition council, not to speak of the public. Why were the contents of the award kept secret between August 8 and 17? It is significant that, during this period, Radcliffe was the guest of Lord Mountbatten in New Delhi. Was the award altered during Radcliffe's stay in New Delhi under the pressure of Mountbatten?

The *Manchester Guardian*, referring three years later in an editorial to Pakistan's sense of resentment at the award of Gurdaspur to India, mentioned what it termed 'an old story' in Pakistan to the effect that '. . . Sir Cyril Radcliffe's award in its first draft gave Gurdaspur to Pakistan but that he was persuaded by the then Viceroy to change his ruling'. 'In support of this', the *Manchester Guardian* pointed out, 'Pakistanis claim that there was a mysterious delay in the publication of the award. The stories are firmly and widely believed. They cause the more resentment because, if India had not held Gurdaspur, it could scarcely have intervened in Kashmir.' The leader writer suggested 'perhaps the best course would be for Sir Cyril Radcliffe to narrate the full story of his mission.'[44] The chairman of the Boundary Commission has not, so far, related the full story as suggested by the *Manchester Guardian*, but Justice M. Munir, the former Chief Justice of Pakistan and one of Radcliffe's colleagues on the Commission, published in 1964 his account of the story. According to Munir, the only explanation possible is that Sir Cyril altered the award some time between August 8 and 17, when he was in New Delhi. Munir believes that the chairman would not of his own accord have made the alteration; he must have known that the original award had been communicated to Sir Evan Jenkins, and no fresh arguments had been addressed to him after August 8 to persuade him to alter his decision.

C

'The irresistible inference, therefore, is that he must have been prevailed upon by Lord Mountbatten to make the desired alteration.' About the award itself, Munir says: 'If the Award was judicial, it lacked every attribute of a judicial decision. And if it was political, why lay claim to justice, fairness and impartiality? Why not say that India belonged to the British and their Viceroy gave it to whomever he liked?'[45]

Mountbatten, it seems, was offended by Jinnah's refusal to make him the joint Governor-General of India and Pakistan. Ian Stephens speculates that 'perhaps he had set his heart on becoming dual Governor-General; the rebuff knocked against his most vulnerable point, his pride'.[46] Pakistanis were also viewing, not without apprehension, the growing friendship between the Viceroy and the Indian leaders, particularly Pandit Nehru. Between Nehru and Mountbatten, Michael Brecher writes, 'there developed a relationship . . . which is rare among statesmen and unprecedented in the annals of British Raj. The friendship blossomed during the tempestuous months leading to the partition and beyond.'[47] The allegations against Mountbatten have, however, been denied by British writers, who consider these doubts and suspicions as unfounded and unfortunate. Nevertheless, regrettable as it may be, these doubts are still shared not only by the man-in-the-street in Pakistan but also (as the present writer can vouch for) by responsible persons there who seem to know a lot of inside stories about the transfer of power. It is almost a conviction in Pakistan that the Viceroy was offended by Jinnah's refusal to make him the Governor-General of both India and Pakistan; that he was greatly prejudiced against Pakistan and her leaders; and that he used his authority during the transition period to the detriment of Pakistan. That this resentment against the Viceroy is deep-rooted can be understood from Pakistan's refusal to allow Mountbatten to visit Pakistan in 1956 as the First Sea Lord of the Admiralty, and then again in 1965 as the chairman of the Commonwealth Immigration Commission.

The Radcliffe award was termed in Pakistan as 'extremely unfair', 'disgusting', 'abominable' and 'one-sided'. Government ministers and all national leaders condemned it strongly. Jinnah called it 'unjust, incomprehensible and even perverse'. However, he pointed out that, as the Pakistanis had agreed to abide by the decision of the Boundary

Commission, it had to be accepted. In a broadcast speech from Lahore on October 30, 1947, he said:

> The division of India is finally and irrevocably effected. No doubt we feel that the carving out of this great independent sovereign Muslim state has suffered injustices. We have been squeezed in as much as it was possible and the latest blow that we have received is the Award of the Boundary Commission. It is an unjust, incomprehensible and even perverse Award. It may be wrong, unjust and perverse and it may not be a judicial but a political Award, but we had agreed to abide by it and it is binding upon us. As honourable people we must abide by it. It may be our misfortune but we must bear up this one more blow with fortitude, courage and hope.[48]

The Pakistanis suffered greatly from the Punjab Boundary Commission's decision; they lost territories which, by all canons of justice, should have gone to their country—territories the possession of which enabled India to annex the Muslim-majority states of Jammu and Kashmir. Yet, such was Jinnah's hold over his people that they accepted the award without reservation and did not agitate against it once they had bound themselves to abide by it. No political party or group in Pakistan has sought to undo the award and reannex the Gurdaspur district. This is in marked contrast with the situation in India, where many political parties and groups cherish the hope of undoing partition and, in particular, of integrating East Pakistan into the Union. If Indian attitudes could become the same as Pakistan's in this matter, many of the disputes between the two countries could be solved.

Another source of bitter friction between the two countries arose from the division of the assets of the former government of undivided India. 'The unwillingness of the British Government to admit the necessity of partition until all hope of preserving Indian unity had vanished', says Sir Percival Griffiths, 'had the unfortunate result that no detailed thought was given to the mechanics of division until June 1947.'[49] The Cabinet Mission of 1946 was so averse to any division of the country that no serious attention was given to examining the difficult task of dividing the country's resources in case of division. During the crucial days of the negotiations from March 1946 to May 1947, this vital aspect of the transfer of power seems to have been ignored, though the Muslims were pressing hard to convince the British of the desirability, if not inevitability, of partition due to deep-seated and growing Hindu-Muslim antagonism. The outcome was that, when at last partition was agreed upon and most hastily executed, by far the greater part of the assets and resources of British India remained in the physical possession of the new Indian government, which could conveniently deprive Pakistan of her legitimate share. As Ian Stephens writes: 'In the division of assets, India started with the advantage of having most of them in her physical possession and she dishonestly retained much of Pakistan's share.'[50] Pakistan suffered greatly under the mechanism for the division of the country's assets, particularly military stores and equipment. In spite of repeated representations from the government of Pakistan, India never gave her sister Dominion its due share of the partition assets. This constituted one of the earliest causes of tension between the two countries.

From June 3 to August 15, 1947, a large number of complicated matters had to be solved, with the result that serious dislocation on a vast scale occurred. Highly complicated issues—such as the partition of Bengal and the Punjab, referendum in the North-West Frontier Province and in the Sylhet district of Assam, the division of assets and liabilities of the Government of India, the fate of six hundred princely states, the division and reorganisation of civil and military services— all these were carried out in great haste and in a confusing and bewildering manner within seventy-three days. Many problems were left unsolved and became the source of conflict and quarrel between Pakistan and India. In Ghulam Mohammad's view, Mountbatten 'rushed partition through with undue haste as if it was a naval operation with the result that administration broke down and the Muslims suffered'.[51]

After the verdict of the legislatures of Bengal and Punjab in favour of the partition, a 'Partition Council' was set up both at the centre and in Bengal and the Punjab, on June 27, 1947. At the centre, the Partition Council worked through a steering committee composed of two officers—a Muslim, Choudhury Mohammad Ali (who later became Prime Minister of Pakistan) and a Hindu, H. M. Patel. In addition, there were appointed ten expert committees which covered the whole field of administration and dealt with important and varied subjects, such as division of armed forces, the administrative organisation, records, personnel, assets and liabilities, problems relating to currency, trade and economic control. It was the function of the steering committee to ensure that concrete proposals were evolved within the time limit by the various expert committees, adequately to examine these proposals and then to present them to the Partition Council for decision; and then, after obtaining these decisions, to take steps for implementing them.

The Partition Council worked smoothly up to August 15, 1947, before which date a number of decisions were made quickly in a fair manner. But the whole atmosphere was changed after the transfer of power, for the government of India had no hesitation in going back on the undertakings it had previously made. On September 27, twenty-eight days after the transfer of power, Field Marshal Auchinleck wrote in his report to the British Prime Minister: 'As soon as British authority was withdrawn [the Indians] disregarded solemn obligations which they had freely incurred ... what mattered to them, above all else, was to cripple and thwart the establishment of Pakistan as a viable independent State.'[52] No records essential to the operation of the various ministries had ever reached Karachi; the first two trains carrying some of the necessary government records from Delhi to Karachi were burnt and nothing could reach the new state. In respect to such simple matters as which citizens possessed passports and which did not, the Indian government did not deliver the papers and the government of Pakistan was without the necessary information.[53] The 'strangulation' procedure was highly successful because all the records and apparatus of the government machinery were in New Delhi. The central government at Karachi had to start from scratch.

While we may ignore some details of this 'strangulation' plan, there are two matters which need to be elaborated, for they continued to embitter the relations between the two countries for many years, and one of these agitates the minds of Pakistanis to the present day. These are distribution of military stores and equipments, and the allocation of the cash balance of the former government of India.

To supervise the division of armed forces and military stores and equipment, a Joint Defence Council was set up with the Governor-General, Lord Mountbatten, as chairman, and consisting of Field

Marshal Lord Auchinleck, the Supreme Commander, and representatives of the two successor authorities. It was charged with the duty of completing the division of the armed forces, with their plant, machinery, equipment and stores. It was an impartial organisation under Auchinleck for ensuring fair division of the military equipment. It was estimated that the Supreme Commander would be able to complete his task by March 31, 1948. Within a very short time after the transfer of power, India was bent on abolishing this instrument for impartial distribution of military equipment, finding it a great hindrance to her plans for depriving Pakistan of any military stores or equipment in order to keep her militarily weak. Soon great pressure was brought to bear on Mountbatten to abolish the Joint Defence Council. It was highly distasteful to him to yield to Indian pressure on this issue; yet, being a constitutional Governor-General, he had to abide by the decisions of his Indian cabinet. In 'the most difficult letter' that he had 'ever had to write' in his life, he informed the Supreme Commander of the decision and pressure of the Indian cabinet. He lamented to Auchinleck: 'One of the most balanced and level-headed Ministers complained recently that you seemed to regard yourself as the champion of Pakistan's interests: such is the reward of impartiality.' 54 Auchinleck himself reported to the British Prime Minister: 'I have no hesitation whatever in affirming that the present India cabinet are implacably determined to do all in their power to prevent the establishment of the Dominion of Pakistan on a firm basis. In this I am supported by all responsible British officers cognizant of the situation.' He referred to India's designs to 'prevent Pakistan receiving her just share or indeed anything of arsenals and depots in India', and spoke of Delhi's opposition to the Joint Defence Council. Concluding that 'if we are removed there is no hope at all of any just division of assets in the shape of movable shares belonging to the former Indian Army', Auchinleck added: 'The attitude of Pakistan, on the other hand, has been reasonable and co-operative.' 55 Pakistan strongly opposed the abolition of the Joint Defence Council before the agreed date (March 31, 1948), but, in spite of her protests, it was abolished on November 30, 1947.

Thus, the Indian government was successful in doing away with the impartial organisation which could have ensured equitable distribution of the military stores and equipment. It undertook, however, that Pakistan's due share of military stores would be delivered, and Mountbatten pledged 'the honour of my Government' at the meeting of the Joint Defence Council on November 7, when the question of its abolition was hotly debated between the representatives of the two governments. 'This pledge', Sir Zafrullah Khan later informed the Security Council, 'like other similar pledges of the Indian Government has not been honoured.' Pakistan's Foreign Minister told the Security Council that, of 165,000 tons of ordnance stores due to Pakistan, only 4,703 tons had been delivered up to March 31, 1948, leaving a balance of 160,000 tons undelivered. Less than 3 per cent of the stores were delivered.[56] Under the partition agreement 150 Sherman tanks were allotted to Pakistan; not one of them, however, was delivered. The small amount of military equipment that Pakistan got from India was 'mostly unserviceable, damaged or obsolete'.[57] The delivery of telegraph stores was also withheld. Despite repeated representations by the Pakistan Post and Telegraph Department, goods valued at less than one million rupees were released out of stores worth 11 million rupees. That was less than 9 per cent, and of this small amount released only one-third was actually received. 'No laboratory equipment, testing equipment, carrier terminals and repeaters', the Foreign Minister complained, 'have so far been released by India despite the repetition of the protest. . . . This is a matter which is causing a good deal of irritation and friction and which continues to produce bad feeling between the two governments.'[58] The government of Pakistan continued to demand the due share of military stores, and the government sent a communication about the matter (dated April 30, 1948) to the Inter-Dominions Defence Secretaries Conference which met in New Delhi on May 3, 1948. Thereafter, the Prime Minister, Liaquat Ali Khan, and other ministers raised this question at subsequent Inter-Dominion Conferences. In 1951, when Liaquat Ali and Pandit Nehru exchanged letters on how to improve the relations between the two countries, the issue was raised, but without effect. Pakistan's due share of the military stores was never delivered. India resorted to all sorts of delaying factors and ultimately stopped even the delivery of the small quantities she had agreed to send. Pakistan had to use one-sixth of her sterling balance by June 1949 in paying for defence stores as a consequence of India's refusal to share the military stores equitably.

The present writer has had access to a number of confidential records of the government of Pakistan, from which it would appear that there can be no question of the genuineness of Pakistan's allegation with respect to non-delivery of military stores from India. In a note which was prepared by the government of Pakistan at the time of the Ayub-Nehru meeting on September 10, 1959, when serious efforts were made to improve the relations between the two countries, it was stated that, under the agreement reached between the two countries, Pakistan was to receive approximately 165,000 tons of defence stores, valued at approximately 487 million rupees. Against this quantity she had received only about 23,000 tons.

In May 1961, at an Indo-Pakistan conference, Pakistan put forward a claim of 370 million rupees as compensation for buying stores abroad at a considerably higher cost due to India's failure to supply Pakistan's share of the defence stores in accordance with the Partition Council's decision. Sir Percival Griffiths says that 'it would not be surprising, in view of the tension between India and Pakistan and the dispute over Kashmir, if India did, in fact, keep back arms which she should have sent to Pakistan'.[59] All the facts taken together do seem to support the general case that India never gave Pakistan her legitimate share of military stores and defence equipment. It was presumably done to keep Pakistan weaker so that India could dictate terms on disputes like Kashmir, the Indus River water and border disputes. It was an act of bad faith and gave rise to deep distrust and misgiving in Pakistan. 'How can we ever trust the word of the government of India after this sort of treatment?', was the question in the minds of the leaders and people of Pakistan. Even today, it rankles in Pakistani minds. Pakistan 'regarded her powerful neighbour from the outset with fear and suspicion, which were strengthened by the belief that she had been unjustly treated by India in the division of the assets and particularly the military stores of undivided India'.[60]

Serious disputes also occurred over the division of financial assets, particularly the cash balance of the former government of undivided India. Pakistan complained to the Security Council that 'ever since the announcement of the decision to carry a partition of the subcontinent of India into Pakistan and India, those responsible for giving effect to the decisions on behalf of India have adopted an attitude of obstruction and hostility towards Pakistan, one of the objects being to paralyse Pakistan at the very start by depriving it of its rightful share of financial and other assets'.[61]

The cash balance of the former government of undivided India on August 14, 1947, was 4,000 million rupees. Pakistan demanded 1,000 million rupees as her share of the cash balance; India did not agree. The matter, therefore, was referred to the Arbitration Tribunal which had been set up to decide such cases of differences. In December 1947, however, the two governments arrived at a financial agreement under which Pakistan's share was fixed at 750 million rupees. Earlier, as an interim measure, 200 million had been awarded to Pakistan. The Indian Deputy Prime Minister, Sardar V. Patel, when announcing the financial agreement in the Indian Parliament on December 9, expressed the hope that the Kashmir dispute would be settled simultaneously. But during negotiations of the financial agreement, which was reached on its own merit, there was never any hint or suggestion that its implementation would be linked with the solution of the Kashmir dispute. The Pakistan Finance Minister, Ghulam Mohammad, who led his country's delegation to the financial talk, stated: 'At no stage of the discussion which led to the signing of the agreement was the question of Kashmir ever mentioned or considered. If it had been, Pakistan would never have been a party to the agreement.'[62] Yet Sardar Patel declared at a press conference on January 12, 1948: 'India cannot reasonably be asked to make payment of cash balance when an armed conflict with its forces is in progress', and he indicated that the Kashmir dispute would be 'likely to destroy the whole basis of the financial agreement'.[63] The Indian government instructed the Reserve Bank of India (which, according to the agreement made at the time of partition, was supposed to act as banker and currency authority both for India and Pakistan up to October 1, 1948) not to credit the government of Pakistan with the 550 million rupees of the cash balance which were due to her under the financial agreement. This produced sharp reaction and resentment in Pakistan, where it was described 'not only as an unfriendly act but as an act of aggression'. Ghulam Mohammad denounced India's action as 'nothing but one of pressure politics and blackmail'. He appealed to international opinion 'to judge how the big brother—India—is treating the infant state of Pakistan'.[64] Liaquat Ali Khan and Sir Zafrullah Khan also spoke in bitter terms of India's failure to honour her obligations under the financial agreement.

Pakistan also accused India of putting pressure on the Reserve Bank not to fulfil its obligations. The pressure, it was alleged, was designed to destroy the monetary and currency fabric of Pakistan, which had not yet set up her own State Bank. It was pointed out that money under cash balance did not belong to India in any sense; it was Pakistan's property. The seizure might conceivably be justified if the two countries were at war and if that war had broken out after the agreement had been signed. But the Kashmir dispute had been going on already for about six weeks when the government of India signed the financial agreement. It was clearly recognised that Pakistan's share of the cash balance was Pakistan's property. It was no gift or aid from India which could be withheld to bring pressure on Pakistan over the Kashmir problem. The action of the government of India in linking the payment of cash balances with the Kashmir dispute, put Indo-Pakistan relations under further strain. The situation took such a grave turn that Gandhi had to intervene, and he started a fast to end communal tensions and fighting in India. Gandhi's fasting was also an indication of his disapproval of the Indian government's dishonouring of the financial agreement on seemingly absurd grounds. At last, India agreed to pay Pakistan her share of the cash balance, but even then an amount of 50 million rupees was arbitrarily deducted as advance adjustment of certain claims against Pakistan. Pakistan considered this deduction as 'untenable and wrong' because the financial agreement did not provide for any such deductions. India described its action in releasing the cash balances of Pakistan as 'an act of generosity' while, in fact, it was a belated act of justice performed after giving rise to bitterness and mistrust.

While the government of India denied Pakistan her share of military stores and defence equipment, and while so much fuss was created before her cash balances were paid, Pakistan gave delivery to India of ninety aircraft (including fifty Tempests, thirty-two Spitfires, three Austers and some aero-engines) which were part of India's share but were in physical possession of the government of Pakistan. The *Hindu* reported from Karachi on January 12, 1948, that 'crates containing planes and plane parts belonging to India are being loaded in ships to be delivered to the Government of India. All these 100 planes were lying in Karachi port even prior to August 15, 1947.'[65] No 'Mahatma' was needed to undertake a fast to induce the Pakistan government to give India her share of aircraft—planes that were used in the Kashmir war—nor did it designate the fulfilment of its agreed obligations as 'an act of generosity'. If India had shown the same attitude and spirit in implementing the various agreements made at the time of partition, much of the dispute, fear and suspicion which still complicate any effort to improve the relations between the two countries could have been avoided.

STRUGGLE OVER THE ACCESSION OF PRINCELY STATES

In the preceding pages we have discussed a number of developments which put Indo-Pakistan relations to severe strain and stress. But the most alarming thing since independence had been the development of direct conflict between the two governments, likely to embroil them in war over the accession of certain princely states. Terrible as had been the bloodshed inflicted on the peoples of the Punjab by communal hatred, the diplomatic capacity of the two governments was to be even more severely tested by their competition for the adhesion of the princely states. Relations between the two Dominions approached boiling point over the fate of three princely states: Junagadh, Hyderabad and Kashmir.

In 1947, there were 562 princely states. These had hitherto preserved a degree of independence, and their rulers had direct relations with the British Crown, the paramount power. With a total area of 712,000 square miles and a total population of 93 million (according to the 1941 census), they occupied two-fifths of the entire Indian subcontinent and contained nearly a quarter of its population. The future of these states was not adequately or fairly dealt with at any stage of the negotiation of transfer of power in 1946–47. Their future was far from clear, and the subsequent near-war tension between India and Pakistan over the future of some of them was exacerbated by what Ian Stephens calls 'the impetuous and (some might reckon) unprincipled haste with which the British, under Lord Mountbatten's lead, extricated themselves in August 1947 from their governing responsibilities'.[66] The

British Cabinet Mission made the following statement on the future of these states on May 12, 1946:

> When a new fully self-governing or independent Government or Governments come into being in British India, His Majesty's Government's influence with these governments will not be such as to enable them to carry out the obligations of paramouncy. . . . His Majesty's Government will cease to exercise the powers of paramouncy. This means that the rights of the States which flow from their relationship to the Crown will no longer exist and that all the rights surrendered by the States to the paramount power will return to the States.[67]

The same policy towards the princely states was reaffirmed in the final plan for the transfer of power as announced on June 3, 1947. Statements made by the British government on February 20 and June 3, 1947, showed that there was no intention of handing over the powers and obligations exercised by the Crown under paramouncy to any successor government or governments of the Indian subcontinent.

As in some other cases, the Congress leaders accepted this part of the plan of transfer of power with great mental reservations. They challenged the right of any prince to decide the future of his state, and declared, not without justification, that the princes were 'anachronisms' and 'medieval despots' (though in the case of Kashmir, as we shall see later, India's leaders were only too willing to rely on the legal rights of a 'medieval despot'). The Muslim League, representing the future government of Pakistan, accepted faithfully the position as laid down by the British government. The Congress leaders, however, soon got the full support and approval of their policy from the Viceroy, Lord Mountbatten. It was reckoned by many that one of the factors which led the Indian leaders to appoint Mountbatten as the first Governor-General of free India was to secure his help in gaining the adhesion of the princely states. At a hurriedly summoned conference with state rulers in Delhi on July 25, 1947, Mountbatten virtually repudiated all the pledges and promises made to the princes and urged them to join either of the two new governments. The princely states had the option, therefore, of acceding either to India or to Pakistan; but the vast majority of states, under pressure from the Viceroy and under threats from the Congress leaders, joined the Union of India.

When the ruler of a state and his subjects were of the same religion, no dispute ordinarily arose. It was different where the ruler was Hindu and the population mainly Muslim, or where the ruler was Muslim and the population mainly Hindus. Unfortunately, there were a number of such cases. It may be recalled that the whole subcontinent was divided on the basis of religion. The Indian leaders, today, claim that they had never accepted religion as the basis of division of India, yet it was they who pressed, successfully, for the division of Bengal and the Punjab on the basis of religion. The Hindu-majority areas were separated and carved out of the Muslim state of Pakistan. Similarly, the Indian government did not allow any princely state to accede to Pakistan if the Hindus were in a majority in that state. It was only in the case of states with Muslim majorities that Nehru and his colleagues advanced the argument of secularism and relied on the legal rights of the princes whose 'medieval despotism' they had denounced. They even resorted to violence and armed conflict. When the Muslim ruler of a small state tried to opt for Pakistan, the Dominion of India made a demonstration with tanks, troops, warships, and planes and forcibly annexed the state which had legally become a part of the Dominion of Pakistan. But when the same problem arose with regard to a state whose Hindu ruler, in spite of its Muslim majority, refused to join Pakistan, India sent aeroplanes with Sikh soldiers to coerce a Muslim people struggling to be free.

In less than five months after the attainment of independence, the two countries were on the verge of war over the accession of some princely states. Of course, India knew that in the event of an all-out war Pakistan would be at a disadvantage. India had all the major industries of the subcontinent and had an army of about 200,000 against an army of 55,000 in Pakistan, which hardly had any military equipment, as mentioned earlier. India had also all the ordnance factories of the subcontinent. A sense of military superiority was manifest on the part of the stronger and larger neighbour. In the struggle for accession of states, India relied heavily on her physical might, making 'a sheer exploitation of superior force'.[68] She resorted to direct action, thereby adding immeasurably to the legacy of suspicion and ill-will, and hastening the outbreak of full-scale hostilities.

Let us now review the near-war tensions and armed conflict that began between the two Commonwealth countries in 1947–48 over the accession of certain princely states. Some of these disputes, like those over Junagadh and Hyderabad, have lost much of their importance and become stalemates, though still provoking bitterness and distrust. But the conflict over Kashmir has proved to be fatal and enduring; it led to serious armed conflict between the two countries twice since 1947, and it still constitutes the most threatening menace to any effort to improve understanding and relations between the two countries.

Junagadh

The first dispute over the accession of the princely states arose over the small state of Junagadh in the Kathiawar peninsula, on India's west coast. Junagadh had an area of roughly 4,000 square miles, with a population of about 750,000, of which about 80 per cent was Hindu and some 20 per cent Muslim. Contiguous to Junagadh was the tiny state of Manavadar, an independent chieftainship, the population of which was also mainly Hindu. Another chieftainship was Mangrol, which was not independent but feudatory to Junagadh. In the Kathiawar region there were also several *talukas* (estates owned by landholders having special privileges), all of which were under the feudatory control of Junagadh. Though Hindus formed the majority of the population of Junagadh, Manavadar and Mangrol, their rulers were Muslims whose sympathies lay with Pakistan. The territory of Junagadh state was not by land contiguous to Pakistan, but it was about 300 miles by sea from Karachi and less than 300 miles from the nearest border of Pakistan. With two fair-sized ports and several smaller ones along its seaboard, Junagadh had good direct communications with Karachi. Though there was great pressure on the Nawab of Junagadh to accede to India, he did not commit himself till August 15, when the transfer of power took place. Subsequently, he expressed his desire of acceding to Pakistan; the moves for accession to Pakistan were made earlier, but the Government of Pakistan accepted the accession on September 15, 1947. The Nawab of Manavadar acceded to Pakistan on September 24, while the ruler of Mangrol, which was feudatory and not independent, joined India, as also did some landholders of the

Babriawad *taluka*. These latter had no independent power of accession but the government of India accepted their adhesion in retaliation against the action of the Nawab of Junagadh. The drama was thus set for an open rupture between India and Pakistan.

As soon as the Nawab of Junagadh had expressed his willingness to join Pakistan, India vehemently protested against his decision. In a telegram to Liaquat Ali Khan, dated September 12, 1947, Nehru argued that 'a state is free to accede to either of the Dominions but the choice of state in regard to accession must, in our opinion, necessarily be made with due regard to ties of geographical contiguity'. 'The Dominion of India would be prepared to accept any democratic test in respect of the accession of Junagadh state to either of the two Dominions', but, he warned, 'if the ruler of Junagadh is not prepared to submit this issue to a referendum and if the Dominion of Pakistan, in utter disregard of the wishes of the people and principles governing the matter, enter into an arrangement by which Junagadh is to become a part of the Federation of Pakistan, the Government of India cannot be expected to acquiesce in such an arrangement'.[69] Less than six weeks after the sending of this telegram, India, in 'utter disregard of the wishes of the people and principles governing the matter', accepted the accession of the Hindu ruler of predominantly Muslim Kashmir. Pakistan was now not only asked to acquiesce in such matter; she was even dubbed 'aggressor' for offering sympathy and moral support to the people of Kashmir. In the case of Junagadh, the Governor-General of India, in a telegram to Jinnah, could argue that the 'acceptance of accession by Pakistan cannot but be regarded by the Government of India as an encroachment of India's sovereignty and territory and inconsistent with the friendly relations that should exist between the two Dominions'. But India was vehemently to deny the applicability of this argument to her own acceptance of the accession of Kashmir.

India did not rest by sending telegrams expressing high principles and paying allegiance to the wishes of the people. As soon as Junagadh's accession was announced, a campaign was started against the Nawab's government which Sir Zafrullah Khan denounced as 'closely reminiscent of the Nazi technique of overpowering weaker neighbours'.[70] 'A technique of aggrandisement had been learnt [in Junagadh]', Ian Stephens observes, 'to be repeated later elsewhere not only in 1961 successfully against Goa and in a modified form in 1950–51 and again in 1961–62 against Nepal, but in 1948 against another of three princely states which on Independence Day had remained undecided and a very much bigger and more important one, Hyderabad.'[71] A 'Provisional Government' for Junagadh was set up by a relative of Gandhi. The Mahatma's early associations with Kathiawar were recalled and it was stated that he was greatly agitated over Junagadh's accession to Pakistan. This 'Provisional Government' under Samal Das Gandhi raised an 'army of liberation' which was equipped with all modern weapons, presumably supplied by the Indian army. The so-called liberation army indulged in all sorts of violence—plundering, killing and looting the border villages of Junagadh. The government of India, of course, expressed its non-recognition of the 'Provisional Government' and pleaded that no encouragement had been given. Yet after the forceful occupation of Junagadh by the Indian troops, Samal Das Gandhi offered his thanks and appreciation to the Indian Deputy Prime Minister, Sardar Patel, and said: 'All the honour goes to Sardar Patel who was kind enough to give me every possible guidance and co-operation. If there had been no Sardar Patel, we could not have achieved such a brilliant success.'[72] India's elder statesman, Sir Chimantal H. Setalvad, on November 3, 1947, made the following comment on the situation: 'The so-called provisional government of Junagadh was openly formed in Bombay and for days it proclaimed its intention of marching to Junagadh to overthrow the Junagadh Government as by law observed . . . the leaders of that provisional government have openly raised a volunteer army and have captured several villages in Junagadh territory.' He lamented that 'the Indian Government themselves have remained passive spectators of all unfriendly and hostile acts against a state which is, together with the Dominion to which it had acceded, at peace with India'.[73]

India's hostile activities were, however, not confined to giving aid and encouragement to the 'Provisional Government'. In utter violation of the standstill agreement with the Dominion of Pakistan, India interrupted and stopped postal and all other communication with Junagadh which had become legally a part of that Dominion. The government of India also imposed an economic blockade against Junagadh; supplies, including food and petrol, were withheld.

In the meantime, there were exchanges of telegrams and messages between the two governments to settle the accession of Junagadh by an impartial plebiscite. Pakistan, to the great surprise and bewilderment of the Indian government, agreed to discuss the terms and conditions for a plebiscite in Junagadh. On October 7, in a telegram to Liaquat Ali Khan, Nehru said: 'We are glad that you are agreeable to our discussing conditions and circumstances under which a plebiscite or a referendum should be held to ascertain the wishes of the people.' The government of Pakistan made it clear that 'Junagadh is not the only state regarding which this question [of plebiscite] arises', and that it was 'prepared to discuss conditions and circumstances in which a plebiscite or referendum should be held in any state or states'. This was a well-calculated step on the part of the government of Pakistan, which was anxious to get the method of plebiscite or referendum accepted as a medium of settling conflicts over the accession of any state when the wishes of a ruler did not coincide with those of its people. If this method had been applied indifferently, there would have been no trouble or armed conflict over the accession of the princely states. It may be recalled that the referendum was already accepted and applied in those parts of British India where there was any doubt about accession to India or Pakistan. It is difficult to see why Lord Mountbatten, who devised this method of ascertaining the wishes of the will of the people of British India, did not suggest or recommend it in the case of princely states.

While the negotiations between the two governments were in progress, one of the understandings reached was that no Indian troops would either enter Junagadh or be moved through Junagadh territory. Delhi, however, was not in a mood to settle the dispute peacefully. When the government of Pakistan suggested to the Indian government that the management of the postal, telegraphic and other communications should be handed over to Pakistan in accordance with the terms and conditions of the standstill agreement between the two Dominions made at the time of partition, India refused to agree, saying that 'we do not recognise the accession of Junagadh and are therefore unwilling to comply with your request'.[74] At the same time, it is certain that the Indian leaders could see the implications of a plebiscite to solve the question of accession. If a free and impartial plebiscite were accepted for Junagadh, how could it be refused in Kashmir or Hyderabad? Hence Delhi put forward the absurd requirement that the terms and conditions for plebiscite in Junagadh should be settled by India and Junagadh; Pakistan, to which the state had acceded was not even to be a party to such arrangement. Lord Mountbatten, as Governor-General of India, stated that 'the Government of India are, however, prepared to accept the verdict of the people of Junagadh in the matter of accession, the plebiscite being carried out under the joint supervision of the Indian and Junagadh Governments'. [75]

India, in no time, blocked all the paths to peaceful solution of the Junagadh dispute, and soon resorted to arms to settle the question. A force of warships, tanks, troops and planes sent by the government reached the port of Porbandar on the frontier of the state of Junagadh on October 5, 1947. The following day, the *News Chronicle* published, under the heading "India sends tanks to warn a State", the news of India's amphibious landing at Porbandar: Indian troops, supported by sloops, minesweepers and fighter planes moved to occupy Junagadh; Indian troops surrounded the state of Junagadh. While moving her troops to occupy Junagadh, India professed that she had 'no desire to take any step which might aggravate an already difficult situation'. India also referred to her adherence to the declaration of September 20, 1947, in which the two governments declared their determination to 'rule out war'. In a communiqué announcing the landing of Indian troops at Porbandar, Delhi declared that it was its wish 'to find a solution of this problem by friendly discussion'. [76] On October 17, *The Times* reported: '3,400 Indian troops, supported by light tanks and a squadron of fighter aircraft are surrounding Junagadh.' Finally, on November 9, Indian troops marched into the city of Junagadh, capital of the state. The ruler had already left for Pakistan. It was stated on behalf of the government of India that its troops had occupied Junagadh in response to a request from the Dewan (chief minister) of the state. The Dewan, Sir Shah Nawaz Bhutto, however, subsequently said: 'Handing over the administration to the India Union was comparable to inviting a thief to tea.' All he had done, he said, 'was to ask the Regional Commissioner at Rajkot to give his assistance to the administration which was threatened from without'. According to him, 25,000 Indian troops surrounded Junagadh and threatened to arrest its ruler. [77]

The legal position was, as later pointed out by Pakistan's Foreign Minister in the Security Council, that, in view of the state's accession to Pakistan, the Dewan had no right to offer, and the Indian government had no right to accept, the so-called invitation to take over the state's administration. 'Hundreds of states, including . . . Kapurthala which has a Muslim majority in the population, acceded to the Indian Union', said Sir Zafrullah Khan, 'but in no case did the Pakistan Government intervene in any way. Junagadh was the first state to accede to Pakistan and at once the India Government started a campaign of vilification, threats and economic blockade', finally leading to its occupation by the armed forces of India. [78]

On November 10, after the military conquest, Pandit Nehru declared that India had taken Junagadh on a 'temporary basis'; while Gandhi, in his prayer meeting on November 11, said that he 'could see no breach of International Law and no occupation'. [79] But for Pakistan the occupation of Junagadh by Indian troops was a 'clear violation of Pakistan territory and breach of International Law'. [80]

It was not only the government of Pakistan that considered it an act of aggression and violation of its territory; many outsiders were also shocked to see India resort to arms to settle a dispute with its neighbour. Thus, *The Times*, in an editorial on November 5, 1947, declared:

> The course of events in Kashmir and Kathiawar is steadily imperilling good relations between the Indian Union and Pakistan. Of the two Dominions, India is by far the stronger in economic as well as in military resources and the action it is taking, however defensible in its own estimation, seems . . . to be sheer exploitation of superior forces. It would be fatal to the future of both Dominions as well as to the larger interest of the people of the Indian peninsula if further encouragement were given by either side to the idea that such differences as have arisen can be satisfactorily settled by strong-arm methods.

The *New York Times* termed the Indian action 'extremely unwise and unfortunate'. [81] But perhaps the most apt comment was made by the *Manchester Guardian*, in an editorial on October 21, 1947:

> There is an old Indian story of a holy man who believed in non-violence and was the inspiration and idol of his people. He hurt

neither man or beast nor even vegetable. But one day, chancing on a piece of iron, he relaxed his principle to the extent of chopping a jungle weed which had grown across the entrance to his cell. The next day he came upon a snake in the forest and growing used to his new tool, protected himself by dispatching it at one blow. Thus he took the first steps to violence. Within a year he was chieftain and within five he had the blood of tens of thousands on his head. Here surely is a parable on which the Indian Government should reflect in its dealing with Junagadh. . . . [This use of force] is a departure from all that Mr Gandhi and Jawaharlal Nehru have preached. It puts the new Government on a level with those states which Congress once despised—it now seems pharisaically.

Diplomatic relations between the Dominions of India and Pakistan had been pushed almost to an open clash by India's action in sending troops to Junagadh and taking over the administration of that state. It may be asked, why did Pakistan accept the accession of Junagadh, which it was not in a position to defend militarily? From conversations with a number of responsible persons—including officers of the Ministry of Foreign Affairs—in the Pakistan administration, it is the present writer's impression that Pakistan's action was governed by two factors: first, she did not expect that India would really resort to arms once the state had become legally part of the Dominion of Pakistan; secondly, and more important, it was expected in Karachi that the affair would lead to a satisfactory formula to decide the question of more important princely states, such as Hyderabad and Kashmir where the religious affiliation of the ruler was not the same as that of the majority of the population. Neither of these two states had acceded to India or Pakistan on August 15, 1947. If the principle of a fair and impartial plebiscite could emerge from the dispute over Junagadh, the fate of those two important states could be settled without any bitterness between the two Dominions. By the principle of plebiscite, India would certainly get Junagadh as well as Hyderabad, but Kashmir would come to Pakistan.

The dispute over Junagadh was brought before the Security Council along with the Kashmir dispute, but no decision was made there sustaining the right of India's action in Junagadh. The Security Council, however, heard the statements of the representatives of Pakistan and India, and its resolution of June 3, 1948 asked the United Nations Commission for India and Pakistan to study and report back to it on appropriate action to be taken over the Junagadh dispute, along with other disputes which Pakistan had brought to the notice of the United Nations in January 1948. But the Commission was so preoccupied with its endless task of finding a solution to the Kashmir dispute that other disputes were never investigated or reported. To complete the story of Junagadh we should, perhaps, refer to the plebiscite which India held after the military conquest. It was as forced as it could be. Samal Das Gandhi, the head of the 'Provisional Government' of Junagadh declared: 'If the Muslims [of Junagadh] vote for Pakistan, we will know who are not loyal to the Union; we cannot keep the serpents and scorpions alive moving under our pillows. We must put them to death. We will see who votes for Pakistan.'[82] Sir Zafrullah Khan stated: 'Many of the Muslim ladies of highly respected and wealthy families escaped into Pakistan with the fronts of their bodices cut off with scissors because the Indian troops were in a hurry to deprive them of their jewelry and gold and could not do so quickly enough except by cutting off their bodices' fronts.'[83] No wonder that, under such circumstances, the plebiscite resulted in 190,799 votes for India as against 91 for Pakistan. The princely state of Junagadh has disappeared from the map of India; it is now a part of the Union State of Bombay. The government of Pakistan, however, still considers Junagadh as a part of Pakistan which is being held illegally by India. The bitterness over the dispute has survived to the present day.

We shall now turn to Hyderabad; although the sequence of events would suggest that Kashmir should be discussed after Junagadh, the dispute over Kashmir is so lengthy that we shall discuss it in a separate chapter.

Hyderabad

Hyderabad was the most important and highly developed princely state. Before the British authority was established in the Indian sub-continent, Hyderabad was an independent power that had established treaty relations with certain European powers, including Britain and France. Under the British *Raj*, Hyderabad, like other princely states, had surrendered its external sovereignty to the British Crown, which exercised political suzerainty. But Hyderabad continued to exercise complete internal autonomy and retained most of the ingredients of a state, controlling her own postal system, currency and communications. In relation to the British Crown the ruler of Hyderabad, the Nizam 'stood in a class distinct from any other ruler', and was officially designated Britain's 'Faithful Ally'. The Muslims of the Indian subcontinent looked on the Nizam as the principal inheritor of the Moghul tradition. The University of Hyderabad was a great centre of Muslim culture and learning. The state had an area of over 82,000 square miles and, under its Muslim ruler, lived a population of over 18 million, the majority of whom were Hindus. Hyderabad was traditionally noted for Hindu-Muslim harmony, and peace was maintained within its borders when the communal massacre on an unprecedented scale began in various parts of British India and also in some Hindu princely states. This harmony, unhappily, was not to survive the aggression of India.

As stated earlier, the agreement reached before the transfer of power was that the Indian princes should have the option of joining either of the two Dominions or of remaining independent, and their obligations under paramountcy were to lapse with the withdrawal of the British. Clement Attlee, speaking on the Indian Independence Bill in the House of Commons on July 10, 1947, said that, 'with the ending of the treaties and agreements, the states regained their independence', while the Secretary of State for India, Lord Listowel, declared in the House of Lords on July 16, 1947: 'From the date when the new Dominions are set up, the treaties and agreements which gave us suzerainty over the states will become void. . . . They will then be entirely free to choose whether to associate with one or other of the Dominion Governments or to stand alone.'[84] The Indian leaders, it may be recalled, did not like the prospect of any independent princely state; yet, when it was convenient, they acknowledged the rights of the princes to remain independent. Thus, the Indian delegate during the debate on the Kashmir dispute in the Security Council said on January 15, 1948: 'When the Indian Independence Act came into force, Jammu and Kashmir, like other states, became free to decide whether it would accede to the one or the other of the two Dominions or *remain independent*.'[85] The Indian delegate even recognised the right of any princely state to 'remain independent with the right to claim membership in the United Nations'. From the legal point of view, there was full freedom for any ruler of state to claim independence after the transfer of power.

In accordance with this legal position, the Nizam of Hyderabad, immediately after the announcement of the plan for transfer of power on June 3, declared on June 11, 1947:

The basis of the division of British India is communal. In my state, however, the two major communities live side by side and I have sought, since I became ruler, to promote by every means good and friendly relations between them. My ancestors and I have always regarded the Muslim and Hindus as the two eyes of the state and the state itself to be the indivisible assets of all the communities inhabiting it. . . . . The subjects of my state have affinities and common interests with both the contemplated new Unions [India and Pakistan]. By sending representatives to either of the constituent assemblies, Hyderabad would seem to be taking one side or other. I am sure I am consulting the best interest of my subjects by declining to take such a course. I have, therefore, decided not to send representatives to either of the constituent assemblies. [86]

Hyderabad had one serious disadvantage if it remained as an independent state: it was landlocked, with no access to the sea. India took full advantage of this geographical handicap. As soon as the Nizam declined to accede to India and indicated his desire to retain a limited measure of independence, India began a campaign of pressure and persecution. The government in Delhi under Lord Mountbatten brought all sorts of pressures to force Hyderabad to accede to India. 'Secular' India's real attitude to Hyderabad was revealed when an Indian spokesman declared that: 'Hyderabad is a Muslim dagger pointed at the belly of India' which must be removed. [87] Considering his state's geographical position, the Nizam was anxious to come to terms with India in respect of external affairs, defence and communications. Delhi, however, demanded nothing less than full accession.

After a period of negotiations, a 'standstill' agreement was reached between the Nizam's government and India on November 29, 1947.

It was to continue in force for a year, and disputes arising under it were to be submitted to arbitration. Like many other agreements with her smaller and weaker neighbours, India showed very little regard to this agreement. With this agreement in force, India started a ruthless and cruel economic blockade which included food, salt, medicine and even babies' food. Winston Churchill told the British House of Commons on July 30, 1948: 'A harsh blockade has been imposed against Hyderabad by the central Government of India which in many aspects is similar to that which the Soviet Government are now throwing around Berlin. But the number of helpless people in Hyderabad is 17 million compared with 2,500,000 in Berlin. The supply of medicine, drugs and hospital equipment to Hyderabad has been cut off.'[88] The Times, in its editorial of July 27, 1948, called the blockade of Hyderabad 'a sorry example of public policy from a country that gave birth to Mr Gandhi'.

In accordance with provisions of the standstill agreement, the Nizam desired that differences between the two governments be referred to arbitration, but India simply ignored his appeal. Further, the Nizam offered to hold a plebiscite in Hyderabad, under the supervision of the United Nations, to ascertain the wishes of the people on the issue of accession to India or independence. The government in Delhi, however, would have nothing to do with a plebiscite because it relied on superior military strength. India's reply was that Hyderabad must accede to India first and then a plebiscite might be held to confirm the accession: the type of plebiscite India gave to Junagadh after the military conquest of that state. As in the case of Junagadh, the Indian government was not content with an economic blockade only; it simultaneously concentrated troops around Hyderabad. Nehru declared on July 26, 1948: 'If and when we consider it necessary we will start military operations against Hyderabad state.' He described the Nizam's government as 'composed of gangsters', and asserted that the only alternatives for Hyderabad were accession or disappearance as a state. He even refused to qualify by the name of war the military operations which India was about to begin, on the ground that 'war can be waged only between independent countries'.[89]

Faced with threats of military operations and a severe economic blockade, the Nizam's government brought the situation before the

Security Council under Article 35, paragraph 2, of the United Nations Charter, and asked for 'swift, authoritative and determined action' by the Council. Such swift action was urgently needed. Even before Hyderabad's appeal could be heard, Indian troops began marching into the state on September 12. Professor Clyde Eagleton, who was a member of the United States delegation at the Dumbarton Oaks conference, subsequently declared that India's invasion of Hyderabad 'represents the most clear-cut defiance which the Security Council has yet faced and if left untouched it will be the United Nations' most humiliating defeat, a precedent very dangerous for the future'.[90]

The Foreign Minister of Hyderabad appealed to the conscience of the world against wanton and entirely unprovoked acts of aggression by India. 'All modern weapons of war are being used against a defence-less state—a state which placed all her resources at the disposal of the allies during the last war.'[91] This use of force against a weaker neigh-bour came badly from a government which owed its existence to the principles embodied in the Charter of the United Nations.

The coercion of Hyderabad was not justified in the eyes of the world either by the quick success of India's military operations or by the chorus of approval raised by Indian public opinion, which had shown itself oblivious of all but narrowly nationalist and even com-munal considerations. Many of India's warmest friends abroad were distressed by her ruthless use of force against a weaker neighbour. In the British Parliament, Anthony Eden said: 'It is beyond dispute that the Dominion of India by invading Hyderabad has committed a flagrant and inexcusable breach of their own agreement with Hydera-bad. The invasion of Hyderabad by the armies and air forces of the Dominion of India is in fact an act of aggression'; while the British Foreign Secretary, Ernest Bevin, expressed in the same debate his regret that 'in this new Dominion a war-like spirit has developed'.[92] The world press was also shocked. *The Times* observed bitterly that 'once again a powerful Government by resort to arms has imposed its will upon a weaker neighbour. [The Indian Government] has, in the judgment of world opinion, violated the moral principles upon which hopes of international security must rest.'[93] To the argument advanced in New Delhi that the invasion of Hyderabad was a 'police measure to restore law and order which the Nizam could not maintain himself', the *Christian Science Monitor* retorted: 'That is the sort of formula Hitler brought into disrepute.'[94]

What happened to Hyderabad's appeal to the Security Council? The appeal was pending when Indian troops marched into the state and occupied it. The Karachi newspaper *Dawn* lamented: 'Paris [the Security Council was meeting in Paris] fiddled while Hyderabad fell.' The Council took '96 hours holiday from responsibility' and when it met India had already achieved its object and presented the United Nations with a *fait accompli*. *Dawn* continued: 'India is making war in Kashmir; India has made war and has over-run Hyderabad. Many Indian leaders and organs of Indian opinion have been openly talking of war against Pakistan. If this war-like spirit, which Mr Bevin deplored, is not checked, large sections of mankind will remain continuously exposed to the danger of further aggression.'[95]

The Security Council heard the Hyderabad complaint at several meetings held in Paris during September 1948, but it contented itself with keeping the question on its agenda without making any effort either to stop the aggression or to terminate the military occupation after India had overwhelmed Hyderabad. India, however, made the Nizam withdraw his complaint. This was obviously done under duress. As Professor Jessup, a US delegate and later a judge of the International Court of Justice, remarked at a later session in May 1949: 'The use of force does not alter legal rights and therefore the situation has not been materially affected by the events of the last hours nor has it been substantially changed from what it was when the Security Council took it under consideration at our last meeting.'[96] The Nizam's withdrawal of complaint after the Indian military conquest was described by Dr Jose Arce of Argentina as 'hearing about the sheep from the wolf'.[97] Several other delegates also asserted that the complaint should be on the agenda. The discussion was, however, not taken up in the face of Indian opposition.

On October 6, and again on November 21 and December 6, Pakistan requested that discussion be resumed and sought to participate in it. The Indian government announced that it would send no representative to any discussion on Hyderabad's complaint after it was 'withdrawn' by the Nizam; it also asserted that Hyderabad was not a 'state' and therefore not entitled to appear before the Security Council.

In any case, India claimed that '*now*', i.e., after the military conquest, Hyderabad was a domestic question over which the United Nations had no jurisdiction. This contention that Hyderabad was wholly a domestic affair could be compared with the Netherlands' contention that the Indonesian Republic was her domestic issue, or South Africa's contention that racial discrimination was a domestic issue. In regard to such arguments from the Netherlands and South Africa, India, rightly, agreed with the world opinion that problems of this kind were not domestic issues; but, in the case of Hyderabad, India could see no justification for a Security Council discussion of her military action against a smaller neighbour. The *Christian Science Monitor*, commenting on India's double standard of morality, said on May 24, 1949: 'What happens to the Indian minority in South Africa, a sovereign state, is a matter of concern to the United Nations, says India. What the Netherlands does in Indonesia, over which it claims sovereignty, is equally a concern of the UN, says India. But what has happened to the recently annexed state of Hyderabad is strictly an Indian affair and no business of the UN, says India.'

As regards India's contention that Hyderabad was not entitled to be heard by the Security Council because she was not a state, Professor Eagleton, after pointing out that the Security Council had heard the representatives of Indonesia and the other non-Sovereign entities— of the Jews in Palestine before Israel became a state—went on to say: 'A case actually in consideration by it [Security Council] was interrupted by a use of force which was itself contrary to or in defiance of the Security Council jurisdiction. . . . The Council was confronted with a *fait accompli* and if disputes can be settled in this fashion, the very purpose for which the United Nations was created is undermined.'[98] Sir Zafrullah Khan declared that, 'if Hyderabad was independent before September 12 of last year [1948], then the mere fact that its independence has been destroyed does not make the dispute a domestic matter for India. If that were so, then after every annexation by a state of territory belonging to another state, once the annexation had been completed as a result of military action . . . the state that had gained the accession might say: "Well, this is now a domestic matter, today it is a domestic question".'[99]

The question of Hyderabad last came up for airing at the meetings of the Security Council held on May 19 and 24, 1949, when the statements of the delegates of India and Pakistan were heard. The matter ended there without any action. The complaint is, however, still pending on the agenda of the Security Council. Such is the fate of a complaint by a smaller state against a bigger state whose forces fully occupied the former and wiped it from the map of the world. Hyderabad as a separate political entity no longer exists, it now forms part of the Union States of Andhra, Bombay and Mysore. The Muslims of Hyderabad were subjected to all sorts of tyranny and harsh treatment. The Prime Minister of Pakistan stated on October 30, 1948 that 'things were still happening in Hyderabad that would shock the world'.[100] The real situation was that the Hindu majority in Hyderabad regarded the Indian military action as the conquest of ruling Muslims by Hindus, and they let loose a reign of terror, suppression and oppression against the Muslims under the protection of Indian military rule. Dr J. Naidu, an independent member of the Indian Parliament, stated on July 23, 1952:

> According to conservative figures 2,000 persons were killed, not less than 50 died in jails and concentration camps, fifty thousand persons were arrested and subjected to all kinds of tortures and indignities, one thousand houses were destroyed or burnt . . . and property worth *lakhs* destroyed and 10,000 raids were made on villages; I do not know the number of women raped, because rightly or wrongly women would not admit rape but only cry.

When the ruling Congress party members challenged the allegation, a Muslim member of the Indian parliament rose and, clenching his fist, said, 'My own sister was raped'.[101]

What was the impact of India's military conquest of Hyderabad: a state with which the Muslims all over the Indo-Pakistan subcontinent had great cultural and historical links? Sir Zafrullah Khan told a press conference in London on September 17, 1948: 'The case of Hyderabad causes us considerable disgust as to future relations between Pakistan and India. If genuine differences are only to be settled by armed forces, how much will international peace be worth?'[102] India's action in Hyderabad caused great resentment and concern among the people of Pakistan, all the more so because it coincided with the death of their predominating influence, the *Quaid-i-Azam*, Mohammad Ali Jinnah. Many Pakistanis feared that the same technique of territorial aggrandisement as applied in Junagadh and Hyderabad was also being vigorously pursued in Kashmir, and might also be applied against the defenceless East Pakistan. Ian Stephens confirms the force of this fear: 'What did at the time actually concern Pakistan, because attempts, she guessed, would soon be made at applying it against herself—as indeed threatened during the war-like crisis of 1950 and 1951—was the manner of Hyderabad's extinction; virtually the same as Junagadh.'[103]

FEARS, ANXIETY AND DISTRUST

Pakistanis followed the course of events after the transfer of power with growing alarm. It began with the massacre of the Muslims under the Sikh Plan; then came the hosts of disputes arising over the process of partition itself and depriving Pakistan of her share of the British India assets; and finally there was India's military action to solve the dispute over the accession of three princely states. Within less than a year, the armies of two Commonwealth countries were engaged in an armed conflict over the mountains of Kashmir. The army of India, a country that acknowledged King George as Head of the Commonwealth, had annexed a territory of the same king's Dominion of Pakistan, and then the armies of two 'brother' states were engaged in warfare in another disputed territory. Apart from the legal niceties confronting the Commonwealth, it created harrowing anxieties in Pakistan. The principal danger to good relations between the two Dominions, product of the events in Junagadh, Hyderabad and Kashmir, lay in the feelings aroused in Pakistan by the spectacle of India's exercise of military strength. The correspondent of the *New York Herald Tribune* thus describes the prevailing tensions and fears in Pakistan in early 1948:

If I can sum it up after two weeks of listening to it here, it comes to this: that the Hindu leaders never really accepted partition but only pretended to do so in order to get rid of the British and that since August 15, last, the independence date for both India and Pakistan, they have tried by every means in their power to strangle this new state before it can fully come into being. . . . I do not take all

Pakistan statements for Gospel by any means. But all the facts adduced, taken together, do seem to support the general case, which is that India wishes to destroy Pakistan as rapidly as possible and to restore it to the dominion of Delhi.[104]

In their public statements Indian leaders frequently made insufficient allowance for Pakistan's susceptibilities. Mahatma Gandhi, while trying to restore communal peace in India, told his countrymen that the persistence of Hindu-Muslim hatred would perpetuate the division of India. By using that phrase he indicated quite clearly—what, indeed, he had said earlier—that to his mind the partition was merely a temporary division. When such were the words of Gandhi, who unquestionably still ruled India through his disciples, there would appear to be ground for Muslim apprehension over the fate of Pakistan. Other Indian leaders were even more explicit. The Congress president, Acharaya Kripalani said on Independence Day (August 15) 1947: 'Let us henceforth bend all our energies to the unification of this land of ours.'[105] Pandit Nehru declared: 'India's heart has been broken but her essential unity has not been destroyed'; and he asked his people: 'How will you repair the broken heart?'[106] Sardar Patel, the Congress's 'strong man', said: 'Today the partition of India is a settled fact and yet it is an unreal fact; the partition would remove the poison from the body politic of India. This would result in the seceding areas desiring to reunite with the rest of India. India is one and indivisible; one cannot divide the sea or split running waters of a river.'[107] Sardar Patel's attitude towards Pakistan was revealed by his close associate, Maulana Abul Kalam Azad, who was president of the Congress for several years; Azad wrote: 'He [Patel] was also convinced that the new state of Pakistan was not viable and could not last. He thought that the acceptance of Pakistan would teach the Muslim League a bitter lesson. Pakistan would collapse in a short time and the provinces which had seceded from India would have to face untold difficulty and hardship.'[108] Gandhi was perhaps more optimistic than anybody; he expressed full confidence that the two parts of India would ultimately reunite again.[109] 'The Muslim League will ask to come back to Hindustan. They will ask Jawaharlal Nehru to come back and he will take them back.'[110]

The real attitude of the Congress was, perhaps, betrayed by the resolution which it adopted while accepting the partition plan of June 3, 1947:

Congress has consistently upheld that unity of India must be maintained. Geography and the mountains and the seas fashioned India as she is and no human agency can change that shape, or come in the way of her final destiny. Economic circumstances and insistent demands of international affairs make the unity of India all the more necessary. The picture of India we have learned to cherish will remain in our hearts and our minds. . . .

The committee earnestly trusts that when present passions have subsided, India's problems will be reviewed in their proper perspective and the false doctrine of two nation theory in India will be discredited and discarded by all.[111]

Could the Congress leaders be more explicit in their desire to undo the partition and eventually bring the 'seceding areas'—Pakistan—back to the union of India? The Pakistanis seemed to be convinced that the policy the government of India pursued since the achievement of independence was directed to this aim of reuniting India.

After the announcement of the partition plan on June 3, 1947, the correspondent of *The Times* summed up the Congress attitude like this: 'Congress will work the present plan in the hope that it will ultimately lead to a restored union of India'; and the paper's editorial commented: 'The Congress party still pins its faith to the conception of an undivided India for which it will continue to work.'[112] Six months after partition, *The Times* again reported in a leading article, entitled "Rise of Pakistan":

Rightly or wrongly, every Pakistani believes that the sovereignty of his country is contested. He fears that the larger Dominion is determined to destroy Pakistan and that the systematic sabotage of partition schemes, stoppage of essential requirements such as coal and rail transport, the deliberate withholding of arms and equipments, and the massacre of Muslims are all part of a prepared but veiled plan to enforce reunion.[113]

The speeches of Indian leaders sometimes appear to indicate that they found it difficult to conceive of Pakistan as a separate state. The belief that 'seceding areas' would later come to their senses was widespread in India. Nehru's biographer, Michael Brecher notes that 'there was a widespread belief that Pakistan would be short lived. Most of the Congress leaders, and Nehru among them, subscribed to the view that Pakistan was not a viable state—politically, economically, geographically or militarily—and that sooner or later the areas that had seceded would be compelled by force of circumstances to return to the fold.'[114] The Indian government seemed to be working hard to create the necessary 'force of circumstances' to compel Pakistan to seek reunion. Brecher concludes: 'Conversation with many Indian politicians strongly suggests that this was a sincere conviction.'[115] It was a general belief in Congress circles, and held strongly, that the North West Frontier Province and East Bengal, in particular, would be compelled by economic pressure to reunite with the rest of India.[116] Congress leaders more readily accepted the 'truncated', 'moth-eaten' Pakistan because they regarded it as only temporary. When the division of the Indian subcontinent into two separate states was proposed as a solution of the Indian problem, serious doubts were expressed that the new state of Pakistan could ever be made a workable proposition from the financial and economic standpoint. Indian economists and experts were forecasting the early collapse of Pakistan, and this strengthened the tendency to assume that in due course Pakistan would seek reunion.

This was an important, if not the guiding, factor in the acceptance of the partition plan by the Congress, and the post-independence policy pursued by India seems to have been directed to hastening the process of reunification. This was certainly the belief in Pakistan. Sir Zafrullah Khan said on January 1, 1948: 'The objectives of the policy of the Government of India towards Pakistan through all these months has been to punish the Muslims for their temerity in demanding the partition of India. They apparently desire to beat Pakistan down to its knees so as to make it sue for readmission into the tender embraces of India.'[117] A communiqué from the Pakistan Ministry of Foreign Affairs on July 29, 1948, stated: 'It is evident that Pandit Nehru is still unable to accept the fact of partition and that his and other Indian leaders' consent to partition was given with mental reservations which are now being revealed. So long as this attitude persists, no number of conferences can succeed in establishing formal and neighbourly relations between the two Dominions which Pakistan so earnestly seeks.'[118]

It is not too much to say that Indo-Pakistan relations since independence in 1947 have been as bad as Franco-German relations ever were and with implications as explosive. The real problem was mistrust; the disputes were open to solution, but the trouble was that mistrust had become too deep. As Professor Quincey Wright said: 'Pakistanis do feel that India does have its eye out for the re-annexation of Pakistan.'[119] Because of mutual distrust and fear, the limited financial and economic resources of both the new countries were frittered away on defence. Pakistan, being the smaller of the two, viewed with anxiety and suspicion the designs behind the expansion of the Indian military machine which was growing fast; and hence felt compelled to spend on defence what its limited resources would justify.

The gravest discord between any two new states in South Asia was that between Pakistan and India. The two neighbours, in fact, looked upon each other as enemies soon after their independence. *Round Table* reported in June 1948: 'There was a large body of opinion in India which regarded Pakistan as an ephemeral and unnatural product doomed to early collapse which could be hastened by all measures of pinpricks.' In an earlier issue, in March 1948, *Round Table* observed: 'The question that has been uppermost in the minds of the peoples of this Dominion [Pakistan] has been whether war between India and Pakistan can long be avoided.' India's Deputy Prime Minister, Sardar Patel, said on January 6, 1948 that 'war between India and Pakistan is inevitable if their present unsatisfactory relations continue'.[120] To this the Pakistan Prime Minister replied: 'Indian Union leaders who have never accepted partition of India sincerely have been making elaborate designs to end Pakistan since its very birth. It is the intensive desire of Sardar Patel to block Pakistan's way to progress and to achieve that end he has been employing all kinds of weapon.'[121] Pandit Nehru aroused enthusiasm among 100,000 listeners, mostly Sikhs at Amritsar, on January 29, 1948, when he hinted at India's armed strength as against Pakistan's. Dealing with the possibility of war with Pakistan, he declared: 'If we have to fight anyone, we have an army strong enough.'[122] It is not surprising, therefore, to find *The Times* reporting

D

on January 5, 1948: 'There is much loose talk in India about the inevitability of war between the two Dominions, not only by men in the street but also by responsible persons who should know better. There are fears in Pakistan that border incidents may provoke India to enter her territory.' A fortnight later, its editorial observed: 'Talk of war filled the air and the anti-Pakistan party led by Sardar Patel with his bitter Gujarati memory of ancient Muslim oppression gained control.'[123]

A plea for good relations between India and Pakistan was made by Ghulam Mohammad, Pakistan's Finance Minister: 'Both India and Pakistan are spending heavily on defence—huge sums which could be spent on education, sanitation and housing. All this money is going down the drain and all because there is distrust.'[124] The Pakistan Foreign Minister, Sir Zafrullah Khan, said at a press conference on January 1, 1948, that the partition of India had left throbbing wounds behind. 'It is the task of true statesmen to seek to bind and heal the wounds rather than by calculated action to seek to convert them into running and poisonous ulcers.'[125]

An initial period of misunderstanding between Pakistan and India was perhaps to be expected, though with good will it could have been considerably reduced, if not altogether avoided. The demand for the partition of India made by the Muslims was not welcomed by the non-Muslims as a whole. The Congress, representing the latter, had vehemently opposed the creation of Pakistan. Only three days before the announcement of the partition plan, Gandhi had declared: 'Even if the whole of India burns, we shall not concede Pakistan, even if the Muslim demanded it at the point of the sword.'[126] The unity or division of India became, as was pointed out in the preceding chapter, the major issue between the two great communities, Hindus and Muslims, living in the subcontinent. When partition was finally announced, it caused great bitterness and anger among the non-Muslims; consequently a feeling of resentment towards Pakistan became evident. The Muslims also had grievances, particularly over the partition of the Punjab and Bengal. But the Muslims accepted the partition scheme with the fullest intention of making it work both in letter and spirit. On the Muslim side, though there was disappointment, it was accepted *bona fide*. There was an apparent lack of such good faith on the part of the Hindus who seemed, as is indicated by the quotations from the speeches of their leaders, to have accepted partition with great mental reservations and with the aim of undoing it in due course after the British had left. The unfortunate utterances of the Indian leaders and some aspects of the policy of the government of India created an image of India in the minds of Pakistanis which complicated further the Indo-Pakistan relations. The image of India in Pakistan, as it emerged in the initial years of 1947–48 and has continued to the present day, depicts her as unwilling and unable to accept Pakistan as a sovereign state. India seems to regard Pakistan as an overt challenge to the ideal of a united India which the Congress leaders continue to cherish and foster. 'Pakistan is the embodiment of all the principles that India denies.'[127]

3

KASHMIR

PAKISTAN-INDIAN relations since 1947 have pivoted mainly on the issue of Kashmir. This dispute is the poisoned well from which infection has spread to every other point of contact between the two countries. The importance of Kashmir to Pakistan can hardly be exaggerated. If in Delhi the Kashmir question represents an issue of prestige or principle, in Rawalpindi it looks like a matter of life and death: any hostile power installed in Kashmir can dominate Pakistan militarily; can threaten at close range the vital road and rail communications from Lahore to Peshawar; and can control the waters of the Chenab and Jhelum on which the economic life of the country depends. For ethnological, economic and strategic reasons, Pakistanis contend that they cannot possibly allow any hostile or potentially hostile country to hold Kashmir; and a Kashmir held by India would put them in the position of Czechoslovakia after Hitler's rape of Austria. Western Pakistan would be surrounded on three sides by India and would become militarily indefensible.

The dispute over Kashmir has lasted now for two decades. It has kept Pakistan and India divided; it has largely influenced the international outlook of the two countries, and has caused embarrassing situations for the friends and 'allies' of the two countries. Above all, it has led to actual armed conflict between the two states: the limited war of 1948, and the major battles of 1965—'the biggest tank war since the Second World War'. Because of Kashmir, the two countries have spent huge sums of money on arms: money that could have financed the gallant aims of both the new nations to raise their peoples' pitiably low standard of living. Gigantic efforts, supported and helped by friendly nations, to improve the economic conditions of the two countries have been greatly hampered and thwarted by the ruinous dispute over the mountains of Kashmir. Until this dispute is settled, the threat of war in the subcontinent is bound to persist. Any effort to improve Indo-Pakistan relations, as made at the Tashkent Conference in Januaty 1966, is likely to be wrecked on the rock of this grievous dispute.

Of the numerous disagreements between Pakistan and India, their conflicting claims to the state of Kashmir, with its predominantly Muslim population, have been most prominent. If the two countries could settle this question they would speedily resolve their other quarrels. The festering sore of this dispute has infected the relations of the two countries so seriously that it is responsible for failure to reach agreement on any other major issues. Although a cease-fire has been twice achieved by the United Nations since 1948, the rival armies are still ranged against each other and it needs only a spark for fighting to break out again. No government in Pakistan, however powerful it may be, can survive if it neglects or tries to evade the issue of Kashmir. The Muslims in Pakistan have shown themselves determined never to accept a state of affairs in which Kashmir, with Muslims composing 80 per cent of its population, would be governed by Hindus from Delhi. The Kashmir issue dominates national thinking. To a Pakistani, Kashmir is not a remote and unknown country; it is near and dear and vital: near in geography; dear in religion; vital in strategy.

Jammu and Kashmir, in area and population, was second only to Hyderabad among the princely states of undivided India; and its proximity to the Soviet Union and the Chinese province of Sinkiang gave it a special strategic importance. Known to the tourist as the 'Switzerland of the East' for its beauty of hill and valley, it was also prosperous. For generations the economic life of Kashmir was bound up with what is now Pakistan. Its principal exports, consisting of raw materials, timber, hides and wool, used to pass down to Lahore and Sind. The census of 1941 estimated the population of Jammu and Kashmir to be 4 million, of whom over 3 million were Muslims.

Islam entered into the state in the tenth century and since then the Muslim culture has been dominant. It was firmly established by the Mogul emperors Akbar, Janhangir and Aurangzeb who paid frequent visits to the state. In race, culture, dress, food and customs, the Muslims of Jammu and Kashmir are closely akin to the Muslims of Pakistan. Only by accident did it happen that a Hindu rule was established in Kashmir: under the Treaty of Amritsar (1846), the British sold the state to Raja Gulab Singh (a petty chieftain of the Sikh tribe of the Dogras of Jammu) for about $7\frac{1}{2}$ million rupees. The Dogras proved to be oppressive and degenerate despots. Amid the natural wealth and beauty of their homeland, the Muslim population endured the tyrannical rule of the Sikh Dogra and of the Hindu Brahmin caste until the autumn of 1947. Like the other rulers of princely states, at the transfer of power the Hindu Maharaja of Kashmir had the option of joining either India or Pakistan or of remaining independent. 'All through the early part of 1947', noted the Asian specialist, M. Philips Price M.P., 'when the British were preparing to leave India, the Maharaja of Kashmir was busy introducing Sikh and Hindu Mahasabha agents into Kashmir "to influence" his subjects.'[1] The Maharaja's policy, which ran manifestly counter to the wishes of the Muslim majority, brought discontent and unrest into Kashmir. Anarchic conditions began to prevail in the state; indeed, as a political and administrative entity it virtually disintegrated during the great political transformation at the time of partition and independence. Muslim subjects in certain areas rose in revolt against the rule of the Maharaja, declaring themselves independent of his authority when they found the situation intolerable. Civil war broke out. In the cases of Junagadh and Hyderabad, as we saw in chapter 2, India did not allow the rulers the option of choosing one or the other Dominion or of remaining independent, arguing that the action contemplated or taken by these rulers was contrary to the wishes of the majority people of those states. But in the case of Jammu and Kashmir, India sent troops, tanks and aeroplanes to uphold the cause of an autocratic ruler who was not only denying the wishes of the majority but actually repressing them by violence.

The trouble in Kashmir began in August 1947, when the Hindu Maharaja, Sir Hari Singh, started applying the same techniques of extermination to the Muslim population as were being employed by the Sikh and Hindu rulers of the princely states of Kapurthala, Faridkot Patiala, Nubha, Alwar and Gwalior. The process of extermination might have been as successful as in Kapurthala, which also had a

Muslim majority population, but the Maharaja of Kashmir experienced some difficulties in carrying out his grand design, because some of his people were ex-soldiers of the Second World War and did not wish to die, and because his state was surrounded by Muslim-majority areas. These factors complicated the Maharaja's plans and he was not as successful in genocide as his fellow-rulers elsewhere. He had to seek the support and help of India's troops and planes. Lord Birdwood has well described the situation:

In August 1947 an anti-Muslim movement within the state was initiated with all the appearance of a systematic persecution. It started on August 26 at Bagh in Poonch when Muslims were set on and killed by the state troops. . . . It continued and increased in tempo with the infiltration of members of the RSSS, Akali Sikhs and the INA* into Jammu province in October. . . . The motives of the Kashmir state Government in prosecuting so disgraceful a campaign of persecution are not difficult to divine. A systematic modification of the population in favour of the non-Muslim elements would obviously achieve popular support for an extension of their own precarious term of office.[2]

The same story is told by Premnath Bazaz,[3] the Kashmiri Hindu leader, in his *History of Struggle for Freedom in Kashmir*: 'In Poonch and Mirpur, populated by thousands of demobilised soldiers of the Second World War, the Maharaja's armies in order to assert the Dogra Rule wantonly plundered whole areas inhabited by Muslims and set fire to their homes. The Government wanted to massacre people without letting the world know what it was doing.'[3]

It was in Jammu province, where Hindus and Sikhs slightly out-numbered the Muslims, that the Maharaja's extermination plan had its main success. 'Within a period of eleven weeks starting in August [1947]', writes Ian Stephens, 'systematic savageries, similar to those already launched in East Punjab, Patiala, Kapurthala, practically eliminated the entire Muslim element in the population, amounting

* RSSS: Rashtriya Swayam Sevak Sangh, the Hindu terrorist group.

INA: Indian National Army, the Japanese-sponsored guerrilla force organised during the Second World War by Subhas Chandra Bose, groups of which maintained terrorist activities after 1945.

to 500,000 people. About 200,000 just disappeared, remaining untraceable, having presumably been butchered or died from epidemics or exposure.'[4] *The Times* reported on October 10, 1947: '237,000 Muslims were systematically exterminated, unless they escaped to Pakistan, by the forces of the Dogra state, headed by the Maharaja in person.' These atrocities took place before the much-publicised 'tribal invasion' in October 1947, which provided the pretext for the Indian military intervention in Kashmir. In terms of human suffering and misery, the incidents in Jammu and Poonch were far more appalling than the inrush of Pathan tribesmen which occurred in October. Political leaders, writers and the press in India have continuously told the world that the Indian soldiers and planes were sent to Kashmir in October to save the Kashmir people from the tribal invasion which, it is alleged, was engineered and supported by the government of Pakistan. Little, if anything, is said by them of the fact that the Muslims of Kashmir were being systematically massacred by the state troops of the Maharaja of Kashmir, against whose oppressive and cruel rule the people had arisen. The trouble in Kashmir started, not with the inrush of tribesmen, but with the systematic massacre of the Muslim population by the state forces, and the Pathan attacks were a direct consequence of this slaughter of fellow-Muslims. As the Pakistan Foreign Minister told the Security Council:

> Apparently the case that it is sought to make out here is that all these troubles came from the tribesmen, that is, outsiders who made an incursion into the state and disturbed the peace of that beautiful and happy valley. That is an entirely untrue picture of the whole situation. The correct picture is that the Maharaja, for purposes of his own, let his troops loose upon his people in certain areas, particularly in Poonch; that he let the bands of Sikh and *Rashtriya Sevak Sangh* volunteers create havoc in certain parts of the Jammu province of his state and that against these barbarities the people of the state rose in revolt.[5]

Indian forces were used, not to rescue the people who were being systematically exterminated, but to protect the autocrat who was inciting the slaughter. If the Indian soldiers and planes were really meant for the relief of the suffering people, they should have been sent

to the province of Jammu in August and not October of 1947 and to
rid Kashmir of Sikh bandits. While more than 200,000 people were
being exterminated in a well-organised genocide by the Hindu
Maharaja, Nehru and Gandhi seem to have raised no protest; it was
only when fellow-Muslims from tribal areas came to rescue the
suffering people that the Indian government sent its forces to protect
the ruler whose savagery had incited the Pathan tribesmen to ven-
geance.

In a telegram to the British Prime Minister on October 29, 1947,
Liaquat Ali Khan, the Prime Minister of Pakistan, said: 'There is no
doubt that the state troops attacked Muslims at Poonch. Women and
children took refuge in Pakistan, and burning villages could be seen from
our border...later they set out to massacre Muslims of Jammu.' Liaquat
further revealed that the Dogra brigadier in command of Jammu had
admitted that his orders were to drive out Muslims from a belt of
territory three miles wide.[6] In the American Missionary Hospital at
Sialkot, hundreds of injured women and children were brought in for
medical help. A harrowing feature of the atrocities, said Sir Zafrullah
at the Security Council, was the maiming of children 'under the very
eyes of their mothers'. At least 25,000 women had fallen into the hands
of Dogra troops and Sikh and RSSS bandits. In a telegram to the Prime
Minister of Kashmir on October 12, the Foreign Secretary of Pakistan
protested to the Kashmir government about this massacre of the
Muslims, but without any result. Indeed, the Prime Minister of Kashmir, far from paying any attention to the complaint, threatened 'to
ask for friendly assistance' to suppress the people's revolt. The Maharaja
had already started secret diplomatic moves in India to secure support
against the popular rising. Pakistan's reply to the Maharaja was that
the only object of such intervention by an outside power would be 'to
complete the suppression of the Muslims to enable you to join the
Indian Dominon as a *coup d'état* against the declared will of the population.'[7]

The Maharaja's design to exterminate the Muslims did not work well
in Poonch. Many of its inhabitants were veterans of the Second
World War who decided to put up a stiff resistance; they evacuated
their families to Pakistan and came back to fight with weapons
collected from their relatives and friends. A press statement issued by

the Maharaja's government on September 12, 1947, admitted the collapse of his regime in Poonch. Despite the savagery and brutality of the Maharaja's forces and that of the RSSS and Sikh bandits, the uprising gained momentum and spread to other areas. In some areas, the forces of the Maharaja were routed or scattered, and ultimately he was compelled to flee from his capital and seek shelter in the town of Jammu, where his troops had already killed or driven out the Muslim population. Having liberated themselves from the oppressive rule of the Maharaja, the Kashmiri Muslims set up a provisional government of Azad (free) Kashmir, under the leadership of Sardar Mohammad Ibrahim Khan, president of the Muslim Conference. The Muslim section of the Maharaja's army gave its allegiance to the Azad Kashmir government. In Gilgit, the local people rose against the Maharaja's rule and liberated themselves from it. They have been successful in retaining their freedom.

At the height of this struggle between the Maharaja and the Muslims of Kashmir, on October 22, 1947 tribesmen from the North West Frontier and Punjab, who had close ties of kinship and religion with the suffering population of Kashmir, crossed the borders of the state. The Pathans swept down to help their fellow-Muslims in distress, but the rising was mainly of the people of Kashmir themselves. 'The historical fact is', wrote M. Philips Price, 'that the initiative for this pro-Pakistan movement came from the people of West Kashmir. Pakistan troops took no part in it and Jinnah, in spite of pressure from his own people, refused to move troops across the frontier, which he could easily have done. Meanwhile irregular tribesmen from the North West Frontier crossed the North Punjab and gave aid to the revolting Poonchis.'[8] The same fact was stressed by the special correspondent of the New York Times: 'The Indian Government constantly refers to the Azad forces as raiders, implying that they are Muslim tribesmen from Pakistan's North West Frontier. Actually, according to reliable private informants, sixty-five per cent are native Kashmiris in revolt against the Hindu Government of the princely state.'[9]

It was from his exile in Jammu that the Maharaja took the final step of acceding to India. But the plans and preparations for accession to India had a long history behind them. While his troops were engaged in killing the Muslim population, the Maharaja was making active and secret moves towards the accession to India, and his overtures met with a prompt and encouraging response in New Delhi. The Maharaja was well aware that the vast majority of his subjects wished to accede to Pakistan. The most important Muslim political party in the state, the Kashmir Muslim Conference, declared itself in favour of accession to Pakistan, and in July 1947 its general council unanimously passed a resolution to that effect. The other important political group, the National Conference, met in mid-August and the majority of its members were reported to have favoured accession to Pakistan. It deferred taking a final decision until its leader, Sheikh Abdullah, could be consulted. Abdullah, like other leaders of both the political groups, was in prison. On September 5, 1947, the Jammu and Kashmir Kisan-Mazdoor (peasant and worker) conference met and approved a statement on the question: 'The overwhelming majority of Kashmir's population is Muslim. The state is contiguous with Pakistan territories. All the three big highways and all the rivers of the state go into Pakistan.' The Kizan-Mazdoor organisation therefore supported accession to Pakistan.[10] On September 18, the Kashmir Socialist Party came to the same decision. 'Hundreds of telegrams', Bazaz records, 'were sent to the Maharaja from all over Kashmir imploring, beseeching and advising him not to accede to the Indian Union.'[11] On August 15, 1947, 'Pakistan Day' was observed with great enthusiasm throughout the state, including the town of Srinagar. Geography, economics and the wishes and sentiments of an overwhelming majority of the people dictated accession to Pakistan, but the Maharaja's personal interests and those of the ruling Hindu elite demanded accession to India, and he pressed on with his plans to achieve this.

Nor were India's leaders and government idle. As soon as the plan for the partition of the Indian subcontinent was announced, on June 3, 1947, the Congress leaders lost no time in assuring the Maharaja of the advantages in joining India. In this task, the Indian leaders were helped by Lord Mountbatten and the Hindu rulers of Patiala, Kapurthala and Faridkot, who all paid visits to the Maharaja during June and July 1947. Mountbatten was an old friend of the Maharaja—they had both been ADCs on the staff of the Prince of Wales when he toured India in 1921.[12] The Viceroy visited Kashmir on June 19 and stayed there for four days. He certainly did not go for a holiday, because he was too busy to have a holiday. His press attaché, Alan Campbell-Johnson, said that one of the reasons for the visit was to dissuade Gandhi and Nehru from going to Kashmir. The fact remains that Gandhi did visit the state in early August, and other Congress leaders went there, including the president of the Congress, Acharaya Kripalani. It has been said that Mountbatten was unable to discuss the issue of accession because the Maharaja was 'very elusive' and, when the final talk was scheduled, sent a message that 'he was in bed with colic'.[13] It seems improbable that Mountbatten, who could persuade and cajole nearly 600 ruling princes when sitting in New Delhi, could not even discuss the future of Kashmir during his four days' visit to the Maharaja. This would argue an incredible indifference on Mountbatten's part towards a very large and strategically important state, and it is difficult to believe that he so meekly accepted the Maharaja's excuses. As Professor Nicholas Mansergh has observed: 'There was no state in the subcontinent the future of which, if left undecided when the independent impartial authority withdrew, was more likely to occasion dissent between the two Dominions. The failure to concentrate more closely on the problem it presented was destined to prove an oversight fraught with grave consequences.'[14] Jinnah and other Muslim League leaders had already found the Viceroy 'cold and indifferent' to them. There was deep conviction among the Pakistanis that Mountbatten from the beginning was conniving with the Congress leaders to secure the accession of the state of Jammu and Kashmir to India.[15] British writers, however, have termed the conviction 'mistaken'.

The Times commented on October 25, 1947: 'The union of India has been taking a lively interest in the subject and indications are that the Hindu Maharaja of Kashmir, Sir Hari Singh, has lately been much influenced by representations made by Mr Gandhi who visited Kashmir three months ago and by other Congress leaders.' This needs to be weighed against statements from Delhi, then and since, to the effect that India had taken no interest in the Kashmir affair until the tribal invasion in October 1947. It is significant that, after these visits took place, there were a number of political developments in Kashmir which were greatly influential in promoting the state's subsequent accession to India. For instance, soon after Gandhi's visit, the Prime Minister of Kashmir, Pandit Kak (who was not pro-Indian and who made a 'standstill agreement' with Pakistan), was replaced by a militant Dogra, Janak Singh, and later by Mehr Chand. Both of them were definitely in favour of Kashmir's accession to India, and it was during their tenure of office that the massacre of the Muslims in Jammu and Poonch started. Further, as a result of Gandhi's talks with the Maharaja, negotiations started with the government of India to build a direct road between India and Jammu. It may be added here that the two main roads connecting Kashmir with the outside world, which remain open throughout the year, lead into Pakistan. The object of these negotiations was to create an alternative route between Kashmir and India so that essential supplies, and troops, could pass from one to the other without crossing the territory of Pakistan. The award of the Gurdaspur district (chapter 2, pages 53–6) to India greatly helped Delhi's design to incorporate the state. The plan to construct the road between Jammu and India was regarded as a state secret, and when a local newspaper sought to report on it, the censor stepped in and stopped publication. It is clear from these negotiations over the road, and from the speed and secrecy of its construction, that the Maharaja had agreed with Delhi that his state should join India. *126021*

The Maharaja's secret agreement with India, made before the onrush of tribesmen, was leaked out when the aircraft of his envoy, his cousin Thakore Hariman Singh, was forced to land at Lahore because of engine trouble. The plane was attacked by a mob and Thakore lost all his suitcases, in one of which was the draft-treaty. According to that treaty, the Indian Union, in return for Kashmir's accession, promised to build communications from Pathankot to Jammu. It was also agreed that Indian troops should be stationed at Gilgit and Indian air force units at new air fields to be built by India at strategic points.[16]

The Maharaja was aware that his was not an easy task; he knew that 80 per cent of the population of the state ardently desired accession to Pakistan. So he moved slowly and with cunning. On August 15, 1947 (Independence Day), he concluded a 'standstill' agreement with Pakistan, which accepted it as a preliminary step to accession to Pakistan. As a result of the agreement, Pakistan stepped into the shoes of the pre-partition government of India and became responsible for the defence, foreign affairs and communications of the state. In pursuance of this agreement, the Pakistan railways continued to operate the small railway line in Kashmir, and Pakistan personnel took over the state's postal and telegraph services.

The Maharaja's object in signing the standstill agreement was to lull the popular demand for accession to Pakistan. He had no desire for relations with Pakistan, and he began to find excuses for picking a quarrel. The standstill agreement was utilised for this purpose. Soon he was complaining that the Pakistan government was not fulfilling its obligations under the agreement, and that supplies of such commodities as food-grains, petrol, cloth and salt were not regularly coming up. It is part of the Indian case that Pakistan was exerting economic pressure on the Maharaja to secure the accession; the correct interpretation is that the Maharaja was trying to find excuses to pick a quarrel with Pakistan as a part of his design ultimately to join India. When his government made the allegation, the Pakistan government sent the Joint Secretary of Foreign Affairs to discuss the whole question in order to reach a satisfactory solution. Jinnah himself made a plea to the Maharaja, but the latter resisted all moves for a peaceful settlement of any issue between the government of Pakistan and that of Kashmir. On October 18, his government asked for an 'impartial enquiry', and the proposal was concluded with a threat that, if it was not accepted, the Maharaja would ask for 'friendly assistance', presumably from India where the plans for such assistance were already laid. The government of Pakistan, notwithstanding the provocative terms of the proposal, accepted it, but the Maharaja's government did not even reply when asked to nominate its representative to the 'impartial enquiry'. Then, on October 20, the Prime Minister of Kashmir informed the Governor-General of Pakistan that he was justified in asking for 'friendly assistance'. This, it should be noted, before the incursion of tribesmen; according to the government of India itself, no tribesmen entered Kashmir before October 23. 'The excuse', said the Pakistan Prime Minister, Liaquat Ali Khan, 'that Indian troops went to Kashmir because of the entry of so-called raiders from the North-West Frontier Province is not an honest one.'[17]

In the meantime, the Maharaja had made another successful move towards his goal. On September 29, he released Sheikh Abdullah, leader of the National Conference, though none of the leaders of the Muslim Conference was released. Liberating Abdullah was not a princely whim on the Maharaja's part; it was presumably done at the behest of the Indian government. Abdullah had long associations with Nehru, and the Indian Prime Minister fully utilised their close personal relationship. Although Abdullah was opposed to the Maharaja's tyrannical rule and had contributed to the political awakening of Kashmir, at the critical moment of his country's history he played the role of an opportunist. Without perhaps fully realising the whole situation, he came to the aid of the Maharaja's design to join Kashmir to India against the wishes of the people. Immediately after his release he went to Delhi, where Nehru persuaded him to support the Dogra ruler whom he had hitherto opposed, and he made a number of speeches which were markedly pro-Indian and anti-Pakistan. Abdullah seems to have been governed wholly by personal factors. He was opposed to Jinnah and the Muslim League. The Kashmir Muslim Conference, rival to his National Conference, was firmly attached to Pakistan. His political rivals would very probably come to power if Kashmir joined Pakistan; since this might well mean his political death, he threw in his lot with India. This sort of narrow consideration led Abdullah to commit the greatest blunder of his career. His reward, ironically, was to be the very political death he had schemed to avoid. As soon as Abdullah's immediate role was played, Nehru required him no longer. His efforts to exercise an independent rule in Kashmir proved highly embarrassing to the Indian government, which eventually, in 1953, imprisoned him. Released in 1958, within a short time he was back in gaol; freed again in 1964, an Indian prison soon received him, and the cat-and-mouse game has continued. But far more important than his personal fate was the outcome of his short-sighted and selfish role in 1947: India's seizure of Kashmir against the will of its people. One of his comrades in the struggle for freedom in Kashmir comments thus on Abdullah's role: 'At the start of revolution in China more than thirty years earlier, the last Manchu monarch did a similar thing when he appointed the opportunist Yuan Shih Kai as his Prime Minister to stem the tide of revolution. The students of history know with what results. Yuan Shih Kai could neither save the Manchu dynasty nor continue himself to rule for a long time.'[18] Similar was the fate of Abdullah.

The Maharaja, having secured Abdullah's support for his plan to accede to India was ready to take the final step. The possibility of a 'smooth' accession was frustrated by the popular rising and the attacks of the tribesmen. But the plan agreed between the Maharaja and the Indian government seemed to allow for all eventualities, including the use of force. A fugitive from his capital, the Maharaja on October 26 wrote from Jammu to the Governor-General of India, Lord Mountbatten, offering the accession of his state to India and asking for the help of Indian forces to crush the rising. Abdullah, he said, had been asked to 'carry the burden of responsibility' of office, along with his Prime Minister.

Mountbatten, in his letter accepting the offer of accession on behalf of the Indian government, stated that the ultimate question of a state's accession should be settled by reference to the people. (This was to be the most crucial point in the ensuing dispute.) The atmosphere at Government House in New Delhi on the eve of Kashmir's accession has been vividly described by Ian Stephens, then editor of the British-owned Indian newspaper, the *Statesman*. He was invited to dinner by Lord and Lady Mountbatten on the same evening, and records his impressions thus: 'I was startled by their one-sided verdicts on affairs. They seemed to have become wholly pro-Hindu. The atmosphere at Government House that night was almost one of war. Pakistan, the Muslim League and Mr Jinnah were the enemy.'[19] Josef Korbel, a member of the United Nations Commission for India and Pakistan (1948), observes:

> Mountbatten's attitude and advice in this case raise critical questions. Why, for example, did he advise that Indian military assistance to the Maharaja must be covered by the legal technicality of accession? . . . He must have known that if war over this issue were to develop between these two Dominions it would not be on the basis of the legality of such a method of accession but rather over the fact itself . . . it is most difficult to understand why no one, particularly Mountbatten, advanced the most obvious idea—that of immediately getting into contact with the Karachi Government for consultation.[20]

Indian troops landed in Srinagar only a few hours after the acceptance of accession on October 27—a factor, which led General Sir Frank

Messervy, then commander-in-chief of the Pakistan army, to assert
that there was 'much evidence that this accession had been deliberately
planned for some weeks before the event'.[21] Liaquat Ali Khan declared,
'It is rather significant that the very day the Governor-General of
India signed the instrument of Accession, Indian troops had landed in
Srinagar by 9 a.m. on October 27.'[22]

Pakistan's reaction to India's military intervention in a predominantly
Muslim state was naturally violent and bitter. In the early hours of
Tuesday, October 28, 1947, Pakistan and India were on the brink of
war. Jinnah telephoned Lieutenant General Sir Douglas Gracey, acting
commander-in-chief of the Pakistan army, at his headquarters at
Rawalpindi and ordered him to despatch troops to Kashmir. General
Gracey, however, wanted the matter to be referred to Field Marshal
Auchinleck. Auchinleck flew to Lahore and told Jinnah that, if the
armies of the two Dominions came to blows, all British officers on
both sides would immediately resign, and he urged Jinnah to withdraw his orders. It is not surprising that, with the experience of
India's intransigence over two decades, a good many Pakistanis today
regret that Jinnah's orders were withdrawn. The present writer put
the question to Field Marshal Auchinleck, in an interview on March 10,
1966, in London: If Jinnah's orders could not be obeyed because
Kashmir had become 'legally' a part of the Dominion of India, how
could British officers continue to serve India when the Indian government occupied Junagadh, which had also become 'legally' part of the
Dominion of Pakistan? No clear reply was given to the question. It is
certain, however, that Auchinleck's intervention was not due to pro-
Indian sympathy. He was thoroughly disgusted with the whole affair
and distressed at the prospect of war between the two Dominions.

Even without the use of force, Kashmir's accession to India would
have been a flagrant denial of the principle determining the division
of the subcontinent between the Indian Union and Pakistan. The
Indian leaders claimed they did not accept the division as being on a
religious basis, yet if such were not the basis, it is hard to know what
was. In Bengal and Punjab, the Hindu-majority areas were carved
out so that they should not be included in Muslim Pakistan. Out of
nearly 600 princely states, and notwithstanding the options promised
to their rulers, India did not allow any state with a Hindu majority

to accede to Pakistan. When Junagadh's ruler opted for Pakistan, India forcibly occupied the state. When Hyderabad's ruler opted for independence, his state was invaded and annexed. India justified these breaches of the agreement reached before the transfer of power by claiming that she was defending the popular will. But the popular will was to be the determining factor only in Hindu-majority states. Kashmir, irrespective of the manifest wishes of the Muslim majority, was at all costs to be joined to India and denied to Pakistan, even if this meant supporting an autocratic and cruel Hindu ruler, even if it meant the use of armed force and the risk of war with Pakistan. Nehru, who had championed the cause of the Hindu people of princely states, put his democratic principles in cold storage when sanctioning the use of troops against the Muslim people of the princely state of Kashmir. He claimed, in the Indian Parliament on March 8, 1949, that he had had Gandhi's 'blessing in the steps we took in Kashmir'. How, Bazaz asks, could Mahatma Gandhi, the apostle of non-violence, 'bless the Indian armies to occupy the state and to defend the Hindu princely state against the obvious desire of the Muslims?'[23]

The government of Pakistan did not, and does not, accept the validity of the accession of Kashmir to the Union of India. Its representative made this plain to the Security Council in 1948:

> The Pakistan Government have not accepted and cannot accept the accession of the state of Jammu and Kashmir to India. In their view, the accession was based on violence and fraud. It was fraudulent in as much as it was achieved by deliberately creating a set of circumstances with the object of finding an excuse to stage the accession. It was based on violence because it furthered the plan of the Kashmir Government to liquidate the Muslim population.[24]

The government of Pakistan also declared that the existence of the standstill agreement between Pakistan and the state, which had never been repudiated, was a bar to the subsequent accession of the state to India. Further, the acceptance of accession by India was conditional, and there was no provision for conditional acceptance under the Indian Independence Act, 1947. The most important fact, however, was that the ruler of the state had no authority left to make any decision; his people had disowned him and the Azad Kashmir organisation was by that time exercising control over a large part of the territory of the state. The 'Maharaja's state' had virtually disintegrated; its ruler had fled, and the forces leading the popular revolt against his tyrannical rule had established themselves successfully in various parts of Kashmir. But for the Indian troops and planes, the process of liberation might have been completed within the next forty-eight hours.

Immediately after the occupation of Kashmir by the Indian army, a conference between the Governor-General and the Prime Ministers of the two Dominions was arranged in Lahore at the instance of Jinnah; but it could not be held owing to Nehru's 'illness' and Sardar Patel's reluctance to talk with the Pakistani leaders. A meeting at last took place between Jinnah and Mountbatten on November 1 at Lahore. Jinnah put forward a three-point proposal for the settlement of the dispute: (i) a cease-fire within forty-eight hours should be proclaimed; (ii) all 'alien' forces, i.e., tribesmen and Indian troops, should withdraw; if the tribesmen did not obey, joint Indo-Pakistani military action would be taken against them; and (iii) the two Governors-General should be vested with full powers by the governments of India and Pakistan to restore peace, undertake the administration of the state and arrange a plebiscite under their joint control and supervision. Mountbatten pleaded his inability to accept the proposals without the consent of the Indian cabinet. It subsequently turned them down. There were at least three more attempts by the government of Pakistan for a settlement of the issue by negotiation. Each attempt was flatly rejected by the Indian government, which seemed to rely on the physical might of its armed forces. The government of Pakistan wanted the withdrawal of all alien forces, the establishment of a neutral administration, and then a plebiscite under the control of the United Nations. The government of India wanted first to occupy the state, then maintain there its armies and its client administration under Abdullah, and then have a plebiscite with UN personnel acting only as observers. Rather than seek a realistic solution of the dispute, India seemed to prefer to continue indefinitely the danger-fraught situation in Kashmir.

In a press statement on November 16, 1947; Liaquat Ali Khan stated: 'It is quite clear now that what the Indian Government are after is permanent occupation of Kashmir. The Indian Government's whole conduct is based on "might is right" and on the belief that Pakistan is unable to fight them. . . . If the Indian Government are allowed to follow their imperialist land-grabbing policy, this will have repercussions not only in Asia but throughout the world.'[25] India's attempt to present the world with a *fait accompli* in Kashmir was regarded in many quarters as a serious breach of the international morality of which Pandit Nehru had always been a foremost advocate, and India's attitude was seen to be governed by a militant nationalism. While Pakistan appealed to moral law and mobilised the principle of self-determination, India buttressed her arguments with 'reasons of state'. Pakistan pressed the right of the people of Kashmir to express their will about their political future; India was, however, resolute in sticking to her guns. Ten years later, a British journal stated that India's role in Kashmir was 'colonialism at its worst'.[26]

In spite of India's resolution, she did not find the task of military occupation in the mountains of Kashmir an easy one. The Indian troops met with determined resistance from the people who were fighting for their very existence against heavy odds. After weeks of fighting, and with the approach of winter, the Indian military operations became a costly and complicated affair. Faced with this grim prospect, India brought the Kashmir dispute to the United Nations on January 1, 1948. Under Article 35 of the Charter, India complained that Pakistan was responsible for creating disturbances in the state. The Security Council was requested to ask Pakistan to prevent tribesmen and its nationals from entering Kashmir, and to desist from giving any material assistance to the rebels. The government of India undertook that, once law and order were established, a plebiscite would be held to ascertain the wishes of the people.[27] As has been noted, India had made this commitment about a plebiscite when accepting the offer of accession from the Maharaja. This pledge had been affirmed by Nehru on several occasions during the preceding three months when Pakistan made repeated efforts to negotiate over the Kashmir dispute.

Pakistan also invoked Article 35 of the Charter in bringing to the Security Council her grievances against India. The statement complained of an extensive genocide against the Muslim populations of India; of India's military conquest of Junagadh and the adjoining states which had acceded to Pakistan; of India's refusal to implement the various partition agreements, thereby depriving Pakistan of her legitimate share of the assets of the former government of undivided India. The complaint stated that India had adopted an attitude of obstruction and hostility towards Pakistan, one of the objects being to paralyse the new state at the very start by depriving it of its rightful share of financial and other assets. Pakistan challenged the validity of Kashmir's accession to India because it was based on 'fraud and violence', involving large-scale massacre of Kashmir Muslims by the armed forces of the Maharaja. She also complained of repeated raids and incursions into her territory by Indian troops and bombing by Indian planes. Finally, Pakistan referred to India's threat of military attack against her.[28]

Thus, in January 1948, the Kashmir dispute was brought before the Security Council. It has been before the Security Council ever since. Problems come and problems go, but the Kashmir dispute seems to go on for ever. Few, if any, post-war problems have enlisted such disinterested, carefully thought-out offers of assistance, and none has failed more dismally. The failure to reach an agreement lies clearly at the door of India. Pandit Nehru consistently made conditions for a plebiscite that would make a farce of it; he rejected every constructive proposal for a solution. India wanted a plebiscite in Kashmir but only if an Indian-installed government were functioning and an Indian army were in control. Although India at first accepted the principle of the right of self-determination and the plebiscite, Nehru soon set his face resolutely against a free and fair plebiscite held under United Nations control. However wise and clever her policy might be, India seemed at the United Nations to be behaving like some of the more sophisticated of the imperialist powers she has often criticised. From this, world opinion could only conclude that, in spite of her declared apparent willingness to let the dispute be decided by a plebiscite, India really had no confidence that a vote would go in her favour. There was no valid reason why a UN-supervised plebiscite could not be held in Kashmir except India's fear of losing the vote. Efforts made by the Security Council to find a solution have come to nothing because of India's obstinate refusal to agree to any constructive suggestion. The main aim of India's policy seems to have been to stalemate the dispute for so long that it ceases to be an issue.

The Kashmir issue has accumulated a literature and a mass of argument for and against that is truly formidable. The full analysis of the debates and deliberations of the Security Council and its various commissions and representatives cannot be attempted in this survey. We shall confine ourselves to the major developments of this ruinous dispute which has bedevilled the relations between the two countries.

UNITED NATIONS' MEDIATION, 1948-52

The Security Council passed a resolution on January 17, 1948, urging both Pakistan and India not to take any steps which might aggravate the situation and to inform the Council of any material change therein; the next step was to establish a commission of three with the task of mediating between Pakistan and India. Though it was proposed that the commission should 'proceed to the spot as quickly as possible', nothing was done to send it within six months. In the meantime, a lengthy debate started in the Security Council; all aspects of Indo-Pakistan relations were discussed by the representative of Pakistan, while the Indian delegation stressed the rights of the Maharaja and the so-called tribal invasion of Kashmir and the alleged help and support of it by the government of Pakistan. Pakistan never denied that some tribesmen and Pakistan nationals had gone to help the Muslims of Kashmir, who were threatened with extermination and who were fighting for their very existence against a tyrannical and oppressive rule. Sir Zafrullah Khan, analysing the situation, told the Security Council that, in a situation where one's father or brother might have been killed or where one's wife had been raped or children butchered, it was difficult to be neutral and to do nothing. 'That kind of thing might be expected of angels but it cannot be expected of human beings. I will say that a man would be despicable coward if, under those circumstances, he did nothing to help.'[29] The Pakistan government did not organise any attack, nor were its troops yet participating in the fight between the forces of Azad Kashmir and the Indian forces, but it was not possible for Pakistan to 'control the movements of those who offer their services in a cause which they passionately believe in'.[30]

While the debate was going on at Lake Success, something approaching 'eve of war' tensions prevailed in the subcontinent as a result of India's threat 'to enter Pakistan territory to take up military action against the invaders' of Kashmir. Pandit Nehru threatened that India would be justified in 'self-defence' in attacking 'bases' in Pakistan. Nehru, true to his usual technique, asserted that sending troops into Pakistan 'need not be considered an *act of war*'. It appeared that the subcontinent might be facing a great upheaval. 'In New Delhi many voices were saying war would soon be declared between the Dominons of Pakistan and India and not all voices were regretful.'[31] India also informed the Security Council that she might send troops to Pakistan, and she appeared already to be applying economic sanctions against Pakistan. Replying to Nehru's threat, Liaquat Ali Khan said: 'Any action taken by India on Pakistan territory would be an act of unprovoked aggression against Pakistan.' He continued: 'India is out to destroy Pakistan which Indian leaders still persist in regarding as a part of India itself.'[32] India was planning for a violation of Pakistan territory on the southern borders adjoining Jammu. The supply route to her forces in Jammu was the poor road from Pathankot; the plan was to seize the road from Gurdaspur through Sialkot. Pakistan troops were moved to Sialkot for defensive purposes.[33]

At Lake Success, the debate continued the whole of January and the early part of February; the consensus of opinion of the majority members of the Security Council was that the only lasting solution of the Kashmir problem lay in holding a plebiscite under UN auspices, to which proposal India professed to agree. On February 10, the president of the Council, General A. G. L. Mcnaughton (Canada) and F. Van Langenhove (Belgium) incorporated the consensus of opinion in a draft resolution which called for the immediate cessation of all violence and fighting; the withdrawal of all forces and armed individuals who had entered the state; the return of all those citizens who had left due to disturbances and violence; the establishment of an administration commanding the confidence and respect of the people; the holding of a plebiscite under UN supervision at the earliest possible date. Pakistan accepted the resolution but India, which had declared itself in favour of a plebiscite, was most unhappy at this prospect of a UN-supervised plebiscite. The Indian delegate sought for an adjournment of the debate, ostensively for consultation, but really to use diplomatic pressure during the time thus gained. Nehru expressed his 'distress and disappointment' at 'the strangely narrow view that the Security Council took of Kashmir'.[34] He now put diplomatic pressure on the British government through the Governor-General of India, Lord Mountbatten. Once more, Mountbatten came to Nehru's aid and was successful in persuading the Labour government of Clement Attlee to favour India's case in the Security Council. The Kashmir dispute might have been settled in early spring of 1948 if Attlee's government had not decided to go back on the plan by which the British Commonwealth Secretary, Philip Noel Baker, had helped to build up a consensus amongst the members of the Security Council. In 1965, Sir Zafrullah Khan, now a judge of the International Court of Justice, told the story of how the constructive plan in the Security Council was sabotaged by the Indian government with the help of Lord Mountbatten. Having once succeeded in coercing the Security Council into abandoning that consensus, India went from one defiance of that body to another.[35]

When the Security Council resumed the debate in March 1948, a new resolution more favourable to India was passed; under the new resolution there was no unqualified withdrawal of Indian forces, but India was asked to withdraw such forces as were not required for the maintenance of law and order in the state; the interim government was to be replaced by an administration in which major political groups of the state would be asked to share. The resolution provided for the appointment of a plebiscite administrator by the Secretary General of the UN with full powers to carry out a free and impartial plebiscite. A commission of five members was set up to place its good offices at the disposal of the two governments. Notwithstanding the concessions to India, the proposal was rejected by her and she refused to implement those parts of it which dealt with the withdrawal of the bulk of her troops and the substitution of the Abdullah government by a coalition government. India agreed, however, to confer with the UN Commission. Pakistan, though resenting the concessions to India, did not reject them. As with every other move of the United Nations, her government agreed to carry out the new resolution. The United Nations Commission for India and Pakistan did not, however, come to the subcontinent until the first week of July 1948.

In the meantime, India, notwithstanding the appeal of the Security Council to both countries not to do anything to aggravate the situation, was making large military preparations in the state for an all-out offensive in Kashmir, apparently seeking to present the United Nations with a *fait accompli*, as she had in Hyderabad. The new all-out offensive was launched in April 1948. This threatened the security of Pakistan and it also led to a large exodus of Kashmir Muslim refugees to Pakistan. The Indian forces advanced towards the border of Pakistan; the head-works of the Jhelum canals, which is situated in Kashmir and on which the irrigation of Pakistan depends so much, was also threatened. On March 15, India's Defence Minister announced in the Indian Parliament that the Indian army would launch a major offensive in Kashmir. *The Times* reported on April 13, 1948, from its special correspondent at Srinagar: 'The Indian army has worked extremely hard during the winter months and its position has been improved . . . the force has been considerably strengthened and it should be soon ready for a limited offensive. Already some units have advanced from Rajanri in Jammu and from Uri . . .' At this stage, the government of Pakistan received a report on the general military situation from its commander-in-chief, Sir Douglas Gracey (who had been appointed on February 11, 1948), in which he stated:

It is obvious that a general offensive is about to start very soon. The present dispositions suggest that it will first start in the south with Bhimbar and Mirpur as the most likely objectives with a view to coming right up to the Pakistan border. . . . If Pakistan is not to face another serious problem of refugees uprooted from their homes; if India is not to be allowed to sit on the doorstep of Pakistan in the rear and on the flank at liberty to enter it at its will and pleasure; if the civilian and military morale is not to be affected to a dangerous extent and if subversive political forces are not to be encouraged and let loose within Pakistan itself, it is imperative that the Indian army is not allowed to advance beyond the general line Uri–Poonch–Naoshera.[36]

The Indian army would sooner or later reach the northern border of

Pakistan and over-run the headwork of the river on which the whole economy of Pakistan depended.

For these and other strategic reasons, Pakistan could not allow the new India offensive to go unchecked. It was futile to look to or rely on the Security Council; India had been emboldened to defy its resolutions and appeals. In accordance with the recommendations of its commander-in-chief, the government of Pakistan in early May 1948 sent a limited number of troops to Kashmir to hold certain defensive positions and to prevent the Indian army from advancing to the borders of Pakistan. The United Nations Commission for India and Pakistan was informed of this development on the very first day of its arrival in Pakistan. India made a great fuss about this development. As to her criticism that Pakistan had not notified the Security Council earlier, Sir Zafrullah Khan replied: 'Did the Government of India, in mounting their offensive, notify the Security Council?' In explaining the presence of Pakistan troops, he said: 'Pakistan would have been justified in sending her troops in October last, but she had not done so in the hope that an amicable settlement would be arrived at. At least, Pakistan had the desire to avoid a general conflagration. But when the hope of an amicable settlement receded more and more, Pakistan, with a view to keeping the conflict in Kashmir localised, had to take immediate action to stop the Indian forces from coming into contact with her frontier.'[37]

Thus began the 'limited war' between the armed forces of the two Dominions and it continued for the rest of 1948. It was the most curious war in modern history. It was compared to a war of manœuvre and limited objectives of eighteenth-century Europe before Frederick the Great began to make war total.[38] This limited war of 1948 was to have its sequel in the total war of September 1965; between the two lay fifteen years of unsuccessful efforts for peaceful settlement of the dispute, both inside and outside the United Nations. It is to these fifteen fruitless years that we now turn.

The United Nations Commission for India and Pakistan came to the subcontinent in July 1948, and its negotiations with the two governments continued for six months. The Commission passed two resolutions—the resolutions of August 13, 1948, and January 5, 1949. These were accepted by both India and Pakistan and endorsed by the Security

Council. They constitute an international agreement for the settlement of the Kashmir dispute; both India and Pakistan bound themselves to honour these commitments to the United Nations. Taken together, the resolutions provide for: (i) the issue of cease-fire orders and the demarcation of a cease-fire line; (ii) the demilitarisation of the state of Jammu and Kashmir; and (iii) a free and impartial plebiscite conducted by the United Nations to determine the question of accession of the state of Jammu and Kashmir to India or to Pakistan. The Commission was successful in effecting a cease-fire from January 1, 1949, and after protracted discussions an agreement on demarcation of the cease-fire line was also reached on July 27, 1949. But the next two stages— demilitarisation and the holding of a plebiscite under UN supervision— could not make any headway because of India's obstruction. Once the cease-fire was achieved, India was not in a mood for co-operation with the Commission. As a result of the cease-fire India had under her physical control the best and major part of the state, and seemed to rely on the principle, *possession vaut titre*. India soon created difficulties and sought to make her own interpretations of the two resolutions of the Commission. She would neither accept the interpretation of the authors of these resolutions, namely the UN Commission, nor an impartial interpretation by any third party. The situation was similar to that in 1946, when the Hindu Congress torpedoed the Cabinet Mission Plan for maintaining the unity of India under a loose scheme of a federal union. The Congress leaders then, it may be recalled, put their own interpretation on the vital feature of that federal scheme (the grouping of the provinces); ultimately the British government had to say that the interpretation given by the Congress leaders was not correct. After independence, the Indian leaders seemed to have become even more uncompromising, and there was now no outside authority to enforce any decisions. The United Nations Commission certainly had no such authority over the Indian leaders. Pandit Nehru could, therefore, flout his obligations to hold an internationally controlled plebiscite in Kashmir.

The first obstacle to the scheme of demilitarisation, as set out under the Commission's resolutions, was India's insistence on the disbandment of the forces of the Azad Kashmir government. Pakistan claimed, and in this was supported by the Commission, that the question of disbandment of Azad forces belonged to a later stage; in the first stage of demilitarisation, it was Pakistan's forces and the 'bulk' of Indian forces that were to be withdrawn. The Commission assured the government of Pakistan that the withdrawal of Pakistan forces and that of the 'bulk' of Indian forces, would be 'synchronised'. It gave the further assurance that the defence of the territory to be evacuated by the Pakistan troops would be the responsibility of the local authorities (i.e., the Azad government). The Commission clearly stated that 'no Indian soldier would tread on the evacuated territory'. The second stage of demilitarisation would come into operation when the plebiscite administrator had assumed charge, and he would determine the final disposal of the remaining Indian forces and state armed forces, on the one hand, and of the Azad Kashmir forces, on the other. This phase of demilitarisation was to be carried out in consultation with India in respect of the forces on her side of the cease-fire and in consultation with the 'local authorities' (i.e., the Azad government) in respect of Azad forces. India, however, would not agree to any withdrawal of her forces until the Azad troops had been disbanded; that is to say, she refused to accept the Commission's ruling that the question of withdrawal or disbandment of Azad forces belonged to the second stage of demilitarisation, between the establishment of the truce and the actual plebiscite. India also claimed to control those parts, 'northern areas' of the state, where the Azad government had been functioning. It was an absurd demand; the Commission itself reported to the Security Council: 'The situation in the northern areas today is such that posting of garrisons by the Indian army at any point beyond those which are now held by it would result in an extension of military activities by the Government of India.' It concluded: 'The cease-fire line which is today a guarantee against resumption of hostilities should be scrupulously observed by the Governments of India and Pakistan and opposing forces should remain behind it.'[39]

In order to overcome the difficulties over the implementation of its resolutions, the Commission submitted its own truce proposals on April 15, 1949. India had failed to submit her truce proposal; Pakistan's was presented on March 9, 1949. The truce proposals were modified on April 28, 1949, to meet some of the objections raised by India, but still India rejected the Commission's truce terms. After exhausting all efforts at mediation, the Commission, as a last resort, proposed on August 30, 1949, that all the points of difference relating to demilitarisation should be submitted for arbitration by Admiral Chester W. Nimitz, who had been designated as plebiscite administrator on March 22, 1949, with the approval of India and Pakistan. This proposal was supported by personal appeals from President Truman and Prime Minister Attlee to the Prime Ministers of India and Pakistan. The government of Pakistan agreed to this proposal, but India rejected it. 'India's attitude', the *Annual Register* for 1949 observed, 'was deliberately obstructionist and colour was lent to this view by a speech of Pandit Nehru in which he declared that Kashmir was part of India and no power on earth could take it away. Many observers also felt that India had unwisely given the appearance of prejudging the issue in defiance of the United Nations by allotting four seats in the new Parliament to representatives of Jammu and Kashmir.'[40] Nehru expressed 'surprise' at the personal appeals of Truman and Attlee and called them 'intervention'. The British government was sorry to note that the friendly appeal of its Prime Minister should have been interpreted as 'intervention'. The *Manchester Guardian*, commenting on Nehru's attitude said: 'If it is to be be considered as beyond question that Kashmir is a part of India, why did India accept the resolutions of the UN Commission in August 1948 and January 1949? Mr Nehru stated that the people of Kashmir had challenged the "two-nation" theory of Mr Jinnah. Though predominantly Muslim, they did not wish to join and instead they supported the ideals of Mahatama Gandhi. This may be so, but it must be proved. It can only be proved by plebiscite.'[41] The *New York Times* observed: 'India is by no means so confident of an election victory and is therefore more distrustful about details and "safeguards" in the plebiscite itself.'[42]

At the end of 1949, the situation in Kashmir was summed up by Pakistan's Prime Minister as follows:

Of three stages in the settlement, stage 1, the cease-fire, has already been reached. Stage 2 is the settlement of the peace terms. These are still under dispute. Stage 3 is the plebiscite. The plebiscite administrator cannot begin his work until the obstacles at stage 2 have been overcome. As to that, there are only four ways of composing a dispute: by agreement—that has been found impossible; by mediation, but the UN Commission has tried to mediate and has failed; by arbitration, but India has refused. Or by war. India knows that it would lose a free plebiscite. If India should remain in occupation of Kashmir, Pakistan would be surrounded; like Hyderabad it would be at India's pleasure before ever the UN could pass a resolution.[43]

Over the next two years, three United Nations representatives came to the subcontinent in search of a formula or basis to settle the Kashmir dispute. On December 17, 1949, the Security Council requested its president, General A. G. L. Mcnaughton of Canada, to try to find a mutually satisfactory basis between the governments of India and Pakistan for dealing with the problem. General Mcnaughton, after months of negotiations with the two parties, put forward his proposal for the demilitarisation of Kashmir and control of the northern areas with a view to overcoming India's objections. He recommended the withdrawal of the Pakistan troops and of all Indian forces, other than those required for civil government on the Indian side of the cease-fire line, and the reduction of the state forces on the one hand and the Azad Kashmir forces on the other. As regards 'northern areas', he agreed with the United Nations Commission's view that the control over these areas should remain with the existing 'local authorities' (i.e., Azad Kashmir government), and that India should remain on its own side of the cease-fire line. Pakistan accepted General Mcnaughton's proposals; India again rejected another constructive move made by the United Nations.

The next development was a resolution by the Security Council on March 14, 1950, which reaffirmed the resolutions of the United Nations Commission for India and Pakistan of August 13, 1948 and January 5, 1949. The Security Council also called upon the two governments to prepare and execute, within a period of five months from the date of the resolution, a programme of demilitarisation on the basis of General Mcnaughton's proposals or of such modifications of those proposals as might be mutually agreed. The Security Council also appointed a UN representative to assist India and Pakistan in the preparation and execution of the demilitarisation plan. Sir Owen Dixon of

Australia was appointed as this representative on April 12, 1950.

When Sir Owen Dixon came to the subcontinent, Pandit Nehru was pressing hard to get Pakistan declared as the aggressor in Kashmir. Dixon took the position that, in the first place, the Security Council had never declared Pakistan an aggressor; secondly, he had not been commissioned to make any judicial investigation of the issue; and thirdly, that such a finding could not be given without going into the history of the Indo-Pakistan subcontinent and the origin of the Kashmir dispute. However, he made a statement, presumably to break the deadlock created by Pandit Nehru, to the effect that the entry of tribesmen in Kashmir in October 1947 and of Pakistan troops in May 1948 was 'inconsistent with International Law.' This comment of Sir Owen Dixon's was given great prominence by the Indian leaders and publicists. Not unnaturally, the Pakistan Prime Minister strongly resented this unwarranted remark, of a kind which the Security Council itself never thought fit or necessary to make. But, even so, Dixon's proposals for demilitarisation, framed principally to meet the Indian point of view, were turned down by India and accepted by Pakistan. His proposals made a significant concession to meet India's objections: Pakistan should commence withdrawing her forces on a named day and then, after a significant number of days, India should begin her withdrawal. It will be recalled that, under the resolutions of the United Nations Commission, the withdrawal of the forces was to be 'synchronised'. Yet Dixon's proposals were not acceptable to India. After spending three months in the subcontinent, he became convinced that 'India's agreement would never be obtained for demilitarisation in such form, or provisions regarding plebiscite of such character, as would guarantee that the plebiscite was held entirely free of intimidation or other forces of influence or abuse'.[44]

Having come to this realisation, Sir Owen Dixon applied himself to finding another basis or formula to settle the Kashmir dispute. He proposed, as a substitute for an over-all plebiscite in the state, a plebiscite in the limited area consisting of the Kashmir valley and adjacent territories; the rest of the state should be partitioned between India and Pakistan. At first India showed interest in this scheme for partition and a limited plebiscite. But, when Dixon coupled it with suggestions for achieving an impartial and fair plebiscite in the limited areas, his scheme was no more acceptable to India than the previous proposals prescribing an over-all plebiscite under United Nations supervision. Hence, Dixon's second formula was also turned down by India, Thus ended yet another attempt by a United Nations representative, and one who had gone a long way to meet the Indian point of view.

In the meantime, a disinterested and earnest effort to solve this unhappy quarrel between two Commonwealth countries was made at the Commonwealth Prime Ministers' Conference in January 1951. The Commonwealth Prime Ministers decided to discuss the Kashmir dispute, not only as a grievous dissension within their family of nations, but also as a source of continuing danger to the peace of Asia. They discussed Kashmir informally for many hours, and were eager to devise conditions and safeguards that would ensure a fair and free plebiscite. To this end, they made a number of suggestions and three concrete proposals. They proposed that India and Pakistan should withdraw all their forces from Jammu and Kashmir and that all the local forces (i.e., the state army as well as the Azad forces) should be disbanded and disarmed. The maintenance of security and law and order would be undertaken by a neutral Commonwealth force. The governments of Australia and New Zealand offered to provide this force at their own expense. This proposal was accepted by Pakistan and rejected by India. Alternatively, it was suggested that the securing of law and order could be achieved by a joint force from India and Pakistan. Again, this was accepted by Pakistan and turned down by India. The third proposal was that the plebiscite administrator might be authorised to raise a local Kashmir force. Its fate was the same: Pakistan's acceptance and India's rejection.

Nehru put himself visibly in the wrong by refusing, while Pakistan accepted, all the most reasonable proposals put forward by the Commonwealth Prime Ministers, who certainly would not and did not suggest anything unfair. In fact, their proposals were so fair and impartial that no man with a good case could have refused. But the difficulty was that Nehru's case was not good. His triple refusal left the impression that he did not dare trust the Kashmiri people to express an opinion. His unwillingness to permit a free plebiscite in Kashmir was part of his power-politics approach to Asian problems.

The contrast between Liaquat's readiness to agree to any reasonable proposal to bring the deadlock to an end and Nehru's refusal to modify his claim to retain Indian troops in Kashmir did much to bring world opinion, as reflected in the press, to the side of Pakistan.[45] 'India has rejected', said the *New York Times* in an editorial on January 17, 1951, 'every suggestion for mediation that has come through the United Nations in the last few years. The plain fact of the matter is that India has consistently made impossible terms for a plebiscite or for any other kind of settlement. It is hard to avoid the conclusion that Mr Nehru would rather see a continuance of the present situation than face a genuine popular verdict.' Commenting on India's rejection of all mediation efforts made by the Commonwealth leaders and by the Security Council, *The Times* noted in an editorial of March 29, 1951: 'The obstacle to any proposals is still India's persistent refusal to submit to any sort of arbitration on the differences of interpretations regarding her claims and commitments on Kashmir.'

India's uncompromising stand on Kashmir exemplified the perplexing dual set of international principles under which she appeared to be operating. In Korea, India preached the Gandhian principle of approaching all disputes in a disposition to agree. But in Kashmir, India was concurrently blocking conciliation with unrelenting demands. Nehru had been giving advice to other countries about the settlement of various disputes; evidently he found it easier to solve the problems of the world than one in his own backyard. The *Christian Science Monitor* wrote on January 22, 1951: 'Mr Nehru in the matter of Korea has enjoined Western nations to be pliant rather than insistent and to recognise human factors involved. More of this approach in India's attitude towards Kashmir would help to substitute settlement for suspension in a very troubled area.'

During the period between the submission of Sir Owen Dixon's report and the Commonwealth Prime Ministers' Conference, India took one more complicating step in the Kashmir dispute. Under instructions from Delhi, Abdullah's government in Kashmir made arrangements to convene a constituent assembly to decide the question of accession. Abdullah's party came out with the demand on October 28, 1950, and it was given prompt blessing from Delhi. The Foreign Minister of Pakistan on December 14, 1950, in a letter to the Security

E

Council, affirmed that the plan to convene a constituent assembly in Kashmir was clearly an attempt on the part of India to wriggle out of her obligations to the United Nations, and that it constituted a grave challenge to the authority of the Security Council.

When the Security Council met in February 1951 to consider the report of Sir Owen Dixon, it was faced with this additional complication. The debate continued until the end of March, when a resolution, jointly sponsored by the United States and Britain, was adopted. The Anglo-American proposal reaffirmed the principle embodied in the Security Council's previous resolutions and the two resolutions of the UN Commission, namely, that 'the future of the state of Jammu and Kashmir should be decided through the democratic method of a free and impartial plebiscite conducted under the auspices of the United Nations'. It also declared that the convening of the constituent assembly would not constitute a disposition of the state in accordance with the above principle. The Anglo-American resolution provided for the appointment of another UN representative to effect the demilitarisation on the basis of the two resolutions of the Commission. The governments of India and Pakistan were called upon to co-operate with the UN representative and, in the event of failure to achieve agreement on demilitarisation, to submit their differences to arbitration by an arbitrator or a panel of arbitrators, appointed by the president of the International Court of Justice. The same old pattern was repeated: Pakistan accepted the resolution, India rejected it. Indian opinion was chagrined and incensed at the Security Council's endorsement of the Anglo-American resolution without a dissentient vote.

Each plan for solution was dashed by what appeared to be an unyielding Indian obduracy. The will of the people of Kashmir could not be ascertained in a 'controlled' election. The policing of a critical part of the state by troops of one party or another would properly be regarded as such a 'control'. The search for a formula, therefore, revolved around the method by which real freedom of choice could be assured. Unhappily, Nehru resisted every suggestion of such an assurance. 'The Indian attitude', wrote the New York Herald Tribune on March 10, 1951, 'is a source of worry and annoyance to most UN delegates, and the further they examine it, the less justification they find for it. The conclusion has become inescapable that the Indian position, cut to its essence, is simply this—Kashmir for India, regardless of expense.'

Notwithstanding India's rejection of the Security Council's resolution of March 1951, the council proceeded to appoint Dr Frank Graham as the UN representative on April 30, and he came to the subcontinent in June 1951. India, however, proceeded with her plan of convening a constituent assembly in Kashmir. Pakistan's Foreign Minister again told the Security Council that the proposal to convene such assembly was 'not only a prejudicial act but . . . deliberately designed to by-pass the United Nations and to prevent the holding of a free and impartial plebiscite'.[46] The government of Pakistan was constrained to note that the hesitancy of the Security Council to assert its authority and to enforce its resolutions relating to Kashmir had encouraged the government of India and Abdullah to persist in their intransigence. Dr Graham, after prolonged discussion with the two governments, presented his first plan for demilitarisation on September 7, 1951: he subsequently made other proposals for this end. Each of these, involving new concessions to India and demanding new sacrifices of Pakistan, was accepted by Pakistan and rejected by India. It was grievous to see the Security Council allowing India to turn down so many constructive suggestions, while refusing to undertake any action to enforce its decisions. The weakness of the United Nations was glaringly revealed; and India, the great champion of international peace and morality, contributed to the undermining of its prestige and authority.

In the meantime, the constituent assembly of Kashmir was set up. Its seventy-five members were elected unopposed, all of them being nominees of Abdullah's party. Korbel comments: 'No dictator could do better.'[47]

On December 23, 1952, the Security Council again passed a resolution asking the governments of India and Pakistan to enter into talks with a view to reaching agreement on the specific numbers of troops within the range of 3,000 to 6,000 on the Pakistan side of the cease-fire line and 12,000 to 18,000 on the India side of the cease-fire line. Dr Graham submitted five reports on his mission to the Security Council. An analysis of these reports would reveal that Pakistan made every possible concession to arrive at a peaceful solution of the Kashmir dispute, but all these proved fruitless because of India's intransigence and obstruction. Dr Graham finally reported the failure of his efforts to resolve the differences over demilitarisation of the state. He suggested that the leaders of both countries should have direct negotiations over Kashmir.

Thus ended an important chapter of the efforts of the United Nations to solve the Kashmir problem. Up to this period, the Indian government did not openly discard the idea of a plebiscite. But while ostensibly paying allegiance to the idea, it created all sorts of obstacles to the holding of a plebiscite and sabotaged at least eight attempts by the United Nations to organise a free and fair vote in Kashmir. 'Much of Mr Nehru's moralising on the conduct of other powers now seems to many people as cant of the most nauseous kind, put up as a smokescreen behind which to practise his own aggression . . . proposal after proposal followed with Pakistan agreeing and India rejecting.'[48] India's attitude and action were presumably based on the calculation that the United Nations would prove as ineffective over Kashmir as it had over some other issues, and that the absorption of Kashmir would gradually be accepted. The result of this defiance of the Security Council was, however, much more serious than India seemed to realise. The uneasy state of armed truce continued to prevail along the explosive frontier of Kashmir. War in suspense is still the order of the day. Further, India was damaging the prospects of a better international order, which Nehru always advocated. If he stood for the machinery of the United Nations, he should have accepted its rules even when they went against him.

DIRECT NEGOTIATIONS, 1953–54

On becoming Prime Minister in April 1953, Mohammad Ali (of Bogra) made an impassioned appeal to Pandit Nehru to settle all outstanding disputes between India and Pakistan. He said in the Pakistan parliament: 'I consider that the maintenance of peace and establishment of friendly relations between India and Pakistan are essential to the peace and stability of Asia.' He stressed the need for the settlement of Kashmir without which no permanent peace or friendship in the subcontinent was possible. The two Prime Ministers met informally in London in June 1953 on the occasion of the Commonwealth Prime Ministers' Conference, and they met again the following month in Karachi. Mohammad Ali (Bogra) sought to urge on Nehru the desirability of settling the Kashmir dispute and thus promote friendly relations between the two countries. Nehru was, as usual, evasive. A high Pakistani official who assisted Mohammad Ali in the negotiations told the author that Nehru would talk on everything, including philosophy and ethics, but not on Kashmir. Mohammad Ali seemed to be impressed by Nehru's charm and started calling him 'elder brother'; but, so far as the Kashmir dispute was concerned, a solution was no nearer. The 'sweetness' of Nehru which impressed Mohammad Ali had its reasons: he was planning to enter the second phase of his scheme to incorporate Kashmir into India.

Abdullah was Nehru's great friend and he proved to be an asset in the crucial days of 1947 when the Maharaja of Kashmir acceded to India. Abdullah was described as the accredited leader of the people of Kashmir, and his support was taken as a token of popular approval of accession. He was also sent to the United Nations, where he indulged in all sorts of provocative, if not abusive, attacks on Pakistan and its founder, Mohammad Ali Jinnah. But, like many other opportunists, Abdullah had to face the consequences of his actions: his services were no longer required. He was now convinced of India's real intentions to seize the state of Jammu and Kashmir. He protested against this and was duly sent to prison. Nehru was apprehensive of a popular uprising in Indian-held Kashmir and, following Abdullah's arrest, the Indian government took steps to repress all opposition. The popular uprising was crushed by force, and an iron curtain fell over Kashmir. Foreigners and press reporters were not allowed to visit the state; all air services between Srinagar and Delhi were suspended; news from the area was heavily censored.

This caused widespread anger and concern in Pakistan. Mohammad Ali dashed to New Delhi to confer with Nehru, who did not at first like the idea of this meeting because the affairs in Kashmir were 'no concern of Pakistan'. The meeting of the two Prime Ministers in August 1953 resulted in a communiqué which stressed: (i) 'it was their firm opinion that this dispute would be settled in accordance with the wishes of [Kashmir] . . . the most feasible method of ascertaining the wishes of the people was by a fair and impartial plebiscite'; (ii) the plebiscite administrator should be appointed by the end of April 1954; (iii) previous to that, the preliminary issues that had held up progress towards a plebiscite so far should be decided and actions in implementation thereof should be taken, and with this object in view committees of military and other experts should be appointed to advise the Prime Ministers; (iv) progress 'can only be made in this direction if there is an atmosphere of peace and co-operation between the two countries'.[49]

The Delhi meeting was followed by exchange of letters between the Prime Ministers; twenty-seven letters and telegrams were exchanged between August 10, 1953, and September 21, 1954. The letters reflected mounting disagreements between the Prime Ministers shortly after the four-day meeting in New Delhi in August 1953, and revealed a failure to reach agreement even on most of the preliminary issues. It showed that, even if a plebiscite were held, India would not accept its full result. In a letter dated November 10, 1954, Nehru wrote: 'One cannot go by the results of plebiscite completely because some *absurd result* might flow.' Any boundary which was to be an international frontier must take account of geography; a handful of persons cannot change a frontier because they wish it. This qualification was met by a reminder from Mohammad Ali that, under the international agreement between the two countries, Kashmir was to be disposed of in accordance with the verdict of the people.

In May 1954, the news of American military aid to Pakistan was published, which gave Pandit Nehru a splendid excuse to go back on his commitments to hold a free vote in Kashmir. So far, India's 'inability' to hold the plebiscite had been a disagreement over demilitarisation; now began the second excuse: Pakistan's new military strength. It was in vain that Mohammed Ali (Bogra) pointed out that India was spending three times as much as Pakistan on its armed forces. Knowing that powerful sections of the Indian public made no secret of their resolve to annul the partition of the subcontinent by force, Pakistan had cause for uneasiness at the rapidity with which India was arming herself. If either country staged a military comeback in Kashmir after demilitarisation, Mohammad Ali wrote, war might engulf the entire subcontinent. and therefore it did not really matter where troops were deployed. The danger to peace in Asia arose not so much out of military aid but from disputes relating to Kashmir and other matters which affected the well-being of millions. But Nehru's objections to military aid to Pakistan dominated the correspondence and ultimately wrecked the direct talks which Mohammad Ali began with great hopes. Pakistan's Prime Minister tried again and again to impress on Nehru that the over-all military strengths of the two countries outside Kashmir could have no bearing on the issue if demili-tarisation were accepted. But, thanks to Nehru's intransigence, no progress towards this goal could be made. The expert committees met once, but no subsequent meeting was held by Nehru on account of this 'new factor': the military aid to Pakistan. The situation was further complicated by the provocative statements of the new 'Prime Minister' of Kashmir, Bakshi Ghulam Mohammad, who succeeded Abdullah—and also followed him into jail in due course. Bakshi said that the plebiscite administrator would never be installed, and that Kashmir's 'accession' to India was 'ratified' by the constituent assembly. In February 1954, Mohammad Ali wrote two letters to Nehru com-plaining of this decision, 'taken in contemptuous disregard of our talks and the agreement you and I reached in Delhi and of India commit-ments under the resolutions of the UN Commission for India and Pakistan'. He appealed to Nehru to repudiate the decision of the 'constituent assembly' and reaffirm his decision to solve the dispute in accordance with the commitments. 'This you have declined to do', he wrote: 'your statement that India stood by her international commitment *subject to such changes as may come about or unless something else happens* puts a novel construction on the sanctity of international commitments.' Nehru did not answer until March 5, when he wrote that India could take no risks and must keep troops in Kashmir. As the 'accession' of Kashmir to India was legally and constitutionally completed in October 1947, there was no question of confirming or ratifying it. The Kashmir constituent assembly, moreover, had every right to express its wishes in any way it chose.

Mohammad Ali soon became convinced that all his efforts for a peaceful settlement of the Kashmir dispute were in vain. Nehru's real reason for these talks was to tide over the popular uprising following the arrest of Abdullah and the imposition of new restrictive measures. Once the situation was brought under control by force, he could conveniently go back on the pledge he made to Mohammad Ali during their meeting in Delhi in the previous year, as he had gone back on his earlier pledges to the United Nations. In his letter of September 21, 1954, Mohammad Ali lamented: 'It is with profound regret that I have been led to the conclusion that our talks regarding Kashmir have failed.' Since becoming Prime Minister in 1953, Mohammad Ali had laboured unceasingly to put the relations between India and Pakistan on a friendly and co-operative basis. He incurred unpopularity in Pakistan for putting too much faith and reliance in Nehru's words.

Thus ended another major and most earnest effort to solve the Kashmir dispute: a dispute which 'continues to create tension and bitterness and suspicion and has resulted in a heavy drain on the meagre resources of two countries—resources which are desperately needed for raising the living standards of our peoples'. Mohammad Ali's concluding words to Nehru were: 'I hope and pray that the conscience and wisdom of man may yet perceive the great injustice and dangers inherent in the continuance of this disastrous dispute.'

BACK TO THE UNITED NATIONS, 1957–62

In 1957, after an interval of five years, the dispute was brought back to the Security Council. Pakistan had no other option. During the previous two years (1955–56), India entered into the third phase of her grand design to absorb the state of Jammu and Kashmir. So far, India had only created obstacles to holding a plebiscite by disagreeing to any scheme of demilitarisation, but by 1956 she was bold enough to declare that the plebiscite was no longer needed.

Delhi now had the blessing and support of a super-power in its new move to defy the United Nations and international commitments. In response to Pakistan's joining the Western military alliance, the Soviet Union started to woo India. There is no easier way to win India than to oppose Pakistan; the Soviet leaders seemed to have fully realised this vital aspect of India's foreign policy. In order to make India her friend and punish Pakistan for joining the Western bloc, the Soviet Union came out with most partisan and palpable support of India's stand on Kashmir (see chapter 6). The Indian leaders took it as axiomatic that the military aid given to Pakistan justified them in denying the people of Kashmir the right of self-determination—as if the foreign policy of Pakistan must be subservient to Delhi in order to secure the right of self-determination for 4 million Kashmiris. 'The Government of India', said the Foreign Minister of Pakistan in the 1957 UN debate, 'has put forward one pretext after another in an effort to justify its intransigent attitude. As the hollowness of one becomes apparent, another is thought up. The latest pretext is that acceptance by Pakistan of American military aid absolves India from her obligations to Pakistan, to the people of Kashmir and to the Security Council to honour her agreement to co-operate in a free and impartial plebiscite.'[50] Mohammad Ali had earlier (1954) told parliament: 'It is extraordinary that the fact that Pakistan should decide to accept military aid from the USA in order to strengthen her defences should be regarded by the Indian Prime Minister as a ground for postponing or abandoning the efforts for an amicable settlement of the Kashmir dispute.'[51] The real situation was, however, that Nehru never wanted a plebiscite in Kashmir as he knew that the vote would go against India; so he was in need of excuses. When in 1962, India also started receiving military aid from the United States, he put forward another novel excuse: Kashmir is the showpiece of India's secularism; if the plebiscite results in a pro-Pakistan vote, the Muslims in India would be massacred by the communal elements in India. So the 3 million Kashmiri Muslims must act as hostages for 50 million Muslims in India. We shall examine this argument when we come to the next aspect of India's strategy.

Pakistan complained to the Security Council in 1957 of India's annexing Kashmir with the help of the so-called 'constituent assembly'. The Security Council adopted a resolution almost unanimously, with ten votes in its favour and only one abstention, the Soviet Union. This resolution, like that of March 1951, reaffirmed the earlier resolutions of the Council and of the UN Commission that final disposition of the state of Jammu and Kashmir should be made in accordance with the will of the people, expressed through the democratic method of a free and impartial plebiscite conducted under the auspices of the United Nations. It declared that any action taken by the constituent assembly of Kashmir would not constitute a disposition of the state in accordance with that principle. The resolution urged the parties to maintain for the time being the *status quo* of the state. But, in spite of the Security Council's 'holding' resolution, the Indian government proceeded with its annexation plan by promulgating the so-called 'Srinagar constitution'.

India's defiance of the United Nations caused widespread resentment and disapproval. *The Times* commented: 'India has set herself up in the eyes of the world as, above all, a guardian of the moral law in international politics . . . for this reason, her apparent inconsistency in the Kashmir dispute seems to outsiders harder to understand.' [52] To the *News Chronicle*, the London Liberal daily, Nehru's actions were in strong contrast with his concern for the sanctity of the moral principle; 'the great internationalist has shown himself as stubbornly nationalist as the worst of them'. [53] The British weekly, *Time and Tide*, declared: 'It is shameful to remember that India is still a member of the Commonwealth. How long can the other nations of the Commonwealth maintain the association with India which has manifestly abused the link with the Commonwealth?' [54] The *New York Herald Tribune* exposed India's double standard of morality: 'See how Mr Nehru, who parades his pure lily-white idealism all over the place, has reached out and grabbed Kashmir. And that in spite of the unanimous vote of the Security Council.' [55] The *Daily Telegraph* asked: 'How can Mr Nehru plead reasons of state when he so consistently demands of others the strictest conformity to the dictates of international morality as interpreted by the United Nations?' [56] But nothing deterred Nehru from defying the United Nations. He knew that, in view of its long record of inertia and vacillation on the Kashmir question, the Security Council would be content with only moral censorship.

Moreover, India by this time had got the protection of the Soviet veto. It was this which thwarted the Security Council's move to take further steps to solve the Kashmir dispute. On February 14, 1957, a draft resolution was moved by Australia, Cuba, Britain and the United States seeking to use a temporary United Nations force for demilitarisation and for holding a plebiscite. The Soviet delegate, objecting to any reference to demilitarisation and to the United Nations temporary force, declared that the introduction of a UN force in Kashmir would be completely at variance with principles of the Charter and would be an outright insult to the national sentiments of the people of Kashmir. He even denounced the idea of a plebiscite in Kashmir. When the Soviet amendments were rejected by the Council, the USSR exercised its seventy-ninth veto but the first one used by any of the 'Big Five' in respect to Kashmir. The Soviet veto against the four powers' resolution on Kashmir extended the dark and ominous shadow of the East-West cold war over the dispute between the two Commonwealth countries of the subcontinent. So receded further any hope of peaceful solution of the dispute through the United Nations.

After the Soviet veto, a new resolution was tabled which omitted any reference to the UN force. It requested the president of the Council, Gunnar Jarring of Sweden, to consider any proposal likely to lead to a settlement of the dispute and for that purpose to visit the subcontinent. The resolution was passed and a new UN representative was added to the long list of mediators. Gunnar Jarring held discussions with the two governments from March 1 to April 10, 1957. He submitted his report—the failure of his mission—to the Security Council in late April 1957. He reported that he had sought to prevail upon the parties to accept arbitration on the crucial point contained in the resolution of August 1948 passed by the UN Commission for India and Pakistan, namely, whether demilitarisation and withdrawal of troops had taken place. India complained that Pakistan had not acted upon the Commission's recommendation that she should withdraw her troops and tribesmen, upon which Indian troops would be withdrawn in agreed stages. Jarring suggested that this point should be referred to an arbitrator or arbitrators, in case they found it necessary 'to indicate to the parties which measures should be taken to arrive at a full implementation'. Although the Pakistan government had given Jarring ample evidence that India's contention was not correct and that it had fulfilled its obligations under the resolution of August 1948, yet it agreed to Jarring's proposal for arbitration to decide this hurdle. But India, who made the complaint, did not agree to Jarring's suggestion. Delhi contended that such arbitration 'would be inconsistent with the sovereignty of Jammu and Kashmir' and, further, that it would give Pakistan what it called a *locus standi* in the dispute. After a decade of negotiations and talks with Pakistan and the United Nations, India now maintained that Pakistan had no *locus standi*; this was yet another argument now manufactured in Delhi.

India made it known to Jarring that she felt Pakistan's membership of military alliances had changed the whole situation—an argument which had been advanced during the talks between Mohammad Ali and Nehru, and which ultimately led to the failure of these talks. Jarring took note of the 'changing pattern of power relations in west and south Asia'—a remark which was interpreted by the Indians to mean that the UN representative was convinced by India's new case for withholding her commitments on Kashmir. An analysis of his report will, however, reveal that Jarring had not passed any judgement on the Indian argument. In fact, like the other UN mediators, Jarring was anxious to settle the Kashmir dispute in accordance with the resolutions of the Security Council and those of the UN Commission. It was not honest or fair to give such interpretation to Jarring's remarks.

Nor would Jarring comment on India's often-repeated charge of Pakistan's 'aggression' in Kashmir. He told the government of India that the Security Council had taken note of India's complaint but, instead of making any pronouncement on it, had succeeded in persuading the parties to reach an agreement whereby the question of accession was to be decided through a free and impartial plebiscite. It was not for him to say at such a late stage why the Security Council did not consider fit to give a judgement on India's complaint. He reminded them that both India and Pakistan, irrespective of the merits of the case, had accepted the UN resolutions and were bound by them to hold a free plebiscite in Kashmir. He seems to have regarded India's charge as irrelevant and frivolous in design. The Pakistan Foreign Minister dealing with India's charge observed in the Security Council when Jarring's report was debated: 'Throughout the previous discussions in the Security Council, the representatives of all the powers, great or small, who considered this issue since January 1948 have all regarded the Indian allegation as unworthy of consideration.'[57] Nehru's lamentations against the Security Council's deliberations would substantiate the statement of the Pakistan Foreign Minister.

After the failure of the Jarring mission, a stalemate developed over the discussion of the Kashmir dispute in the Security Council. Dr Frank Graham was sent once more to the subcontinent in 1958. He put forward a new set of proposals which, as usual, were accepted by Pakistan and rejected by India. India's rejection had, by now, become a matter of routine, and the Security Council's inertia and inactivity had also become obvious—which, in turn, increased India's intransigence. Dr Graham's latest report was not even discussed in the Security Council, as if not to offend India. Moreover, Pakistan's Western allies had, by 1960, become sensitive to India's objections. The growing rift between China and India led them to support a policy of boosting India in Asia, even if it meant disregarding her continued defiance of international commitments, and even if it was vigorously opposed by their 'ally' Pakistan. The object of the wrath of the Soviet Union, Pakistan now had to suffer coolness from her allies. Such is the plight of a smaller country in power politics.

In the meantime, President Ayub had come to power in Pakistan, and under him a strong and stable government was formed. Ayub was most anxious to have better relations with India; he even offered a plan for joint defence with India. He made it clear, however, that without a settlement of the Kashmir issue the chances of any lasting friendship between the two countries were remote. Ayub soon realised, like his predecessors, that Nehru had no real intention of solving the Kashmir dispute. In 1962, the dispute was brought once more before the Security Council. The Irish delegate, Professor Bolland, put forward a constructive resolution envisaging direct negotiation between India and Pakistan on the basis of previous resolutions of the Security Council and the UN Commission, and of Article 3 of the Charter. The Soviet veto, once more, came to the rescue of India.

The whole situation was, however, dramatically changed with the outbreak of the Sino-Indian border conflict in 1962, when the Indian forces were defeated and routed by the Chinese. India, in desperation, begged Western arms—beseeching that military aid from the West which she had so stubbornly opposed when Pakistan became its recipient in 1953. These developments opened another chapter of the unfortunate Kashmir dispute.

DIRECT NEGOTIATIONS, 1962-63

The Sino-Indian border war seemed to have melted away, for a time, Nehru's long resistance to any negotiation of the Kashmir dispute either with the United Nations or Pakistan. Nehru had been saying that the 'Kashmir issue had been settled' and that therefore 'there is nothing to discuss'. But the Sino-Indian border conflict of 1962 transformed the whole political atmosphere of the subcontinent. Though India's relations with China had been growing tense, Nehru's main military deployment was still against Pakistan. This was a serious handicap to him in his dispute with China, when the Indians 'were edging forward in [the] disputed area' of the Sino-Indian border.[58] The Chinese reply to Nehru was so terrible that he had to have second thoughts on his 'closed' chapter on Kashmir. The British Commonwealth Secretary, Duncan Sandys, and the United States Assistant Secretary of State, Averell Harriman, went quickly to the subcontinent. The Chinese crisis enabled the envoys to break down Nehru's resistance to a reopening of the Kashmir question. The Anglo-American move sought to make Nehru realise the serious consequences that could develop from India's failure to settle the Kashmir dispute and build close friendly relations with Pakistan.

In the circumstances that developed over the Sino-Indian border dispute, it would seem incumbent on Nehru to take the initiative and settle the Kashmir issue with Pakistan, if, as seemed to be the case, India's military strength was greatly compromised because the majority of her troops were deployed against Pakistan. Instead of taking such initiative, India tried to put pressure on Pakistan, through the United States and Britain, not to press the Kashmir problem. In fact, President Kennedy and Prime Minister Macmillan were understood to have written to President Ayub Khan suggesting a 'freeze' on Kashmir until the Indo-Chinese border conflict was solved. This was too much to ask from Pakistan and she could not agree to it. Yet Ayub gave Nehru indications, through the United States and Britain, implying that Pakistan would not do anything to make India's military problems worse.[59] As a result, India transferred at least one-third of her troops from areas near Pakistan to where they could be useful against the Chinese. All the same, India maintained a large force against her 'customary enemy'. Sandys and Harriman tried to convince Nehru that the great advantage to India of a settlement with Pakistan would be a state of peace on their common frontier enabling her to concentrate on the Sino-Indian border. Nehru was under constraint: the classic constraint of having an enemy on two fronts.

Even during the Sino-Indian border conflict, the hostile attitude towards Pakistan was never relaxed. The deep-seated differences and suspicions that subsisted between the two countries continued to be vituperatively expressed. Though India could hardly face the crisis with China without a settlement with Pakistan, Nehru was not in a hurry to reach the conference table. He said on December 13, 1962 that he thought that there could be no real settlement of the issue until India's border dispute with China was over. Nehru was 'enormously surprised' by Pakistan's attitude towards India during the border conflict with China.[60] He would perhaps have found less occasion for surprise if he had given thought to his own people's attitude towards Pakistan over her difficulties with Afghanistan. The Indian press and government have always been generous in giving paternal blessing and encouragement to Afghanistan's demand for 'Pakhtoonistan', a claim involving a substantial part of Pakistan's territory. The sad fact is that, since independence in 1947, both India and Pakistan have looked upon one another as potential enemies, and in their external relations the friends of the one country are looked upon as hostile by the other.

However, the Anglo-American move was successful in extracting a joint communiqué on November 29, 1962, issued simultaneously from Rawalpindi and New Delhi, stating that a renewed effort was to be made to resolve the Kashmir dispute and, with that end in view, ministerial talks would be held between India and Pakistan to pave the way for an eventual meeting between Ayub and Nehru. Yet even before Harriman and Sandys left the subcontinent, Nehru came out with the bald statement that his readiness to discuss Kashmir did not mean that India would 'by-pass or ignore her basic principles'. Duncan Sandys, who was in Karachi at that time on his way back home, cancelled his journey and rushed to Delhi to meet Nehru in the middle of the night to apprise him of the serious repercussions which his statement had caused in Pakistan. At the instance of the British Commonwealth Secretary, Nehru sought to explain away his earlier statement, saying that it was incorrect to read into it any intention of limiting the scope of the Indo-Pakistan discussion or to exclude consideration of any solutions which either government might propose. However, soon afterwards, Nehru's Home Minister, Lal Bahadur Shastri, declared that India's willingness to have talks with Pakistan on the question did not mean that the negotiations would be resumed on the basis of suggestions for partitioning any 'part of India'. 'We are not prepared to partition Kashmir.' A few days later, Nehru told his parliament that pressures were being brought on him to settle the Kashmir dispute.[61] The statements of the Indian leaders seemed to have jeopardised the prospects of the talks.

Even so, talks began at ministerial level at Rawalpindi on December 27, 1962, between Z. A. Bhutto, the Pakistani Minister for Industries, and Sardar Swaran Singh, the Indian Minister for Railways. (Both subsequently became Foreign Ministers of their countries.) The discussions opened against a background of profound scepticism; six rounds of ministerial talks were held from December 27, 1962 to May 16, 1963. In a sense, these talks on Kashmir were a quadripartite affair because Britain and the United States—while maintaining, of course, a correct aloofness from the matter of issue—were deeply committed to promoting a successful outcome. 'Three of these four were pressing for brisk progress towards substantive negotiations on Kashmir. But the fourth party, India, soon manifestly lost some of the urgency that was forced upon her at the height of her border conflict with China.'[62] Since he could not break off these distasteful discussions, Nehru was trying to keep just enough life in them to mollify his Western armourers. But the Western arms only buttressed India's intransigence on Kashmir. The Times reported during the talks: 'To India a settlement means confirming the cease-fire line as frontier and letting bygones be bygones.'[63] Kenneth Galbraith, the United States Ambassador to India, was said to have reported to Washington that India was continuing the talks largely out of fear of American wrath. The United States and Britain applied diplomatic pressure on both India and Pakistan for a settlement.[64] 'The crux of the problem', the New York Times remarked, 'lies in the failure of India to manifest any readiness to make any important concession.'[65]

Let us now review the course of these desultory and unfruitful talks in alternate capitals until May 16, 1963, when a formal failure was announced. At the first round, the Indian delegation, while admitting that the resolutions of the United Nations Commission of August 14, 1948 and January 5, 1949, had envisaged a plebiscite, put forward various pleas and excuses to explain why such a plebiscite could not be held. The Pakistan delegation made it clear that, if the Indians had entered into these talks only to confirm or adjust the existing cease-fire line, it would not pursue these talks any further. To this, the Indian delegates replied that such a proposal was not in their minds and that they would seek an honourable and equitable solution. The Pakistan delegation emphasised that its government regarded a fair and impartial plebiscite under the supervision of the United Nations as the best solution. Nevertheless, Pakistan was prepared to consider any other constructive and fair proposal. The Pakistan delegation drew the attention of India to the informal proposals—particularly those of General Mcnaughton of Canada in 1948 and of Sir Owen Dixon of Australia in 1950—which envisaged a limited or regional plebiscite and the partitioning of the state between India and Pakistan: proposals which had been informally discussed during the direct talks between the Prime Ministers in 1953–54.

During the second round of talks, the Indian delegation engaged in a protracted academic discussion of these proposals, and then told the Pakistan delegation, towards the end of a three-day conference at Delhi, that it did not consider any ideas contained in these proposals to be of any value or interest, because all formulas involved, in some way or other, the idea of ascertaining the wishes of the people of Kashmir. The Indian government was opposed to any reference to the people. Its main argument against a plebiscite, either an over-all or a limited one, was that, if a vote were held and if it went in favour of Pakistan, the Hindus of India would take this as proof of their belief that Muslims in India are not loyal; riots would start and India would be bathed in blood. Thus, India's new argument against a plebiscite in Kashmir was that it would destroy India's 'secularism': an argument which reflected the truth that the masses of India do not believe in secularism as embodied in their constitution, that the Indian government cannot control the religious emotions of its people, and that the Indian nation is sitting on a powder barrel. This argument, the Pakistanis contend, is blackmail of the most despicable sort; any stick seems good enough in Delhi to beat down the right of the Kashmiris to self-determination. Nor has the absence of a vote in Kashmir, they point out, prevented persecution of Muslims in 'secular' India; how many riots have taken place in 'secular' India? The argument means that the Muslims of

Kashmir must be hostages, in political bondage for the 50 million Muslims in India. There is a strong flavour of political immorality in this argument.[66]

After elaborating its objections to any form of reference to the people of Kashmir, the Indian delegation proposed what it called 'political settlement'. By 'political settlement', it meant partition of the state without any attempt to ascertain the wishes of the people. The Pakistan delegation did not reject the proposal but emphasised that, without prejudice to Pakistan's basic stand for an over-all plebiscite in Kashmir in accordance with the resolutions of the United Nations, it was prepared to consider any territorial division provided this took into consideration certain important factors or principles, such as (i) the composition of the population of the state; (ii) the economic and strategic interests of Pakistan; (iii) an international boundary should be so drawn as to be acceptable to the people of the state. At the end of the second round of talks, it was agreed by both sides that a 'political solution' must be explored, and that a political settlement must be honourable, equitable and final, taking into account the following factors: (1). India and Pakistan should seek the delineation of an international boundary in Jammu and Kashmir. Pakistan urged that territorial division should take into account the composition of the population of the state, control of rivers, requirements of defence and other considerations relevant to the determination of an international boundary and acceptable to the people of the state. India urged that the division should take into account geographic, administrative and other considerations, and that the settlement should involve the least disturbance to the life and welfare of the people. (2). There should be a disengagement of the forces of India and Pakistan in and around Kashmir, and the removal of all tensions. It was further agreed that the settlement should embody in a solemn declaration the determination of the two countries 'to live side by side in peace and friendship and to solve all other problems peacefully and to their mutual benefit; and that ways and means should be considered of removing other major irritants between the two countries.[67]

In the third round of talks, held in Karachi in February 1963, the Pakistan delegation pressed the Indians to indicate their plan for 'political settlement'. After considerable reluctance, they presented their plan for the partition of the state of Jammu and Kashmir towards the end of the Karachi talks. To the great surprise and disappointment of Pakistan, this plan amounted to nothing more than the mere readjustment of the existing cease-fire line. India had assured Pakistan at the first parley that her proposed 'political settlement' would not offer only an adjustment of the cease-fire line. Yet, after two months of negotiations, it was merely this that the Indian delegation had to offer. Z. A. Bhutto, reminding it of its promise not to make such a proposal, rejected the Indian plan and emphasised again the essential principles on the basis of which Pakistan had agreed to consider the 'political settlement'. 'Some progress' at Rawalpindi had faded into 'slight progress' at New Delhi; and now, at the end of the third round of talks in Karachi, 'the differences that emerged' were 'quite considerable'.

With whatever seriousness Nehru had agreed to the discussions—and the integrity of his intentions is open to question—it was now becoming clear that the Indian government was no more interested than before in an honourable and equitable settlement. By the beginning of 1963, India had begun to feel more secure. The mediatory explorations of the Colombo powers had indicated that China would not renew border hostilities. 'As the Chinese troops withdraw and fear of renewed fighting recedes, the Indian Prime Minister is reverting to his old form.'[68] Moreover, India's prospects of receiving Western military aid were getting brighter, particularly in the light of the Kennedy-Macmillan talks at Nassau in December 1962.

During the fourth round of talks at Calcutta in March 1963, much time was wasted by the Indians on the Sino-Pakistan border accord. India got further encouragement from Washington's displeasure at Pakistan's 'flirtations with China'. Dean Rusk, in a statement on March 8, just on the eve of the Calcutta parley, assured Nehru that United States military aid to India would not be conditional on successful negotiations over Kashmir.[69] Nehru reacted strongly to the Sino-Pakistan frontier agreement, which he described as a realignment of the boundary between China and 'areas of Kashmir illegally occupied by Pakistan'.[70] The Times questioned his argument: 'In moving to settle her borders with China, Pakistan has done nothing more than what has been done unresented by Burma and Nepal.'[71]

At the Calcutta meeting, the Pakistan delegation presented its plan for the partition of the state. This proposed a boundary that would follow the peaks of the Pir Punjal range in northern Jammu and give Pakistan the districts of Riasi, Mirpur and Poonch. Under the *de facto* boundary created by the present cease-fire line, India controls Riasi and parts of the other two districts. Riasi is important to Pakistan because it includes the middle reach of the Chenab River and much of its watersheds, which are vital to her economy. Pakistan was willing to postpone consideration of the Vale of Kashmir and Srinagar, her delegation indicating that it would want an agreed solution of the Vale but that its implementation might be postponed. This suggestion of delayed implementation was made to meet India's contention that Srinagar controls communications with Ladakh and is therefore essential to her defence against China.[72] As an alternative, President Ayub proposed to Duncan Sandys that the Vale be internationalised as a 'five to ten year interim solution'; but Nehru turned this down.[73]

During the last two rounds—in Karachi in April 1963 and in New Delhi in May 1963—no further progress could be made due to the fact that the partition plans submitted by India and Pakistan were utterly divergent. India would not make any concession. One aspect of India's attitude is particularly significant. The Pakistan plan would have removed from India certain areas of Jammu where Hindus had a majority; India would never agree to part with these areas because they were populated by Hindus. And yet, at the same time, the Indian leaders were saying that the religious affiliation of the people of Kashmir should not be taken into consideration as this would affect India's 'secularism'. That India felt under no obligation to amend her 'double-standard' attitude may be attributable in part to the relaxation of American and British pressure on her. Shortly before the last round of talks was concluded, Lord Mountbatten, who is held responsible by many Pakistanis for the origin of the Kashmir dispute, visited India and *The Times* correspondent from Delhi reported: 'Misunderstanding between Britain and India has been nipped in the bud by the intervention of Lord Mountbatten and an attempt to use the Sino-India border war as a lever to force a settlement of the Kashmir dispute has been written off.'[74]

The British and United States envoys had assisted in the talks throughout their duration. While the British High Commission stoutly insisted that it had no plan for a Kashmir solution, the American Embassy had been more forthcoming. The Galbraith plan (the 'Harvard Exercise' as it was called) was put forward. Briefly, the plan proposed that the road across the cease-fire line between Rawalpindi and Srinagar should be reopened; that there should be freedom of trade with both Pakistan and India; that India's military rights in the Vale of Kashmir should be respected because on them depends her defence of Ladakh; that citizens of Kashmir should be free to choose either Indian or Pakistani citizenship, which would be in itself a sort of silent plebiscite without attendant political shouting.[75]

Unfortunately, when serious efforts were being made to improve the Indo-Pakistan relations, Nehru made a statement to the correspondent of the *Washington Post* that Indo-Pakistan 'confederation remains our ultimate aim'. This immediately aroused Pakistan's deep-rooted suspicions of India's ultimate aim of reuniting the subcontinent. It produced sharp reactions and comments; President Ayub, who was already being accused in Pakistan of making concessions to India over Kashmir, had to face further domestic embarrassment.

When the deadlock proved unbreakable at the sixth and final round of talks, India came forward with her often-repeated 'no-war' pact. Pakistanis have always considered this as a hoax in the absence of a settlement of the Kashmir issue, and as a convenient tool manufactured by the Indian government, which uses it to sidetrack any serious effort to solve the Kashmir problem. We shall discuss it in a subsequent chapter.

Thus ended the fourth phase of the unsuccessful efforts to resolve the Kashmir dispute. Plebiscite, partition, internationalisation, 'political settlement': all the textbook solutions for a territorial dispute have been proposed for Kashmir and all have proved fruitless. They have failed because the party in possession of everything that matters has felt strong enough to resist 'the concessions that any solution would require'.[76] From an analysis of the 1962–63 negotiations, it becomes clear that India was a reluctant party to the conference table. There was no change in India's attitude; it was simply that the diplomatic pressure of the Western powers whose military aid she needed compelled her to appear amenable to negotiation. India was never at any stage of the talks serious about a fair and honourable settlement. Nehru was playing for time in order to watch developments regarding the outcome of the mediatory efforts of the Colombo powers and to ensure the passage of arms aid legislation by the United States Congress. With the relaxation of the crisis created by the Sino-Indian border conflict, and with the assurance of military aid from the Western countries, particularly from the United States, Nehru had no need of these distasteful talks and one excuse after another was offered to paralyse the negotiations. 'As the talks went from one round to another, there was more and more evidence of a hardening of the Indian attitude.'[77] On the eve of the final round of talks, the *Observer's Foreign News Service* reported from New Delhi on May 14, 1963: 'Now that India no longer has its back to the wall against China, everybody here expects an early breakdown of the Kashmir negotiations.'

After six rounds of talks on Kashmir, Pandit Nehru declared: 'Kashmir was, is and will continue to be an integral part of India.'[78] But the people of Kashmir did not seem to accept his assertion. They rose in revolt against Indian rule in Kashmir in December 1963, when 'less than ever does it seem possible that the valley can ever be peaceful without some open test of public feeling'.[79] India tried to make the world believe that all was settled in Kashmir. From the outside, the issue might seem unnecessary, unintelligible and interminable, but inside the subcontinent all discussions of the future, of world affairs, of economic developments, come back to this unfortunate and miserable dispute which poisons the whole life of the two countries.[80] We shall discuss in our concluding chapter the developments in Kashmir between the direct talks of 1962–63 and the all-out war over Kashmir between Pakistan and India in September 1965, when the forecast made in the *Christian Science Monitor* on August 21, 1951, seemed to be near to realisation: 'The storm clouds which might spell the outbreak of World War III are gathering over the beautiful Vale of Kashmir, famed in song and story.'

4

TRADE AND WATER DISPUTES

THE economic situation in the subcontinent was hardly taken into account when the scheme for partition was being decided on the basis of religious affinities. The result was that 'the economy of the Indian Empire was violently vivisected'.[1] Partition dislocated the whole basis of the subcontinental economy which had been developed as a single unit; this was a circumstance for which the two parties concerned were to blame. There resulted a Pakistan which might be regarded as 'the perfect example of a colonial economy'.[2] Pakistan fared very badly in the distribution of the industrial sector of the subcontinent's economy. All the major industries were concentrated in areas assigned to the new Indian Union, leaving Pakistan an under-developed country.

Of the 405 cotton mills, Pakistan got only 16; of the 153 sugar factories, her share was only 11; and all the jute mills went to India. In short, India had 86 per cent of the total industrial establishments, and 90 per cent of the total industrial population.[3] The best coal and iron mines also fell to India's share; and other important minerals, like manganese, copper and mica, were located in India. Pakistan has some coal mines, but the quality is poor and inadequate to meet her requirements. With regard to mineral oils, Pakistan's share was little better. She got minerals like chorimite, salt and saltpetre, limestone, etc. There were many gloomy forecasts about the economic viability of the new state; in many quarters its early collapse was predicted on economic grounds, if not on any other factors. The situation was further aggravated by the political disputes between India and Pakistan, which had adverse effects on their economic relations.

While Pakistan fared badly in the distribution of industries, she inherited a fairly balanced and sound agriculture. She received the bigger share of irrigated areas of the subcontinent; 40 per cent of Pakistan's cultivated area is irrigated, as against India's 18 per cent. Whereas India suffers from chronic deficiency of food, Pakistan is self-sufficient in this respect, and in a normal year has a surplus for export. In the production of cash crops, such as jute and cotton, Pakistan's share was far better than that of her neighbour; in 1947–8, she produced 78 per cent of the total yield of raw jute in both countries, though she had not a single jute-manufacturing plant. Similarly, in cotton Pakistan produced 40 per cent of the total output of raw cotton in undivided India, and was the largest exporter of raw cotton in Asia and the fourth largest in the world.

The common-sense solution of the economic situation that prevailed in the subcontinent in 1947 would have been some sort of arrangement under which Pakistan would supply raw jute, cotton, hides and food grains to India, receiving from her neighbour cloth, iron and steel, coal, jute manufactures, paper, etc. The facts of history and geography dictated that the economies of the two countries should not be treated as mutually exclusive and separate. The ideal situation would have been a customs union with free trade, but it was unpractical to think in terms of such a union because of the prevailing tensions. Indeed, as a result of strained political relations between them since their inception, the two countries have been drifting apart economically, and a tariff war has created exasperating impediments in inter-Dominion trade. India declined to grant rebates of excise duties on exports to Pakistan, while granting such rebates to other countries. This discriminatory policy was raised by the Pakistan delegate to the Agency Conference on World Trade in 1949, who alleged that India's action was a violation of the Geneva Agreement on Trade and Tariffs (GATT). Because of the constant political tension, each country has always tended to follow policies designed to make itself as economically independent of the other as possible, and to turn to trade agreements with distant states in Europe or North America for supplies of commodities which are actually within easy reach in the subcontinent.

In 1947, Pakistan made a proposal to India under which Pakistan would supply and India would manufacture jute and cotton on the basis of sharing the export duties and the foreign exchange earnings.[4]

India, however, was not willing to enter into such an arrangement. When the question of apportionment of the revenue on jute was discussed by the joint expert committee, India insisted on the retention by each country of the revenue collected at its own ports: a principle which would have given Pakistan less than 20 per cent of the jute duty, though producing 78 per cent of the raw jute. Pakistan could not possibly agree to such conditions. At the time of partition, a standstill agreement was made by the two countries under which goods moving from one country to another would be exempt from customs duty; and, in fact, what amounted to a customs union was set up. This, however, was an interim arrangement. As a result of India's refusal to give Pakistan any share of the export duty on jute, the temporary 'customs union' came to an end in less than three months. Since then, Indo-Pakistan trade relations have never been free from the strains and stresses of the political disputes which bedevil the relations between the two countries.

On November 13, 1947, the government of Pakistan announced the application of an export duty on raw jute transported across the land frontier of Pakistan. The official press statement noted:

> In the current year's budget, the total revenue from the export duty on jute was estimated at $5\frac{1}{2}$ crores [55 million] of rupees. These duties have hitherto been collected only at the ports with the result that, although three-quarters of total jute crop of India and Pakistan is grown in East Bengal [Pakistan], over 90 per cent of the revenue was accrued at Calcutta and less than 10 per cent at Chittagong. The Pakistan Government cannot afford to lose so large a proportion of the revenue which is derived from Pakistan products and which belongs to them. They are, however, most anxious to settle the matter by agreement, if possible, and they have made every effort to arrive at a settlement even by offering a share of this jute revenue to the Indian Dominion. The Indian government refused to agree to any such agreement.

The government of Pakistan made it clear in the press note that this was not a new or additional duty; it merely authorised the collection on the land frontiers of a duty which was already payable on jute exported by sea. The government of Pakistan expressed its willingness to refer to arbitration the whole question of the distribution of customs and excise revenue and abide by the decision.[5] We have made this reference to the press statement of November 13, 1947, because the imposition of this duty was on many occasions referred to by the Indian government as an example of Pakistan's putting obstacles in the way of smooth Indo-Pakistan trade in the early years of independence. The real situation, however, was that the government of Pakistan was quite willing to enter into an arrangement under which the *status quo* could be maintained, but insisted on a legitimate share of revenue and foreign exchange. The Indian government seemed to be eager to take full advantage of Pakistan's initial economic and financial difficulties, and it was not in a mood to discuss any rational and just system by which the economies of the two countries could be saved from complete dislocation after partition. As India had possessed the greater financial and economic strength, she sought to dictate terms to the weaker neighbour. The same technique of strangulation as we have noted in the preceding chapter was applied vigorously in trade and economic relations.

The government of India declared the Dominion of Pakistan to be a 'foreign country' for the purpose of levying customs and excise duty with effect from March 1, 1948. India's trade with Pakistan also came under the scope of the Imports and Exports Control Act. The 'standstill agreement' between the two countries came to an end. Pakistan took reciprocal actions to counter India's move. The Pakistan Finance Minister said that his country was most anxious to avoid the imposition of any unnecessary barriers on trade between the two countries, but India's action left no choice. The first unfortunate effects of this inter-Dominion failure to come to terms over customs and excise were visible in the spate of orders issued from Delhi and Karachi. As soon as the new Dominions could find time to organise their customs posts, they declared each other 'foreign countries' as far as trade was concerned, thereby adding enormously to their respective difficulties. The net result of the trade deadlock was that Pakistan spent part of her meagre foreign exchange reserves in buying coal from the United States and Britain, and India looked beyond the seas for cotton of a type grown in West Punjab and Sind.

In May 1948, however, there was convened an Indo-Pakistan conference on the supply of essential commodities between the two countries, which resulted in a trade agreement providing for the supply of essential commodities between Pakistan and India for one year. India would supply coal, steel, cloth, paper, chemicals and railway materials, while Pakistan would supply raw jute, raw cotton, food grains, hides and skins. The agreement was not, by any means, a comprehensive trade agreement but merely emphasised the need for exchange of essential commodities subject to custom and other regulations that might exist in each Dominion.

There were charges and counter-charges about the implementation of the trade agreement, and it did not work satisfactorily. It was perhaps too much to expect any Indo-Pakistan agreement to work without a hitch because of the prevailing tensions. The two countries were already engaged in a 'limited war' over Kashmir, and it is no wonder that trade and commerce should be affected by it. An attempt to iron out the difficulties in the implementation of the agreement was made at a conference in October 1948, but the situation showed no improvement. The real difficulty, as in the case of political disputes, was lack of mutual trust and understanding. Even so, despite the difficulties, the trade agreement continued to work and in 1948–49 India was Pakistan's most important buyer as well as seller, consuming 60 per cent of her total exports and supplying nearly 43 per cent of her total imports. The complementary character of the economies of the two countries was still dominant. The working of the agreement, in spite of all stresses and strains, indicated the immense volume and importance of inter-Dominion trade.

When the agreement expired, a fresh agreement for the exchange of essential goods was signed on June 30, 1949, and came into operation on July 1. A disquieting feature of trade under the previous agreement was India's enormous adverse balance of trade. This was good neither for India nor Pakistan. The new agreement sought to achieve an equilibrium between India's export to and import from Pakistan; a 20 per cent import cut was imposed on raw jute from Pakistan and a 30 per cent cut on raw cotton imports. On the export side, India included several new items and the duties on existing items were increased.[6] Yet the new agreement showed that inter-Dominion trade was still regarded as important by the two countries.

At the beginning of 1949, it became apparent that India was the chief sufferer from the customs regulations and trade barriers. The

Indian Commerce Minister, Mr Neogy, made a plea for the customs union which India had wantonly destroyed in the previous year. But his suggestion was coolly received in Pakistan because of the unhappy experiences in relations with India. The trade agreement of 1949, however, revealed business acumen on both sides. The chief problem was how to reduce India's adverse balance with Pakistan (about £35,250,000). India's jute industry was facing increased foreign competition in a diminishing world market. This situation was partly the result of the earlier phase of India's trade policy against Pakistan when she tried to insist on a low price for jute. This led to a severe temporary shortage of the Indian jute industry's raw materials which was freely taken advantage of by manufacturers elsewhere in the world, including those of Dundee, who found the Pakistanis only too willing to sell them raw jute at a more favourable price. The trade agreement of 1949 provided an elaborate machinery whereby India's deficit of payments was not supposed to exceed Rs. 35 crores (Rs. 350 million). It also allowed various categories of goods to cross the frontiers without export licences. The prospects for improving and rationalising Indo-Pakistan trade seemed to be bright, but unhappily the full implementation of the new agreement was frustrated by a fresh development which led to a trade war between the two countries.

In September 1949, the British government decided to devalue the pound sterling. India followed Britain in devaluing her currency, but Pakistan decided not to follow suit because of her economic circumstances and requirements. The government of Pakistan in a press note stated that account had been taken of the 'intrinsic position' of the country's economy and the interests of producers of exportable raw materials, and that particular regard had been paid to the need for reducing the general cost of living and the maintenance of conditions favourable to the country's development. The statement of the Pakistan government added: 'Our balance of payments position is not such as to necessitate devaluation, nor do our exports, which consist almost entirely of raw materials, admit of any appreciable expansion. The decision not to devalue will mean cheaper imports which should have a welcome effect on the general cost of living.' As regards exports, the Pakistan government confidently expected that, after an initial period of adjustment, trade would resume its normal course. Non-devaluation would enable Pakistan to buy, without additional cost, capital goods and essential raw materials from countries where they were plentiful. Pakistan's decision not to devalue her currency was promoted by her compelling economic interest. Her main contribution to world trade consisted of raw materials which were in short supply; she was largely self-supporting in food; her urgent need was for capital goods— all these factors dictated the decision against devaluation. The Finance Minister said that Pakistan's decision not to devalue its rupee was primarily based on the desire to earn dollars. There was no desire or intention to leave the sterling bloc. He further stated that 'Pakistan wants to live at peace with India'.[7]

The Economist commented on Pakistan's decision on September 24, 1949: 'The Pakistan government no doubt felt justified in trying to maintain its rupee at the old dollar value. The new Dominion needs capital equipments and by maintaining its rupee rate no doubt expected to be able to reduce the rupee cost of such imports.' Pakistan was not, at that time, having any problem of a dollar deficit; on the contrary, she was a net earner of dollars. There was no intrinsic reason for depreciating the Pakistani rupee, and it did not seem good sense for Pakistan, with a favourable trade balance, not only with the sterling area but also with the United States, to take a step which would mean higher costs of imported goods without bringing any compensatory advantages in the volume of exports. There was hardly any elasticity in the demand for Pakistan's export commodities, for these were already in keen demand and she had no difficulty in selling them.[8]

But Pakistan's decision not to devalue her rupee was received with indignation and anger in India. At once, the Reserve Bank of India informed all banks functioning in India that it would not quote any rate for the purchase and sale of the Pakistani rupee. India seemed to consider that to accept any other rate than par between the two rupees would endorse the suggestion that Pakistan was in a stronger economic position than India—a suggestion which Indians stoutly denied. A decision, which was wide open to economic debate, had been turned into a question of national prestige. India's reaction to Pakistan's decision was almost hysterical. Sir Percival Griffiths relates that one of the most intelligent Hindus in Delhi told him: 'I would rather see both countries ruined than agree that the Pakistan rupee should be worth one iota more than the Indian rupee.'[9] India's Deputy Prime Minister, Sardar Patel, said: 'We do not mind if our mills remain idle but we are not fools to pay Rs. 145 for Rs. 100 worth of Pakistani jute.'[10]

Because of India's attitude, an economic war of attrition was waged between the two new Dominions. Anger, bitterness and misery were the dominant emotions. India harassed Pakistan with noxious embargoes and added more complications to the corrosive political friction between the two countries. The ensuing economic war of attrition made the 1949 trade agreement a dead letter. Inter-Dominion trade (60 per cent of Pakistan's trade was with India, and 30 per cent of India's trade was with Pakistan) came to a dead stop in September 1949 when India refused to accept Pakistan's decision not to devalue her currency.

Mr Neogy, the Indian Commerce Minister, announced in the Indian parliament that all supplies of Indian coal to Pakistan were being suspended in retaliation for what he called illegal seizure of Indian-owned jute. There were complaints in the Indian press that Pakistan had refused to deliver 300,000 bales of jute to India under contracts made before devaluation. These contracts were, however, between private parties of both Dominions and the payments were to be made in Pakistani rupees. Because of the refusal of India's Reserve Bank to have any transaction in Pakistani rupees, deliveries of jute under these private contracts were suspended. The government of Pakistan had no responsibility for these contracts. The Pakistan Commerce Minister pointed out that the withholding of jute in East Pakistan was due to the failure of Indian purchasers to provide proof of payment to the Pakistan jute board.

Pakistan faced the cessation of coal supplies from India with grim stoicism. The 'trade war' became, for the time being, the most dominating aspect of Indo-Pakistan relations. The Pakistan Commerce Minister accused India of violating the inter-Dominion trade agreement of 1949 by suspending coal supplies. India's next move in the economic 'war' was to cut off the Ferozepur canal waters, and to follow up her coal embargo on Pakistan by stopping the transit of petrol, oil and kerosene into East Bengal (Pakistan) which relied on shipments through Calcutta (India).[11] India's decision to suspend coal supplies to Pakistan and Pakistan's failure to deliver raw jute in 1949 seemed likely to precipitate a full-scale economic war between the two countries. Newspapers on both sides were clamouring for reprisals. There was talk on the one hand of Pakistan's stopping goods traffic on the railway from Assam through East Bengal and petrol supplies for East Punjab through Karachi and Lahore; on the other hand, Indians were threatening to cut off Pakistan's supplies of canal waters and electric power from headworks and stations in Indian territory. In the meantime, the Hindu Mahasabha made its demand for taking steps 'to restore the seceding areas [i.e., Pakistan] as an integral part of India'.[12]

Trade between Pakistan and India was wholly at a standstill as a result of 'the battle of the rupees'.[13] Both sides had been losers. Scores of thousands of jute and cotton mill operatives in Bombay and Calcutta faced starvation; on the other side of the border, jute growers had difficulties. More than a hundred cotton and jute mills in India closed down. The impasse was the despair of all thinking men in both countries. The trade deadlock was a distraction of the first magnitude and wholly unnecessary. Both countries had to adopt a number of extraordinary measures to meet the crisis created as a result of India's refusal to accept Pakistan's decision regarding her currency. A very onerous responsibility had to be shouldered by Pakistan's jute board to prevent the fall of prices of jute, while the Indian Ministries of Agriculture, both central and provincial, had to make plans, not only to make India self-sufficient in food, but also to supply her mills with the varieties of cotton and jute until recently imported from Pakistan. All these extraordinary measures and the resultant suffering for the ordinary citizens in both countries could have been avoided had not political misunderstanding been allowed to disrupt the economic relations between the two successor states of the British *Raj*.

The Economist, analysing the trade stalemate between the two countries, wrote:

Political argument apart, however, Pakistan had good economic reasons for maintaining the parity of its rupee with dollar. These reasons can be broadly summarised under four heads. First, Pakistan's balance of payments with the rest of the world, including the United States, is favourable. Secondly, Pakistan has embarked on a programme of industrialisation and therefore she needs to import capital goods as cheaply as possible. Thirdly, the Pakistan government believes that its exports (and again particularly those to hard currency markets) have certainly an inelastic supply. Finally, Pakistan wants to bring about a fall in domestic price level. . . . India has apparently accepted the Pakistan decision not to devalue as a declaration of economic war. . . . To sum up, if the exchange rate between the two rupees were to be determined by economic considerations alone, the present official parity of Indian Rs. 144 = Pakistan Rs. 100 would probably not be an overstatement of Pakistan's economic strength.[14]

But no amount of argument or rational consideration could change India's hysterical attitude. India's reluctance to accept Pakistan's decision to maintain the ratio of its rupee was a typical example of her attitude towards her neighbour. Pakistan must not make any decision; whether it relates to her foreign relations or her defence or her economic relations, if it has not the approval of New Delhi. India seems to be unable to reconcile herself to any independent action of Pakistan. India's extraordinary response, in not recognising the Pakistani decision and in effect imposing an economic blockade, says Ian Stephens, was of psychological interest as an early disclosure of the mental attitude that caused the acute controversy of 1954, when Pakistan signed her defence agreement with the United States. He concludes: '[India] could not bring herself to regard her small neighbour as entitled to evolve its own financial or other policies.'[15]

As a result of 'the battle of the rupees', trade between India and Pakistan was drifting towards different channels and the belief that the economies of the two countries were complementary was seriously challenged. The impact of this economic conflict on the trade patterns of both countries was profound and far-reaching. India suffered serious interruption in the normal working of her jute mills, and this reduced the foreign exchange receipts of her biggest dollar-earner; her textile industry's need of raw materials also required the expenditure of valuable foreign exchange on raw cotton. Trends in Pakistan's foreign trade indicated that she was vigorously seeking alternative sources of supply of goods such as coal and cotton piece goods, which caused strains on her foreign exchange also. An important feature of Indo-

Pakistan trade before the deadlock had been that only a few commodities on either side accounted for the bulk of trade. For instance, 75 per cent of Pakistan's exports to India were accounted for by raw jute and raw cotton; India's chief exports to Pakistan were cotton textiles, jute manufactures, coal and mustard oil. The *Karachi Commerce* observed: 'Now that there is "total blockade", Pakistan has an opportunity to find other markets for her jute and other raw materials.'[16] Business circles in Pakistan were of the opinion that, in view of past experiences, they must be prepared to arrange alternative sources of supply and avenues of disposal if the economic stability of the country were not to be subjected to sudden and arbitrary strains. Pakistan took vigorous steps to set up mills to process her own cotton and jute, while India tried hard to become self-sufficient in jute and cotton supplies. Although it was not an easy task for either country to become economically independent of the other in a short period, each made the strongest possible efforts to achieve self-sufficiency. The conflict over the rupees had a permanent effect on the economic relations of the two countries and the old patterns of trade were never resumed.

The chief criterion of the soundness of Pakistan's decision of non-devaluation was whether she could dispose of her export commodities without a serious drop in prices. She did not find much difficulty in disposing of her raw cotton after the loss of the Indian market. There had been an expanding market in many regions of the world for Pakistan's long and staple cotton, and buyers were prepared to pay more for 'non-dollar' cotton. Wool had provided an even more pleasant surprise: there was an unprecedented demand for Pakistani wool, which was mainly used in carpet manufacture. It was in the disposing of jute that Pakistan had worries and problems. On October 22, 1949, the Pakistan government announced new measures to protect the interests of the jute growers in East Pakistan. An ordinance was passed prohibiting the purchase and sale of jute below a minimum price, which was fixed at Rs. 23 per mound (80 lb). The government also arranged to purchase jute through the Jute Board, and the Pakistan National Bank was established to finance the jute purchases. In the field of inter-Dominion trade, it was clear by January 1950 that the loss of the Indian market for Pakistani jute, cotton and other commodities was not serious. India used all sorts of threats and pressure—a protest

F

to the International Monetary Fund against the recognition of the higher value of the Pakistani rupee; suspension of supplies, of coal in particular; threats of more economic sanctions—but the government of Pakistan was determined to maintain the ratio of its rupee. The trends in the world market following the Korean war seemed to favour Pakistan in her resistance against India's economic pressures.

One of the causes of communal upsurge in West Bengal in the early part of 1950, which brought India and Pakistan to the verge of war, was the economic hardship in Hindu business circles in Calcutta. Anti-Pakistan feelings were roused high as a result of the 'trade war' between the two countries. Taking advantage of this explosive situation, the Hindu Mahasabha and other extremist groups fanned the flames of communal hatred. The result was a major catastrophe which will be discussed in the next chapter.

When the Prime Ministers of Pakistan and India met in April 1950 to discuss the threats of war as a result of the Bengal crisis in March 1950, the whole atmosphere was changed for the better. Indo-Pakistan relations entered into a harmonious phase for a short time. Advantage was taken of this 'sweet interval' to solve the trade deadlock, and a truce was effected by a three-months' trade agreement, signed on April 21, 1950. An official statement issued on April 21 said that negotiations had resulted in the reopening of trade 'in a defined sphere as a first step to attainment of the objective of the Indian and Pakistan governments of promoting good will and reviving trade between the two countries'.[17] Under this agreement, Pakistan would supply India with 800,000 bales of raw jute, and India would supply Pakistan with cotton textiles, steel, jute manufactures and mustard oil. The most significant aspect of this agreement was that it did not deal with the dispute over the different exchange rates of the two rupees. Instead, to avoid this difficulty, the two governments agreed as a temporary expedient that transactions would be accounted for in Indian rupees, through a special account to be kept for this purpose. In addition, the governments agreed to permit the movement of certain commodities without any restrictions. The intention was that a balance of trade should be maintained in the transactions covered by the agreement. It was not to be expected that the dismantled machinery of Indo-Pakistan commercial intercourse would be quickly put together again, but the agreement for reopening of trade along a limited sector was welcomed in both countries. But just as the Liaquat-Nehru pact on minorities was not favourably received in West Bengal, so also was this trade agreement 'somewhat critically received there';[18] and there were extremists who urged carrying the 'trade war' with Pakistan to the utmost. The trade agreement was, however, welcomed by many outside observers who were dismayed at the exacerbation of Indo-Pakistan friction by the deadlock over the exchange ratio between the two rupees. An editorial in *The Times*, observed: 'The most significant indication of improvement in relations between India and Pakistan is the recent breaking of the trade deadlock which has caused so much economic loss and political bitterness.'[19]

The dispute over the rate of exchange, however, remained the main obstacle to the full resumption of trade between the two countries. When the temporary trade agreement expired, the Indian government was not inclined to renew or extend the principle of a balanced exchange of commodities. With 'good improvement' in the production of raw jute in India, it was not willing to show any 'weakness' to Pakistan. The dispute over the ratio had already been referred to the International Monetary Fund. Early in July 1950, Pakistan joined the IMF, and this involved declaring to the Fund the par value of the Pakistan rupee. When this was done, the IMF had the right to suggest (though not to enforce) any alteration in the declared exchange rate that might seem appropriate in the light of Pakistan's economic position. India urged the Fund to declare that the exchange rate of Pakistan's rupee was 'artificially' higher. Like other Indo-Pakistan questions, the exchange deadlock was found too complex to be solved without lengthy delay. Pakistan requested India, in the words of its Commerce Minister, to 'fall into line with the rest of the world' and recognise her currency; but India still seemed unable to reconcile herself to any higher value of the Pakistan rupee. Pakistanis maintained that, if India allowed trade to flow freely at the different rates of exchange, Indian prices would prove to be competitive.

The 'battle of rupees' differed from the other Indo-Pakistan disputes because in the end a solution was enforceable by the laws of economics. Both governments appeared to be awaiting the decision of the IMF. The Pakistan Finance Minister claimed that the government of

India had actually agreed to recognise the value of the Pakistani rupee towards the end of September 1949, but that it suddenly went back on this. On September 28, the Pakistan government received a telegram from the Indian government stating that 'with a view to facilitating resumption of business between the two countries, we are prepared to allow transactions to proceed on the basis of the new rate of 100 Pakistani rupees equal to $143\frac{15}{16}$ Indian rupees'.[20] Subsequently, without assigning any reason, the Indian government changed its mind and initiated the 'trade war' between the two countries.

While the decision from the International Monetary Fund was awaited, the compelling economic circumstances made India accept Pakistan's new exchange rate. The incipient famine and threat of mass unemployment in the jute and cotton industries made India give up her attitude with regard to Pakistani currency. The spirit of economic realism seemed ultimately to have triumphed; negotiations were reopened at India's request for a trade agreement, and a new trade agreement ending seventeen months of deadlock was signed on February 25, 1951. The new agreement amounted to India's acceptance of the par value of the Pakistani rupee. The Indian Finance Minister told the Lok Sabha: 'The economic situation in the world has undergone a radical change in favour of primary producing countries like Pakistan. The government of India has, therefore, in the altered circumstances agreed that exchange transactions between India and Pakistan should be permitted on the basis of the par value of the Pakistan rupee as declared by the Pakistan government.'[21] The Pakistan Finance Minister declared: 'While Pakistan can feel justly happy over the acceptance of her rupee ratio by India, India is also to be congratulated over this act of realistic statesmanship shown by her government.'[22] He hoped that the new trade agreement would mark an easing in economic relations between the two countries. Although acceptance of the higher exchange value of the Pakistani rupee was unpopular with doctrinaire opinion in India, the new agreement was a realistic appreciation of the economic situation prevailing in the subcontinent, and it removed a serious embarrassment from the sterling area. It also removed serious threats to the economic development programmes of the two countries under the Colombo Plan. *The Times* spoke favourably of the 1951 trade agreement:

Hard facts have now prevailed over considerations of politics and prestige . . . it would be imprudent to attach too many political hopes to this commercial agreement but at least it removes an irritant from relations between India and Pakistan and, it is possible to hope it, should be reflected in calmer and more co-operative discussion of the grave political issue still between them.[23]

The Reserve Bank of India announced on February 26, 1951, an extension of exchange control to Pakistan; the Pakistani rupee would be treated as 'foreign currency' for all purposes of financial transactions and would be subjected to the restrictions imposed under foreign exchange regulations. Remittances from one country to the other could be made only through authorised dealers in foreign exchange. Similar measures were taken in Pakistan with regard to the Indian currency. In the meantime, the International Monetary Fund endorsed the par value of the Pakistani rupee. It was a vindication of the growing economic strength of Pakistan, whose economic viability had been in great doubt in many quarters at the time of partition in 1947.

Since the 'trade war' of 1949–50, Indo-Pakistan trade has not regained its former dimensions. Though several trade agreements have been signed between the two countries since 1951, the volume of trade between them does not now assume the same importance that it had before the trade deadlock. The two countries, because of mutual distrust and conflicts, have sought to be independent of supplies from each other; this has shattered the complementary character of the economy of the subcontinent. It is hardly possible to evolve any rational or sound economic arrangement without first solving major political grievances and without eliminating mutual distrust, if not hatred. With their armies glowering at each other over the disputed frontier, it is too much to expect India and Pakistan to come together in some sort of a 'common market'.

INDUS WATERS DISPUTE

Distribution of the waters of the Indus river basin, on which tens of millions depend directly for their livelihood, had rankled ever since partition as one of the great issues dividing Pakistan and India. Since 1947, the Indus waters had raised bitter feelings between the two countries. The Indus and its five tributaries (the rivers Jhelum, Chenab, Ravi, Beas and Sutlej) supply the largest irrigation system in the world. This system, built by the British rulers of India, supports about 50 million people. Its annual flow is twice that of the Nile and three times that of the Tigris and Euphrates combined; it amounts to almost 170 million acre-feet—enough water to submerge, to a depth of one foot, the whole area of the state of Texas or the whole area of France.[24] There are 'hundreds of canals criss-crossing an area almost as large as New England'.[25] The Punjab canal irrigation was started by the British engineers in the 1860s, and it proved to be one of the greatest achievements of the *Raj*; yet it received very scant attention at the time of the partition of British India into two independent and separate states.

Elaborate as it is, the system has some shortcomings. The rivers are notoriously temperamental; they spring chiefly from melting snow and their flow varies from torrent in summer to trickle in winter. There are no adequate storage dams on the rivers to hold back the waters in time of flood or augment them in time of drought. Lack of proper drainage is another shortcoming.[26]

It was, however, the partition of 1947 which constituted the most serious threat: the total disruption of the system. The partition line cut across the Indus; the upper waters of the rivers are in India and in the disputed territory of the state of Jammu and Kashmir, but they all flow into Pakistan. Two-thirds of the irrigated areas and 40 million people dependent on them are in Pakistan, but partition left the head works of the major irrigation systems of Pakistan in Indian territory. The rivers Sutlej, Beas and Ravi, whose waters flow into some of the major irrigation projects in Pakistan, originate and run for long distances in Indian territory before they enter Pakistan. The boundary as drawn under the Radcliffe award put India in a position to deprive Pakistan of the waters of the rivers on which depended the economic prosperity, if not the whole existence, of West Pakistan. As Eugene R. Black, president of the World Bank for Reconstruction and Development, has said: 'The relations between India and Pakistan were thus thrown into a crisis which was to continue along the border intermittently throughout the decade that followed. Five long years after partition Indian and Pakistani troops were still facing each other behind sandbags and barbed wire at irrigation headworks along the frontier . . . this was most likely to lead to all-out war.'[27] The Indus waters problem also adds special importance to the dispute over Kashmir, because the Jhelum and Chenab, whose waters flow into Pakistan from Kashmir, can be seriously interfered with by India through her hold in the state.[28]

Sir Cyril Radcliffe, the chairman of the Boundary Commission, was assured by his Indian and Pakistani colleagues that any arrangements existing at the time of partition as to sharing the waters of the canals would be respected by whatever governments acquired jurisdiction over the headworks concerned until new joint arrangements were made. A similar assumption guided the Arbitration Tribunal set up to deal with claims and counter-claims. Sir Patrick Spens, the chairman of the Tribunal, made it clear that, while he was dealing with India's claim to be compensated for what the former government of India and the former Punjab government had spent upon the canal colonies in West Punjab, he was invited by the Attorneys General of both India and Pakistan to make his award on the basis that there would be no interference with the existing flow of water.[29]

But, as in other commitments under the partition agreements, India did not hesitate to go back on this pledge. The Arbitration Tribunal was dissolved on April 1, 1948. The next day, the government of East Punjab (India) suddenly and without prior intimation stopped the supply of water flowing into Pakistan's central Bari Doab and Dipalpur canals. For five weeks $1\frac{1}{2}$ million acres in Pakistan received no water; thousands of cultivators were faced with starvation. No less serious were 'the psychological effects on Indo-Pakistani relations at a time when bitter feeling had sprung from other causes. . . . Pakistan's trust in India's good intentions had been shaken; the vulnerability of her own position had been tragically demonstrated.'[30] Pakistan criticised the Indian action as an attempt to strangle her; it was regarded not only as violation of the commitments made at the time of partition but also as contrary to international law and morality. This move by India also made Pakistan nervous and insecure as to the future of her irrigation works. Her helpless condition was described by David E. Lilienthal, former chairman of the Tennessee Valley Authority, who visited the subcontinent in 1951: 'No army, with bombs and shellfire, could devastate a land so thoroughly as Pakistan could be devastated by the simple expedient of India's permanently shutting off the sources of water that keep the fields and people of Pakistan alive.'[31]

Indians seemed to be aware of this devastating power against Pakistan; under the title "How Strong is Pakistan?", an article was published in *Vigil* (New Delhi) on August 8, 1951, in which it was pointed out:

> . . . though Pakistan has one of the largest irrigation systems in the world, she is entirely dependent for water on the rivers of East Punjab and Kashmir. . . . If India were to cut off the waters, it is bound to impair Pakistan's strength considerably. Even her very existence would be in danger. Whether India would adopt such a *perfectly legitimate* but ruthless attitude without grave provocation is another matter. Pakistan produces plenty of food but that production depends on canal water which, in a sense, is the gift of India and is in her power to stop.[32] (Our italics.)

These were not only threats; India seemed to be moving ahead to exercise what was termed as 'perfectly legitimate powers'. Faced with the grim prospect of the disruption of millions of acres of fertile land, Pakistan was forced to sign a document with India in which she agreed to 'India's progressively diminishing water supplies to these and to West Punjab's government tapping alternative resources'.[33] A specific reservation was made in the document with regard to India's claim to possess full rights over waters flowing within her territory. The basic issue of the Indus waters dispute was not settled by this agreement; the representatives of the two countries met on several occasions in 1948 and 1949 but failed to reach any settlement. The government of India, however, registered with the Secretariat of the United Nations, as Treaty No. 794, the interim agreement of May 4, 1948. The government of Pakistan informed the United Nations that the agreement was made under duress, and declared in its statement: 'The withholding of water essential in an arid region to the survival of the millions of its inhabitants is, in the view of Pakistan, an international wrong and a peculiar use of force contrary to the obligations of membership in the United Nations. Any concession obtained by such means cannot confer upon the offender any enforceable rights.'[34]

The right to divert water from rivers into irrigation canals has been governed by several principles, such as the law of riparian rights, the doctrine of prior appropriation and the principle of equitable distribution.[35] Pakistan sought to base her case upon recognised rules of international law governing riparian rights. Her government claimed that an upper riparian cannot deny water to a lower riparian; it also referred to India's commitments at the time of partition. India argued that the absence of any specific allocation of Indus water resources at the time of partition meant that Pakistan must be taken to have acquiesced in India's control over the waters. The argument continued; the matter figured prominently in the correspondence between the Prime Ministers of Pakistan and India in 1950: Liaquat Ali Khan proposed that the whole matter be referred to the International Court of Justice, as the dispute was obviously justiciable, but Nehru turned down this proposal since he felt that any reference to an outside authority would be unbecoming to 'proud and self-respecting nations'.[36] Instead, he suggested that the dispute might be referred to an *ad hoc* tribunal consisting of an equal number of judges from both countries. The proposal, however, made no headway as there was no agreement about its jurisdiction, rules of procedure or whether its award would be binding. The deadlock over the sharing of Indus waters continued with its attendant ill-effects on the already strained relations between the two countries.

In 1951, Pakistan alleged that India was seeking to gain time to complete dams and irrigation schemes obviously designed to divert supplies of water vital to Pakistan.[37] 'Suspicion and fear have ever since run like a thread of angry crimson.'[38] In the summer of 1951, Pakistan was planning to take the matter to the Security Council. It was at this time that David E. Lilienthal made an extensive study of the dispute. He suggested that a solution might possibly be found if Indian and Pakistani technicians would together work out a comprehensive engineering plan for the joint development of the waters of the system, and if the World Bank would undertake to assist in financing the necessary works.[39] Lilienthal added that Pakistan's fear that India wanted to turn Pakistan's fertile fields into desert should be set at rest. He felt that if the dispute were referred to the International Court of Justice, Pakistan's stand would be sustained but a decision of the court would not be adequate. He therefore recommended an 'engineering solution' so that the greatest amount of water could be used for the benefit of the people living there, irrespective of the political frontiers which might divide them.

Lilienthal's views inspired Eugene R. Black.

The dispute [Black later wrote] was of deep concern to the World Bank. This was natural enough. For one thing, as long as the dispute was unsettled, the Bank would be unable to help with projects sorely needed to develop the use of the Indus water . . . the basic feasibility of the Bank's mission, that of promoting the growth of the less developed countries, would be thrown into question as long as two of the biggest of these countries were in such sharp conflict.[40]

On November 8, 1951, Black wrote to Nehru suggesting that a 'working party' of engineers should tackle the problem as a co-operative operation, 'not in a political climate, without relation to past negotiations and past claims and independently of political issues'.[41] His suggestion was accepted by both governments; there followed two years of study by a technical group consisting of Indian, Pakistani, and World Bank engineers under the direction of General Raymond A. Wheeler. A temporary agreement was signed in 1952, under which each side undertook to take no action which might diminish the existing supplies of water as long as the negotiations under the auspices of the Bank could continue.

While the World Bank's mediatory efforts were going on, however, India reduced the supplies of water to Pakistan in 1952 and 1953, damaging her crops and causing hardship to the people. One of the factors of the food shortage in Pakistan in 1953 was India's interference in the supply of water in that year. In view of India's violation of the agreement that water supplies would be unaffected during the negotiations for settlement of the dispute under the auspices of the World Bank, Pakistan proposed that a commission of the Bank be set up to maintain the existing water supplies. India did not agree to this suggestion but reaffirmed her obligations under the agreement of 1952; a 'special commissioner of canal waters' was appointed to ensure that the local authorities carried out these obligations. In July 1954, India opened her Bhakra canals to store waters from the Sutlej river; its opening served to increase Pakistan's suspicions that India had designs to draw upon the waters of the Indus basin in such a way as to throttle Pakistan's economy. Her Prime Minister termed the diversion of waters from the Sutlej a potential threat to peace.[42]

At first, the World Bank explored the possibilities of working out a plan for the development, on a joint basis, of the water resources of the system. But after exhaustive negotiations with the two parties, it became apparent that no progress could be made towards a settlement until there was agreement on the basic issue: how was the use of the waters to be divided between the two countries? The Bank therefore directed its efforts to finding a solution which would ensure the independence of the two countries in the matter of the operation of supplies of water falling to the share of each. In February 1954, the Bank made the following proposals: (i) the waters of the eastern rivers (Ravi, Beas and Sutlej) should be for the use of India; (ii) the waters of the western rivers (Indus, Jhelum and Chenab) should be for the use of Pakistan; (iii) there should be a transition period during which Pakistan would construct a system of link canals to transfer water from the western rivers to replace the irrigation uses in Pakistan hitherto met from the eastern rivers; and (iv) India should pay the cost of constructing these replacement link canals to the extent of the benefit derived by her therefrom.

India found in the World Bank plan most of what she wanted; Pakistan, however, had grave doubts about the effect on her interests of such an absolute division. 'The doubt that worried Pakistan was whether it was in fact possible to make use of the water the plan assigned to her in the way the World Bank team had assumed.'[43] She wanted to investigate the full implications of the plan before accepting it. Her doubts and fears were confirmed by the findings of independent hydrological experts.[44] The World Bank, therefore, found it necessary to make some important amendments to its original plan. It was clear, the Bank said, that even the proposed transfer of flow supplies from west to east by link canals would leave Pakistan faced with water shortage of a severity and duration which the Bank could not regard as 'tolerable'.[45] The difficulty was that most of the water in the western rivers which were allotted to Pakistan's use under the Bank's plan is discharged during the months of June-August; in the remaining months of the year, the western rivers do not have enough water. Eugene Black himself later pointed out that the World Bank's plan would have left much of Pakistan's irrigation system without water.[46] To solve this, an extensive scheme had to be evolved for canals and works to bring down water from the upper rivers into the canals once fed by the lower.

There followed more than four years of discussion and negotiation in Washington between the delegations of the two countries and a group of technical experts of the World Bank under the guidance of Sir William Iliff, its vice-president. Both parties, while presenting their claims and counter-claims, agreed to continue the negotiations under the auspices of the Bank which hoped that by March 1957 some comprehensive scheme would be formulated on the basis of suggestions received from each side on the modified plan. Provisional allocations of water to keep Pakistan going were agreed with India, but India continued to interfere or reduce the flow of waters to Pakistan. 'Pakistan became more and more restive under the feeling that India, as it were, had her by the throat.'[47] Pakistan complained that, even when water did come, it often came at the wrong time, causing great inconvenience and harm to her peasants.

Then, in August 1957, the India government warned Pakistan that by 1962 India would take all the water she needed from the eastern rivers. Pakistan considered this a threat to her security and indeed to her existence; she pointed out that, even under the original 1954 plan of the World Bank, which India had accepted, water supplies from the eastern rivers to Pakistan were to be continued until proper replacement arrangements had been made at India's expense. Pakistan made a formal protest to the World Bank against India's warning issued in the Indian parliament in August 1957. A bitter controversy arose and negotiations risked a total breakdown. The situation was further complicated by a fresh wave of bitter feelings over the Kashmir dispute, which was brought back to the Security Council in 1957, nine years after its first tabling at the United Nations.

When a resolution was passed almost unanimously (only the Soviet Union abstaining) against India's move to integrate the state, India's reaction was violent and negotiations between the two countries on all other major disputes were affected. Pakistan was the more apprehensive at India's growing designs over Kashmir because, as pointed out earlier, the sharing of the waters of the Indus is interlocked with the Kashmir problem; India's hold in Kashmir enables her to interfere with the flow of the Jhelum and Chenab, whose waters were allotted to Pakistan under the World Bank's plan. 'The successful solution of the problem of finding more water in west Punjab', wrote Dr F. J. Fowler, 'must ultimately depend upon the provision of reservoirs in the upper valleys of the Chenab and the Jhelum. The difficulties of constructing dams in the Himalayas are formidable and few suitable sites are located in Indian-held Kashmir. It is to safeguard her right to carry out such projects that Pakistan is vitally concerned with the outcome of the Kashmir dispute.'[48]

The good offices of the World Bank, however, survived the strains and stresses of Indo-Pakistan relations during the decade of complicated negotiations over the water dispute. By May 1959, the main issues standing in the way of a settlement had crystallised, although numerous controversies over the financial and technical issues had to be overcome. Eugene Black has recorded: 'Element by element the plan was contested through every stage of its development.'[49] Black and Iliff visited the subcontinent in 1959 to hold discussions with President Ayub and Prime Minister Nehru, when agreement was reached on the general principles of the proposed water treaty. A system of works was to be constructed as part of the settlement arrangements, and the financial contributions were to be made by India.

Even at the drafting stage of the treaty, which began in August 1959 under the auspices of the World Bank, there were many hurdles to overcome. The good offices of the Bank were required at every stage in securing agreement on many complicated technical and financial details which had to be incorporated in the treaty. Meanwhile it had become apparent that the cost of financing the system of works in India and Pakistan, which was part of the proposed agreement, was far beyond the capacity of the two countries. The Bank, therefore, undertook to formulate a plan envisaging financial participation by a number of friendly governments; the basis of this participation entailed an independent series of negotiations and preparation of the Indus Basin Development Fund Agreement.[50]

At last the patient, impartial and imaginative mediation of the World Bank proved successful in the decade-old dispute over the

Indus Valley waters. It seemed to be a major triumph of reason over mutual suspicion. Douglas Dillon, Under Secretary of State, said that the United States government believed the solution of the dispute ranked in importance with Berlin. His government promised generous aid, so did those of Britain, Canada, Germany, Australia and New Zealand. Thus ended nearly 'ten years of on-again, off-again negotiation that had taxed the patience and statesmanship of diplomats, economists and engineers of the World Bank and the countries involved'.[51]

The preamble to the Indus Waters Treaty of 1960 recognises the need for 'fixing and delimitating in the spirit of good will and friendship the rights and obligations' of the government of India and the government of Pakistan concerning the use of the waters of the Indus river system. The treaty allocates the water of the three eastern rivers —Ravi, Beas and Sutlej—to India, with certain specified exceptions. The main exception is the ten-year transition period while the works are being constructed in Pakistan for the replacement of eastern river water; during this period, India will continue to deliver water to Pakistan from the eastern rivers in accordance with a schedule set out in an annexe of the treaty. The waters of the western rivers—Indus, Jhelum and Chenab—are for the use of Pakistan, and India undertakes to let flow for unrestricted use by her neighbour all the waters of these three rivers, subject to the provision that some of these waters may be used by India in areas upstream of the Pakistan border for the development of irrigation, electric power and certain other uses spelled out in detail in annexes to the treaty. During the transition period, Pakistan undertakes to construct a system of works, part of which will replace from the western rivers those irrigation uses in Pakistan which have hitherto been met from the eastern rivers. India is to contribute to the Indus Basin Development Fund about $174 million.

In the treaty, both countries recognise their common interest in the optimum development of the rivers, and declare their intention to co-operate by mutual agreement to the fullest possible extent. Meteorological and hydrological observation stations are to be established, and the treaty provides for a complete exchange of information from these stations. It also provides for an exchange of information about proposed river works to enable each party to estimate the effects these works may have on its situation. The treaty sets up a permanent Indus Commission composed of two persons, one appointed by each government. The Commission will have general responsibility for implementing the provisions and will seek to reconcile any points of disagreement that may arise. Once every five years, its members will make a general tour of inspection of all the works on the rivers and they may, on the request of either commissioner, at any time visit any particular work in either country. The Commission will report at least once a year to each of the governments. Where differences or disputes cannot be resolved by agreement between the commissioners, the treaty establishes machinery for resort to a 'neutral expert', who is to be a highly qualified engineer, for a final decision on technical questions, and for resort, in certain circumstances, to a court of arbitration.

The Indus Waters Treaty has nine annexes. The principal matters covered in these are: agricultural use by Pakistan of water from the tributaries of the Ravi river, and agricultural use by India of water from the western rivers; generation of hydroelectric power by India on the western rivers; storage of water by India on the western rivers; questions that may be referred to a 'neutral expert'; appointment and procedure of a court of arbitration; and transitional arrangements relating to the delivery of waters to Pakistan from the eastern rivers during the transition period.

The division of waters provided for in the treaty necessitates the construction of works to transfer waters from the three western rivers to meet the irrigation uses in Pakistan hitherto met by water from the three eastern rivers. The effect of the transfer will eventually be to release the whole flow of the three eastern rivers for irrigation development in India. The following works are to be built in West Pakistan: (i) a system of eight link canals nearly 400 miles in total length, transferring water from the western rivers to areas formerly irrigated by the eastern rivers; (ii) two earth-fill storage dams to provide the water-storage potential to meet the irrigation supplies of the Pakistan canals; (iii) power stations at the Jhelum Dam with a capacity of more than 300,000 kilowatts; (iv) works to integrate the present canal and river system into the new inter-river link canals; (v) some 2,500 tubewells and drainage to overcome waterlogging and salinity in irrigated areas. The area affected totals 2·5 million acres, and the cost of the works in

Pakistan will be financed out of the Indus Basin Development Fund.

A large earth-fill dam is to be built in India on the Beas river with a reservoir capacity of 5 million acre-feet and a hydroelectric potential for generating 200,000 kilowatts of power. Together with the Bhakra Reservoir (which was nearly completed by the time the treaty was concluded) and with the newly constructed Rajasthan canal system, the Beas Dam will serve to irrigate large areas in the East Punjab and in the Rajasthan desert. The Beas project will not be financed from the Indus Basin Development Fund but by loans from the World Bank and the United States. The Indus Basin Development Fund, administered by the World Bank, has resources of foreign exchange and Pakistani rupees in the order of $894 million. Its foreign exchange resources come from the grants of six friendly countries—Australia, Britain, Canada, Germany, New Zealand and the United States—and from loans by the United States and the World Bank. India's contribution is a little over £62 million, Pakistan's £440,000.

The Indus Waters Treaty was called a 'billion-dollar investment in peace' by Eugene Black, who was the moving spirit in its formulation. It is the greatest irrigation and water-power project in the world. The storage dam on the Jhelum river will be one of the largest earth-fill dams ever made, containing as much earth as has been excavated from the whole Suez canal, and it will create a lake more than 4 million acre-feet in extent.[52] It is expected to enrich the lives of some 50 million people.

In a broadcast to his people on the treaty, President Ayub said: 'The solution that we have now got is not the ideal one—the ideal solution when negotiated can seldom be obtained—but this is the best that we could get under the circumstances, many of which, irrespective of merits and legality of the case, are against us.'[53] Ayub added that the basis of the agreement was realism and pragmatism; though there was no cause for rejoicing, there was certainly a cause for satisfaction and thanksgiving that the crisis which might have arisen in the absence of such an agreement had been averted. The treaty was described by a Pakistani spokesman as essentially a compromise. The only guarantee that India would fulfil it, he said, was goodwill between the two countries. Explaining the advantages of the treaty to Pakistan, the spokesman said that the interlinking of the western rivers would ensure better and more rational use of water supplies. The disadvantages to Pakistan from the treaty included the loss of the Sailab cultivated area, a matter of some 400,000 acres. Feeding the areas now dependent on the eastern rivers with water brought over long distances from the western rivers would involve transit losses; moreover, by carrying large supplies of water over long distances (in some cases more than 200 miles), West Pakistan would be exposed to further waterlogging. The link canals would also be subject to flood hazards. [54] But the most important point is that division of rivers has changed the character of the Kashmir dispute. 'Since rivers exclusive to Pakistan have sources in Kashmir, it has become all the more necessary for Pakistan to control them.' [55]

Pandit Nehru said that the agreement was memorable, not only for the material benefits which it would bring to the cultivators in India and Pakistan, but also for its psychological and even emotional effect. He praised the spirit of co-operative endeavour which had shown the way for further collaboration between the two countries. [56]

Pakistan gave Nehru the warmest welcome when he went there in September 1960 to sign the treaty. President Ayub was urging that the agreement on the division of the Indus waters and the general improvement in the climate of relations between the two countries made it imperative to take up again the problem of Kashmir. Similar views and hopes were expressed in many quarters which were encouraged to see the end of the one major irritant of Indo-Pakistan relations. There had been some preliminary and long-distance sparring about this between Ayub and Nehru. On the eve of the latter's visit to Pakistan, Ayub said: 'The very fact that we will have to be content with the waters of three western rivers will underline the importance for us of having physical control on the upper reaches of these rivers to secure their maximum utilisation for the ever-growing needs of West Pakistan. The solution of Kashmir, therefore, acquires a new sense of urgency.' [57] He expressed the hope that the settlement of the canal waters question would lead to a 'realistic appreciation' of Pakistan's stand on Kashmir. Nehru, before coming to Pakistan, said in the Indian parliament that he was 'prepared to discuss any subject, including Kashmir'. [58] Hopes were roused by these utterances that the friendly atmosphere following the agreement on the Indus waters might lead to a solution of the most serious dispute that had poisoned the relations between the two countries since their inception.

When Nehru came to Pakistan on September 19, 1960, there appeared to be an atmosphere of genuine good will and mutual understanding, and in the seclusion of the president's summer bungalow at Muree, the two leaders discussed the Kashmir issue. But the joint communiqué issued after their meeting, on September 23, was a great disappointment to Pakistanis for it did not disclose any new approach to the problem of Kashmir. The communiqué did not go further in the matter than to record that 'this is a difficult question which requires careful consideration', and that the two leaders 'agreed to give further thought to this question with a view to finding a solution'. The communiqué made it quite clear that Nehru's mind was to all intents and purposes a closed book on Kashmir. Ayub expressed his sense of disappointment when, after bidding farewell to Nehru, he said: 'Kashmir is keeping the two countries apart, and unless this is settled we would remain apart. So long as we remain apart, the solution of other problems stands in danger of being nullified.'[59]

Pakistan's anxiety to remove the threat of a possible diversion of her waters from the western rivers is to be understood in the light of her unhappy experiences in the past over water supplies. The fact that India's hold in Kashmir enables her to interfere with the flow of the Jhelum and Chenab rivers bulks large in Pakistan's estimation of the agreement on sharing the waters of the Indus basin. The 1960 treaty cannot give full satisfaction and security to Pakistan as long as India is in possession of Kashmir.

The country's attitude and fears were expressed by the Pakistan delegation to the direct negotiations on Kashmir which were initiated by the Western powers after the Sino-Indian border conflicts in 1962. When proposals were made during these talks for partitioning the state of Jammu and Kashmir, Pakistan urged that territorial division of the state should take account, among other factors, of 'control of rivers'. The Indian delegation, however, held the view that the Indus Water Treaty had precluded Pakistan from putting forward such a claim. But the treaty expressly provides that its conclusion is to be without prejudice to the rights, interests and claims of either party in other disputes. Pakistan, therefore, considered it *ultra vires* for India to invoke the treaty and to claim that the economic interests of Pakistan had been protected under the Indus Water Treaty.

It may be added that, during the presidential election in Pakistan in 1964, the Combined Opposition Party attacked President Ayub for what it termed as 'selling' the historical rights of Pakistan over the common rivers. This was not a fair criticism. Ayub and Nehru showed statesmanship by removing one major cause for the unhappy relations between the two countries, and they should be congratulated on this constructive move towards peace in the subcontinent. It is no small cause for satisfaction that the Indus Water Treaty has considerably removed the constant threat of economic ruin of the two countries. Pakistan has been assured of a supply of 110 million acre-feet of water from the western rivers as against the 74.5 million she used to receive from her irrigation works. For India also the treaty provides immense opportunities for expansion of her irrigation facilities, and thus helps to solve her chronic deficiency of food.

5

RELIGIOUS MINORITIES

WHEN the subcontinent was split into two separate states on the basis of religion in 1947, it was not possible to make the division so as to create two homogeneous and compact national states. As has been noted in chapter 2, the two communities, Muslim and Hindu, were so intermingled in many parts of the subcontinent that any frontier line was bound to leave millions of Muslims in India and millions of Hindus in Pakistan.

Even with the migrations of 1947, there are still about 47 million Muslims in India and about 12 million Hindus in Pakistan. These religious minority groups are the worst sufferers of the partition of the subcontinent. Their loyalty to their new polity is often questioned; their status as citizens of the two new countries—whatever the legal and constitutional framework might be or whatever might be the professions of the two governments—is never free from strain and stresses. Their economic conditions have gone down in both the countries, while their cherished culture and way of life often seems to be in danger. Worst of all, they live in perpetual fear and anxiety. It should be noted, however, that, while in 'secular' India there has hardly been a single year when Muslim minorities have not been the victim of large-scale and often organised riots, in so-called 'theocratic' Pakistan there have been major riots in only two years: 1950 and 1964.

The existence of religious minority groups in the two countries has added further complexity to Indo-Pakistan relations. The mental image that each has formed of the other has greatly been influenced by the attitude that each country is alleged to have taken towards the religious minority. For instance, it is widely believed in India that

Pakistan is an intolerant, theocratic state, where the Hindu minorities 'may at best live on sufferance as helots or, worse, face genocide'. Similarly, it is widely held in Pakistan that Muslim minorities are systematically and continuously suppressed and oppressed in India; that they are in perpetual fear of being butchered by the Hindu extremist groups; and that they have lost all possibility of security and dignity. These notions create a highly emotional factor in Indo-Pakistan relations. The Muslims in Pakistan feel a strong sense of kinship for their co-religionists in India, with many of whom they have close blood relations. The Hindus in India likewise have strong attachment and sentimental affinities for the Hindus in Pakistan. The news of maltreatment of Muslims in India causes deep resentment in Pakistan, and the same is the case with regard to any news about Hindus in Pakistan. The two countries were on the verge of war—'on the edge of a precipice'—over this issue of religious minorities in 1950, as will be described in the next chapter.

India's latest argument for her continued refusal to hold an internationally organised plebiscite in Kashmir is (as noted in chapter 3) that, if the vote goes in favour of Pakistan, the lives of nearly 50 million Indian Muslims would be in jeopardy. This argument, based on political blackmail, means that the people of Kashmir must be hostages for the Indian Muslims. It also reveals the constant insecurity of the Indian Muslims and proves the hollowness of India's claim of secularism.

The religious minorities are often exposed to dangers and threats whenever there is any worsening of Indo-Pakistan relations. It is a vicious circle: the effect of the hold which memories of an unhappy past still have over people's minds. Nationalism is entangled with religious conceptions. Majorities and minorities do not fully form a community with one another in either country. The present phase of the problem arises from the persistence of traditional suspicions and resentment.

SECULAR INDIA?

India claims to have built a secular state, and the Indian constitution seeks to erect the structure of such a state. The chief architect of the constitution, Pandit Nehru, perhaps believed in secularism, but India does not consist of Nehru only and a few liberals who may have faith in the Western concept of secularism. In an Asian country like India or Pakistan, secularism cannot be established by mere legal declaration; the communal outlook in the Indo-Pakistan subcontinent has very deep roots in behaviour patterns and mental attitudes; it has also a history of 600 years behind it. Any promulgated declaration of secularism cannot change the situation overnight; habits and patterns of behaviour would have to be changed, and such a change cannot occur in the prevailing atmosphere of communal tensions and bitterness. In a country where age-old customs and prejudices still play a dominant role, where religious feelings are, by far, more important than the proclaimed policy of the government, secularism has no secure foundation.

India's secularism can be judged best by an analysis of the fate of its largest religious minority group: the Indian Muslims. Their position has pitiably deteriorated since 1947. Though the Indian constitution, in theory, guarantees the right of equality to all citizens, the Indian Muslims have, in reality, gradually been relegated to the status of second-class citizens. Speaking in the Indian parliament on June 6, 1962, an independent Muslim, Syed Badruddoza, described the plight of his community:

> Minorities can get no quarter, no shelter, no facilities, no opportunities for self-expression, politically, socially, culturally, economically, and even physically; in the executive, in the police, the judiciary, in the Army, the Navy and Airforce, in every department and domain of administrative activity, Muslims present a pathetic commentary on the glorious past and an eloquent testimony of the ravages of all . . . in the service we are nowhere; we have no appointments but disappointment only.[1]

A convention of the Indian Muslims was held in June 1961 to discuss their condition. Dr Syed Mahmud, a well-known Congress leader who held a ministerial post in Nehru's government, told the convention that, despite constitutional guarantees, the Muslims did not find their lives, honour and property safe. Dr Mahmud added that, in the recruitment of services, the Muslims were discriminated against and the doors of entry into the police and army were practically closed to them. The same was happening in commerce. He regretfully concluded that Muslims were treated as 'suspects, criminals, traitors'.[2]

The Indian Muslims have made sincere attempts to identify themselves with the hopes and aspirations of the new India. They have nothing to gain by adopting a communal attitude; they are sincerely trying to think in terms of national integration; they fully realise that Pakistan cannot accommodate nearly 50 million Muslims even if she wanted to. Their loyalty and change of attitude, however, have never been appreciated. They are being discriminated against in all spheres of life for no other reason than that they are followers of Islam; in social life they are segregated; in the economic sphere they are greatly losing place. There are no new large-scale business or industrial establishments started by them anywhere in India; old ones are struggling for survival and facing handicaps at every level. Many Indian Muslim graduates seek employment in Pakistan because they have no avenues in their own country.

In the cultural sphere, there have been attempts at changing the cultural and historical heritage of the Muslims in the form of rewriting Indian history. School textbooks are increasingly projecting the scope of Hindu culture as the mainstream of Indianism; Islamic faith and culture is represented as alien and odd. Such books are replete with highly exaggerated stories of tyranny, torture and vandalism alleged to have been done by the Muslim rulers of India. The Muslims of India are portrayed as descendants of an intruding, alien people and of those of the lower castes in Indian society who were forcibly converted to Islam. Muslim rule in India is depicted as a dark period of oppression and persecution.

In the political sphere, the Indian Muslims have lost completely and they find themselves utterly frustrated and helpless. The Muslim population in new India is so scattered that they cannot, on the basis of numerical strength, play any significant role in the politics of the country either on a national or state level. After partition, the majority of them supported the Congress party, though a few sided with the communists and one or two other parties. The preaching of secularism by the Congress attracted the Muslims, yet the deep-rooted and long-standing Hindu prejudice and suspicions against Islam and its adherents has proved too strong to allow them any significant participation in the political life of the country. But 'Indian Muslims, like American

Negroes, have their uncle Toms'.[3] Thus the world hears of Muslim representatives of India vituperatively attacking Pakistan at the United Nations. Then, there are Muslims occupying high positions, like cabinet ministers and vice-president. But these few Muslims who occupy prominent positions in India have too often stood apart from their community, denying the injustice and discrimination which is being suffered by the community as a whole. On the grounds of the secular constitution, the Indian Muslims lost all the political safeguards and special protection which were given to the minorities in India during British rule. The most important of these safeguards was the provision for a separate electorate under which the Muslim voters could choose their own representatives to central and provincial legislatures. The Indian constitution abolished it in the name of secularism. What has been the result? The Muslims constitute 11 per cent of the population in India; in the 1951–52 election, only 4 per cent of the seats in the Lok Sabha were held by Muslims; in the 1962 election, this percentage fell. The numerical representation of the Muslims has been even poorer in the state legislatures.

It is, however, the communal violence in India which constitutes the most serious threat to the existence of the Muslims there, and it is the recurrent upsurge of communal violence which is embittering Indo-Pakistan relations. In 1947, influential groups in India were not reconciled to partition. Their anti-Muslim activities resulted in communal murders and mass migration on a scale unprecedented in modern history. The continued and persistent anti-Muslim policies of the militant Hindu organisations in India, such as the Hindu Mahasabha, the Jan Sangh and the RSSS, have resulted in hundreds of riots. The government of Pakistan in a report in 1964 catalogued the communal riots in India since 1947; this report was based on findings drawn from the Indian press, which reported as many as 105 riots during the period January 1948 to March 1950. Then the Liaquat-Nehru pact was signed in New Delhi, providing a 'bill of rights' for minorities in both countries. Between the signing of the pact in April 1950 and January 1964, there were 550 communal riots. Notable examples were the serious outbreaks in Madhya Pradesh in February 1961, in Uttar Pradesh later in the same year, in West Bengal and Assam in 1962, and over vast tracts of eastern India early in 1964. The riots in West Bengal in 1964 caused a havoc much greater than that of the riots of 1961 at Jabalpur city which, according to the Madhya Pradesh Chief Minister, looked like a 'cremating ground'. The renewed communal upsurge in various parts of India in the 1960s, after a decade of Nehru's seeming experiment in secularism, was the result of organised activities by militant communal groups. Frank Anthony, an Anglo-Indian member of the Indian parliament, stated on April 14, 1964:

> These revivalist bodies are not only well-organised but they have their own press; it is a gutter press. It is a press which drips poison . . . the cult of violence is openly inculcated. . . . Each general election intensifies not democracy but each general election has intensified theocracy; it has intensified castocracy. . . . The vote in every state is cast along religious and caste lines. . . . With this spread of the virus of revivalism and religious and caste-communalism, the Congress party has been increasingly infected. . . . When the great Calcutta killings were on [in 1964], the police were afraid to intervene to stop the Goonda elements because it was said that most of the MLAs [members of the state legislature] had their respective retinues of Goondas to whom they gave political protection. This is the truth. It has been published in many papers.[4]

This is the true picture of 'secular' India. The constitution may be secular in inspiration, but Indian society, government and state cannot be described as 'secular'. India may be lay but is surely not secular. Gandhi himself had declared:

> I can say without the slightest hesitation and yet in all humility that those who say that religion has nothing to do with politics do not know what religion means. . . . Thus it will be seen that for me there are no politics devoid of religion. They subserve religion. Politics bereft of religion are a death-adder because they kill the soul.[5]

Pandit Nehru, no doubt, believed in secularism, but he also had to admit:

> Ever since the partition, the spirit of communalism and a certain revivalism have been encouraged in India. Organisations which

dared not preach them in earlier years now flaunt them in public and even challenge the very basis of our constitution. What is more distressing is the fact that the spirit of communalism and revivalism has gradually invaded the Congress and sometimes even affects government policy.[6]

The All-India Muslim Convention held a two-day session in Lucknow after the widespread communal riots in India in 1964; it passed a resolution saying that the government of India had failed to discharge its duties of protecting the life and property of the Muslims in West Bengal, Orissa, Bihar and Madhya Pradesh. In urging action against the State government and the district officials concerned, the resolution affirmed that, behind the communal disturbances, there was the hand of some political organisations and even of some government officials.[7] Similar allegations were made by the Muslim members of the State legislature in West Bengal. The president of the Convention, Dr Mahmud complained: 'On the one hand, the Muslims are made the victims of aggression on all sides, it is also a reality on the other that such barriers of estrangement and hostility have stood between the Muslims and the people of this country as do not allow the majority community even to sense the gravity of these aggressive activities.'[8]

The New Delhi correspondent of *The Times*, in reporting the Convention, analysed in depth the problems of India's Muslims and pinpointed the political blackmail which makes them hostages for the Hindu minorities of East Pakistan. His report described 'the plight of Muslims, their manifold injustices and prejudices'. 'The situation of Muslims in India has sensibly worsened in the past three years. . . . The chief cause of this deteriorating position of Muslims is no doubt the strong swell of nationalism in India in recent years which in north India has had its undercurrents of Hindu nationalism.' A speaker at the Lucknow Convention said that Indian Muslims had been repeatedly reminded that 'their fate in India was dependent not on their behaviour but on that of people of a foreign country, in other words that they would be made to pay in like coin for the sufferings of Hindus in East Pakistan'.[9]

One of the most disquieting features of communal disturbances in India is that, whenever a riot takes place in India, the blame is automatically put on Pakistan even if there is perfect communal peace in that country. The Indian press, political groups and even the highest officials have sought not only to minimise, if not hide, unfortunate atrocities in their country, but also sought to find excuses or justification for these riots by manufacturing stories about the ill-treatment of the Hindu minority in East Pakistan. It is neither claimed nor pretended that everything has been satisfactory for the Hindus of East Pakistan; they also have reasons for feeling frustrated and insecure; but it is conceded by impartial observers that there have been very few major communal riots in Pakistan since 1947. As mentioned earlier, on two occasions—in 1950 and 1964—communal riots in Pakistan took place on a large scale. 'It may be remarked', says Ian Stephens, 'that except during the spring of 1950 and 1964 when grave anti-Hindu disorders in East Pakistan synchronised with equally grave anti-Muslim disorders in India, the Hindu minority in Pakistan has not been the victim of any serious major attack, whereas in India rioting against the Muslim minority has been frequent.'[10]

This tendency to put all blame at the doors of Pakistan not only aggravates the insecurity of the Muslim minority in India; it also produces unfortunate tensions and bitterness in the relations between the two countries. When communal hatred, murder and arson were rife on a vast scale in various parts of India in 1964, President Ayub made an urgent appeal to the Indian head of state, Dr Radhakrishnan, to take effective steps to restore order and peace in Calcutta and other areas of West Bengal, so as to create a sense of security in the minds of the Muslim minority and enable the Muslim refugees to return to their houses. Ayub emphasised that this was in the interest of both India and Pakistan.[11] The Indian President's reply was distressing and disappointing. He put the entire blame for the killing and destruction in Calcutta and West Bengal on 'incidents' in East Pakistan, and accused the Pakistani leaders and press of doing 'everything to rouse communal passions to an uncontrollable pitch'.[12]

To prevent the issue's becoming a verbal war of charge and counter-charge, Ayub told the Indian President:

It would, I think, be most unfortunate if you and I should get involved in an exchange of recriminations. This would deflect attention from our real purpose. This purpose is that lives and property of the minority community must be fully protected; that communal peace must be maintained and that the minority community must not be looked upon as a hostage. By blaming and thus impliedly condoning communal killings and destruction in one or similar instances in the other, we might unwittingly lend encouragement precisely to the evil forces which it is the government's duty to curb. . . . We are faced with a grave human problem. It will not be solved by shutting our eyes to it, nor can we solve this problem by blaming others for creating it. Let leaders in each country look into their own hearts and resolve to put their own homes in order.[13]

The Indian leaders, however, continued to shift on to Pakistan all blame for the failure to protect the lives and properties of their Muslim minorities. One Indian central minister said that 'Pakistan is India's enemy number one and its challenge has to be met';[14] the Indian Defence Minister declared: 'We shall see that India becomes a graveyard of Pakistan';[15] and Pandit Nehru blamed Pakistan for the existence of all evils in India.[16] During the debates in the Indian parliament and in the State legislatures on communal riots in India, the main theme of various speakers was to find excuses for the communal frenzy in India by accusing Pakistan of maltreatment of the Hindu minority and thereby lending further encouragement to those who had been responsible for atrocities and crimes against the Indian Muslims. While the blood bath was going on in India, there were demonstrations to 'save the minority community in East Pakistan', and a "Save Pakistan Minority Committee" was fanning further disorders and bloodshed. The government of Pakistan watched these developments with great distress and concern.

EVICTION OF INDIAN MUSLIMS

The Indian government's policy of evicting thousands of Muslims from Assam and Tripura, driving them to East Pakistan, is yet another factor in the tense and explosive relations between Pakistan and India. The systematic campaign for the eviction of Indian Muslims inhabiting the border states of Assam and Tripura started in 1960, but the tempo was accelerated in the middle of 1962 when, on the plea of strategic border security measures necessitated by developments along the Sino-Indian border, India stepped up the evictions. Up to the end of May 1964, the figure rose to 164,746.[17] The government of India seemed to have adopted this policy for the following reasons: (i) to clear the border areas of Muslims for strategic purposes; (ii) to create administrative and economic problems for Pakistan; and (iii) to distract Pakistan's attention from the Kashmir problem.

Muslims had settled in Assam and Tripura some fifty to sixty years ago, the administration in these areas encouraging their immigration as helpful in agricultural and economic development. After decades of hard work, the migrants succeeded in reclaiming several hundred thousand acres of jungle and marshy land. These settlers are Indian nationals in terms of Articles 5 and 6 of the Indian constitution and of the relevant provisions of the Indian Citizenship Act, 1955. Justification for the expulsion is sought on the pretext that the evicted are residents of East Pakistan who infiltrated into the Indian border districts surreptitiously. The government of East Pakistan appointed a commission headed by a retired judge of the High Court to ascertain the nationality of the evicted. In its report the commission stated: 'We have very carefully examined the case of each of the heads of the deportee family whose statements on oath have been recorded by the commission and we have found that 95·8 per cent of them are Indian nationals, within the meaning of Articles 5 and 6 of the Indian constitution read with provisions of Indian Citizenship Act of 1955.'[18] It is not only the report of a Pakistani commission that finds that the evicted are Indian nationals; the Indian Muslim leaders have also challenged the validity of their government's contention. The All-India Jamiat-e-Ulema-e-Hind sent a delegation to Assam in October 1962 to probe into the mass eviction of Muslims from these areas to East Pakistan; the delegation urged the government of India to stop the expulsion of what they called *bona fide* Indian Muslims. Similar views were expressed by other Indian Muslim leaders.

Foreign observers also were not convinced by India's case for expulsion of so many Muslims from Assam and Tripura. In a despatch from Comilla, East Pakistan in December 1963, *The Times* special correspondent there reported:

In camps and compounds in the Comilla district there are thousands of Muslims who have been forcibly evicted from their homes in India and driven to East Pakistan. The pretext for the evictions is that these people had illegally entered the Indian territory of Tripura within the past ten years and they have now simply been sent back, but the evidence available from them shows that most were long settled in Tripura, even for generations. . . . Putting it at its best, the established residents of Tripura, Indian citizens by right, who have been uprooted and dumped over the borders with no formalities or only the sketchiest, are the victims of local authorities in that territory whose excesses are not fully appreciated in New Delhi. They may be acting in response to local forces of communal enmity and greed for land but they are acting with injustice and inhumanity. . . . some [Muslims] received 'show cause' notices warning them that they would be expelled unless they could prove that they had been in India before 1952. They say that they went to court with their papers and were told that the magistrate would make further investigations, but that a day or two later the police and lorries came to their villages and they were forced in and driven to the border. Others received no notices or warning before the police vehicle arrived. Some of their papers were kept by the court or destroyed by the police who expelled them. . . . It is undeniable that a great wrong is being done to the Indian Muslims in Tripura.[19]

The *New York Times* wrote on March 20, 1964: 'The critics of Indian policy have charged that India is abandoning the principles of secularism written into her constitution by expelling Muslims from Assam on the ground that they are illegal immigrants from Pakistan, while welcoming Hindu refugees who have the same national legal status as the persons being evicted.'

The Foreign Minister of Pakistan, Z. A. Bhutto, raised the issue in his speech in the General Assembly of the United Nations on September 30, 1963. His reference to the evicted Muslims was challenged by Mrs Pandit, the leader of the Indian delegation, who contended that the evicted were 'Pakistani infiltrators'. This led to a heated and unhappy debate between the delegations of the two countries—a phenomenon not uncommon in the United Nations. In order to resolve the conflict over the issue of eviction, the Pakistan Foreign Minister said that Pakistan was willing to accept the adjudication of the United Nations, or of an international commission, or of a commission composed of Commonwealth countries or of any other third party acceptable to both India and Pakistan. This offer of settlement was, however, turned down by India. When, in the early part of 1964, communal riots broke out on a large scale in various parts of India, Ayub Khan had to tell the Indian President: 'I cannot help feeling that, in thus taking the law into their own hands with a view to drive the Muslims out of West Bengal into East Pakistan, certain elements in the majority community in West Bengal have drawn encouragement from the policy that the government of India has been following over the past two years, despite our protest and appeals, to drive out Indian Muslims living in districts bordering East Pakistan.'[20]

Pakistan had been trying to get down to the root cause of the fresh wave of communal violence in both countries. After much hesitation and persuasion, India eventually agreed in March 1964 to Pakistan's suggestion for holding ministerial talks on the eviction of Muslims from Assam and Tripura. The Home Ministers of Pakistan and India met in New Delhi from April 7 to 11, 1964, to discuss the issue. The Pakistan delegation stated that the basic factor in the recent communal upsurge was the eviction of the Muslims from Assam and Tripura; and as such the eviction should be stopped forthwith. The Indian delegation maintained that since 'legal remedies' were available to the evicted, no injustice was being done. But, as *The Times* special correspondent pointed out, these 'legal remedies' were hardly of any help to the evicted, and the local authorities in Assam and Tripura had shown very little, if any, regard to the process of law. Since the views of the two delegations were widely divergent, Pakistan's representative proposed that the issue should be investigated by a joint tribunal consisting of one Pakistani judge, one Indian judge and a mutually agreed impartial judge from another country. The tribunal should decide if the evicted were really infiltrators from Pakistan; if not, steps should be taken to restore them to their homes in India. India was not agreeable to the proposal for a joint tribunal, arguing that it would infringe her sovereignty. There are many precedents for the settlement of questions of disputed nationality by impartial joint commission, and this procedure is not regarded by fair-dealing governments as infringement of national sovereignty. But to the Indian government, all these arguments were meaningless; it seemed to be determined to clear the border areas of Indian Muslim citizens. Its attitude also betrayed India's lack of confidence in her own religious minority groups, and revealed the shaky and insincere character of secularism. India's secularism is mainly for outside consumption; in dealings with religious minorities like her Muslim citizens, she is no better than any narrow nationalist state—nationalism being entangled with religion.

THEOCRATIC PAKISTAN?

Pakistan has never claimed to be secular. The framers of the Pakistani constitution designated the country as 'the Islamic Republic of Pakistan', and its leaders take delight and pride in calling it the largest Muslim state in the world. The *raison d'être* of the emergence of Pakistan as an entity independent of the rest of India had been the distinction in the rights, interests and cultures of Hindus and Muslims considered as different nations.

When, however, Pakistan emerged as a nation on August 14, 1947, its population was not exclusively Muslim but contained several millions of non-Muslim citizens. What would be the status of non-Muslims in a state that had come into being pre-eminently because the Muslims had sought a homeland wherein they could lead a life of their own based on the religion and culture of Islam? The Constituent Assembly of Pakistan came into existence on August 10, 1947, and, within two days of its establishment, it set up a committee to advise on the fundamental rights of Pakistan and on matters relating to the minorities. In his inaugural speech at the first session of the Constituent Assembly, Jinnah laid down the policy of the new state towards its minorities:

> You may belong to any religion or caste or creed—that has nothing to do with business of the state . . . we are starting in the days when there is no discrimination between one community and another, no discrimination between one caste or creed and another. We are starting with this fundamental principle that we are all citizens and equal citizens of one state . . . you will find that in due course of time

Hindus would cease to be Hindus and Muslims cease to be Muslim, not in the religious sense, because that is the personal faith of each individual, but in the political sense as citizens of the state.[21]

It was a very good beginning and an excellent ideal. The minority leaders, in defending their claim, have referred to this memorable speech on many occasions. It has been regarded as the 'Magna Carta' of minority safeguards in Pakistan.

But a single declaration or a speech cannot solve the minority problem in a state made up of various religious groups; in the hard workaday world of stern realities there occurs a falling-off from the ideal. The problem of religious or racial minorities is one of the most perplexing and intriguing problems of a modern national state.

In Pakistan, the problem of non-Muslim religious minorities was further complicated when the framers of the constitution decided to establish a state on Islamic principles. This decision made, the position of non-Muslim citizens in Pakistan presented itself as a complex and difficult problem. What should be the rights and status of a non-Muslim in an Islamic state? The supporters of the Islamic state point out the broad principles of Islam towards the minorities. There is in Islam an equality of all races and colours; all are alike in the spirit of God, all can aspire to any position or vocation; there is also in Islam a doctrine of respect and toleration for other religions.

The critics of the Islamic state, on the other hand, maintain that, whatever may be the theory of tolerance in Islam, history belies it. They say that in an Islamic state the best status that the non-Muslim can have is that of the *Dhimmi*. *Dhimmis* have their lives, laws and property assured to them, but they have a definitely inferior status; they are not full citizens but enjoy the status of protected wards. The non-Muslim citizens in Pakistan naturally expressed apprehension with regard to their position in the proposed Islamic constitution. They were given some grounds for their apprehensions by some of the orthodox religious groups. According to some *Ulema* (religious teachers), the non-Muslims in Pakistan cannot be full-fledged citizens.

But neither the government of Pakistan, the framers of the constitution, nor the Pakistani intelligentsia have ever accepted the views of

G

the *Ulema*. The founder of Pakistan had already formulated the principle of equality of all citizens irrespective of caste, creed and religion, and the framers of the constitution followed this principle. Except for the provision that the head of state must be a Muslim, there is no discrimination in the constitution on the grounds of race, caste or religion in respect to citizenship or rights in the constitution. The provision relating to the head of the state is a justifiable recognition of the predominantly Muslim character of the people; nobody could contemplate the possibility of a Hindu President in Pakistan any more than he could think of a Muslim Prime Minister in India. Professor Wilfred Smith, in analysing the problem of the non-Muslim minorities in the Islamic constitution of Pakistan, remarks:

> It is fundamental to remember that the rights accorded to any minority or other non-powerful group in any state depend on the ideal of those in power. . . . A state may be democratic in form but unless it is democratic also in ideal, unless the majority of its citizens are actively loyal to the transcendent principles of democracy recognizing the ideal validity of every man's status as a man, then the arithmetical minority has, through the democratic form, no rights at all. . . . Many outsiders and several Pakistani Christians and Hindus have stated or supposed that these minorities would be better off if Pakistan were simply a 'democratic' instead of an Islamic state. This is irresponsibly glib. For if Muslims do, in fact, treat non-Muslims unjustly, then a democratic form (without the Graeco-Roman and religious traditions of democracy to vitalize it) would merely give them as majority the constitutional authority for doing so without let or hindrance.[22]

Reference is made to the Islamic constitution in Pakistan, not to claim that it has conferred all the protection and privileges to the non-Muslim citizens, but to affirm that there is nothing basically wrong in having an Islamic constitution in a state like Pakistan where there is a non-Muslim minority. Whether they are treated well, or whether their fate is no better than that of the Muslims in India, depends not so much on having an Islamic or a secular constitution, as on the attitudes and behaviour patterns of the majority community. As we have seen, the 50 million people composing the Muslim minority in India are not equal with the majority in the exercise of the right and privileges of citizen-ship—and this despite the fact that India has a secular constitution. The Indian government, however, lost no opportunity for discrediting Pakistan in the eyes of the world as an 'intolerant theocratic state', where the non-Muslim minorities were alleged to have suffered hard-ships because of Islamic ideology and the Islamic constitution. This is not fair or correct. If the minorities are not well off in Pakistan, the form of constitution, as in India, has little to do with it. After the conference on minority problems between Liaquat Ali and Pandit Nehru in Delhi in 1950 the Indian Prime Minister told parliament that Liaquat Ali had declared that Pakistanis looked upon their ideal of an 'Islamic state' in exactly the same sense that Indians referred to 'Ram Rajya' (rule of Ram, or God) as the goal of their government. 'In other words, Liaquat held that Pakistanis did not associate the term "Islamic state" with the Muslim religion in the narrow sense, any more than Indians associated the slogan "Ram Rajya" with the Hindu religion in an exclusive sense.'[23]

But, in spite of repeated clarifications like this, widespread distrust and prejudice exist in India against Pakistan as a Muslim state. A for-bidding image of Pakistan is being deliberately created because of her adherence to the broad ideals of Islam. As we have stated, it is neither claimed nor pretended that all is well with Hindus in East Pakistan. Before the partition of the subcontinent, the Hindus in East Pakistan, though constituting a minority, had the predominant share in trade, commerce and in other professions. They occupied a very important position in the economic life of East Pakistan; most of the landlords were Hindus; all save one or two of the region's textile mills were owned by them. They dominated the legal profession and occupied very important places in the educational services of East Pakistan. After independence, the Muslims got political power and they sought to adjust economic relations for the majority population. It cannot be denied that this was a threat to the privileged position which the minority had enjoyed so long, and is at the root of its grievances. The Hindus in East Pakistan had been in the precarious position of an elite—precarious because, even before partition, Muslim education and social reforms were undermining their position, and after independence their position became more untenable. It was hard for the Hindus of

East Pakistan, who constituted an upper class, to adjust to the political ascendency of the Muslims, and it was particularly difficult for them to be reconciled to the mere idea of Pakistan. Moreover, they were confident that India could accommodate them. Their situation in this respect is markedly different from that of the Muslims in India. If the Hindus migrated from East Pakistan, they would add only one-twenty-fifth to the population of India—a country whose size and resources are great; but the Muslims of India would add one-half to the population of Pakistan. These facts are to be remembered in any analysis of the problem of minorities in the two countries. The psychology of the Hindu exodus from East Pakistan can be better appreciated in terms of these facts. Pandit Nehru once said in the Indian parliament, à propos of this problem, that 'lack of confidence among minorities was partly psychological'.[24]

It is not to be implied, however, that East Pakistan's Hindus had no grievances, no lack of security. There were cases of harassment by local authorities. They also had panics like Indian Muslims whenever there was a deterioration in Indo-Pakistan relations. Perennial quarrels between the two countries over various issues have exposed the religious minorities in India and Pakistan to constant insecurity and frustration. Pakistan can, however, claim that threats or actual outbursts of communal violence have been less frequent than in India. Nor is there any such powerful organisation in Pakistan as the Hindu Mahasabha, the RSSS or the Jan Sangh: the religious extremist groups which openly preach violence against the Muslims in India. The Bengali Muslims and Hindus have tried to avoid the cult of violence as preached by the extremist Hindu groups in India.

6

'EDGE OF A PRECIPICE'

A MAJOR crisis arose between India and Pakistan over the resurgence of communal troubles in West Bengal (India) and East Bengal (Pakistan) in early 1950. The hate-charged atmosphere of 1947 was again prevalent. The crisis in the two Bengals during February and March 1950 brought India and Pakistan, in Pandit Nehru's words, 'to the edge of a precipice'. So grave was the situation that many observers feared that an attack on East Pakistan by India was imminent. Professor Norman Brown, for instance, observed: 'Active communal organisations—the Hindu Mahasabha, the Rashtriya Swayam Sevak Sangh, and the Council for Protection of the Rights of Minorities—demanded that partition be repudiated and East Bengal be forcibly made a part of India or that it be constrained by economic pressure.'[1]

How did this crisis start? The press and the propaganda machinery in India were proclaiming that the Hindu minorities in East Pakistan were oppressed and that the trouble which flared up in West Bengal was due to 'sympathy' and 'concern' for the Hindus of East Pakistan. The following account in the London *Annual Register* of 1951 gives the correct picture of the situation:

It was . . . in West Bengal that the trouble first broke out. Admittedly in December 1949, there had been an incident in the Khulna district of East Bengal, but this was entirely non-communal in character and was deliberately misrepresented by the irredentist elements in Calcutta. The president of the Hindu Mahasabha at a conference held in Calcutta at the end of that month had openly declared that Pakistan must be reabsorbed into India and this view had many supporters in right-wing Hindu circles. . . . the Prime Minister of India, on his visit to Calcutta, was publicly subjected to pressure to declare war on Pakistan.[2]

The *Annual Register*'s account further stated that 'tensions increased to such a pitch during March following renewed riots that war seemed almost inevitable'.[3]

The whole crisis in West Bengal seemed to have been originated by a highly provocative speech in Calcutta by the Indian Deputy Prime Minister, Sardar Patel, on January 14, 1950. Addressing the Hindus of Bengal, he said: 'How can Bengal ever forget those days of direct action and the situation in Calcutta which followed in its wake [in 1946]. Then came the tragedy of Noakhali: how can India or you [Bengali Hindus] forget those dark days?' Referring to the partition of the subcontinent, Patel declared: 'What an irony of fate: we resisted the partition of Bengal when it was planned by the British forty years ago. You sacrificed your all to avoid the catastrophe of partition; India was with you. Subsequently we had to accept partition of another conception.' Turning to the Hindus of East Bengal, he said:

> Those friends who were with us yesterday have now become foreigners today. But how can that be in practice? They are still what they were before. Artificial boundaries cannot separate them from us. Our relationship and economic ties cannot be broken. Difficulties are there but they must be removed. How can we go to their help? If we can express sympathy with the people of South Africa and run to their assistance, it is easier to do so in the case of people in East Pakistan. Do not forget that important limbs of your mother India have been cut.

He urged Bengali Hindus to 'show courage, bravery, in full expectation of the good days to come'; and concluded: 'Bengalis want more room for expansion. It is my earnest desire to help Bengal in its hour of need to the maximum of my capacity.'[4]

By this speech, Sardar Patel opened a vista of wild imagination for the West Bengal Hindus. He seemingly aroused the hope that his government would give support to their attempts to annex East Pakistan, and thus he stirred up all the passions attendant upon such thoughts and fancies. The speech was made against a background of communal tension and hatred which were stoked up by the Hindu extremists who had been agitating for direct or 'police action' in East Pakistan. Their hostility to the very existence of Pakistan, expressed in reckless statements in the previous weeks (December 1949) was encouraged by this unfortunate speech of India's Deputy Prime Minister. It set the match to the Bengal powder-keg. A 'Council for Protection of Rights of Minorities' in East Pakistan was formed; even a provisional government for East Bengal was set up; while the Council, along with the Hindu Mahasabha, raised and trained an irregular army to organise 'police action' of the type employed in Hyderabad in 1948. At a later stage in the crisis, on March 28, 1950, the *New York Times* observed: 'The Hindu Mahasabha's objective was to create conditions in which the Government of India would be forced to act.'

The echoes of Sardar Patel's speech had hardly died away in the streets of Calcutta when hundreds of pamphlets and posters appeared in West Bengal demanding 'action'. The mobs attacked the Muslim minorities, burning their houses, looting their shops; the mosques were desecrated. Over 150,000 Muslims poured into East Bengal in an appalling condition. When these refugees came to East Pakistan, with their horrible tales of persecution and prosecution, communal riots broke out in certain places there. This, in turn, led to further explosive situations in West Bengal. Nehru had to admit: 'Recent happenings in West Bengal have been a matter of deepest shame and sorrow for us'; and a colleague, Maulana Abul Kalam Azad, affirmed that 'planned attacks were made by Hindus on the Muslims of Calcutta with the deliberate intention of terrorising them into running away from their hearths and homes'.[5]

The communal rioting in West Bengal, which began after Patel's speech on January 5 and continued throughout January and February 1950, took a most serious turn on March 27, when West Bengal had to impose martial law in Howrah, a densely populated satellite town of Calcutta. As a press note of the West Bengal government of March 27 admitted: 'The situation continued to deteriorate and went out of the civil authorities' control. Brutal murders had been committed and mob attacks on innocent persons had been made.'[6] Riots also spread to Assam and other parts of India, such as Bombay and Uttar Pradesh.

E. M. Philips, a Christian member of the legislature of Uttar Pradesh told the Chief Minister, Pandit Pant, in the legislature that district officers were creating a situation in which the Muslims would be forced to migrate to Pakistan.[7] In the words of Liaquat Ali Khan:

> Human values which emerged from ceaseless striving, continued over centuries, are being destroyed by inhuman barbarities; the edifice of civilization, built on the principles of justice and peace, is being demolished by hatred and malice. Tens of millions of men, women and children are spending a life of misery and woe. For a large number of them, the future holds nothing but perpetual misery and fear. When the day dawns, they do not know what their fate will be at its end. When the sun sets, they do not know whether they will live to see another day. In this state of terror, they have lost their self-respect and sense of honour.[8]

As a result of riots in the two Bengals, 400,000 Muslim refugees came to East Pakistan, and a similar number of Hindus left Pakistan for India.[9]

The most menacing development of this situation was 'war hysteria' in India, which found its gravest expression in Nehru's threat of 'other methods' to Pakistan. On February 23, 1950, he told the Indian parliament of his proposal to Pakistan that delegates of the International Red Cross, accompanied by ministers or officials of each government, should visit the affected areas in East Pakistan and West Bengal. Nehru warned that, if the methods suggested to Pakistan on that issue by the Indian government were not agreed to, 'it may be that we shall have to adopt other methods'. He added: 'To me it appears that what has happened in Kashmir and what is happening in East Bengal are all interlinked and we cannot separate them.'[10] This attempt to connect the Bengal situation with that in Kashmir was an ominous hint. On the pretext of tribal invasion, India had sent troops to Kashmir in October 1947; many Pakistanis were alarmed that, on the pretext of communal riots in East Pakistan, India was planning to send an army there. By placing the Bengal situation on the same plane as Kashmir, where Indian and Pakistani forces were facing each other at a time when tensions between the two countries were at their worst, Nehru was certainly not taking a step towards peace in the subcontinent. His talk of 'other methods' and the comparison of Bengal with Kashmir sounded like a threat to Pakistan, and it heightened the ill-feeling between the two states. His statement revealed the extent to which the old spectre of communalism was, once more, exacerbating the conduct of relations between India and Pakistan. Speaking on Nehru's threat, Liaquat Ali Khan said: 'I invite all the peace-loving people of the world to note this threat. . . . The truth of the matter is that the leaders of India have not accepted Pakistan and keep on devising methods of undoing it. But Pakistan is an unalterable fact. The sooner this is realized by the leaders of India, the better it will be for the stability and progress of this subcontinent.' Liaquat charged India with preparing for war.[11]

Commenting on Nehru's threat of 'other methods', the *New York Times* wrote on February 24, 1950:

Prime Minister Nehru issued a warning in parliament yesterday that, although Indian policy was founded on peace, it may be 'we have to employ other methods'. . . . what is surprising about Mr Nehru's sombre threat is that it should be made by a leader who had adopted neutrality as his policy and who insisted during his visit to this country that peace between East and West could be achieved without show or threat of force. . . . It is understandable that the successor of Gandhi should believe in passive resistance but not that he should expect it to work with the Soviet Union when he admits it does not work in Pakistan.

Explaining, or rather elaborating, his threat of 'other methods', Nehru said in a broadcast on March 3: 'Anyone who knows me should know that I hate war and will go to the furthest limits. But to talk complacently of peace, when there is no peace and something worse than war is possible, is to be blind to facts.'[12] The *New York Times* published this explanation under the heading "Nehru disavows war but renews warning".[13] The Indian leader's unfortunate words added greatly to the already tense and bitter atmosphere. The war hysteria increased in intensity. The New Delhi correspondent of *The Times* reported on March 24, 1950: 'One widely circulated Calcutta newspaper has conducted a "war poll" and continues to press for military action to protect the minority in East Bengal, while another Calcutta newspaper advocates the setting up of an *Azad* (free) eastern Pakistan Government in India.'[14] Three days later, *The Times* published the results of the 'war poll' of the Calcutta newspaper: 'The people's verdict is 82·7 per cent in favour of armed intervention, or "police action" as it is euphemistically termed, as the only permanent solution of the East Bengal problems.'[15] After Nehru's threat of 'other methods', the Indian press openly preached war between India and Pakistan. In its editorial of February 24, 1950, the *Free Press Journal*, under the caption "March into Pakistan", urged India to declare that 'India will march her troops into Pakistan to restore law and order.' Members of the Indian parliament, such as R. K. Choudhury, openly declared that India should go to war with Pakistan, while the Indian socialist leader, Jayaprakash Narayan, said on March 7, 1950: 'The only alternative left is to send our own forces into East Bengal [Pakistan] to protect our minorities there. If Pakistan takes it as a declaration of war, which it is not meant to be, it cannot be helped.'[16] A precedent for this was already there. When India sent troops to occupy Hyderabad in 1948, her government had said the same thing; it was not war, merely a 'police action' to deal with local disturbances. *The Times* stated in an editorial of March 8: 'Mr Nehru has met organised demonstrations in favour of armed intervention for the protection of Pakistani Hindus.'

The outlook was grim. The war hysteria had spread to other parts of India, and there was alarm throughout the subcontinent. The Council for Protection of the Rights of Minorities was vigorously conducting its campaign for the forcible seizure and annexation of East Pakistan. The cancellation of all Indian army leave brought the 'edge of the precipice' in sight, and war between these two Commonwealth countries was now openly canvassed. To Nehru's threat, the Pakistan Prime Minister replied: 'If India wants war, Pakistan is prepared.' The *Daily Telegraph* reported: 'Considerable troop movements by the Indian army took place in March 1950 near the borders of Pakistan, both East and West. The Indian army had sent armoured forces into Firozpur district. Two or three infantry divisions had moved into East Punjab.'[17] During March the Indian army was feverishly reinforcing its concentration on the borders of East Pakistan from one end to the other. Major-General J. Choudhury, who until recently had been the Military Governor of Hyderabad, was reported to have taken a comprehensive reconnaissance tour on the borders of East Pakistan facing the districts of Dinajpur, Rahshahi and Jessore.[18] The whole situation has been well summed up by Ian Stephens, at that time the editor of the only British-owned newspaper in India, the *Statesman*: 'By the first week of March, whatever Delhi's intentions, war had nearly come. The two countries were within a hair-breadth of it. Troops had been moved, not only in Bengal but—more perturbing—in the Punjab. India's armoured division, to which no real Pakistani counterpart existed, was pushed forward in a way which threatened Lahore.'[19]

The flare-up of religious riots had, thus, gravely aggravated the ill-feeling that was already running high over Kashmir and the economic cold-war. The Pakistan Prime Minister made a strong plea to end the tensions; in a statement on March 29, 1950, he said:

As long as war hysteria in India continues unchecked, its effects, particularly on the minds of the minority communities in Pakistan, cannot but be disastrous. For weeks past, the Indian press and several Indian leaders have been demanding that India should declare war on Pakistan. The dangerous possibilities of continuance of such a campaign are obvious and cannot be over-emphasised. Unless vigorous action is taken to put an end to this agitation, dangerous consequences might ensue.[20]

Liaquat did not simply issue a statement; he proposed a meeting with the Indian Prime Minister to determine how to end the communal riots and the fears of war. Nehru responded in a splendid way; notwithstanding the pressure from the extremist Hindu leaders and press, he reciprocated Liaquat's overture.

The historic meeting between the two Prime Ministers took place in New Delhi on April 2, 1950. Imaginative statesmanship had, it seemed, drawn the two countries back, for a while at least, from the brink of a yawning abyss. The news of the Liaquat-Nehru meeting came like a glimpse of blue sky in the overcast atmosphere of Indo-Pakistan relations. The conference continued for six days, and on April 8 the Liaquat-Nehru Agreement was signed. This could be called a 'bill of rights' for the minorities of the two countries. It was divided into three parts: it sought, first, to allay the fears of the religious minorities on both sides; second, to promote communal peace; and third, to establish a climate in which other differences could be amicably settled. The Agreement declared: 'The Governments of India and Pakistan solemnly agree that each shall ensure, to the minorities throughout its territories, complete equality of citizenship, irrespective of religion; a full sense of security in respect of life, culture, property and personal honour.' It also guaranteed basic human rights to the minorities, such as freedom of movement, of speech, of occupation, of worship. Especially important was the provision that minorities would have 'equal opportunity with members of the majority community to participate in the public life of the country, to hold political or other office and to serve in their country's civil and armed forces'. The Prime Minister of India pointed out that these rights were already guaranteed in the constitution of India, while the Prime Minister of Pakistan pointed out that similar provisions were made in the objectives resolution as already adopted by the Pakistan Constituent Assembly in 1949.

The Liaquat-Nehru Agreement also provided for implementatory machinery that included drastic measures for dealing, when necessary, with oppressive elements. Each government decided to set up a Minority Commission, a major function of which would be to observe and report on the implementation of the Agreement, to take cognisance of breach or neglect and to make recommendations to ensure its enforcement. Both Minority Commissions would be headed by a minister of the provincial government and would include representatives of Hindus and Muslims. It was laid down that the recommendations of each commission would normally be binding upon the government concerned but that, should there be disagreement between commissions or between ministers specially assigned to assist them, the dispute should be referred to the Prime Ministers of India and Pakistan, who would either settle the dispute themselves or set up a special agency to settle it. Further, in order to restore the confidence of the minorities, the two governments decided to include representatives of the minority community in the cabinets of the two Bengals; and they decided to depute two central ministers, one from each government, to remain in the affected areas for such period as might be necessary.

Both governments, however, emphasised that the allegiance and loyalty of the minorities were to the state of which they were citizens, and that it was to the government of their own state that they should look for the redress of grievances. This was a salutary provision, because minority problems in both countries were complicated by the fact that the Hindus in East Pakistan looked to India for protection and Muslims in India expected support and help from Pakistan. The relations between the two states have often become tense as a result of this attitude. It was, however, difficult to avoid such an attitude in view of long-standing Hindu–Muslim differences and the creation of two states on the basis of religion.

Liaquat, in presenting the Agreement to the Pakistan parliament, said that he looked upon it as the precursor of a new understanding between India and Pakistan. He appealed for understanding of the minorities' problem, adding that 'the lives of millions depend on how we conduct ourselves in this matter'; and he urged his people and the press to help make the Agreement work.[21] Similarly Nehru told the Indian parliament: 'We have stopped ourselves at the edge of the precipice and turned our back to it. . . . The brief course of our history as an independent nation has been bedevilled by our strained relations with Pakistan and conflicts that have resulted therefrom. It is now up to us, as it is up to the government and the people of Pakistan, to live up to our professions and face all our problems with sanity and good-will and a fixed determination to put an end to the vicious atmosphere that has surrounded us for these two and a half years.'[22]

The Agreement was widely hailed as a hopeful beginning to improved relations between the two countries. The two leaders had taken their countries back from the drift towards what might have become a war. They had made a supreme appeal to reason, and their accord was acclaimed in the world press as 'the dawn of reason in the east', as a 'turning point in Asia'. Walter Lippman described it as the 'Light of Asia', and added: 'It is the first great demonstration of high states-manship by the new independent powers of Asia.'[23]

It is true, however, that communal insecurity, mistrust and strife in the Indo-Pakistan subcontinent have very deep roots in behaviour patterns and psychological attitudes. These cannot be changed over-night by an act of legislation or by formal agreements. The statutes and accords are necessary, and certainly they were imperatively so in the spring of 1950. But there must be a change in the hearts of men to make formal undertakings valid. The Liaquat-Nehru Agreement was a feat of statesmanship and moral courage; the spirit and understanding of the pact were genuinely democratic and humane. But whether it really marked a turning point in Indo-Pakistan relations was by no means certain. Under the pressure of major disputes like Kashmir, it ran the risk of being merely one more in a series of agreements between India and Pakistan which had been broken in practice by one side or the other.

While men of good will and the press all over the world welcomed the high spirit and noble principles underlying the Agreement, the Hindu extremists in West Bengal and their press reacted to it in the most hostile way. The *Hindustan Standard* of Calcutta termed it 'an elaborate attempt to cheat history . . . a truly extraordinary piece of make-believe'. The *Amrita Bazar Patrika* and the *Nation* commented in similar terms, the latter describing it as 'fruitless and a triumph for Pakistan diplomacy'. Most of the Bengali newspapers in West Bengal expressed similar opinions. The two Bengali ministers in Nehru's cabinet—Dr Shayamaprasad Mukerjee and K. C. Neyogi—resigned in protest. Dr Mukerjee declared in the Indian parliament: 'Pakistan's failure to protect minorities challenged the basis of the partition of the subcontinent into two Dominions in 1947. Therefore a "police action" would be justified.'[24] He made his remarks two months after the Delhi meeting between Liaquat and Nehru, when sincere attempts were made to improve the relations between the two countries.

In contrast, the press and the people in Pakistan without exception gave loyal support to the Agreement. This was testified by variou[s] 'good will' visitors from India, notably by a special correspondent of the *United Press of India* who made a seventeen-day tour of Pakistan after the Delhi meeting and reported on his impressions in the *Hindu*:

The correspondent, who met a cross-section of the people there [Pakistan], including officials, political leaders, minorities members, commoners, journalists, students, tradesmen and others found an avowed determination among them to perpetuate the spirit of friendliness generated by the pact. Another indication of the good will created by the pact is the complete change in tone of the Pakistan press. Propaganda against India has now given place to a friendly and cordial tone.[25]

Surveying the working of the Agreement, *The Economist* wrote in a leading article:

> By the end of its first and most crucial two months, from mid-April to mid-June, the agreement had succeeded in completely stopping the net flow of Hindus from East to West Bengal. The flow of Muslims, in the reverse direction, was not stopped. . . . West Bengal stands out as the main source of danger to the agreement. Even now, the tone of its press—apart from the *Statesman*—is ugly and bitter. Mischief makers in West Bengal might, once more, bring all India to the brink of the abyss. The truth is that many West Bengalis do not want the agreement to work. . . . The Pakistan Government is to be congratulated on having done what it can through trust committees to restore Hindu middle class property without attempting to bargain about the Muslim position in West Bengal.[26]

The Times reported: 'The number of Hindus returning to East Pakistan during the past few days has been averaging over 10,000 a day; in contrast to this encouraging tendency the number of Muslim refugees entering West Pakistan is still showing a slow increase.'[27]

Pandit Nehru told the Indian parliament: 'The central Government of Pakistan has anxiously and to the best of their ability tried to give effect to the April Agreement just as the Government of India has done. The Government of East Bengal has, on the whole, tried to do so.'[28] Nural Amin, the Chief Minister of East Pakistan, claimed: 'My Government have spared no pains to implement in every detail the agreement and thereby to create such conditions as will ensure that minorities can live in complete peace and security. Since the agreement, we have welcomed numerous outside observers, and the consensus of opinion of these observers has testified to the success of my Government's efforts.'[29] While the opposition to the Agreement in West Bengal was deplored in Pakistan, Nehru's sincerity about implementing it was never doubted. His main difficulty was lack of co-operation from West Bengal.

The Prime Ministers met again, this time in Karachi, April 26-28, 1950, to explore the possibilities of solving their problems and to review the Agreement. There was also an Indo-Pakistan newspaper editors' conference in May in Delhi which sought to bring about an atmosphere of good will. Urged by Nehru to create a friendly atmosphere, the editors pledged themselves to stop fault-finding and recriminations in the press of both countries. Nehru's appeal was responded to by a Pakistani editor, who said: 'Let us not compete in narrowmindedness but in the fields of tolerance, far-sightedness, good neighbourliness and advocacy of peace.'[30]

A close review of the operation of the Agreement was made at meetings in Delhi on August 3, 4 and 5, and in Karachi on August 9 and 10. The two central ministers for Minority Affairs and the chairmen of the Minority Commissions of East and West Bengal were present at both conferences. The governments of both countries sought to strengthen the Agreement by adding a ten-point supplement to the original pact. Each government agreed to investigate promptly every communal incident brought to the notice of the authorities and to take effective and deterrent action against offenders, including government servants found guilty of dereliction of duty. The presidents and members of the local self-government bodies (Union Boards) were charged with special responsibilities in preventing communal incidents in rural areas and in promoting unity between Hindus and Muslims. Also agreed were proposals for the appointment of special constables from the majority community, and the imposition of collective fines and the stationing of punitive police forces in areas frequently affected by communal incidents. A detailed procedure was devised for restoring urban and rural property to returning refugees. Commendable provisions were made to expedite the restoration of abducted women; it was agreed that police officers be given powers to search, without warrant, any house where it was suspected an abducted woman was being kept.

Thus, the original Agreement of April 8, 1950, was strengthened to restore confidence among the minorities and to prevent recurrence of communal incidents. These were admirable steps. Yet it must be stressed again that an agreed programme, or any promulgated declaration of intent, could not of itself remove intercommunal strife.

While the Liaquat-Nehru Agreement achieved the immediate objective of removing the threat of an imminent war between the two
countries, it could not achieve the long-term objective of giving a full
sense of security to the minorities. To achieve this, habits of mind and
patterns of behaviour would have to be changed, and these could be
modified only by usage and long habituation. Between the signing of
the Liaquat-Nehru Agreement in April 1950 and January 1964, 660
communal riots occurred in various parts of India. The news of these
riots was published in the Indian papers; there might have been more
which remained unreported. On January 15, 1964, fourteen years after
the Agreement, the *New York Times* correspondent reported from
Calcutta: 'Clashes between Hindus and Muslims have produced
tensions unparalleled here since the partition of India and Pakistan in
1947. The army took control tonight of several areas of Calcutta where
civil administration had failed to check a wave of arson and murder.'
The next day, the same correspondent wrote: 'India's sixteen years'
struggle, led by Prime Minister Jawaharlal Nehru, to establish and
maintain a secular state with freedom and equality for all religions has
received a grave set back in the Hindu-Muslim riots of the last five days.
The killing, burning, and looting continued so fiercely that Gulzarila
Nanda, the Home Minister, flew to Calcutta last night to proclaim
what amounted to martial law in five of the city's twenty-five police
districts.' The *Observer* condemned the criminal negligence of the
police in Calcutta:

> Those who have lived through this black week know many examples
> of police laxity. While the rioters made no secret of their plans, the
> police forces in the first few days seemed always to be everywhere
> except in the streets attacked. The official slackness is partly respons-
> ible for the heavy toll Calcutta has had today. Nobody accepts the
> official figures which sets the numbers of dead at no more than 100,
> and the usual estimate is around 500 killed while tens of thousands
> have lost their homes through fire.[31]

It is against this sort of police or official laxity that the Liaquat-Nehru
Agreement of 1950 sought to build a defence.

Indo-Pakistan relations have always been strained since they gained
independence in 1947, but there have been some brief intervals of

'sweet periods'; the Liaquat-Nehru Agreement of April 1950 ushered in such an interval. Unhappily, it lasted for a few months only, and then followed the old tensions and bitterness. Six months after the Agreement was made, the correspondent of *Round Table* wrote from Pakistan: 'It will be a happy day when any chronicler of Pakistan affairs feels no necessity of making more than a passing reference to relations between Karachi and New Delhi. From the birth of Pakistan, the factor of inter-Dominion tension has dominated all others, both in political and in the economic field. During the last quarter hopes of improvement, from both aspects, have been dashed.'[32] The Kashmir dispute and the trade deadlock had shown no signs of improvement. India, on the contrary, took a provocative step by summoning a 'constituent assembly' for Kashmir.

WAR PREPARATIONS AGAIN

In the summer of 1951, India and Pakistan were passing through another acrimonious phase of their long-standing differences and disputes. 'The danger of war between India and Pakistan is, once more, becoming acute', observed *The Economist* on July 21, 1951; while the correspondent of *Round Table* from Pakistan reported, 'In August [1951] Pakistan, inured as she has been to the atmosphere of recurrent crisis in which her four years of existence have been spent, was facing perhaps the gravest crisis of the many she has encountered on her way.'[33] Friction between India and Pakistan was as fierce in July 1951 as in March 1950, just before the signing of the Liaquat-Nehru Agreement; they were again moving towards an abyss and on the brink of war.

The Prime Minister of Pakistan, Liaquat Ali Khan, disclosed in a press statement on July 15, 1951: 'Heavy concentration of Indian armed forces is taking place in East Punjab and in Jammu and Kashmir. As a result of these troop movements, the bulk of the Indian army is now concentrated against the Pakistan borders. In particular, all its armoured formations have been moved forward within easy striking distance of West Pakistan. This constitutes a grave threat to the security of Pakistan and to international peace.' Liaquat recalled that a year before concentrations of the Indian armed forces against Pakistan had led to so grave a situation that the two countries were brought to the brink of war. He pointed out that the press and prominent personalities in India had indulged in violent incitement to war. A few minor border incidents had been magnified beyond all proportions and taken out of their context as a propaganda measure against Pakistan, but the truth was that Indian forces along the cease-fire line in Jammu and Kashmir had been responsible for hundreds of incidents during the previous two and a half years. In the light of the heavy concentration of Indian forces on Pakistan's borders, Liaquat said, it could now be seen that all this propaganda was intended as a cover for the movement of India's forces. 'Last year [1950] India had concentrated very large forces on the borders of East and West Pakistan and in spite of the fact that under the Delhi agreement of April 1950 I was assured that these big concentrations would be removed, they were not, they were kept throughout and now on top of that they have concentrated their armoured units plus other divisions that were in reserve in the interior of India.' According to reliable information, India's armoured force comprised one armoured division and an independent armoured brigade. Asked if he was sure that aggression was the object of the concentration, the Pakistan Prime Minister replied: 'Unless the object is to have a swim in the river Ravi, what other purpose can there be?'[34]

Liaquat made a triple appeal: to Nehru 'to remove the threat'; to the Security Council to take notice of the position; and to the people of other countries to judge India's aggressive designs. Indian forces were massing aggressively on the frontier in the Punjab; practically the whole of India's armour was massed on the borders of Pakistan. 'The general truth of this assertion was not denied by Nehru who, however, affirmed that the action was purely defensive and had been necessitated by Pakistan's war-mongering tendencies. No one could suppose that Mr Nehru had any fear that Pakistan, being so much the weaker of the two, would launch a direct attack on Indian territory.'[35]

This concentration of Indian forces on the Pakistan border led to an exchange of telegrams between the Prime Ministers of Pakistan and India. It revealed Pakistan's great anxiety and the depth of mutual suspicion, hostility and hatred. In his first telegram to Nehru, on July 15, Liaquat appealed: 'I would most earnestly urge you to remove the threat to the security of Pakistan created by the forward move of your armed forces.' In reply to this appeal, Nehru said: 'India's policy continues to be to preserve and ensure peace and to avoid war.' He referred to 'an intensive and astonishing campaign of *Jehad* and war against India in Pakistan' and said that his government 'cannot ignore this continual talk and preparation of war in Pakistan'. Nehru then made a most significant admission: 'It is true that certain troop movements have been ordered by us for defensive purposes.'[36] This denial of Liaquat's charges provoked strong comments from observers who found it difficult to believe that India had moved her entire armed forces on the borders of Pakistan just because there was talk of *Jehad* or war in Pakistan. Anyone who had any knowledge of the military strength of India and Pakistan would find this explanation wholly inadequate. India had four times the population of Pakistan, was much larger, more prosperous and much more industrialised. Moreover, India acquired at partition all the arsenals and arms factories of the *Raj*, and maintained much larger armed forces. Liaquat told Nehru:

> The strength of India's armed forces at the time of partition was double that of Pakistan. You have since persistently tried to increase that disparity, not only by constantly building up your armed forces, but also by attempting to hamstring Pakistan forces by denying them the stores which were their rightful share under the partition agreement. Pakistan has, therefore, been forced to spend considerable sums on the purchase of equipment wrongfully withheld by India. In spite of this, the increases in Pakistan's defence budget are less than half of those in India's defence budget. Because of the disparity between the armed forces of the two countries, it is fantastic to suggest that there is any danger of aggression against India from Pakistan.'[37]

The greater size of India's armed forces and the manner in which they had been used since 1947, causing repeated threats to Pakistan, could leave no doubt as to where the potentiality of aggression lay.

Pakistan's Foreign Minister, Sir Zafrullah Khan, said that Nehru's reply had only 'intensified Pakistan's apprehensions; the reply is far from reassuring'; it was 'either incorrect or half-truth or fallacy'. He asserted that the massing of India's troops on the border of Pakistan and the forward move of her entire armoured units within a few miles of Pakistan's border indicated 'aggressive intentions'. Referring to Nehru's assertion that the movement of the Indian army was for defensive purposes, Sir Zafrullah asked: 'Against whom is the Indian army trying to defend?' He emphatically declared that Pakistan did not move a single soldier until the concentration of Indian troops and this, he claimed, could be investigated by any impartial observer.[38] Liaquat offered Nehru the same suggestion. Referring to Nehru's assertion that India's policy was to avoid war, Liaquat pointed out that 'the use of military force in Junagadh, Hyderabad and more recently in Nepal are grave warnings against acceptance of these assertions at their face value. The continued denial by force of arms to the people of Kashmir of their right of self-determination and repeated threats to the security of Pakistan by massing of Indian troops against its borders are hardly indications of a desire for peace.'[39] Sir Zafrullah Khan pressed home the same point: 'Take Junagadh, take Hyderabad, take Kashmir, take even Nepal; if they are illustrations of ensuring peace and avoiding war, Pakistan's apprehensions are fully justified.'[40]

To Nehru's accusation of 'talk of *Jehad* and war in the Pakistan press', Liaquat replied: 'You have been at pains to distort the significance of expression of discontent which has appeared in the Pakistan press over your persistent refusal to allow a peaceful solution through a free plebiscite in Kashmir. You have construed the expression of the natural desire for the liberation of Kashmir as propaganda against India.'[41] He drew attention to the continuous and blatant propaganda for war against Pakistan, and indeed for the very liquidation of Pakistan, carried on by the Indian press, prominent leaders and political parties which openly adopted as an article of creed the undoing of partition—which meant nothing but liquidation of Pakistan. No doubt, there had been talk of *Jehad* or liberation of the Muslim population of Kashmir in Pakistan, but there has never been any political movement or agitation in Pakistan which wished to annex any part of India. The Pakistanis' grievances have always been confined to Kashmir which, according to the findings and the resolutions of the United Nations, is a disputed territory. It was wrong to construe expressions giving vent to feelings of frustration over the failure of peaceful methods of solution in Kashmir as a desire for war against India.

But, in India, the creation of Pakistan itself is still regarded as a 'tragic mistake' which ought to be corrected.

The Pakistanis were not alone in being unconvinced by Nehru's 'denial'. Outside observers also did not seem to be impressed by it. Nehru's 'denial' was published in the *Manchester Guardian* under the heading, "Mr Nehru's admission: army movements";[42] while the *Daily Express* headline ran, "Nehru answers 'lies', then admits troops are on border."[43] Other important newspapers gave similar captions: the *New York Times*, "Nehru says troops mass for defense as he confirms recent army movement towards border"; the *New York Herald Tribune*, "Nehru admits army masses near Pakistan but says move is security action and not aggressive". World opinion, as reflected in the editorial comments on India's troop movements, confirmed Pakistan's fears and anxieties. *The Times* wrote:

> Mr Nehru may be determined that India shall never attack Pakistan but his consciousness of his own peaceful intentions is not itself an adequate guarantee that war can be avoided. He will not admit the possibility that his policy over Kashmir may be misconceived. He makes no allowance for the effect on Pakistani opinion of his benevolent attitude towards the 'Pathanistan' movement, of his encouragement of 'Red Shirt' refugees from the frontier province, of Mahasabha propaganda that Pakistan is merely 'India irredenta' and above all of troop movements along the frontier between the two Punjabs which include armoured units that Pakistan does not possess.[44]

The *Manchester Guardian* did not mince words:

> India has made a deplorable impression by its troop movements against Pakistan, all the more so because of its denials. What has caused India's action? The world has not forgotten Hyderabad. India complains of recent frontier incidents. But the principal United Nations observer has said that these have not been as serious as others in the past. It complains that Sir Zafrullah Khan, the Pakistan Foreign Minister, made a menacing speech against India. But this speech could not by any conceivable interpretation be read as a threat of imminent action by Pakistan . . . the most plausible explanation is

that India is putting itself in an advantageous position before the meeting of the Kashmir constituent assembly.[45]

'In the opinion of the best military observers', the *Observer* stated: 'India has taken aggressive action in placing her armoured division and an armoured brigade north-west of the river Beas in the neighbourhood of Amritsar where they have the freedom for defensive manœuvring.'[46] The *Daily Telegraph* wrote: 'Mr Nehru did not deny that there had been such movement [of troops]. . . . It is surely unwise, if one has no intention of drawing the sword, to rattle it loudly in the scabbard.'[47] The *New York Herald Tribune* asserted: 'India imperils the peace . . . there is no doubt that India's conduct throughout the entire dispute has been a sore disappointment to its friends in the Western world.'[48]

Pakistan protested to the Security Council on July 17, 1951, against the massing of Indian troops on her borders. To outside observers, it appeared the more sinister that troop movements were not only in Kashmir but on the international boundaries between the two countries. As a result of India's troop movements, Pakistan took a number of precautionary measures, and four battalions of the National Guard were assigned to supplement the Pakistan army. The government of Pakistan also promulgated ordinances making provisions for civil defence and air-raid precaution services. The whole atmosphere in the Indo-Pakistan subcontinent again became tense and surcharged with fear and anxiety. The possibility that a chance incident might plunge the two countries into war—a consummation devoutly wished by the Hindu Mahasabha and other extremist bodies in India—could by no means be overlooked. The border areas were infected with 'eve of war' tensions. Any movement of troops, even if promoted by a genuine and legitimate desire for security, was fraught with danger. Pakistan army officials on the border feared that a crisis might be precipitated within a few days. The danger was that, with two armies facing each other, a minor incident might precipitate events that both governments would be powerless to stop. Communal riots in the two Bengals or trouble between two forces on the Punjab border, where an estimated 200,000 Indian troops faced 70,000 Pakistanis, would be sufficient to set light to the tinder.

The Defence Minister of the government of Pakistan disclosed that, while Indian troops were moving to new positions in the Amritsar area on July 11, the Pakistani forces, in order to avoid a crisis, did not move until July 15. His view was that India contemplated a pincer movement against Lahore with infantry-backed armour striking direct for the town; and the Indian fifth division was reported to be planning to cut the Karachi-Lahore railway. Two Indian destroyers were in the Gulf of Kutch, only 300 miles south of Karachi. A cruiser was stationed at Bombay, and three extra infantry brigades from Calcutta and Assam had been moved to the East Pakistan border. Foreign observers confirmed that Indian troops moved first in the Punjab area and that the movement, especially that of armoured units to the Amritsar area, could well be interpreted as a potentially hostile act.[49] High tension between India and Pakistan had continued from 1947 and, though their bad relations during the previous four years (1947–51) had not led to war, there was no certainty that the catastrophe of an Indo-Pakistan war could always be staved off.

India was indignant because the outside world condemned its troop concentrations. Yet it was an extraordinary freak of history that Nehru, advocate of international peace and morality, should pursue the old-fashioned policy of making troop demonstrations. India justified her military adventures on six grounds. *First*, there had been frontier incidents. But the chief United Nations observer reported that the blame was on both sides. *Second*, Pakistan was alleged to have infiltrated sabotage agents into Indian-held Kashmir. But what was the evidence? Had India caught any agent? None was produced to substantiate the accusation. Did this justify a formidable troop concentration? *Third*, Pakistan was alleged to have begun the troop movements, but impartial and outside observers said that the whole affair was started by the Indians. Pakistan did not make a single troop movement towards India's frontier until India moved her forces to Pakistan's borders. In fact, months before, India had been collecting equipment and stores, establishing bases and making roads in preparation for the moving of her forces to Pakistan's frontiers. *Fourth*, Liaquat was alleged to have refused a 'No-War Declaration'.* But he offered one as part

---

* See below, page 216 *et seq.*

of a general settlement which would include mediation or arbitration on all outstanding disputes, including Kashmir, and this was turned down by India. If Liaquat was guilty of not signing a vague and meaningless 'No-War Declaration', Nehru was guilty of turning down a practical plan for a solution of all disputes and for avoiding war. *Fifth*, it was claimed that Pakistan's Foreign Minister had made an inflammatory speech and threatened war. But the speech in its totality to any impartial interpreter did not threaten India with war or invasion. *Sixth*, it was alleged that there had been agitation for a *Jehad* or holy war against India in Pakistan. The truth was that, though irresponsible leaders and organs of the press in both countries had indulged in loose talk of war, there was in Pakistan no powerful political body or organisation which intended to wage a war against India or annex any part of her territory. In India, however, there was—in addition to the Hindu Mahasabha and the RSSS, which urged war and annexation— a considerable section of opinion which had been agitating since the spring of 1950 for 'police action' in East Pakistan. This movement continued even after the signing of the Liaquat-Nehru Agreement which made a strong plea against provocative talk and agitation. The extremist leaders and press in West Bengal were never tired of suggesting the annexation of East Bengal. In any case, India produced no evidence of any special movement or agitation in Pakistan in July 1951 which might have provoked her to concentrate her armed forces on Pakistan's borders. What had shocked the world was that a step had been taken by India which increased the risk of war; that it was taken without adequate cause, and initiated very soon after the Security Council had exhorted both sides to refrain from measures which would aggravate the quarrel. To rattle the sabre was as irresponsible as to draw the sword.

India's international repute was not enhanced by Pandit Nehru's unworthy accusation that the activities of British military advisers, officers and ex-officers in Pakistan had added greatly to the prevailing tensions. In refuting this charge, the British Prime Minister, Clement Attlee, told the House of Commons on August 1, 1951: 'I regret Mr Nehru should have lent the weight of his authority to such unfounded allegations.'[50] Nehru was also resentful of the British and American press comments on his military moves. India seemed to have the

opinion that, if the Security Council and the outside world were disinterested in Indo-Pakistan quarrels, Pakistan would have no recourse
except to submit to India's supreme force, and 'peace' would prevail in
the subcontinent. Hence, outside 'intervention' appeared to the Indians
the main obstacle to peace. Commenting on this attitude of India, an
editorial in the *Manchester Guardian* bluntly declared: 'In the same
terms, Hitler demanded that Britain and France should disinterest
themselves in Czechoslovakia.'[51] When the United States urged India
and Pakistan to withdraw their troops in order to lessen tensions,
Nehru's reaction was one of anger over 'American intervention'. The
All-India Radio announced on August 2, 1951, that Nehru would not
send even a written reply to the State Department's note advising
withdrawal of forces. India's reply was given 'verbally' to a United
States embassy official in New Delhi.[52] Suggestions were also made that
UN observers should be posted on the frontiers where troops in heavy
concentration were lined up against each other; but no such suggestion
was acceptable to India.[53] The Australian Prime Minister, Robert
Menzies, offered his good offices to ease the tension between India and
Pakistan, but Mr Nehru, as usual, turned down the offer, telling
Menzies that 'there is no need for Australia's good offices at this stage
in relations between India and Pakistan'. 'India', he added, 'had no
aggressive intentions towards Pakistan. It had merely taken certain
precautionary measures.'[54]

In the meantime, the correspondence between the two Prime
Ministers, Liaquat and Nehru, dragged out into a lengthy argument
and finally petered out fruitlessly. In the course of this correspondence,
the Prime Minister of Pakistan repeatedly urged Nehru to withdraw
Indian forces to their normal peacetime stations, in return offering to
rescind the orders for troop movements which he had been obliged to
make after the concentration of Indian forces against Pakistan's borders.
The Prime Minister of India, however, persistently refused to do so. In
fact, the Indian forces moved against Pakistan's borders were further
strengthened.

An outstanding feature of this correspondence was the five-point
peace plan which Liaquat Ali Khan, on July 26, 1951, put forward
for the creation of a peaceful atmosphere and the firm establishment of
friendly relations between India and Pakistan.

For the restoration of a peaceful atmosphere and the establishment of friendly relations between our own two countries on a permanent basis, I make the following proposals:

(i) The troops now concentrated on the borders should immediately be withdrawn back to their normal peacetime stations.

(ii) As soon as this has been done, both India and Pakistan should reaffirm their agreement that 'the question of accession of the state of Jammu and Kashmir to India or Pakistan will be decided through the democratic method of a free and impartial plebiscite held under UN auspices'. To this end both Governments should state their readiness to implement without obstruction or delay the obligations undertaken by them under the UNCIP [United Nations Commission for India and Pakistan] resolutions of 13th August, 1948 and 5th January, 1949, which include the observance of the cease-fire line agreement and withdrawal of their armed forces from the state and to accept the decision of the Security Council in the event of any differences in regard to the interpretation and execution of these agreed resolutions.

(iii) Both Governments should also declare their renunciation of the use of forceful methods in the settlement of any other disputes and to refer such disputes to arbitration or judicial determination if they are not resolved by negotiation or mediation.

(iv) Both Governments should reaffirm the obligation undertaken by them in the Delhi Agreement of April 8th, particularly in clause C (8) that they 'shall not permit propaganda in either country directed against the territorial integrity of the other or purporting to incite war between them and shall take prompt and effective action against any individual or organisation guilty of such propaganda'.

(v) Both Governments should make a declaration that they will on no account attack or invade the territory of the other.[55]

The 'peace plan' of Liaquat ruled out war and aggression by India and Pakistan, not only against each other's territory but also in Kashmir. It provided for a peaceful settlement of the Kashmir dispute under the auspices of the United Nations and of all other disputes by mediation or arbitration—which the constitution of India lays down as a directive principle of state policy in settling international disputes. The plan imposed no obligations on India which Pakistan was not equally prepared to accept. *The Times* commented: 'Mr Liaquat Ali Khan has made a characteristically bold effort to stop the drift towards a collision between India and Pakistan', and added that the peace plan contained 'practical and constructive proposals for a comprehensive settlement between the two countries'.[56]

But Nehru turned down this peace plan. Reaffirming India's 'peaceful intentions' and desire to avoid war with Pakistan, he yet made it clear that India would not withdraw her troops from Pakistan's borders. As to Liaquat's proposal for the withdrawal of troops, there were 'compelling reasons to continue precautions'. He repeated his original case: 'Pakistan had nothing to fear from India, which would never be the first to attack; India did not want war; but "open war preparations" in Pakistan obliged India to maintain precautions against Pakistan.'[57] India, it was to be concluded, could not leave her frontiers unguarded even if Pakistan's troops were withdrawn to their peacetime stations. Liaquat suggested to Nehru that, after the first step of withdrawing forces on both sides had been taken, the two Prime Ministers might discuss any aspect of the peace plan and he invited Nehru to come to Karachi. Nehru termed Liaquat's invitation as 'conditional' and refused to accept it. Liaquat sought a harmonious atmosphere for top-level discussions, and a necessary first step towards this was the withdrawal of troops by both sides. It was futile to expect that the leaders could talk about peace when their armies were menacing each other. He was also willing to withdraw Pakistan's armed forces. Liaquat's offer was sincere and honest; it was not fair to call it 'conditional'.

Nehru's rejection of the five-point peace plan kept alive the explosive situation in the Indo-Pakistan subcontinent, with the armed forces of India and Pakistan ranged against each other on the hot plains of the Punjab and along the hundreds of miles of mountain truce line in Kashmir. Karachi and New Delhi, however, continued to proclaim their intentions not to open fire. *The Times*, commenting on Nehru's profession of peace and rejection of Liaquat's peace plan, wrote editorially:

Nobody doubts that these admirable sentiments are an honest expression of Mr Nehru's conviction. The real difficulty is that whenever he is asked by Pakistan or for that matter by a mediator working for the Security Council to translate them into positive action, his own interpretation of them seems to come in the way. Last year, he invited Mr Liaquat Ali Khan to join him in a declaration that all disputes between India and Pakistan must be settled peacefully. Mr Liaquat Ali Khan was quite willing to do this, but he wanted to give positive meaning to the declaration by embodying in it a plan for the settlement of all outstanding differences by negotiation, reference to judicial bodies and in the last resort by arbitration. Mr Nehru did not agree. Again Mr Nehru was the first to suggest the settlement of the Kashmir question by a plebiscite but, while Mr Liaquat Ali Khan is willing to accept any arrangements for the pebiscite that strike the United Nations as fair, Mr Nehru insists that Indian troops must stay to 'protect' Kashmir while the plebiscite is being held and that Sheikh Abdullah's government must exercise supervisory authority. Lastly, in his letter to Mr Nehru, Mr Liaquat Ali Khan pointed out that the best way of lowering the temperature between India and Pakistan is to withdraw the forces of both sides from the border where the risk of explosion, however unpremeditated, is plain. Mr Nehru has found excellent reasons for keeping Indian troops where they are. Mr Nehru's reply to Mr Liaquat Ali Khan's invitation to Karachi does little or nothing to relieve tensions between India and Pakistan. [58]

Why did India insist on keeping the troops on Pakistan's border, and why did Nehru turn down every constructive suggestion for reducing the tensions? If he had no intentions of attacking Pakistan, why did he show such reluctance in taking reasonable steps to reduce tensions? The reason for massing and maintaining Indian troops on the frontier would seem to be that Nehru wanted to keep Pakistan overawed while the Kashmir 'constituent assembly' played its preordained part of formally voting for accession to India. By emphasising that his government regarded Kashmir as an integral part of India, he perhaps wanted to make clear that, if Pakistan would be provoked to start trouble in Kashmir, India would take it as an act of aggression and would react accordingly on the frontiers of the Punjab. This seemed to be the main reason for Nehru's continuing the confrontation.

Fortunately for the peace of the two countries, the communal situation in the two Bengals during the crisis months of July and August, 1951 was somewhat quieter. A new flare-up in Bengal might have created complications and tensions beyond control. Several Hindu leaders of East Bengal spontaneously issued statements making it clear that they had thrown in their lot with Pakistan and deploring the action of the government of India in threatening her with troop movements. This was a most encouraging indication of the growing integration of the Hindu minority in Pakistan. It was commonly attributed to the fact that, having had a very unhappy experience of an abortive migration in the spring of 1950, the Hindus had decided that refugees got the worst of both worlds and that considerations of self-interest made it advisable for them to stay in Pakistan. According to the authentic information available, the number of Hindus returning to East Bengal during this period actually exceeded the number of those migrating to West Bengal.[59]

By the end of September 1951, the 'eve of war' tensions had slackened; the monsoon in the Punjab seemed to have put an end to the idea of immediate military action. And so, this crisis, like its predecessors, passed away. But the memories of the Indian military adventures in the spring of 1950 and in July-August 1951 had made a great impact on the minds of Pakistanis. The subsequent development in Pakistan's foreign policy was greatly influenced by the unhappy experiences of the 1950s.

In the meantime, while the monsoon in the Punjab brought down the temperature and averted immediate military action, the Indian press became increasingly virulent. The government of Pakistan published in late summer 1951 a White Paper on the crescendo of war hysteria in the Indian press, and gave quotations from newspapers, books and broadcasts on how war was sought to be carried into the 'granary of the Punjab and the jute fields of East Pakistan'.[60] Most of these quotations related to the period after the signing of the Liaquat-Nehru Agreement of April 8, 1950 under which India and Pakistan undertook not to permit propaganda in either country directed against the territorial integrity of the other or seeking to incite war between the two countries. The government of Pakistan initiated twenty-seven complaints of flagrant violation of the Agreement by a number of influential Indian newspapers, but no effective action was taken by the Indian government, the plea being that its scope for action was limited by the Indian constitution. The Pakistan government pointed out that, if this were the position, the government of India should not have undertaken an international obligation which it was not in a position to carry out. The government of India made only eight complaints about alleged violation of the Agreement, and it was claimed in the White Paper that the government of Pakistan took effective and prompt action in all eight cases.

It was pointed out that the government of Pakistan had all along been systematically discouraging any movement directed against the territorial integrity of India. There was, for instance, great dissatisfaction and resentment over the cession of the Muslim majority areas of Gurdaspur district to India under the Radcliffe award of 1947, yet there had never been any public agitation against it in Pakistan. When the Khaksar party leader, Inayatullah Marshraq, included in the objectives of his organisation certain features to which objection could be taken in India, the government of Pakistan took drastic action against the organisation and it ceased to exist. Similarly, the so-called Hindustan Hamara ('India is Ours') party was not allowed to grow beyond a paper organisation.

In contrast to this, a number of influential Indian political organisations adopted as their declared goal the undoing of partition and thus the liquidation of Pakistan. The Hindu Mahasabha, the Rashtriya Swayam Sevak Sangh (RSSS), the Young India, and the people's party of the late Dr Shayamaprasad Mukerjee were actively campaigning for the amalgamation of Pakistan with India. As mentioned earlier (page 189), in the spring of 1950, a 'provisional government of East Bengal' was set up in India. The election manifesto issued by the central parliamentary board of the Hindu Mahasabha in April 1951 stated: 'The indivisibility of India is an article of faith and Mahasabha shall strive its utmost to bring about a reunification of India and Pakistan into a consolidated home to be called *Akhand* (United) *Hindustan*.' The election manifesto of the All-India Forward Bloc, issued on September 8, 1951, outlined the Bloc's objectives as 'the unification of India and Pakistan on the solid foundation of national and cultural unity. This means that the new state will be a Union of socialist republics, a people's state unifying all shades of differences and autonomy in a federal Government.' Prominent Indian socialist leaders, such as Jayaprakash Narayan and Dr R. M. Lohia, also lent support to this policy. Their views, however, were expressed in more subtle ways than those of the Hindu Mahasabha; they used expressions like 'reunion of India and Pakistan' and 'confederation of India and Pakistan'.

The government of Pakistan complained that, in spite of the acceptance of the partition of the subcontinent under the plan of June 3, 1947, the Indian leaders had never really reconciled themselves to the creation of Pakistan, hoping that the new neighbour would be a temporary political phenomenon, soon to be absorbed by India, if necessary by force. Instances are not lacking when Indian leaders, including those belonging to the ruling Congress party, have made no secret of their desire to undo the partition of Indo-Pakistan subcontinent. Pandit Nehru said on July 8, 1951: 'Pakistan continues to be a communal state which by the very nature of her objective and ideology is aggressive in its outlook . . . we cannot ignore the effect of this on millions of people in Pakistan and indirectly in India'.[61] This statement was made fifteen months after his formulating the terms of the 1950 Agreement with Liaquat. Nehru's sister, Mrs Vijaya Lakshmi Pandit, India's Ambassador to the United States, predicted that India and Pakistan would become 'one nation'. 'We agreed to partition,' she said, 'because failure to do so would have perpetuated foreign rule.'[62] The Congress president, Purshottamdas Tandon, stated on December 12, 1950, eight months after the signing of the Liaquat-Nehru Agreement: 'Partition has proved to be a tragedy. It has separated millions of our own brothers from their kith and kin and subjected them to untold miseries.' In another speech, he said: 'I for one had stoutly opposed partition.'[63] Acharaya Kripalani, former president of the Congress, urged that 'the government of India should follow an iron policy to deal with this question [the minority problem in East Pakistan]. This may well lead us into such circumstances *where we may have to resort to military action.*'[64] (Our italics.) The Pakistan Ambassador in the United States had to state: 'The whole course of Indo-Pakistan relations since partition is full of evidence that the Indians have not honestly and sincerely accepted the fact of partition.'[65]

Militant remarks and statements against the creation of Pakistan, its

continued existence, its policies and its founder, *Quaid-i-Azam* Mohammed Ali Jinnah, were not confined to the newspapers, nor were they
routine utterances of political leaders; these ideas were also expressed
in a number of books written by Indian authors. An English-language
publication, entitled *What Shall We Do?*, with an introduction by
Sir C. P. Ramswami stated: 'Let the sons and daughters of *Bharatmata*
[Mother India] note the boundaries of emperor Ashoka which covered
the whole of Afghanistan and Western Pakistan.'[66] The Indian socialist leader, Dr Ram Manohar Lohia, in a book entitled *Agla Kadam*,
wrote: 'We cannot wait for long; perhaps in the next two or three
years the boundary line between Amritsar and Pakistan may vanish.
We have to finish off this poison [of Pakistan] and undo the partition
of the country. I believe that this artificial division will end and India
and Pakistan again become one.'[67]

Many more such hostile remarks about Pakistan could be cited from
the Indian press, from books and from publications of principal
political parties. Reference has already been made in chapter 2 to the
statements made at the time of partition in 1947 by major leaders of
India—including Gandhi, Nehru and Patel—expressing the hope of
'reunion' between India and Pakistan. At that time, however, such
statements, though giving rise to fears and suspicions in Pakistan,
could be regarded as natural, and even understandable, on the lips of
men who throughout their lives had believed in the unity of India.
It was sincerely hoped and expected that, once Pakistan became an
established fact, the Indian leaders would gracefully adjust their
thinking. But unfortunately, during the succeeding years Indian
leaders showed very little change of view in their utterances and
statements regarding Pakistan. They continued to express the hope that
partition would ultimately be undone; in particular, they envisaged
the possibility of 'annexing' East Pakistan. Similarly, paternal patron-
age and encouragement were given by India to the 'Pathanistan', or
'Pakhtoonistan', movement of Afghanistan which sought to detach a
substantial part of West Pakistan. Certainly, there were extreme remarks and statements in the Pakistan press and by Pakistan leaders;
but the most significant aspect of anti-Indian propaganda in Pakistan
was the absence of any movement against the territorial integrity of
India. Pakistan's resentment, as pointed out earlier, was confined to a

H

disputed area: the state of Jammu and Kashmir. When, as a result of India's intransigence, the prospects of a peaceful solution of the Kashmir issue seemed bleak, there were outbursts of anti-Indian feelings in Pakistan; and voices were heard urging a resort to force 'to liberate' the Muslims of Kashmir. But there was never a suggestion to 'annex' or 'occupy' any part of India. Alleged talk of 'holy war' or *Jehad* referred to the disputed territory of Kashmir. But in India, leaders, press and even scholars had no hesitation in expressing the hope of undoing the partition and thus annihilating Pakistan.

Nothing has contributed more to the fear and anxieties of Pakistanis than these militant utterances and the apparent furtherance of irredentist hopes by the Indian government. No one can read these statements without feeling oppressed by their spirit of hatred and animosity towards Pakistan. Such utterances of the Indian leaders, years after a mutually accepted partition, have cast a deep shadow on the minds of Pakistanis, and have contributed greatly to the common stock of fears, suspicions, prejudices and anxieties. They have also hampered the settlement of outstanding disputes between the two countries. 'Pakistan had good reasons for believing that many Indian leaders, despite their acceptance of partition, thought of it as fundamentally evil, the vivisection of their motherland, something to be undone as soon as fate might allow and that they prayed for the failure of Pakistan to open such an opportunity of reunion.'[68] 'It is broadly true to say that in many Indian minds the mere existence of Pakistan gives rise to a feeling of something like resentment.'[69]

It is no wonder that, in view of this Indian attitude, the prime objective of Pakistan's foreign policy has been to obtain a shield against a possible Indian aggression.

NO-WAR DECLARATION

An interesting phenomenon of Indo-Pakistan relations during the 1950s was a proposal for a 'No-War Declaration' between the two countries. This was first mooted in November 1949, when Sir Girja Shankar Bajapai, Secretary General of the Ministry of Foreign Affairs of India, suggested such a declaration to M. Ismail, the then Pakistan High Commissioner in India. The Prime Minister of Pakistan asked the High Commissioner to tell the Indian government that the Pakistan government welcomed the proposal that all outstanding disputes between India and Pakistan should be settled by peaceful means and not by war. He added that this had been Pakistan's stand all along. The Pakistan government was convinced that a just and peaceful settlement of outstanding disputes would remove both the causes and fear of war between the two countries. The main disputes as listed by the Pakistan government were: (i) Jammu and Kashmir; (ii) Junagadh and neighbouring states that had acceded to Pakistan; (iii) Indus waters; (iv) Evacuee property; (v) Assets of Pakistan withheld by India.

Over a period of ten months (January to November 1950, with an interval in March when the two countries were on the brink of war), the Prime Ministers of India and Pakistan discussed the proposed 'No-War Declaration' and the manner in which some of the principal disputes between the countries could be expeditiously settled and the feelings of mutual distrust that afflict the two countries be removed. Twenty letters were exchanged between the two Prime Ministers from January 18 to November 27, 1950. In the end, the letters showed a 'dismal record of failure to agree'.[70] Throughout the correspondence, Liaquat Ali Khan maintained the attitude that, if the two countries were to achieve the substance and not merely chase the shadow, and if a 'No-War Declaration' was to carry any conviction to the peoples of both countries, something more than a mere declaration was required.

The draft of the proposed declaration was sent by India to Pakistan on December 22, 1949, and this was followed by a letter from the Prime Minister of India on January 16. Pandit Nehru said that the whole object of the proposed declaration was to remove or lessen the unfortunate tension that existed between the two countries and to produce an atmosphere which would be favourable to the settlement of major disputes. 'A firm declaration will itself be a great service to our two countries, and the world because it will remove fear of war from the minds of our people.'[71] In his reply, Liaquat readily welcomed the proposal to issue a joint declaration, the primary object of which must be to carry conviction to the peoples of the two countries and of the world as to the sincerity of both governments in renouncing war as a method of settling their disputes. 'To attain this objective,' he rightly pointed out, 'it is essential that there should be tangible action to match the spirit of declaration, since peoples and governments are judged by their action rather than by their words.'[72] Liaquat, therefore, recommended a definite procedure to settle the Indo-Pakistan disputes. He wanted to give positive meaning to the declaration by embodying in it a plan for the settlement of all outstanding differences. His plan was as follows: two months would be allowed for negotiation; the next two months would then be allowed for settlement by mediation of those matters which negotiation had failed to resolve. If any matters remained unresolved at the end of this second period of two months, they should automatically be referred to arbitration by a method agreed in advance. In cases where a matter was to be referred to arbitration, it should be agreed that *all* points of difference, including those relating to procedure, should be referred to arbitration so that it should not be possible for either party to hold up or obstruct a settlement. Both governments should agree to abide by the award of the arbitrator. When Nehru raised objections to the 'rigid' timetable in this plan, Liaquat conceded: 'If you think this is too rigid, we need not lay down a timetable but provide that, if either party comes to the conclusion that no further progress can be made by negotiation or mediation, it may refer the matter to arbitration.'[73] The essential point was the firm provision for resort to arbitration if negotiation and mediation failed to produce results. Liaquat emphasised that there was no danger of the premature submission of any matter to arbitration, for, if either party could obtain a fair deal by negotiation or mediation, it would not go to arbitration where it would have no hand in shaping the decision.

But to Nehru, the idea of any procedure for peaceful settlement, particularly one allowing for arbitration, was abhorrent. He was in favour of a 'short declaration'. 'Differences between our two Governments should be settled peacefully'; but he was unwilling to define the word 'peacefully'. Nor did he hold Liaquat's belief that 'the declaration will lose in value and significance unless it describes the procedure by which disputes will, in actual fact, be resolved peacefully'.[74] Nehru's indignation over arbitration by an impartial third party was expressed as follows: 'To think *ab initio* of a third party . . . will also be a confession of continued dependence on others. That would hardly be becoming for proud and self-respecting independent nations.'[75]

Pakistan's insistence on an agreed procedure for the settlement of disputes, one allowing for arbitration, was influenced by her unhappy experiences with India. 'In all disputes', said Liaquat, 'there is danger that the party which is in possession of and wishes to withhold the rightful dues of the other may so conduct itself as either to prevent a fair settlement or to cause such delay in settlement as to give the same result. Either course produces a sense of injustice, frustration and despair of securing a remedy by peaceful means which is one of the most frequent causes of conflict.'[76] The Kashmir dispute was clearly in Liaquat's mind when he wrote those words. Delay in the settlement of a dispute is often in favour of the unlawful or unjust possessor, seldom in favour of justice. If a 'No-War Declaration' was to be sincere and meaningful, it needed to have provisions to deal with a situation in which one party indulged in procrastinating, as India did over Kashmir. As to India's objection to arbitration on the ground that it would be derogatory to her sovereignty and her 'proud' sense of nationalism, Liaquat reminded Nehru: 'Undoubtedly, all references of disputes to international bodies are to some extent a surrender of national sovereignty. But this is a concept which has now been accepted by all nations and is the foundation of the United Nations Charter. . . . sentiments of national prestige should not, in my view, be allowed to stand in the way of a just and speedy settlement of disputes with one's neighbours; such sentiments have inflicted enormous misery and suffering on mankind.'[77] It is extraordinary that Nehru, the great 'internationalist', needed to be told these basic truths of internationalism.

An analysis of the correspondence between the two Prime Ministers would reveal that both India and Pakistan apparently agreed that all disputes between them should be settled by 'peaceful means'. But this agreement came to an end when a definition was sought for the expression 'peaceful means'. According to the Indian government, a simple declaration that the two countries would not go to war was enough. It was not willing to consider any definite procedure for the settlement of outstanding disputes, and in particular it would not commit itself to arbitration, being averse to arbitration either in any particular case or as a general principle. The Indian government avoided committing itself to arbitration except in platonic terms. It put stress on 'peaceful negotiations' but would not answer as to what would happen if negotiations were deliberately procrastinated by one party.

As the correspondence progressed, charges and counter-charges thickened: all the old familiar features of Indo-Pakistan controversy. Liaquat Ali told Nehru: 'Reviewing our correspondence, it becomes quite clear that the crux of the difficulty is the reluctance of your government to substitute on any issue impartial arbitration for threatened and actual use of force.' Nehru replied: 'I am greatly surprised at your reference to force and must deny categorically any suggestion that, at any time, we have threatened to use force to settle a dispute with Pakistan.'[78] Liaquat responded: 'Your categorical assertion that you have never resorted to or threatened to resort to force to settle disputes with Pakistan has surprised me even more.'[79] He reminded Nehru how Indian forces occupied Junagadh and its neighbouring states which had acceded to Pakistan, and referred to the large-scale concentrations of Indian military forces on the borders of Pakistan in the spring of 1950 when Nehru threatened 'other methods' to deal with Pakistan. The assertion that India did not threaten or resort to force against Pakistan could hardly be acceptable to any neutral observer of Indo-Pakistan relations since 1947.

Thus, the ten-month negotiations on a proposal for a 'No-War Declaration' ended with the usual exchange of sharp words. Six years later, the proposal was renewed. In March 1956, the Pakistan Prime Minister, Choudhury Mohammad Ali, declared in parliament: 'Let both countries sign an agreement that they will not go to war against each other and will settle all their disputes by negotiations and mediation and failing these by arbitration. . . . I make this offer in all sincerity and in all earnestness so that the people of India and Pakistan might live as friendly neighbours.'[80] Nehru welcomed the offer in a letter on March 21, 1956, and this was followed by a fresh exchange of letters between the two countries. India renewed her arguments for a simple and short declaration denouncing war between the two countries, and Pakistan, while welcoming it, wanted to strengthen the declaration with an agreed procedure to settle outstanding disputes. India repeated her objections to arbitration. Pakistan would not have anything to do with a statement which would have no meaning, and insisted on provisions for the peaceful settlements of all disputes. Choudhury reminded Nehru that the principle of settling all international disputes by negotiation, conciliation and arbitration was recognised in the Bandung Communiqué to which India and Pakistan were signatories. The principle was also embodied in the United Nations Charter, and the constitution of India also professed allegiance to this method for the peaceful settlement of international disputes. Nehru, however, would not change his attitude towards arbitration, and pointed out that certain disputes could not be referred to arbitration.

Discussion of a 'No-War Declaration' was revived by General Cariappa, former chief of the Indian army, in a letter to President Ayub on July 17, 1959. Ayub told Cariappa: 'So long as one dispute which embitters relations between our countries remains unresolved, a mere declaration of faith abandoning war as an instrument of settling disputes without ensuring that dispute will in fact be peacefully eliminated carries no conviction.' He emphasised: 'It should not be inferred that simply because we have not agreed to sign the "no-war declaration" we are planning conquest or military adventures against India. Nothing is further from our thoughts. We are determined to settle all our disputes peacefully and are going to persist in our peaceful efforts.'[81]

India has refused to give a positive meaning to the proposal for a 'No-War Declaration', and therefore this could never be accepted by Pakistan. But the Indian leaders seem to have made much use of this proposal to prove their 'peaceful intentions' towards Pakistan. Pakistan's refusal to sign it unless it has proper meaning and significance has been interpreted as a sign of her reluctance to avoid war with India. Yet India's willingness to sign and willingness to avoid war are different things. Her philosopher president, Dr Radhakrishnan, on many occasions stated the virtues of a 'No-War Declaration'; one such occasion was during the war of September 1965, when Indian forces crossed the international boundary of Pakistan and were aiming for Lahore. After employing the entire military strength of his country against Pakistan, Dr Radhakrishnan preached the gospel of a 'No-War Declaration'! As Z. A. Bhutto, Pakistan's Foreign Minister had observed in 1964, when the proposal was again in the air:

History shows that the initiative for proposals for 'no-war pacts' has generally emanated from prospectively aggressor states—states with an aggressive intent such as Nazi Germany. The Ribbentrop-Molotov pact is a classic example of a 'no-war pact'. If India were to embark on aggression against Pakistan and we were to defend ourselves, which is a right permitted under the UN Charter, India would turn round and tell the world in its characteristic histrionic fashion that it was Pakistan that had committed aggression, for 'peace-loving' India had offered a 'no-war pact' and having done that, how could India commit aggression? The purpose of India in making the present offer of a 'no-war pact' is a deceptive one. It is to advance India's interests. Pakistan cannot be an accessory to further self-aggrandisement by India.[82]

7

DIVERGENT FOREIGN POLICIES: I. 1949–59

'Pakistan and India, if they acted together', said Sir Zafrullah Khan, 'would be able to make a very valuable contribution to the maintaining of international peace. But from what might have been a position of positive and constructive beneficence for the human race, they have been pushed into one that threatens the peace and prosperity of the whole of South Asia and in its turn constitutes a grave menace to international security.'[1]

These words of Pakistan's elder statesman very aptly describe the sad impact of Indo-Pakistan disputes on the foreign policies and international relations of the two countries. The feeling of mistrust between them is perhaps nowhere more prominent than in the conduct of their foreign affairs; mutual fear and distrust have conditioned the whole international outlook of the two nations. The main aim of Pakistan's foreign policy has been to obtain a shield against a possible attack from India, while the main aim of India's foreign policy seems to be to isolate and weaken Pakistan. The fact that Pakistan's foreign policy from the outset has been largely dictated by its fear of India is readily conceded by the Pakistan leaders and authors. Thus, in his analysis of the basic factors of Pakistan's foreign policy—after quoting the remark by the French statesman, Robert Schuman, that since 1871 French foreign policy had been continuously dominated by one main preoccupation, that of ensuring her security and independence from her neighbour, Germany—Sarwar Hasan adds: 'Unfortunately, the foreign policy of Pakistan has in a similar manner been dominated by considerations of security and independence from its neighbour, India.'[2]

In the last resort, the foreign policy of a country must be a 'policy of survival'. Pakistan's existence as a sovereign state has been threatened from the very beginning. A part of her territory, comprising Junagadh and the adjoining states which legally became a part of Pakistan, was forcibly occupied by India. Hyderabad, another state with which Pakistan had great cultural and historical links, was annexed by India by means of military conquest. Kashmir, whose overwhelmingly Muslim population was eager to join Pakistan, was also forcibly occupied and annexed by India. Then, in 1950 and 1951, India made huge concentrations of troops on the borders of both East and West Pakistan, and her Prime Minister threatened 'other methods' to deal with Pakistan. These facts were uppermost in the minds of those who framed Pakistan's foreign policy. Explaining the main objectives of his foreign policy, Liaquat Ali Khan said: 'Firstly, the integrity of Pakistan. Having established an independent state after many years of struggle . . . the last thing that the Pakistanis are likely to acquiesce in is that the slightest dent should be made in the territorial integrity of their country.'3

'Dents' in Pakistan's territorial integrity were obviously threatened from one specific quarter. In the light of her experiences in the 1950s Pakistan was worried less by the contemporary fear of international communism than by the designs of her fellow member of the Commonwealth. 'Pakistan believes', wrote I. H. Qureshi, the distinguished Pakistani scholar, 'that Indian hostility poses a far greater problem to them than Chinese expansion or Soviet threats, neither country having a dispute with Pakistan. Besides, Pakistan is too small to worry them.'4 When Pakistan sought Western arms in 1953, her Prime Minister, Mohammad Ali (Bogra), declared: 'Mr Nehru asserts that there is no danger of aggression to Pakistan. This is a matter wherein, I think, he must leave the judgement to Pakistan.'5 In 1957, the then Prime Minister, H. S. Suhrawardy, in explaining to parliament the objectives and basis of Pakistan's foreign policy stated the grounds of Pakistan's distrust and fear of her big neighbour:

India denied Pakistan her share of arms and ammunitions after partition with the result that partition found us weak and feeble and unable to defend our borders, our independence and our territorial integrity. We took India at its word that it had no desire to undo partition, although we were fully aware that there were several important parties and personages in India who had made it very plain that they will unite Pakistan and India and undo partition. We were, therefore, alarmed when in spite of the temporary settlement which led to the cessation of hostilities in Kashmir in the beginning of 1949, India, for some reason, which it considered to be justifiable, massed her troops on the borders of Pakistan in March 1950, poised for attack. At that time, Pakistan was practically defenceless and it was necessary for our Prime Minister to go to India and arrive at a settlement to stave off this impending invasion. But again in July 1951 India considered it necessary to resolve certain disputes to mass its troops on our borders. Again, we were caught unprepared because we could not conceive that a government which had solemnly pledged to recognise Pakistan should make an attempt to overawe us and to invade us.[6]

Suhrawardy added that Pakistan's foreign policy was dictated by the instinct of self-preservation in view of threats from India. In fact, the threats were referred to again and again by the various political groups and leaders of Pakistan. Here there has hardly been any difference of opinion. There were many changes of government in Pakistan, but none of these governments failed to respond to the fears of India that have always dominated national thinking in Pakistan.

Soon after the emergence of the new regime in Pakistan in October 1958, President Ayub told his country's 'friends' in the United States:

I would beg our friends that when commenting on our problems, they should at least understand our position clearly. Because of India's aggressive intentions and a massive military build-up, we are forced to maintain forces that, whilst catering for external defence, can at least act as a deterrent. True, it is causing us a lot of expense, but what else can we do? We are victims of circumstances. We have repeatedly offered to settle our differences with India on honourable terms and have extended our hand of friendship, but we regret that there has not been any appropriate response. Is it realized that 80 per cent of Indian forces are sitting almost on our border and could move to forward concentration areas which are fully stocked and launch a major offensive against us at ten days notice?[7]

The Foreign Minister, Z. A. Bhutto, told the Pakistan National Assembly: 'The main driving force behind a nation's foreign policy is its urge to maintain its independence and territorial integrity. Pakistan situated as it is, surrounded by hostile neighbours, must seek arrangements guaranteeing its territorial integrity and permitting it to preserve its distinct ideological personality.'[8] Dealing with Indo-Pakistan relations and their impact on foreign policy, Bhutto said that there was almost a military confrontation between India and Pakistan which aggravated the poverty of their respective peoples and cost the United States and other countries, giving military aid to the two countries, billions which could be utilised for better purposes.

It would, however, be an oversimplification to say that there is no other consideration in Pakistan's foreign policy than the fear of Indian aggression. There are, of course, genuine desires to promote friendly relations with new nations of Asia and Africa, and more particularly with the Muslim countries. Similarly Pakistan has constantly and vigorously supported the causes of people under colonial rule. Like many other new nations of Asia and Africa, Pakistan feels a deep sense of sympathy towards the aspirations of the people under colonial rule. Then there is the desire and dire need for economic development of Pakistan. At the time of partition, Pakistan was a poor and under-developed country; it produced raw materials but had very little industry and not much control over her commerce. She urgently needed the good will and co-operation of the advanced countries in her efforts to build up economic foundations, and this constituted one of the major objectives of her foreign policy.

But the *raison d'être* of Pakistan's foreign policy has been her anxiety to maintain the territorial integrity of the country which has been repeatedly threatened by her bigger and more powerful neighbour. 'The fear of India', says Qureshi, 'has always dominated Pakistan's foreign policy. The problem of Pakistan defence in the eyes of Pakistanis is mostly the problem of defence against India. . . . the immediate and continuing danger seems to come from India . . . [and] the history of Indo-Pakistan relations shows that India has made every effort to make it difficult for Pakistan to exist.'[9]

India, however, maintains that her policy towards Pakistan has been 'no different from its policy towards all other nations: a policy of mutual friendship and accommodation'.[10] It is claimed that India's attitude towards Pakistan is dictated by a general foreign policy which is based on *Panch Shila*, the Five Principles of Peaceful Coexistence. These are: (i) mutual respect for each other's territorial integrity and sovereignty: (ii) non-aggression; (iii) non-interference in each other's internal affairs; (iv) equality and mutual benefit; and (v) peaceful co-existence. It is significant that the Five Principles do not include the right of self-determination—the right which Pakistan claims for the people of Kashmir—or any provision for the peaceful settlement of disputes, to which again Pakistan attaches great importance. Significantly, the *Panch Shila* also exclude provision for any collective self-defence. It may be added here that Pakistan's adhesion to collective self-defence arrangements, such as CENTO and SEATO, were constantly and vigorously opposed by India. India also cites her offer of a 'No-War Declaration' as an example of her policy of peaceful coexistence with Pakistan. We have shown in the preceding chapter that Pakistan was most willing to agree to a 'No-War Declaration', and sought to give a positive meaning to it by providing in it a procedure for the peaceful settlement of all outstanding disputes. India would have nothing to do with any such positive meaning of a 'No-War Declaration'; she would keep alive the major disputes, such as Kashmir, and would engage in military adventures on the borders of Pakistan. Then she would offer a vague and meaningless 'No-War Declaration', advancing it as a demonstration of her peaceful intentions towards Pakistan.

Speaking in the Indian parliament, Nehru claimed that, ever since independence, it had been India's policy to have friendly relations with Pakistan—'not, of course, giving up our vital interests'.[11] Perhaps Nehru's 'vital interests' included his continued occupation of Kashmir by Indian troops; his paternal encouragement to the 'Pakhtoonistan' movement; 'special care' for Hindus in East Pakistan; and his constant vigil against any increase of Pakistan's military strength. India also refutes the allegation that the main aim of her foreign policy is to weaken and isolate Pakistan and eventually to undo partition. 'Anything more unrealistic and devoid of fact I cannot imagine', Nehru replied to Pakistan's allegation. Nevertheless, India's assertion that her relations with Pakistan are based on the Five Principles of Peaceful Co-existence is not only challenged by Pakistanis but also by many impartial observers and foreign scholars. No amount of Pandit Nehru's idealist oratory about *Panch Shila*, 'a third area of peace' in Asia or the 'Bandung Principles' could obscure India's unfriendly, if not hostile, policies and actions towards Pakistan. Even Nehru's policy of non-alignment was being perverted into anti-Pakistan attitudes. Analysing India's foreign policy, Geoffrey Hudson, Fellow of St Antony's College Oxford, writes:

> Antipathy to Pakistan is the pivot of Indian foreign policy. . . . India would be genuinely neutral in the cold war as long as Pakistan was also unattached, but any alignment of Pakistan with either bloc was likely to push India in the opposite direction. Had Pakistan turned towards Russia—as a faction in Karachi advocated—India would have moved to the side of the West. But, as it was Pakistan which became a recipient of American military aid and signatory of the Manila Treaty, India became responsive to approaches from Moscow.[12]

Keith Callard states: 'Many Indians feel that the creation of Pakistan was a tragic mistake which might still be corrected, at least as far as East Bengal is concerned.'[13] 'India has continued to treat the basic motive force behind Pakistan as heretical and an affront to reason and sanity.'[14] Callard further points out that in many matters Pakistan has seen herself playing the role of victim; India was doing everything possible to make life difficult for Pakistan.[15] Michael Brecher, in his sympathetic interpretation of India's foreign policy, admits: 'It is inevitable that Indian foreign policy should be influenced by the struggle for Kashmir.' India's objection at the United Nations to the proposal to send UN observers to Hungary and for a UN-controlled election in Hungary was 'because of the precedent it would have created for Kashmir'. Dealing with Indo-British and Indo-American relations Brecher says: 'Since 1948 Indo-British relations have been strained as a result of London's support for the Pakistani view of Kashmir . . . [while] the outstanding example of Kashmir's impact on Indian foreign policy is to be found in the realm of Indo-US relations. Nothing has done more harm to friendship between them than American arms aid to Pakistan.'[16]

When the Security Council in 1957 passed a resolution, with ten votes in its favour and only one abstention (the USSR), disapproving India's plan to integrate Kashmir, India threatened to quit the Commonwealth. Nehru stated in the Indian parliament on March 25, 1957 that, for the first time in several years, he had recently felt that the question of India's membership of the Commonwealth might require further consideration. This was due to the 'painful shocks' India had experienced recently over Kashmir.[17] Similarly, in 1965, when the British Prime Minister, Harold Wilson, criticised India for sending troops across the international boundary of Pakistan and invading Lahore, there was an upsurge of anti-British feeling in India. Any country which has shown sympathetic understanding of Pakistan's problems and difficulties has been the target of attack by India. *The Times* in 1956 spoke in an editorial of 'India's two faces'.

> There are two views of Indian foreign policy. Stripped of its aspirations and noble sentiments for Asia and the world at large, the realist might argue, Indian foreign policy amounts to little more than the containment of Pakistan. In this task, India has precise aims and they are vigorously pursued; positions are tenaciously held—as in Kashmir—and at all times policy has had the backing of force and has been quick to recognize and react to the force that might be used against it. . . . India's attitude to Pakistan is still determined by the circumstances and the lasting emotion of the partition of 1947. To many Indians this was a dismemberment, which they still look back on as a tragedy.[18]

Similar views were expressed elsewhere. The *Observer* wrote in an editorial of November 4, 1962: 'Indian people often seem to have had a double standard—indignantly anti-imperialist abroad but quite ready to apply a little imperialism within their own historic frontier.' C. L. Sulzberger, the well-known columnist on international affairs, says that 'Nehru's foreign policy is peace at almost any price—except perhaps where Pakistan is concerned'.[19] Dr Wayne Wilcox points out the fact that 'Pakistan's history was played out in the shadow of India's hostility and, together with the struggle for survival, Pakistan's external policy was directed at asserting its international personality and escaping isolation by India.'[20] Turning to India's foreign policy, he says: 'The Indian government continued to believe that it was in the interests of the country to organize a foreign policy in such a way as to neutralize or isolate Pakistan. . . . the dichotomy of Indian foreign policy was thus compounded. To the world and on world issues, India was the dove of peace, whereas within the region she stood accused of power politics.'[21]

The fact is, as Wilcox rightly points out, that India considers Pakistan a hostile state and Pakistan considers India 'a proven aggressor'. The foreign policies of the two countries have, therefore, been directed by mutual hostility and acrimony. It is not suggested, indeed, that Indian foreign policy has no other objectives. The establishment of India as a great power; solicitations of foreign aid; the retention of some degree of control over the foreign relations of its neighbour Nepal; leadership in Asia; the fight against colonialism—these are some of the other discernible objectives of India's foreign policy.[22] But antipathy to Pakistan seems to overshadow these other objectives. Apart from the disputes over Kashmir, India's hostile attitude towards Pakistan is also fostered by the latter's continued opposition to any scheme of India's hegemony in South Asia. 'Indian leaders', said President Ayub, 'somehow feel that every country from Afghanistan down to Indonesia, where there is a semblance of Indian culture, forms a part of Indian heritage and so it must form a part of Indian political empire.'[23] Pakistan reacts, almost violently, to any suggestion of Indian 'leadership' in South Asia. This is natural in view of her experiences with India since independence. It is perhaps too much to expect that Pakistan would acquiesce in any scheme of Indian hegemony in the presence of so much mutual distrust. After all, 'India and Pakistan have been involved in a stage of undeclared war, with varying degrees of intensity, throughout their brief history as independent members of the family of nations.'[24] But, while the Pakistani leaders have frankly stated that the aim of their policy has been to obtain a shield from Indian threats to their country's independence, thereby frankly acknowledging their feelings of distrust and fear against India, the Indian leaders and publicists, on the other hand, have tried to conceal their real feelings towards Pakistan under the preaching of *Panch Shila*, 'non-alignment', 'Bandung spirit' and so forth. They would never concede that India's relations with Pakistan constitute a breach of these high-sounding principles. Pakistan, being aggrieved, has to make more noise, and the result is that Pakistan sometimes appears to be more intolerant. In a dispute, the aggrieved party has to express its views sometimes more bluntly and boldly; the party in power can more easily maintain an outward appearance of being pleasant and benevolent. But to any fair-minded and impartial observer of India's foreign policy, her real designs and intentions towards Pakistan become sufficiently clear as is borne out by the remarks and observations quoted in the preceding pages. Whatever might be the outward semblance, 'a cardinal under-lying purpose of Indian policy was to keep her smaller neighbour weak and isolated, for eventual reabsorption'.[25]

In the early days of her existence, Pakistan's internal conditions were most serious. Millions of Muslims, uprooted from India, were pouring in at an alarming rate. Similarly the non-Muslims in West Pakistan were leaving the country. The central government in Pakistan had to start from scratch. There was no money in the national exchequer; as pointed out in chapter 2, Pakistan's share of the cash balance of British India was withheld, and her due share of other assets under the partition agreements was not given. Commerce and trade were paralysed. There were gloomy forecasts about the collapse of Pakistan. But Jinnah roused the confidence of the people, proving himself indeed to be the 'father of the nation'. He proclaimed firmly: 'Pakistan has come to stay.' This became the creed of all Pakistanis. It is this fact which needs to be appreciated for an evaluation of Pakistan's foreign policy. The first duty of a government under such circumstances was to organise itself and seek security. It had also to protect itself from the 'strangulation process' of the Indian government. Pakistan then hardly had any time to think seriously of her role in international affairs. However, Jinnah, as the first Governor-General, made a policy statement on external relations. In a broadcast to the people of the United States in February 1948, he declared that Pakistan's foreign policy was 'one of friendliness and good will towards all the nations of the world'.[26]

The first phase of Pakistan's external relations was devoted to affirming the credentials of Pakistan statehood. There were formidable handicaps to this. The new state was regarded in many quarters, thanks to 'massive Indian propaganda', as 'a monstrosity and a transient pheno-menon'.[27] Pakistan laboured under an additional disadvantage in that 'the world tended to identify the new India . . . with the entire subcontinent'.[28] Yet gradually these handicaps were overcome. The debates and deliberations in the Security Council on the various aspects of Indo-Pakistan relations in the early part of 1948, and the near-war tension between the two countries, focused the attention of the world on the subcontinent. Pakistan's case was most ably represented in the world forum by Sir Muhammad Zafrullah Khan, who made a deep impression in the Security Council. To many delegates of the United Nations, the depth of the Indo-Pakistan quarrel and the lack of understanding between the two Dominions aroused great dismay. Pakistan's struggle to establish credentials was won in those first agonising years of her existence, 1947 and 1948. But her diplomatic isolation was not over. She turned to the Commonwealth for help and advice in the tragic circumstances which were created as a result of communal murder and mass migration. India, however, resented any 'outside interference', and the Commonwealth countries could not be of much assistance and help to Pakistan in her early critical days.

Similarly, Pakistan's attempt to foster brotherly relations with the Muslim countries of the Middle East was vigorously challenged by India. From the beginning, Pakistan's foreign policy reflected a strong desire for closer friendly relations with Muslim countries. She constantly championed the causes of Arabs and Muslim countries both inside and outside the United Nations. India did not view this move with equanimity. The word 'partition' became poison to the Arabs after the partition of Palestine and the creation of Israel in 1948. India took full advantage of the prevailing feelings over 'partition' in the Arab world. The notion was vigorously propagated that the 'British, out of vicious parting spite and in accordance with the old policy of "divide and rule", sought to lacerate the Arab world, in a manner similar to what they had done in India'.[29] This propaganda was quite successful in creating in some Arab countries resentment against the division of the Indo-Pakistan subcontinent and consequently against Pakistan. India made constant efforts to brand Pakistan as a stooge of imperialism. Nevertheless, Pakistan was successful in making firm and friendly relations with such Muslim countries as Turkey, Iran, Jordan and Saudi Arabia.

During the first phase of her foreign relations, in the years 1947-52 when she tried to maintain non-involvement in the East-West cold war, Pakistan felt isolated and friendless. This increased her sense of insecurity, and she felt the need of the support of some bigger power. The link with the Commonwealth and friendly relations with the Muslim countries could not solve the problem of security, and they failed to give Pakistan the freedom from fear which is needed for a country's progress and stability. This led to the abandonment of the policy of non-alignment, and in 1953 there opened the second phase of Pakistan's foreign policy. 'India and Pakistan as factors in each other's foreign policy and relations' became more prominent, and the shadow of the East-West cold war was cast over the disputes of the two countries. The quest for security, the search for friends and allies, and the anxiety to maintain territorial integrity, led Pakistan to pursue a policy of alliance with the West, particularly with the United States. In the early part of 1954, Pakistan accepted new international commitments which dramatically redefined her position in world affairs. First of all, there was the military, economic and cultural alliance with Turkey. The Turco-Pakistan Pact was followed in May 1954 by the United States-Pakistan Mutual Security Programme Agreement. According to this agreement, 'the Government of the United States will make available to the Government of Pakistan such equipment, material, services and other assistance as the Government of the United States may authorise in accordance with such terms and conditions as may be agreed'. Military assistance to Pakistan was given under the American Mutual Defense Acts of 1949 and 1951. The next steps in the alliance with the West were her joining SEATO on September 7, 1954 and the Bagdad Pact (now CENTO) on September 23, 1955.

The United States informed the government of India on November 17, 1953 that it was considering a military agreement with Pakistan. India was thus informed six months before the actual agreement took place. Full advantage was taken by India of this advance information. An all-out campaign against the proposed agreement and Pakistan was started. The Pakistan government was at a considerable disadvantage during these six months in replying to India's vilifications, since it was not yet sure of Washington's final decision. There was the real possibility that the agreement would not materialise, or would at least be postponed, due to India's opposition. Anti-Pakistan feelings were expressed vituperatively all over India. The Indian Prime Minister initiated the campaign against the proposed agreement, which was 'a bitter pill for Mr Nehru to swallow'.[30] When unconfirmed news had appeared towards the end of 1952 of a possible military alliance in the Middle East with Pakistan as one of its members, India raised vigorous objections. Nehru said that the proposed defence pact was a matter of 'grave concern' to India. 'We have been following this with close attention and we shall naturally have to adapt ourselves to the changing conditions and developments.'[31] Even when there was no confirmed news of any negotiations between the United States and Pakistan, India raised a hue and cry. Then, when the Indian government was told of the proposed agreement, the campaign assumed its full dimensions, and Nehru told the Pakistan Prime Minister, Mohammad Ali (Bogra), 'An expansion of Pakistan's war resources with the help of the United States of America can only be looked upon as an unfriendly act in India and one that is fraught with danger.'[32] Obviously, Pandit Nehru was anxious to maintain the disparity between the military strengths of the two countries, which he had aggravated by depriving Pakistan of her share of military assets at the time of partition. It was this disparity which had enabled him to overawe Pakistan in 1950 and 1951 by concentrating Indian troops on her frontiers. It is interesting to note that Nehru during this campaign said that Indians would be 'hypocrites and unprincipled opportunists' if they accepted military aid from the United States;[33] but in 1962–63 he sought, and got, massive military aid from Western countries, particularly from the United States. Nehru, however, is not the only political leader who has had to swallow his own words.

According to Nehru, any addition to Pakistan's military strength as a result of her pact with the United States would disturb the 'area of peace' in Asia, bring the East-West cold war to the subcontinent and upset the balance between India and Pakistan. These three objections merit close examination.

1. The pact would disturb the 'area of peace' in Asia which India was sponsoring. What did this 'area of peace' in Asia mean? It meant, perhaps, that India was aspiring to a 'sphere of influence' in Asia and regarded Pakistan as the main obstacle to this. As stated earlier, Pakistan would never entertain any idea of India's leadership in Asia;

this is based on age-old Hindu-Muslim antagonism, suspicions and fears, and also on her post-independence experience with India. A strong and stable Pakistan would never agree to India's hegemony in Asia. It seemed, therefore, imperative to Indian diplomacy to weaken and isolate Pakistan and to oppose any move to strengthen her. India seems to be unable to accept that any country in South Asia should have a foreign policy which is not approved or influenced by Delhi. Nehru, in expressing his objections to Pakistan's new phase of external relations, wrote to the Prime Minister of Pakistan: 'In view of the developments that appear to be taking place, Pakistan's foreign and defence policy will become diametrically opposed to the policies we have so consistently and earnestly pursued.'[34] Nehru obviously wanted that Pakistan's foreign policy should not be 'diametrically opposed' to that of India. But the truth is that, since their independence in 1947, both India and Pakistan have pursued 'diametrically opposed' external relations, due to their unhappy and unfortunate quarrels, particularly over Kashmir. India, however, always resented any independent action on the part of Pakistan. When Pakistan, for instance, refused to devalue her currency following India's devaluation, a trade war, as we have already discussed, was started against her. The attitude was similar when Pakistan wanted to give up non-alignment while India still continued to pursue it. In Ian Stephens's analysis, India seemed to be telling Pakistan that 'she must not devise a foreign policy of her own; her destiny was to be an Indian satellite. This inference seems strengthened by reflecting on India's own contrary eagerness in taking American (and British) military aid, when herself under dangerous pressure from a big neighbouring power, China, nine years later.'[35] When it suited India's interests, she could make friends with China, and *Hindi-Chini Bhai-Bhai* flourished; but when the Sino-Indian quarrel blew up and Pakistan tried to avoid a similar dispute by demarcating her frontier with China, this was regarded in Delhi as 'provocative' and 'unfriendly'.

The implication that Pakistan, at best, should have a satellite status arouses the ire of Pakistanis; they find such a patronising, bossing attitude intolerable. 'India is progressively gaining ground as a coming Eastern power. As such, she has a big responsibility in taking active measures to remind her Asian neighbours of the need to provide jointly for the defence of this region for their mutual security.'[36] These words of General Cariappa, the former commander-in-chief of the Indian army, illustrate India's designs for leadership in South Asia. Nehru also gave expression to such aspirations: 'India is the only stable and progressive nation in the whole of Asia, [and] as such is the natural leader of Asian countries.'[37] Similar views were expressed by Indian writers. K. M. Panikkar, in *India and the Indian Ocean* (1945), had advocated a theory of Indian leadership before India became independent and after independence similar views appeared in a book entitled *Defence and Security in the Indian Ocean Area*, written in 1958 by a study group of the Indian Council of World Affairs. Here it was stated: 'India may one day find herself morally bound to act as the protector of small powers of this region.'[38] The region was defined to include countries like Burma, Ceylon, Nepal and Pakistan. Pakistan's sense of national prestige and honour make it impossible for her to be a party to such schemes of Indian hegemony in Asia. Her wish to assert an independent status in external relations is regarded in Delhi as a threat to India's leadership. This is the background of their 'diametrically opposed' foreign policies and external relations.

2. The proposed United States–Pakistan pact would bring the East-West cold war to the doors of India. The cold war was already at India's doorstep: in Tibet, in China; yet Nehru said that, with the pact, 'the cold war comes to India's borders'.[39] 'It is a step not only towards war, even world war, but one that will bring war right up to our doors.'[40] Nehru's Congress party described the United States–Pakistan pact as 'full of most dangerous possibilities'. American military aid to Pakistan was compared by Indians with 'American help to Kuomintang troops in Burma, the occupation of Formosa and crossing the 38th parallel in Korea'; and US policy in Asia was called the 'greatest danger for India'.[41]

3. The pact would upset the balance between India and Pakistan. This was the real ground for India's opposition to it. Such an alteration of the balance, Nehru declared, was 'dangerous to India's security'.[42] This argument merits close attention, for the whole campaign against the agreement mainly centred round it.

There had never been any parity between the military strengths of India and Pakistan. As we have pointed out, Pakistan had very little share of the undivided India's military assets and stores. Then, all the ordnance factories of undivided India fell into the hands of the new India. These factories had been expanded and were working to the fullest capacity to increase India's war potential. The relative weakness of Pakistan was too obvious. Sir Dashwood Strettle described the situation: 'Pakistan is entirely dependent on India for ordnance store, ammunition, guns, etc. She has no factories for guns, ammunition, etc. and has no surplus store to replace or maintain herself, which renders her tanks and aeroplanes pretty unserviceable. In the division, [India] has got more than twice the strength of Pakistan in troops, navy and air force.'[43] Yet the fact remained that 'Indians just don't want Pakistan, of all countries, to increase her armed strength'.[44] Any increase of Pakistan's military strength would make India unable to achieve her objectives by use or show of force as she had been accustomed to since 1947. This was the main reason for the furious indignation that swept all over India in 1954 at the news of Pakistan's military assistance from America. The Indian correspondent of the *Round Table* put the case bluntly: 'As long as Pakistan is the enemy, any strengthening of the enemy is to be resisted violently. This is after all a reasonable attitude, as the West confirms in its policies on trade with the communist bloc in strategic goods. . . . It is of no avail to point out that India is already much more powerful militarily than Pakistan; that she is spending twice as much on arms as her neighbour.'[45] The same journal's correspondent from Pakistan, writing on Nehru's opposition to Pakistan's receiving arms aid, stated: 'The answer lies either in the fact that he does not wish to see Pakistan strong because he ultimately wishes to see Pakistan disappear altogether or that he fears that his policy of postponing as long as possible, perhaps for ever, a decision in Kashmir will be endangered if Pakistan is in a position to argue from strength.'[46] Nobody could read the India's arguments against arms aid to Pakistan in 1954 and Pakistan's arguments against arms aid to India in 1962 without concluding that both countries look upon one another as enemies, and any increase of military strength of one would be viewed by the other as a threat to its security.

It is interesting to note in this context that, for all the dust raised in India over the American arms aid to Pakistan, the first United States military advisory mission to function in the subcontinent was not in

Karachi but in New Delhi. This news was withheld from most Indians by military secrecy, otherwise India's furore over Pakistan's arms from the same country would have sounded ridiculous. Military secrecy concealed the arrival of six United States Air Force officers and enlisted men who were to instruct Indian crews in New Delhi for six months; similarly, the arrival there of the first pair among twenty-six C119 Flying Boxcars, sent through the good offices of the Pentagon, was classified as 'secret' by the Indian air force. India was understood to be negotiating the purchase of about twenty more C119 Flying Boxcars from the United States, who also provided at least thirty Sherman tanks and undisclosed numbers of the latest type of multi-place military helicopters. India had been licensed by the United States to use certain exclusive American processes in the manufacture of military equipment in India. All these weapons of war were acquired through a section of the United States Mutual Defense Act which authorised 'friendly nations' to use American military procurement facilities to obtain arms on a cash basis.[47]

No doubt, India 'purchased', while Pakistan got 'aid'. But what enabled India to buy? Amid all the opposition to the American arms aid to Pakistan, Nehru quite readily accepted United States economic aid. His Finance Minister announced foreign aid of about $90 million for 1954–55, most of which came from the United States. Referring to Nehru's statement that American arms aid to Pakistan would lead to 'colonial subjugation' of the Asian countries, the Pakistan Prime Minister pointed out: 'It is strange that Mr Nehru, whose government received hundreds of million dollars as American aid by way of grants and loan, should prefer such a charge. That this aid is economic and not merely military is purely a matter of form and does not affect the issue. But for this aid, I doubt whether it would have been possible for India to set apart as much as 200 crores [2,000 million] of rupees a year for expenditure on her armed forces.'[48] India was receiving huge and massive economic aid from the United States and other countries which enabled her to buy military equipments from her own resources. Both forms of aid, economic and military, effect savings in foreign exchange which then becomes available for purchases abroad, either of machinery and capital goods or of military equipment.

Pandit Nehru seemed to be resentful of anything in South Asia of which he was not the initiator. His feelings in this matter became a marked feature of India's foreign policy. It seemed to the Indian government that, if its policy or advice was not heeded in any matter relating to South Asia and more particularly if any concession was made to its rival, Pakistan, it must be due to 'imperialist wickedness'. If India's national interests were served by such dubious methods as denying the right of self-determination to Kashmir, there was no threat to 'peace' or 'solidarity' in Asia; but if Pakistan's legitimate fears or grievances were taken into account, it was to bring 'cold war', 'revival of colonialism', the 'imperialists' old game of 'divide and rule'. In similar ways, the legitimate hopes and aspirations of the Muslim minority in undivided India had been threatened; whenever Muslims' grievances were considered, the British government was accused of following the policy of 'divide and rule'. Unless this attitude and its behaviour patterns are changed, there is no hope of peace or stability in South Asia.

When, notwithstanding India's vehement opposition, the United States finally decided to give arms to Pakistan, anti-American feelings on an unprecedented scale began to be expressed all over India. President Eisenhower's special assurances as to the uses of arms in Pakistan could not mollify Indian wrath, and Americanophobia in India reached its peak. 'India now is more anti-American than at any time within memory', reported the *Christian Science Monitor* on April 28, 1954; while the *New York Times* observed on March 7, 1954: 'The recurring friction between India and the United States reached an unprecedented tempo with President Eisenhower's announcement of American military aid to Pakistan. This move followed months of protests by India against the arming of her nearest neighbour and principal adversary in international quarrels.'

Relations between India and America sank to their lowest depths when Nehru, with great indignation and with applause from his people, declared on March 1, 1954: 'American military observers attached to the United Nations on either side of the cease-fire line in Kashmir can no longer be treated as neutrals by us and hence their presence appears improper.'[49] To this Dag Hammarskjold, the United Nations Secretary General, replied that observers attached to cease-fire groups, as in Kashmir, owed their allegiance to the United Nations; 'from any point of view the question of nationality does not arise',[50] he added. The Soviet Union, however, gave quick support to Nehru's demand for withdrawal of the American members of the UN observers team in Kashmir. *Pravda* wrote on March 23 that the chief aim of the American observers in Kashmir was 'to meddle in Kashmir affairs and propagate the idea of independent Kashmir, which they hoped to exploit as a military base of the United States'.[51] An 'exposure' of the United States 'conspiracy' in Kashmir, allegedly involving many officials of the US embassy in India, was made in a book entitled *Conspiracy in Kashmir* written by two members of the so-called 'Kashmir Constituent Assembly'. When Sheikh Abdullah was dismissed from his 'prime ministership' in Indian-held Kashmir and was sent to jail, there was talk of a conspiracy between Abdullah and the Americans. It was alleged that the United States aimed at the independence of Kashmir and strategic air bases.[52] India also raised objections to the appointment of Admiral Nimitz as plebiscite administrator in Kashmir—which both parties had approved earlier.

More important than this was India's refusal to consider any proposals to hold a plebiscite in Kashmir in view of the 'changed circumstances', as if India's obligations to the United Nations and to the people of Kashmir were dependent on Pakistan's following a subservient policy to New Delhi; we have already discussed this in chapter 3.

The most significant effect of the new phase in Pakistan's foreign policy was the Soviet-India friendship and the direct involvement of the Indo-Pakistan dispute over Kashmir in the East-West cold war. 'The Soviet government appears to have perceived more clearly than the British or American have ever done that antipathy to Pakistan is the pivot of Indian foreign policy.'[53] The Soviet Union began actively to woo the Indian government. The essence of her policy was to take advantage of anti-Western feelings in India as a result of American arms aid to Pakistan. Moscow's interest in India was regarded as a reply to America's interest in Pakistan. Malenkov made a statement on March 13, 1954, in which he complimented Nehru on his Asian policy: 'A great contribution to the cause of strengthening peace has been made by the great nation of India. We welcome the vigilance displayed by the Indian leaders in connection with attempts of forces of aggression in Asia.'[54] The Indian Ambassador to Moscow was assured of Soviet support for India. [55] Marshal Zhukov visited India with a 'message of sincere love and friendship from the Soviet peoples'. *Pravda* wrote on June 13, 1954 about 'India's contribution to the cause of peace'. 'The Indian government', the paper continued, 'has chosen as the basis for its foreign policy the principle of the peaceful coexistence of countries, it has condemned aggressive blocs. India has advocated and continues to advocate the use of peaceful methods.' *Pravda*, if it had cared for the truth, should have added that India only 'advocates' but does not practise 'peaceful methods' in her dealings with smaller neighbours.

This sudden upsurge of Soviet-Indian friendship in 1954-55 illustrates the fact that Pakistan is the most important and dominating factor in India's external relations, just as India is the main problem for Pakistan's external relations. If any observer is surprised to see the new Pakistan-China friendship since 1962, the Soviet-India friendship in 1954-55 should provide a clue to its understanding.

The Soviet government's wooing of Nehru continued, accompanied by offers of technical assistance. The Soviet Union provided technical help in building a steel plant and in developing diamond mines, and India also received Russian farm tractors. At the same time, Ajoy Ghosh, the General Secretary of the Indian Communist party, went to Moscow and came back duly instructed. The Indian Communists gave approval to Nehru's foreign policy. In early 1955, when elections were taking place in the Indian state of Andhra, the Congress party candidates electioneering against the Communists were able to distribute a pamphlet quoting from a *Pravda* editorial which expressed admiration for the domestic as well as the foreign policy of the Nehru Government. [56]

By this time, Pakistan had become the target of attack in the Soviet press and propaganda machinery. The creation of Pakistan was described as the result of the use of Islam by 'the American-British imperialists for the purpose of fighting the revolutionary and national liberation movement'. [57] *Izvestia* wrote on October 20, 1954: 'Pakistan's inclusion in the military bloc which is being knocked together in Asia by the United States leads to the isolation of Pakistan from other countries of the Middle East and South-East Asia, in as much as this bloc is directed against the majority of Asian countries.' When negotiations were in progress in 1953 for a military pact between Pakistan and the United States, the USSR sent a note protesting against such move. It warned Pakistan that 'the Soviet Government could not regard with indifference reports of negotiations between the United States and Pakistan concerning the establishment of American air bases in Pakistan nor reports that the Pakistan and US governments were negotiating on the question of Pakistan joining in plans to set up a military aggressive block in the Middle East'.[58] Indian publicity organs and propaganda machinery were also geared in Asian and African countries against Pakistan, which was depicted as the 'stooge' of Anglo-American imperialism.

The Soviet-India entente reached its zenith with the visit of Nehru to the Soviet Union in June 1955 and the return visit of Khrushchev and Bulganin in December 1955. It was during this visit that the two Russian leaders openly declared that Kashmir was an integral part of India. They also gave support to the Afghan demand for 'Pakhtoonistan'. As a result of Russia's open support to India on Kashmir and to Afghanistan on 'Pakhtoonistan', Pakistan sought the help of her allies at the second annual meeting of the Council of SEATO held in March 1956. The foreign ministers of SEATO were invited to consider the situation in Kashmir and troubles on the Pakistan-Afghanistan border. The Council at a closed session on March 7 unanimously declared its support for the solution of the Kashmir dispute on the lines of the Security Council resolutions. In the communiqué issued at the end of the meeting on March 8, the Council affirmed the need for an early settlement of the Kashmir question through the United Nations or by direct negotiations. It refrained, however, from passing any opinion on the Kashmir dispute because it was before the United Nations and therefore *sub judice*. On the 'Pakhtoonistan' dispute, the Council members severally declared their governments' recognition of the Durand Line as defining the sovereign area of Pakistan in relation to Afghanistan. This endorsement of the Durand Line as the international boundary entitled Pakistan to evoke the treaty in the event of an attack on her north-western territories.[59]

Although the reference to Kashmir was innocuous, according as it did with the various UN resolutions on the subject, India professed to be deeply affronted by it.[60] The Indian government sent protest notes to the SEATO governments contesting the propriety and legality of their considering the 'so-called Kashmir dispute'. The Indian government claimed that 'Kashmir is in law and fact part of India and the discussion of its future was outside the scope of SEATO'.[61] Mere reference to the Security Council resolutions by SEATO was considered in India to be provocative and disturbing of 'peace' in Asia, but the Soviet Union's partisan attitude on the same issue at that time was accepted as perfectly proper. Similarly, at the second Council meeting of the Bagdad Pact held in 1956, Kashmir was mentioned and an immediate settlement of the problem was urged. Again the Indian government protested against the reference to the Kashmir issue.

When, in 1957, the Kashmir dispute was brought back to the Security Council, India was assured of the Soviet veto on any suggestion for a solution of the dispute. Hitherto Russia had stayed outside the UN efforts to settle the Kashmir quarrel and systematically abstained from voting on all major resolutions. But after the Indian–Soviet entente following American military aid to Pakistan, Kashmir became an issue in the East-West cold war and the Soviet Union helped the obstinate attitude of India over Kashmir by her veto power. On February 20, 1957, the Soviet Union exercised her seventy-ninth veto, but the first one cast by any power on the Kashmir question. This gave India the opportunity to denounce openly her previous commitments on Kashmir to the people of that state, to the United Nations and to Pakistan.

In the 1960s, the global interest of the two super powers made great changes in the alignment of India and Pakistan. To the West, India's significance for the policy of containment of China became more and more important, while friendship with Pakistan became of less moment with the easing of much of the tension in the East-West cold war. Similarly, the Soviet Union seemed to have second thoughts on her partisan attitude towards India-Pakistan disputes. However, before we turn to these developments of the 1960s, there are certain further aspects of the divergent policies of the two countries which require examination, notably Middle Eastern and South-East Asian policy.

As we have stated at the beginning of this chapter, Pakistan since independence had pursued a policy of friendliness towards the Muslim countries of the Middle East, seeking to foster closer and deeper bonds with them. Pakistan's joining the Western sponsored Bagdad Pact was not liked by some of the Arab countries, particularly Egypt, which considered the pact as a threat to her hegemony in the Middle East. Nor did Egypt welcome Pakistan's enthusiasm for Muslim solidarity and unity, looking upon Karachi's moves to this end with suspicion and jealousy. India also contributed substantially to this lack of mutual understanding between Pakistan and Egypt. Relations between Delhi and Cairo had always been close and friendly. When Iraq, an Arab country, decided to join the Bagdad Pact, Egypt's reaction was violent. She did not want any Arab country to pursue a policy which was not approved in Cairo; President Nasser had the same ambition of establishing a 'sphere of influence' in the Middle East as Nehru had in South Asia. In denouncing the Western military pacts, both were speaking with the same voice and working in close co-operation. When Iraq announced its intention of entering into an agreement of mutual co-operation with Turkey in June 1955, Nasser condemned it strongly and called a meeting of Arab Prime Ministers; the meeting, which was not attended by Iraq, attacked the proposed pact. Subsequently on many occasions Nasser, like Nehru, spoke strongly against the military pacts, particularly the Bagdad Pact which was described as a threat to Egypt's 'vital interests' and as 'foreign domination in the Middle East'. The participating countries became the target of abuse and were termed agents of the Western imperialists. A whole barrage of calumny and abuse was unleashed against them.

It was, however, the Suez crisis of 1956 which provided India with the best opportunity to vilify Pakistan in co-operation with Egypt in the Middle East. A brief account of Pakistan's role in the Suez crisis is in place here. There was spontaneous and widespread sympathy for Egypt in Pakistan; the press there, almost without exception, joined in a chorus of protest against the Anglo-French action. 'Bleeding Egypt', 'murder in Egypt', 'a crisis for mankind'—these were typical expressions in the Pakistan press, manifesting sympathy for a country which hitherto had harboured hostility towards Pakistan and had never reciprocated her gestures of friendship. When the crisis started, the Prime Minister, H. S. Suhrawardy, was in China; immediately on his return he denounced Israel as the aggressor. Nehru had not yet done so. When arrangements were made to send a United Nations force to

Egypt, Pakistan offered troops. The four Muslim members of the Bagdad Pact—Iraq, Iran, Turkey and Pakistan—held meetings at Teheran, Bagdad and Ankara, and criticised the senior partner of the pact, Britain, for her intervention in Egypt. Pakistan thereby risked her own national interests, for up to that time she had always received support from Britain in demanding a plebiscite in Kashmir—which Egypt, under the influence of India, had seldom supported. At these special meetings of the Muslim members of the pact, resolutions were passed pressing for the withdrawal of Anglo-French forces from the Suez Canal. The British government acknowledged that it weighed these resolutions in reaching its decision to withdraw. The resolutions also urged that a permanent international force be maintained in the region between Egypt and Israel, and deplored the damage done to pipelines in Syria and urged their rapid repair.[62] Before the outbreak of hostilities, Pakistan had played a prominent part in the twenty-power London conference on the Suez Canal, and the proposals adopted at the conference were known as 'the Pakistan plan'. She stayed out of the second eighteen-power London conference when she thought there was a possibility that Egyptian sovereignty might be compromised.

But nothing could please or satisfy Nehru's trusted friend President Nasser. After all Pakistan's concern and sympathy for Egypt, Nasser could yet declare: 'Suez is as dear to Egypt as Kashmir is to India.'[63] This was a rude shock to Pakistan. It also illustrated again that the best way to be on good terms with India is to support her case against Pakistan. As the Russian leaders pleased the Indians by attacking Pakistan and supporting India on Kashmir, so Nasser did by comparing Suez to Kashmir in this fashion. His stand in this matter brought Pakistan to a sensible appreciation of her aspirations for Pan-Islamic unity and solidarity. After six years of endeavour to this end, Pakistan's Foreign Minister found it necessary to tell parliament: 'Basically, the forces of nationalism clashed with the spirit of resurgent Islamic sentiment that flowed from the new state of Pakistan.'[64] Nasser's attitude towards Pakistan in 1956 helped the latter to 'be more realistic' and 'to be guided more by facts and less by theories and sentiments'.[65]

It was, however, in South and South-East Asia that India was most actively working to build up an 'area of influence' for herself. Pakistan was resolutely opposed to India's hegemony in these areas. Even before independence, Nehru had called a conference in New Delhi—the Asian Relations Conference of 1947—where he preached the ideals of Asian solidarity and unity. In his speeches on external relations, Nehru was never tired of asserting his right to speak on behalf of Asia. A study group of the India Council of World Affairs affirmed that 'by its very size, potential resources and strategic situation India has some leadership thrust upon it whether it likes it or not'.[66] But to her smaller neighbours, India is in fact an ominously large country; to many of them India's scheme for a 'peace area' is either profitless or suspicious.[67] During the Prime Ministers' conference of the Colombo powers (Burma, Ceylon, Indonesia, Pakistan, India) in April 1954, Nehru made a serious bid to assert his leadership, 'but', as *The Times* reported from Colombo, 'Ceylon and Pakistan have made it quite clear that they are not prepared to follow unquestioningly Mr Nehru's leadership.'[68] In Burma also 'Indian economic exploitation before independence has not been forgotten.'[69]

At this first conference of Colombo powers, Pakistan's Prime Minister, Mohammad Ali (Bogra), said: 'If we are to make our contribution to the promotion of peace, we must address ourselves first and foremost to the resolution of our differences.' He added that, so long as the Kashmir dispute remained unresolved, it was a little presumptuous for the Asian countries to preach peace to others. Similarly, any pledge to renounce war and aggression would be unrealistic.[70] But Nehru was fond of trying to solve all the problems of the world except those in his own backyard. In dealings with Pakistan, 'India's behaviour has not always been on the high moral level which she expects from others'.[71] Nehru's reaction to Mohammad Ali's words was reported to be 'hot and immediate'. Because of India's unwillingness to face squarely the problems and tensions of the area, the conference of the Colombo powers failed to accomplish the principal task which it was expected to tackle: to secure effective political and economic co-operation between the five countries represented at the conference, and thus to strengthen them and to make their joint voice heard more effectively in international affairs. Nothing could be done in this direction except record the hope that each government would consider plans for economic co-operation and mutual aid; no standing machinery was set up. Having failed to deal with the problems and tensions of their own, the conference went on to deal with other people's business. The problem of Indochina were the most dominant in the discussion. Finally, the five Prime Ministers issued a 'long but colourless' communiqué condemning colonialism, interference by all external agencies, communist or anti-communist, asking for the admission of the Chinese People's Republic to the United Nations, supporting self-determination in Tunisia and Morocco and expressing sympathy for the Arabs.

Commenting on the communiqué, *The Times* noted:

> Not a word was said about Kashmir, American aid to Pakistan, the Turco-Pakistan pact, the position of Tamils in Ceylon. Yet until the strain of these questions is eased by tolerance and goodwill, regional unity will remain an illusion and the voice of Asia will be correspondingly weakened in the councils of nations. . . . the conclusion which emerges from the communiqué is that five Colombo countries can only agree when it comes to telling the rest of the world how it shall deal with problems over which they themselves have little or no control—like hydrogen bombs—the nearer home a problem comes to them the more chary they are about facing it squarely.[72]

The reason for this justifiable criticism is to be found in India's unwillingness to discuss the real threats to peace in Asia, and in Nehru's consistent refusal to practise himself what he preached to others.

The Prime Ministers of the Colombo powers considered a proposal for holding an Afro-Asian conference; the proposal was further examined at their second meeting, held at Bogor in Indonesia in December 1954, where it was decided that the proposed Afro-Asian conference should be held at Bandung in Indonesia in April 1955. The purposes of the Bandung Conference were defined as the promotion of good will and social, economic and cultural co-operation between all nations of Asia and Africa. Communist China was invited to attend the conference. Among the countries excluded were Korea, Israel, South Africa, Formosa and the Central Asia republics (these last because they were politically part of a European unit, namely the Soviet Union). Twenty-nine countries participated: Afghanistan, Burma, Cambodia, Ceylon, the Chinese People's Republic, Egypt, Ethiopia, Gold Coast (Ghana), India, Indonesia, Iran, Iraq, Japan, Jordan, Laos,

I

Lebanon, Liberia, Libya, Nepal, Pakistan, the Philippines Republic, Saudi Arabia, the Sudan, Syria, Thailand, Turkey, the Democratic Republic of Vietnam, the Republic of Vietnam and Yemen. In sessions from April 18 to 24, 1955, this was, in the words of President Sukarno's opening address, the first intercontinental conference of coloured people in the history of mankind. The nations represented at the conference amounted to nearly two-thirds of the human population.

Nehru's main object at the Bandung Conference was to get an endorsement of his 'Five Principles of Coexistence' and to condemn collective security systems, such as SEATO and the Bagdad Pact. Because of Pakistan's adhesion to these alliances, Nehru lost no opportunity, in vilifying them, to lower Pakistan in the estimation of Asian and African countries. Most of these countries were still under colonial rule, and as such they were hostile to any suggestion of Western domination. Nehru exploited this sentiment to make them look with disfavour on Pakistan. Even so, things did not move according to Nehru's calculations at Bandung. On April 2, 1955, *The Times* special correspondent at the conference reported: 'Indians were somewhat depressed by the turn the conference had taken when the main session of the political committee resumed after luncheon to discuss what might be regarded as the main problem for the conference—world peace and co-operation.'[73] As a substitute for Nehru's 'Five Principles', Mohammad Ali (Bogra) proposed 'Seven Principles of Peace', these were: (1) sovereignty and territorial integrity of all nations; (2) equality of all independent and sovereign nations; (3) non-interference in the internal affairs of one country by another; (4) non-aggression; (5) rights of self-defence of each country to be exercised singly or collectively; (6) self-determination for all peoples and abhorrence of colonial exploitation in every shape; (7) settlement of disputes through peaceful means, that is, by negotiations, mediation and arbitration.

It was quite evident that, although all these principles were in accordance with the United Nations Charter, and though Nehru could hardly disavow them openly, it was difficult for him to accept the principle of the right of self-defence, exercised singly or collectively, because it would take away much of his argument against the pacts of which Pakistan was a member. Similarly, he was not inclined to accept the right of self-determination because he had constantly denied it to the people of Kashmir; nor could he gracefully accept the implications of the commitment to peaceful methods of settlement of disputes because he had turned down all the methods for peacefully settling disputes with Pakistan. In speaking of Mohammad Ali's 'seven principles', Nehru unleashed a whole barrage of calumny and abuse against SEATO and Pakistan. But, to his great surprise, Chou En-lai, the co-author of the 'Five Principles', was quite prepared to add to or modify them. He also revealed that he had been assured by the Pakistan Prime Minister that Pakistan had no aggressive designs in entering SEATO. It was at the Bandung Conference that the first attempt was made to foster better relations between Pakistan and China, and Chou En-lai invited the Pakistan Prime Minister to visit Peking.

In the final communiqué, the 'Five Principles of Coexistence' were expanded to 'Ten Principles'. The Bandung principles recognised the right of each nation to defend itself singly or collectively, in conformity with the Charter of the United Nations, though a clause was added urging the Afro-Asian states to abstain from using a collective defence arrangement for the benefit of any of the great powers, and to abstain from exerting pressures on other countries. Nehru was unhappy at the endorsement of collective defence, but he had to accept the compromise formula. When 'colonialism' was discussed, and the Prime Minister of Ceylon referred to Russia's satellites in Europe and wanted to condemn colonialism of all shades, old and new, Nehru vehemently opposed any reference to Russia's satellites. In the end, it was agreed that colonialism in all its manifestations was an evil and should speedily be brought to an end.

The lengthy communiqué issued at the end of the conference was a compromise. In general, the principles of the United Nations were supported. India's hopes for Asian leadership receded at Bandung. *The Times* special correspondent reported at the end of the conference: 'It has been Mr Chou En-lai's week. Mr Chou En-lai found no need for Indian intervention in making his contacts from one of the continents to the other. From Turkey to the Philippines, Mr Chou En-lai spread his apparent reason and tolerance.'[74] In its editorial on the conference, *The Times* observed: 'Indian diplomacy displayed all its customary adroitness but could not have succeeded in overcoming the distrust which Delhi's neutralism implies in such powers as Turkey,

Iraq, and Thailand . . . it was rather [Chou En-lai] than Mr Nehru who became the focal point of the conference.'[75] Nehru, in fact, failed to impress his Asian colleagues; indeed, his reputation seems to have diminished during the course of the conference. According to many reports, he lost his temper in arguments with his colleagues from Pakistan and Ceylon, and this created a bad impression among delegates at the conference. *The Economist* regretted that he had allowed himself to be 'provoked into the moment's unworthy childishness'. On the other hand, Chou En-lai made an excellent impression by his declaration that the Chinese had no desire to subvert neighbouring countries or to force their views on others; he expressed readiness to settle the problem of the overseas Chinese in a friendly manner. 'Even the delegates from states which had not recognised the Communist regime were favourably impressed by his attitude, and in general greater respect for and sympathy with Communist China was generated.'[76] There was dismay in New Delhi that the leadership at the conference was stolen from Nehru by Chou En-lai.

Nehru's policy of containment against Pakistan in Asia and Africa was not as successful as he had expected. Our discussion of India's foreign policy during this period may fittingly close with an illuminating observation in an article in *Round Table*:

With Pakistan, which India still does not usually treat as a foreign country, Mr Nehru is tough, he is strong enough for that. With Russia, he is polite and correct but aloof, for this is the only line he can take with them; he is not strong enough for anything more and knows that borrowed strength has serious weakness. With Britain and America, he need not be either polite or correct. He can even indulge in such hypocrisies as 'one of the reasons why we have not said that we shall not accept aid from outside is that our saying so would itself be a question of lack of friendship, if not hostility'.[77]

8

DIVERGENT FOREIGN POLICIES: II. 1959–65

THE active involvement of the United States and the Soviet Union in the subcontinent, and the rise of China as a major power in Asia, further aggravated the tension between India and Pakistan in the 1960s. India's external policies continued to seek the 'containment' of Pakistan; the latter's reaction to this cannot be justly described as 'unreasoning hysteria'. The Western powers seemed to regard Nehru and Mao Tse-tung as the only alternatives in Asia, and they began desperately to woo Nehru, even at the cost of sacrificing the interests of the loyal but weaker Pakistan. It was reported that, after his tour of Asia in 1958, Henry Cabot Lodge, United States Ambassador to the United Nations, had advised his government to strive for India's friendship and not offend her on such issues as Kashmir.[1] When Ayub Khan became president in October 1958, he was quick to assure Pakistan's Western allies of the country's commitment to the SEATO and CENTO regional pacts, declaring that he did not believe in hunting with the hound and running with the hare. Pakistan would follow a clear and unambiguous path. But Ayub soon realised that the situation did not lend itself to simple solutions, and that Pakistan under his leadership would have to make a lot of readjustments in her thinking on foreign policy.

Soon after Ayub came to power, the Pakistan-USA agreement of co-operation for security and defence was signed at Ankara in March 1959. This treaty is, in a sense, more significant than the earlier one of May 1954 because it contains clear guarantees for the defence and security of Pakistan. Its operative provisions are not limited to instances of Communist aggression. The preamble states that 'the government of the United States of America regards as vital to its national interest and to world peace the preservation of the independence and integrity of Pakistan'. Article 1 says: 'In case of aggression against Pakistan, the government of the United States of America, in accordance with the constitution of the United States of America, will take such appropriate action, including the use of armed forces, as may be mutually agreed upon . . . in order to assist the government of Pakistan at its request.'[2] Pandit Nehru immediately demanded 'clarification' of the new pact, and concern over it was voiced in all sections of the Indian parliament during a debate on foreign policy on March 16 and 17, 1959. The new bilateral agreement was described as aggravating the tensions and accentuating the differences between India and Pakistan, and Nehru declared that it would come in the way of a solution of Indo-Pakistan disputes. Soon he got the assurance from the American Ambassador in Delhi that the bilateral agreement contained no new or additional commitments. Commenting on Nehru's objection to the pact, Ayub said:

> India demanded and, according to Mr Nehru, received a specific assurance from Washington that this pact 'could not be used against India'. Short of sophistry, this demand amounted to seeking an assurance that, if India should commit aggression against Pakistan or threatened Pakistan's security, the United States would not come to the assistance of Pakistan under this pact. There could not be a more illuminating commentary on India's historical attitude to Pakistan.[3]

Notwithstanding her grievances, Pakistan still continued to follow a policy of unqualified alignment in 1959–60. But, as the war with India in September 1965 was to demonstrate, the agreement's guarantee of Pakistan's territorial integrity and independence was a hollow provision. The United States not only failed to give her any help to resist Indian aggression, but even stopped the normal flow of arms and equipment, while the Soviet Union continued to supply India with military aid without any so-called treaty of mutual security and defence.

President Ayub made sincere efforts to put an end to the corrosive quarrels between the two countries. He seemed genuinely convinced that the sour heritage of hatred and suspicion, dating from the partition of India in 1947, must be swept aside. Just as he applied himself vigorously to some of the internal problems of Pakistan, such as economic development, he made a similar conscious effort to lessen the Indo-Pakistan tensions. In October 1959, he expressed the hope that once the basic differences with India were honourably settled, Pakistan would not hesitate to enter into any form of mutual co-operation with the neighbouring country. He ruled out the possibility of an armed conflict between India and Pakistan; as a military man he pointed out 'neither can Pakistan attack India and get away with it nor can India attack Pakistan and get away with it in spite of her numerical superiority'.[4] He wished that both countries would realise this and stop thinking in terms of war. Ayub expressed concern over developmentt on the northern and north-west borders of the subcontinent, referring to what was happening in Tibet and to the roads which were being built by the Russians in Afghanistan. Wisdom demanded, he said, that India and Pakistan should begin to realise that their position could be defended only if they were united. The main dispute over Kashmir should be got out of the way so that Pakistan and India did not face each other with loaded pistols. 'What have we gained from these quarrels? They have resulted in misery to millions of people and wastage of development resources.'[5]

While the 'great debate' on Tibet was going on in the Indian parliament in May 1959, Ayub offered Nehru a plan for joint defence of the subcontinent against external threats. He believed there was a threat to both India and Pakistan from the north; the two countries should therefore settle their outstanding differences and come to a joint defence arrangement. An agreement for joint defence was possible with good will and understanding between the two countries; it need not be a covenanted pact. 'The crux of the whole thing is that Indian and Pakistan forces are at the moment facing each other; if differences between them were resolved, these forces could be released to the job of defending their territories.' He added that India could continue its policy of non-alignment in case she joined hands with Pakistan to defend the subcontinent. But prerequisite to such an arrangement is the solution of big problems like Kashmir and the canal waters. Ayub pleaded that 'both Pakistan and India should look outward instead of facing each other inward'.[6] An analysis of this proposal indicates that it was, first, a plan for the disentanglement of the Indian and Pakistani armies from the cease-fire line in Kashmir and their deployment in other border areas where they were needed by the two countries. Secondly, the joint defence agreement envisaged a common plan for any attack against the subcontinent.

Ayub's offer of joint defence was turned down by Nehru with ridicule and contempt. He was reported to have said, in a message sent through the Pakistan High Commission in New Delhi, that the question of joint defence did not arise because the broader approaches of India and Pakistan to world affairs were fundamentally different.[7] In a statement in the Indian parliament on May 4, 1959, he ridiculed the idea of joint defence by saying: 'I do not understand when people say "let us have a joint defence"—against whom? Are we to become members of the Bagdad Pact or the SEATO or some other alliance? We do not want to have a common defence policy; the whole policy we have pursued is opposed to this conception.'[8]

The Indian press also laughed at the proposal. The *Indian Express* called Ayub's offer a 'stunt', while the *Hindustan Standard* described it as 'the sedative voice of the cold-war logic'. The *Times of India* said: 'It is quixotic if not downright dishonest to think that India and Pakistan can develop so much mutual trust as to become allies while festering issues which divide them remain unresolved.'[9] It is true that some Indian leaders, like Jayaprakash Narayan, Rajagopalalachari and M. R. Masani, supported Ayub's proposal for joint defence, but the ruling Congress party and the vast majority of the Indian leaders and press were opposed. Yet the proposal testified to Ayub's earnest desire to have a real understanding with India. Nobody could doubt the sincerity and honesty of his overture to India in 1959 following the big events in Tibet and elsewhere.

Nehru's main objection to Ayub's proposal was that 'India is unaligned whereas Pakistan is a member of a particular bloc'. To this his critics could point out that, if India found it possible, as was the case, to have all kinds of economic and political ties and arrangements with the United States—the leader of this bloc—then why not a defence arrangement with one of its members? Similarly, if it was until recently possible to share *Panch Shila* with China, a prominent member of a military bloc, why was it not possible to have an understanding with Pakistan? The real explanation was the lack on India's part of any genuine desire to have an understanding with Pakistan and settle disputes with her. Nehru's attitude towards Pakistan was not changed by any external pressure or factor. 'Containment of Pakistan' still seemed to be the most important aspect of India's foreign policy.

President Ayub, while on a trip to East Pakistan, made an extremely important 'fuel halt' at the Palam airport in New Delhi on September 1, 1959. During the previous decade there had been several 'summits' between the leaders of Pakistan and India, each of which had raised high hopes for improved relations. Yet the Ayub-Nehru meeting in September 1959 has a special significance. In the first place, it occurred soon after the Tibetan crisis which provoked Sino-Indian tensions and conflict; secondly, the new leader of Pakistan was a military man who recognised the vital importance of a plan for the joint defence of the subcontinent against external threats. *Dawn*, commenting on the developing Sino-Indian conflict, wrote in November 1959:

> The relationship between Pakistan and India having been what it was almost continuously since partition, the developing conflict between India and China could very well have been welcomed here, in as much as it exposed an unfriendly neighbour to new risks and hazards. . . . But Pakistan's revolutionary regime headed by President Ayub has been inspired by the highest idealism and noblest motives in matters of internal as well as external policy. In consequence the general attitude of our people towards India has lately undergone a reorientation and the hope is now commonly shared that, in the not distant future, the outstanding problems between the two countries will be amicably settled and it will be possible for them to live as friends instead of as enemies.[10]

Similar hopes were being expressed in certain quarters in India. The *Times of India* had noted in April 1959: 'The new government in Pakistan is one with which we can do business; its leaders have on more than one occasion made conciliatory references to India and recognise the danger and futility of continued enmity with this country. This is something that must be explored.'[11] The crisis in Tibet seemed to have shaken India's confidence in the security of her northern frontier, and this gave rise to demands for a reconciliation with Pakistan. Ayub had already made his offer of joint defence in May 1959 and he had tacitly, if not expressly, indicated sympathy with India in her border conflicts with China. It was a bold step, and one which should have refuted the oft-repeated allegation that Pakistan's policy is always based on hostility towards India. In the present-day Pakistan-China friendship, many seem to forget Ayub's gestures to India in 1959–60. By siding with India on the Chinese question in 1959 and offering a joint defence of the subcontinent, Ayub gave a new orientation and significance to Pakistan's policy. It was India's cold response to Ayub's offer of friendship, together with the failure of Pakistan's Western allies to appreciate her genuine fears and anxiety, that led Pakistan to closer ties with China. She has been in search of security from her inception and her eventual moves to normalise her relations with her powerful neighbours, China and the Soviet Union, are nothing but the expression of the same search for security.

At the Ayub-Nehru meeting in September 1959, the President of Pakistan was reported to have told Nehru: 'Your country and my country are pursuing policies which are dictated by drift more than any rational design. The reason is that we have no plan of neighbourliness with each other. . . . In consequence, poor and innocent people in millions on both sides have suffered and will continue to suffer unless we have a rational plan of neighbourliness.' Ayub said that, unless relations between India and Pakistan improved, one side or the other might invite an outsider to come. 'This was the lesson of the past history of the subcontinent. Human beings are curious; when in difficulties they are quite capable of even wanting to sleep with the devil.'[12]

The communiqué issued after the meeting emphasised the need for relations between the two countries to be conducted 'on a rational and planned basis, and not according to the day-to-day exigencies as they arose'. The two leaders agreed that outstanding issues and problems should be settled in accordance with justice and fair play and in a spirit of friendliness, co-operation and good neighbourliness. One immediate result of the meeting was the conference of ministers and military commanders of the two countries to resolve what Ayub called 'pinpricks, firings, and other things on the eastern borders'.[13] Other pointers to improvement in Indo-Pakistan relations were the successful conclusion of an agreement on border questions, a renewed attempt to define and resolve the financial issues, and a comprehensive trade agreement.

After his meeting with Nehru, Ayub told the special correspondent of the *Daily Telegraph*: 'We have got to have a general settlement between Pakistan and India. Mr Nehru is now beginning to realise the gravity of the situation with which his country is liable to be faced in the near future. These things [the Chinese incursions] are a pointer to what may happen in time to come.'[14] Ayub's reading of Nehru's mind, however, proved to be incorrect. Professor Norman Palmer, analysing Nehru's foreign policy after the Chinese troops 'hit India like an icy blast from the high Himalayas', finds that the Indian leader 'rejected all suggestions that India should reorient its foreign policy and should operate more closely with other non-Communist countries, including Pakistan, in mutual defence measures and other matters of policy'.[15] Not that Ayub, for all his optimism, was unaware of the difficulties: '[Nehru] has to reorientate his mind and attitude. No matter how pressing the circumstances may be, this is not easy.'[16] There was such a long history of disputes and bad feeling between India and Pakistan that a dramatic improvement was unlikely. The Indian correspondent of the *Round Table* wrote in August 1959: 'Not even the threats of China, which is now widely realised, can effect much change in Indo-Pakistan relations.'[17] This, unhappily, was a correct assessment. The current Indian troubles with China were not sufficient to change Nehru's basic attitude towards Pakistan. *The Times* correspondent in New Delhi reported in January 1960: 'There have been signs that the tentative warmth engendered by President Ayub's overtures last September have begun to drain away.'[18]

Nevertheless, on both sides individuals began to make efforts to build what they hoped would be firm bases for a new era of lasting friendship. Most active in this context was the Indian socialist leader Jayaprakash Narayan who, after meeting with Ayub and other Pakistani leaders, had been touring India preaching the need for a new entente. General Cariappa, the former Indian commander-in-chief, endorsed Ayub's plea for a common defence arrangement and was advocating Indo-Pakistan friendship; moreover, the two leading parties in the non-Communist opposition—the Praja Socialists and Swatantra—came out with a plea for an India-Pakistan accord. It was distressing, however, to note that even some of the most enthusiastic Indian supporters of Pakistan's joint defence proposal had read into it very much more than was or could have been intended. Acharaya Vinoba Bhave, for example in welcoming Ayub's gesture, suggested that India and Pakistan should come together by combining defence, foreign affairs and communications. Similarly, Narayan saw in the proposal 'the prospect of two countries joining in a confederation'. These utterances aroused in Pakistan the old suspicion that the Indian leaders wanted to undo partition and reunite the two countries. To talk of such things was to create unnecessary complications and thereby to retard the cause of Indo-Pakistan amity. As has been mentioned in preceding chapters, Indian leaders often fail to recognise Pakistan's sense of national values and sentiments, and in their public utterances often create suspicion in the minds of the people of Pakistan, many of whom feel that their country's separate entity is not yet recognised in many quarters in India.

The attitude of the government of India, particularly of Nehru, showed little inclination for any change. 'To understand [Nehru], his reluctance and reticence in this particular sphere, it is necessary to realize that he was bitterly opposed to the 1947 partition. . . .'[19] Although some sections of public and political opinion in India came to the conclusion that the pressure of China provided a very good reason for a new chapter of friendly relations with Pakistan, Nehru seemed to react otherwise. He was unwilling to give the appearance of being moved into any entente with Pakistan under pressure from China. He often said that the Indian government must not take any action in 'fear' or 'anger'; any reconciliation between India and Pakistan, he felt, would be interpreted as an Indian commitment to the Western camp. The real situation was that, even in the 1960s, he felt no need for Pakistan's friendship or co-operation. To his growing supporters in the United States, he tried to give the appearance of taking a new look at Indo-Pakistan relations, but a close scrutiny of his words and action reveals no change of heart. Ayub, like his predecessors, was soon disillusioned and disappointed. A similar disappointment had attended the efforts of Mohammad Ali (Bogra) to have friendly relations with India in 1954–55.

A second Ayub-Nehru meeting—in September 1960, at the time

of signing the Indus Waters treaty—reaffirmed Nehru's cool attitude towards Ayub's overtures. The joint communiqué issued after this meeting was a sore disappointment to those who were expecting a new turn in Indo-Pakistan relations. Ayub regretfully acknowledged that India had shown little enthusiasm either for his suggestion for a joint defence plan made in May 1959 or his plea for the settlement of outstanding disputes, particularly that over Kashmir. Mutual fear and suspicion persisted, and both governments continued to spend millions of rupees on defence against one another. Pakistan's over-riding problem remained unresolved, and her external relations and policies continued to be directed in search of security against her neighbour. All hopes of ending the long, costly dispute between Pakistan and India under external pressures were dashed to the ground. In a broadcast on the eve of the thirteenth anniversary of Pakistan's independence President Ayub had said:

> We have made every conceivable effort to go out of our way to resolve our problems with India. In some matters we have met a measure of success but our major dispute with India, Kashmir, does not look like getting anywhere near its solution. . . . The future of South-East Asia depends to a large extent on the relationship between India and Pakistan. If there is real peace between the two, what is there to prevent an integrated development and economic policy between Iran, Pakistan, India, Burma, Malaya, Ceylon and even Indonesia and other countries of that region? . . . [But] this can only happen if India can inspire confidence in her peaceful intentions and is prepared to resolve her quarrels with her neighbours in a spirit of large-heartedness.[20]

This fresh dashing of the hope of a settlement with India was to add to Pakistan's anxieties about developments in the policy of her Western allies. As has been mentioned already, American strategists and policy-makers seemed to welcome the growing Sino-Indian dispute as offering them a good opportunity for utilising 'non-aligned' India in their policy for the containment of China. At the same time, the attitude of the United States towards its allies underwent profound changes. After the crisis in Tibet in 1959 and the Sino-Indian border conflicts in the same year, President Ayub wanted to normalise his country's relations with both India and China. This was a reasonable policy for a small country like Pakistan, which is surrounded by bigger neighbours. As we have seen, Ayub's offers of friendship were received coolly in New Delhi, while his attempts to normalise relations with China earned extreme displeasure at the State Department in Washington, where it was denounced as 'Pakistan's flirtation with Communist China'.

All these factors—changed attitude towards 'allies' and 'neutrals'; developing Sino-Indian rivalry; Pakistan's attempts to normalise her relations with China—led to major changes in American policy in the subcontinent. The changed attitude was summed up by the American columnist C. L. Sulzberger:

> Washington recognizes Pakistan's loyalty to the two Asian alliances arranged by the Eisenhower administration and rather less enthusiastically endorsed by Kennedy. But we also recognize that Pakistan represents only 20 per cent of the subcontinent and is divided into distant halves. The sole hope of establishing a viable competitor to China is in India. So our affection for an ally is tempered by geographical reality.[21]

Moreover, Americans needed Pakistan as a base for strategic bombers, until nuclear strategy was transformed by ICBMs and the Polaris submarine.[22]

John F. Kennedy's election as President of the United States in November 1960 brought a new era in Indo-USA relations. For years Kennedy had been associated with Senator John Sherman Cooper, a former US ambassador to New Delhi, in advocating a massive programme of aid to India. In Kennedy's view, the long-range struggle with communism in Asia depended on how India solved its economic problems. His goal was described as an attempt to turn India into a 'showplace' for his ideas on what the Western world should do for an Asian country.[23]

The news of proposed amendments to the United States Mutual Security Act to facilitate the flow of arms to neutrals like India caused anxiety in Pakistan. India had got twenty-nine C119 Flying Boxcar transport planes in June 1960. It was understandable that, after her border war with China in 1959, India should make a major effort to strengthen her defences. But no less understandable was Pakistan's anxiety on observing that, though India complained that China had seized 'vast stretches of Himalayan border', 80 per cent of New Delhi's military strength was still deployed along the frontiers with Pakistan. There was genuine fear in Pakistan that India might, once the terms of the Mutual Security Act were reframed (as they were by the Kennedy administration), secure additional arms from the United States on terms almost as advantageous as those enjoyed by a loyal ally.[24]

Pakistan could not watch the prospect of an Indian arms build-up without grave concern. President Ayub spoke of the proposed amendments to the Mutual Security Act as opening the floodgates of armaments to India whose armed strength was already three times that of Pakistan and which was being augmented by arms supplies from Russia. (By 1962, India had signed the first of what was to become a series of military agreements with the Soviet Union.)[25] Ayub said that it was difficult to explain to Pakistanis a situation where 'people like us who are in open friendship with the United States', and who had as such taken on 'certain added commitments', were put on a par with those 'who do not assume any commitments'.[26] The Indian military purchasing mission in the United States discussed with officials there the possibility of obtaining Side-winder air-to-air missiles. India's military build-up began, in fact, before the Sino-Indian border conflicts of 1962 and at a time when Pandit Nehru was denouncing Pakistan for her military alliance with America.

Then came a most disquieting statement in 1961 from the American Vice President, Lyndon Johnson: 'At President Kennedy's request, I had urged Mr Nehru to extend his leadership to other areas in South-East Asia.'[27] As noted in chapter 7, Pakistanis react strongly against any suggestion of Indian hegemony in South Asia. The roots of their feelings in this matter lie far back in history and in their unhappy experiences with India since Pakistan gained her independence. Ayub, while explaining 'the Pakistan-American relation', gave expression to the feelings of Pakistanis:

India regards herself as a big power in Asia. Her eventual aim has been and still is to have her sphere of influence in South-East Asia. The Indian leaders have stated that their true border extends from the Hindu Kush mountains to the Me Kong river, that is to say, wherever the influence of Hinduism has existed in the past. Their early friendly overtures to China were based on the hope that there would be an understanding between them and China over their respective spheres of influence in Asia and that China would recognise and endorse India's claim.[28]

Johnson's statement provoked in Pakistan strong criticism of American policy in South Asia. Subsequently, a clarification of the statement was made by the United States Ambassador in Pakistan, but not before much damage had been done. One Pakistani daily wondered whether in America 'a movement has been started already for [the] . . . political reunification' of the subcontinent; and it referred to Louis Fischer's *Russia, America and the World*, in which was set forth a plan for 'undoing much of the evil of partition'. Fischer wrote: 'Confederation would correct the 1947 blunder of allowing religious policies to sever India from Pakistan.' He suggested a plan for confederating India, Pakistan and Kashmir, with Srinagar as the capital of the new Union.[29] Pakistan's national sentiment and honour are highly sensitive to such suggestions; Johnson's statement and Fischer's proposal caused bitterness and misunderstanding in Pakistan–USA relations.

A similar view was expressed by Hubert Humphrey, on the eve of his election to the Vice Presidency in November 1964. In an interview with the *New York Times* Humphrey disclosed an American plan for South-East Asia—'a coalition of Asian powers with *India as its main force* to counterbalance Chinese power'. According to this plan, America was to make India 'strong enough to exercise *leadership in the area*'. (Our italics.) Humphrey asserted that 'the future of South-East Asia cannot be predicted upon the infected finger of Vietnam; it must include the palm of the hand from India to Pakistan'.[30] *Dawn* expressed Pakistan's reactions to this sort of plan in bitter terms: 'Just as Americans have ruined South Vietnam by their military intervention . . . and just as they made scores of thousands of South Vietnamese fight and die against their wish, so the same story is to be repeated in India and Pakistan.'[31] This might be an extremely harsh remark, but Pakistanis in general were dismayed by the swift turn of American policy in the subcontinent. They were as much distressed as angered.

Pakistan might not have shared America's enthusiasm for fighting 'international communism', but she was sincerely and genuinely loyal to the West. Hence this kind of response from her 'allies' was a rude shock to her. The Soviet Ambassador to Pakistan, Mihail Kapitsa, told the Pakistanis: 'We support India and Afghanistan against you because they are our friends, even when they are in the wrong. But your friends do not support you, even when they know you are in the right.'[32] It was very difficult for President Ayub to explain his unqualified loyalty to Western friends in the changed circumstances.

By 1962, it was clear that the Pakistan-US friendship, which had its heyday in the Eisenhower-Dulles period, was coming to an end. The United States seemed to be firmly determined to boost India's military power and strength as part of her global strategy against Communist China. Thus began the third and most recent phase in Pakistan's external policies: a transition from an unqualified to a qualified alignment; while in India non-alignment was succeeded by bi-alignment.

Ayub began a 'win friends' campaign, particularly among the Afro-Asian countries, and sought to normalise Pakistan's relations with the Communist countries. He intensified his personal diplomacy and paid visits to a number of countries including Burma, Indonesia, Japan, the United Arab Republic, Ceylon, Philippines, Yugoslavia, West Germany, Jordan, Lebanon, Nepal and Saudi Arabia. All these visits aimed at strengthening Pakistan's standing with these countries. While there was yet not much change towards the West and Pakistan's commitments in the regional pacts, there was definitely a changed attitude towards the Communist countries. The modification in Pakistan's policy was not of the kind that could be formally announced, but it could be felt and observed; a 'reorientation' of her foreign policy had taken place. Ayub's government was prepared to explore the benefits that might come from more amicable relations with the Soviet Union and China.

In the meantime, the Sino-Indian border conflicts were drifting into a serious crisis whose impact on Pakistan's foreign policy and on Indo-Pakistan relations in general was profound and far-reaching. The Sino-Indian border is divided into three areas: the Western, Middle and Eastern sectors. The Western sector is the boundary between the Ladakh area of Indian-held Kashmir and China's province of Sinkiang and Tibet. The Middle sector, much shorter in length, involves the boundary between three Indian states—East Punjab, Himachal Pradesh and Uttar Pradesh—and Tibet. The Eastern sector separates the Indian state of Assam from Tibet. The Chinese contention is that the entire length of the disputed boundary is undefined and unsettled and that the entire alignment requires negotiation. The McMahon Line, which demarcated the Western sector, is regarded by the Chinese as the product of unilateral action by the British government in 1914 when China was weak and powerless. On the Middle and Eastern sectors the Chinese contention is that no attempt at legal definition was made at all and hence the need for settlement. The Indian case is based on treaty, administrative usage and tradition.

India adopted what is known as the 'forward policy' to establish her claims in the Western sector. However, it was not as easy to carry out the 'forward policy' against China as it was to annex Junagadh and occupy Kashmir, Hyderabad and Goa. The techniques which had been successful with a weaker neighbour could not be effective against a bigger neighbour. 'The forward policy', Ronald Segal points out, 'depended on a vast miscalculation.'[33]

The next development was large-scale fighting between India and China in October 1962. The result of the Sino-Indian armed conflict of 1962 was a military débâcle for India. 'It was rout in remote mountain country, a lost engagement, but it carried with it almost the consequences of a lost war. From these dismal months of the frontier war came a sharp downward lurch of India's prestige in Asia.'[34] The Indian government had resorted to arms on four occasions since independence, and had made troop demonstrations on many other occasions against weaker neighbours, but this was the first great shock to the Indian military leaders. To her political leaders the shock was no less. India, which considered herself to be the leader of the non-aligned countries of Asia and Africa, got no support from them in her hour of distress; it was rather the so-called imperialist powers of the West, whom Nehru had denounced so conveniently, who came to his rescue with massive arms aid. Nehru was 'enormously surprised' at Pakistan's attitude towards India. He forgot, however, that it was to deal with precisely such a crisis that Ayub had made the offer of joint defence three years before, which he had turned down. The Sino-Indian border dispute was watched with deep concern and anxiety by Pakistan. She did not take advantage of India's military reverses; on the contrary, President Ayub gave indications through the American and British that he would not make India's military problem worse by any action in Kashmir. This enabled India to withdraw some of her troops deployed against Pakistan and to use them against China. Yet Pakistan was accused of an unfriendly attitude.

When the fighting started, President Ayub made the following assessment:

> Broadly speaking we are seriously disturbed that the differences between India and China have erupted into an armed conflict. However, we believe that the scope of this conflict, because of the terrain over which it is being waged, can perforce be limited. If it were otherwise, then the contestants would have started it with considerable campaigning period ahead of them. It was no time to start it in October when the weather will progressively bring military operations to a halt.[35]

Ayub's assessment, made in consultation with his top military advisers, was proved correct by subsequent events, which culminated in the unilateral declaration of a cease-fire by China.

Even after the military débâcle in both Ladakh and the Eastern sector, the bulk of India's land and air forces was posed to strike at Pakistan. Her three infantry divisions, backed with tactical air support, were still manning the cease-fire line in Kashmir. In addition, there were two infantry divisions against the borders of East Pakistan.[36] Ayub told the Americans: 'Until the outbreak of fighting with China and even during most of that fighting, more than three-fourths of India's best equipped forces remained massed on Pakistan's borders.'[37] He referred to Nehru's statement in December 1962 that Indian military preparedness had been directed primarily against Pakistan. Explaining the reasons for Indian reverses in the fighting against China, Nehru had said that 'most of our military thinking' had been conditioned to the possibility of a war with Pakistan. Ayub thought that this remained India's basic position, and added that, even after the Sino-Indian border conflicts, the collective strength of Indian forces

massed on the borders of West and East Pakistan remained formidable.[38] Under such circumstances, how could Pakistan do other than
view with extreme concern and anxiety the huge military build-up in
India?

The Sino-Indian conflicts of 1962 induced the United States to
rush to India huge arms aid on the age-old basis: the enemy of my
enemy is my friend.[39] The British and some other countries also joined
in what was called emergency assistance to India. On December 29,
1962, after the cease-fire on the Indian-Chinese border, President
Kennedy and Prime Minister Macmillan agreed at Nassau to continue
to supply India on an emergency basis with military aid up to a total
amount of $120 million. In accordance with the Nassau agreement a
United States–British–Canadian air mission went to India to
examine her requirements; so also did a separate American military
mission. Subsequently, on June 30, 1963, at Birch Grove, the United
States and Britain decided on a further substantial programme of
military assistance to India, in addition to that agreed to at Nassau;
and in 1964, additional aid worth $60 million was committed. Then
came the announcement of a long-term agreement between the
United States and India whereby the latter would receive military aid
to the value of $100 million a year for a period of five years.[40] In
addition to this massive arms aid from the West, India also got substantial military supplies from the Soviet Union.

Thus the Sino-Indian border conflicts gave India the opportunity
enormously to augment her military build-up. The so-called leader
of the non-aligned group got very little support from influential
non-aligned states such as Algeria, Burma, Ceylon, Ghana (who, in
fact, opposed the Western military aid to India), Guinea and Indonesia.
But India was highly successful in obtaining support and encouragement from some bigger powers. She fully exploited the 'containment
policy' of the United States against China and the Sino-Soviet ideological conflict to expand her military build-up. What were the effects
of this massive arms aid to India on political alignment and military
balance in the subcontinent?

Pakistan joined the Western military alliances not merely to make
her contributions to the defence of the 'free world'; she was also
anxious to protect herself from the military imbalance existing to her

disadvantage in the subcontinent. As a result of American military aid after 1954-55, she was able to improve her dangerous military deficiency. By 1962, Pakistan had about five active army divisions as against India's eleven; in certain departments, she even had superior equipment, for example, a squadron of supersonic F104 fighter bombers. After many years of serious weakness in relation to India, this was enough to reassure Pakistan, though the over-all military balance of the two countries was still in favour of India.

But the whole situation was changed to the detriment of Pakistan's security and defence by the Western and Soviet supply of arms to India after the Sino-Indian border conflicts. India also had a tremendous advantage over Pakistan in ordnance potential, manpower, industrial infrastructure and general economic growth. Six armed divisions (five mountain and one infantry) were equipped by the Western powers to augment India's armed forces. By the end of 1965, India would have twenty active and well-equipped divisions in the field. Her target was to raise her standing army from eleven to twenty-two divisions as rapidly as possible and to expand substantially her air force and navy as well—'all ostensibly for use against China' (Ayub). Apart from the massive Western arms aid, India's own defence expenditure in 1963 was doubled to reach a figure of over 8,000 million rupees against Pakistan's 1,380 million.

An Indian defence mission left for Moscow in 1963 to negotiate defence purchases, including MIGs, submarines and arms manufacturing plants. Arms supplies to India from various sources included provision for extensive communications, air transport and training facilities as well as assistance for expanding her own armament production. The United States was reported to have undertaken to supply sophisticated high-power radar equipment; two mobile radar stations were provided by 1964 and another six were scheduled to be delivered by 1965. These are intended to be deployed to provide an intensive radar coverage over the whole of northern India, including most of West Pakistan; it would also be extended to the whole of East Pakistan. The existing radar units of the Indian air force would be deployed to extend India's radar coverage over Pakistan. India decided to equip its intercepter squadrons with guided or Side-winder type air-to-air missiles. Since Pakistan's acquisition of F104 fighters, India was trying hard to acquire the same for her own air force. The United States refused India's request for supersonic aircraft; she seemed to be inclined to offer a guarantee rather than aircraft for India's air defences by deploying in the Indian Ocean some elements of the Seventh Fleet, including an aircraft carrier. India did not consider this adequate, though she welcomed the presence of the American fleet in the Indian Ocean as an additional aid. She then turned to the Soviet Union for MIGS. With the proposed expansion of the Indian navy and the development of bases at Port Blair and Marmagao, the Indian navy would be in a position to dominate the Indian Ocean and the Arabian Sea, and interfere with Pakistan's sea communications between East and West Pakistan.[41]

India thus embarked upon an ambitious plan of expanding her armed forces, air force and navy. It was quite evident that this huge expansion of her military strength would completely upset the balance of power in the subcontinent and pose the most serious threat to the existence of Pakistan. The latter's reactions to the Western arms aid to India were bitter and resentful; it put her relations with the West to further strain, almost to breaking point, compelling her to search for a new security and to reappraise her foreign policy.

The West rushed arms to India and expected Pakistan to forget past injustices and insults, present wrongs and future threats and dangers from India. This was, however, not possible. An emergency session of the National Assembly of Pakistan was summoned in November 1962 to discuss the situation arising out of the West's decision to arm India. Pakistan's Foreign Minister, Mohammad Ali (Bogra), began the debate:

I speak in anguish and not in anger when I have to say that one of our allies [sc. USA] had promised us that we would be consulted before any arms assistance is given to India; I regret to have to observe that this was not done. . . . The Indian leadership has been openly hostile to us. They went to the extent of declaring us as their enemy number one. Our safety and security have been under constant threat for the last fifteen years by the bulk of the Indian armed forces, deployed in a state of battle readiness along our border . . . they preach non-violence and practise aggression . . . the present augmentation in Indian military strength and warlike stores and the assistance now being extended by our friends to India is going to seriously aggravate the situation against us and to our great disadvantage. This is a matter of very grave concern to us and we cannot afford to accept this position complacently.[42]

Speaker after speaker joined Mohammad Ali in expressing Pakistan's grave anxiety and concern. The speeches exhibited a deep sense of frustration against the Western 'allies'.

The Indians reacted strongly to Pakistan's opposition to India's military aid, just as Pakistanis had done against India's opposition to Pakistan's aid in 1954. Consequently, there was a further worsening of Indo-Pakistan relations, already strained after Nehru's rejection of Ayub's offer of joint defence and refusal to settle the disputes between the two countries. In May 1962, an American analyst summed up as follows the state of Pakistani attitudes to India before the outbreak of Sino-Indian conflict in the October of that year: 'The days when the President [Ayub] spoke so forcefully in favour of a joint Indo-Pakistan defence of the subcontinent against potential intruders . . . are gone. India's continued refusal to budge from Kashmir, the persistence of anti-Muslim riots in India, the Indian take-over of Goa and the lumping by Indian leaders of Pakistan and Communist China as two of India's enemies have sharpened anti-India feeling.'[43] This feeling was greatly strengthened by the change in Western policy after the Sino-Indian border war.

During 1963-64, President Ayub made a number of speeches pinpointing the dangers of a serious military imbalance in the subcontinent. In an interview with an American journalist in January 1963, he complained: 'We are very old friends of the United States and Britain and allied to them, and they did not even care to consult us over a matter of this nature. We do not claim any right of veto or anything like it in the foreign policy of our friendly countries. But we had some right to expect what the United States and Britain were going to do in a crisis like this.'[44] To a British journalist, the 'deeply aggrieved President Ayub' declared: 'Britain and the US let Pakistan down by arming India; their policies are really driving Pakistan against the wall.' India's new military strength would be used against Pakistan because, basically, India had no desire to fight China. He argued that India would not need to assault Pakistan outright to humiliate her; it was enough simply to possess a greatly superior military force and threaten, bully and tease the vulnerable halves of Pakistan in order to neutralise and isolate the country and turn it into a satellite of India.[45]

Pakistanis felt, not without justification, that the military imbalance would be changed drastically and permanently. Whether overt aggression would come or not, this would strengthen India in her resolve not to settle her outstanding disputes with Pakistan, and in particular her intransigence over Kashmir would be further increased. Part of the American arms aid was being funnelled into Ladakh in Indian-held Kashmir, and the United States was building a military airfield at Leh. Pakistan strongly protested to the United States over this.[46]

In an article published in *Foreign Affairs* in January 1964, President Ayub put forward Pakistan's problems. He examined whether the arming of India 'on this extensive scale is necessary or justified', and observed:

> Even in the unlikely event of a recrudescence of border fighting between China and India, India could not, considering the mountain terrain, deploy more than 3 to 4 divisions against the Chinese. One may justifiably ask then why India is doubling the size of her standing army to 22 divisions. Even allowing for the necessary reserves, what are these divisions aimed against? The fact of the matter is that, taking advantage of the favourable Western response to her demands for arms, India is planning to raise two armies, one with which to face China and the other to use against Pakistan and her other smaller neighbours in pursuance of her expansionist objectives. It should also be noted that any army meant for China would by the nature of things be so positioned as to be able to wheel round swiftly to attack East Pakistan. Thus both the armies pose a grave threat to this country.[47]

India raised objections to Pakistan's military aid in 1954–55; Pakistan did the same with regard to India's military aid in 1962–63. There was, however, one big difference in the expressions of resentment by the two countries. Nehru couched his opposition in all sorts of idealist arguments: destroying the 'peace area in Asia'; bringing the 'cold war' into Asia; creating a 'new domination' of 'wicked' Western imperialist powers in Asian countries; and so forth. Pakistani leaders put their case in a more straightforward way: a militarily stronger India is a threat to their country; Pakistan had been 'neglected', if not 'betrayed', by her allies. India would never put her case against Pakistan in closer terms, preferring to appear to be guided by high ethics and moral principles while, in practice, devising her policy in terms of military strength and balance of power.

Pakistan's Western allies were, no doubt, sorry to note her vehement opposition to their policy of arming India. Initially, Britain and the United States tried to bring about an understanding between India and Pakistan by putting pressure on Nehru to settle the Kashmir dispute. Under this pressure, a new attempt was made to solve the quarrel but, as was shown in chapter 3, Nehru agreed to this negotiation only to facilitate the flow of Western arms to India; as soon as the arms deal was assured, he turned his back and the old stalemate on Kashmir reappeared.

While Pakistan was drifting away from the United States, India was moving closer to her. Washington could now greet with relief the end of the irritating era of India's left-leaning neutralism, symbolised by Krishna Menon (whom Nehru had to drop from his cabinet after the Indian military débâcle in the Sino-Indian border conflict of 1962). The United States was now building its anti-China policy around India.[48] Robert McNamara, the American Secretary of Defense, in stating that military assistance to India was in the interest of the United States, admitted that it had 'deeply troubled Pakistan'.[49] India, self-appointed leader of the non-aligned group, gave tacit recognition to the legitimacy of an American nuclear presence in the Indian Ocean despite the opposition to this from other Asian countries like Burma, Ceylon, Indonesia, Nepal and Pakistan. Nehru, who had always been vocal in denouncing any sign of Western military influence in Asia, now quietly acquiesced in the presence of the American Seventh Fleet in the Indian Ocean by saying, 'it does not apply to us in any way'.[50] In the larger global arena, India began 'a conscious effort to avoid working at cross purposes with the United States'.[51] In turn, there developed an American willingness 'to take a dispassionate view of Indian regional ambitions and to let South Asian relationships develop unimpeded'.[52] Made wary by such straws in the wind as the statements by Lyndon Johnson in 1961 and Hubert Humphrey in 1964, endorsing the idea of India's 'leadership' in South Asia, it is not surprising that Pakistanis saw in the new Indian-USA entente the basis, not only for India's 'leadership' but for her actual hegemony. Letting 'relationships develop unimpeded' also carried with it the implication that the West would no longer take even an honest broker's part in the vital question of Kashmir.

India, moreover, was very careful to retain the friendship of the Soviet Union. Far from deploring Indian ties with Moscow, the United States seemed to have given tacit recognition to it in the expectation that it would intensify Sino-Soviet differences. 'Indeed', Ayub said, '[India] has been given to understand that it is in the Western interest that she should continue to remain "non-aligned" and receive aid from the Soviet Union as well.'[53] There was, therefore, no conflict between the global interests of the United States and the national interests of India. 'Just as India has a psychological vested interest in a stalemate with Pakistan', observes Selig S. Harrison, 'so there is utility in the China impasse as a factor keeping alive Soviet and American interest in New Delhi.'[54] India's policy of bi-alignment was thus blessed both in Washington and Moscow. The result has been that 'India is cast today in the status of a client in its dealings with the super powers. Instead of striking an elusive, equidistant pose midway between the extremes of commitment, the object now is to remain as near as possible to both of her patrons while displeasing neither.'[55]

While India has been highly successful in developing closer ties with the two super powers, her influence and prestige among the Afro-Asian states have been rapidly declining. That India maintained only one facet of non-alignment has in the end become only too clear to many Afro-Asian countries. Her changed attitude and role among them could be discerned even before the Sino-Soviet conflicts of 1962. 'As India became more absorbed by her own vast economic problems and with mounting anxiety sought substantial aid from the West, the Nehru government grew less concerned about colonial liberation.'[56] This decreased enthusiasm on the part of India for colonial liberation could be seen from her luke-warm attitude towards the freedom fight in Algeria and Guinea. Then came the rude shock after the Sino-Indian conflicts of 1962, when India seemed to have decided that the friend-ship of the super powers was of greater value than the 'leadership' of the non-aligned groups. China was also doing havoc to India's image among the new nations of Africa and Asia. The growing conflict between Indonesia and India also contributed to the latter's declining prestige among the Afro-Asian bloc. The Indian government's aware-ness of this helps to explain its unwillingness to support the proposal for a second Afro-Asian conference of the Bandung type.

As India's position was declining, Pakistan made a vigorous bid to strengthen her position among the nations of Asia and Africa, which had been severely affected by Indian propaganda against her as the 'stooge of Western powers'. Pakistan's new trends in foreign policy since 1960, from an unqualified allegiance to qualified links with the West, also helped her greatly to win friends among the new nations. 'In the field of external affairs the year [1963] was notable for further deterioration and a hardening of attitudes in Indo-Pakistani relation-ship and the marked attention by Pakistan to other Eastern states— Nepal, Indonesia, Burma, Ceylon and most of all China. . . . Each of the new countries with which Pakistan sought closer friendship had major or minor grievances against India.'[57]

The old rivalry and competition of the 1950s were vigorously continued in the 1960s. India's policy of 'containment of Pakistan' and Pakistan's search for security against a potential Indian aggression continued unabated and unchecked. India's tactics against Pakistan with the West, particularly with the United States, were to stress Pakistan's 'sinister' and 'provocative' ties with China; while, with the Soviet Union, Pakistan's continued membership of the 'aggressive' military alliance of the West was emphasised. With the Afro-Asian community, India tried to establish that no change in the international outlook of Pakistan had taken place and that she was still an 'agent' of the Western powers.

Under the impact of the big events of 1962—the Sino-Indian border conflicts, and Western rearmament of India—three important trends in Pakistan's foreign policy are discernible: continued friendship towards the aid-giving West, with political reservation; normalisation of relations with the Soviet Union, and a friendly attitude to China; and cultivating friendship with Afro-Asian countries.[58] These trends received a further impetus from the post-1962 policies of the great powers in the subcontinent. Pakistan now seriously studied the implications of the new American policy towards India. Why, it was asked in government circles and the press, should Pakistan continue to pursue a policy of firm adherence to the West when such a policy was not solving her problems of security and defence against India? Now that the Dulles policy was dead for good, and the 'Harvard intellectuals' of the Democratic administration of the United States were denouncing pacts, there seemed no longer any reason for total commitment to the West. It was not that Pakistan's withdrawal from SEATO and CENTO seemed imminent (though some opposition groups in the Pakistan National Assembly were clamouring for immediate withdrawal). For some years, at least, Pakistan would continue her association with these alliances. But in the United Nations and in her relations with China, with the Soviet Union and with Afro-Asian countries, the new trends in Pakistan's policy were clearly noticeable.

The most important and controversial aspect of the reorientation of Pakistan's foreign policy in the 1960s was the 'China policy', which roused great resentment both in New Delhi and Washington and also caused some thought and concern in Moscow. The 'China policy' of President Ayub was not as sudden and dramatic a shift as is alleged in some quarters. Pakistan's relations with China have always been correct, though not cordial. Even in the heyday of the Pakistan-American alliance, there had never been in Pakistan-China relations the same rift as in Pakistan-Soviet relations.

On January 15, 1961, the Pakistan Foreign Minister disclosed that the People's Republic of China had agreed in principle to the demarcation of its border with Pakistan. Pakistan has no common frontier with China except in relation to areas of Jammu and Kashmir which are under Pakistan's control—Azad Kashmir. The Sino-Pakistan frontier agreement therefore meant that Peking did not accept India's claim to sovereignty over Kashmir. India asserts that the territory linking China and Pakistan is hers, while the United Nations and Pakistan say it is disputed, along with the rest of Kashmir, between India and Pakistan. India protested against the boundary talks. President Ayub argued that Pakistan was very much in legal occupation of the territory which runs along China and had every right to hold talks with China on border demarcation, while Nehru declared that India would not accept any decision arrived at between Pakistan and China relating to the border. Pakistan and China formally announced on May 4, 1962 their decision to negotiate on border demarcation and to sign 'an agreement of provisional nature'. The announcement said: 'The two sides have further agreed that, after the settlement of the dispute over Kashmir between India and Pakistan, the sovereign authorities concerned should reopen negotiations with the Chinese government regarding the boundary of Kashmir so as to sign a formal boundary treaty to replace this provisional agreement.'[59]

This announcement was a diplomatic gain for Pakistan in that China formally dissociated herself from the position taken up by the rest of the Communist bloc, which had recognised India's claim over Kashmir. However, in the announcement Pakistan, 'laid no sovereign claims over the contiguous territory which it now occupies and administers'.[60] Pakistan seemed to bank on the theory of 'effective control' in its negotiations with China.

The announcement produced sharp comments in India, whose government and press accused China of giving 'legal and moral encouragement to an aggressor state and prejudicing the prospects of a *peaceful settlement* of the Kashmir issue'.[61] (Our italics.) It was rather strange to hear from India about a 'peaceful settlement' of the Kashmir dispute after her record of fifteen years of obstinacy over any constructive suggestion advanced both inside and outside the United Nations. Nehru condemned Pakistan's policy of establishing friendly relations with China as 'opportunistic' and 'adventures'.[62] He was also 'surprised' to find Pakistan's attitude changed. Pakistan's Foreign Minister replied: 'If India were to abandon its attempts to encircle and isolate Pakistan, [Nehru] would cease to be surprised. . . . Our relations with China are based on the spirit and letter of the ten principles proclaimed at Bandung in 1955.'[63]

Pressed by India and disillusioned with her allies, Pakistan during 1963 edged her way towards closer relations with China.[64] It was a cautious advance but a perceptible trend nevertheless. On July 4, 1963, Ayub said that Western arms aid to India would drive the smaller nations of the region into the shelter of China.[65] A few days later his Foreign Minister, Z. A. Bhutto, told the Pakistan parliament that an attack on Pakistan would involve the largest state of Asia.[66] He was obviously referring to China. This was the first reference to the possibility of Pakistan's receiving Chinese assistance in the event of aggression against her. The officials of the State Department in Washington were reported to be distressed and annoyed at the implication that Pakistan would look to China for help in her defence against India. However, though Bhutto's statement implied the existence of a defence treaty against India between China and Pakistan, all available evidence pointed the other way. Bhutto was seeking only to impress the Western powers with the gravity of the situation and the extremes to which they were forcing Pakistan.

Pakistan steered her course in the new direction 'very warily and circumspectly'; she had not abruptly gone from one extreme to another.[67] But Pakistan's China policy was greatly resented in Washington and New Delhi. In Britain there was better appreciation of her problems and worries, and the new 'China policy' did not provoke there such hostile comments. *The Economist* observed:

> It is no coincidence that as India has drifted closer to the West, after the Chinese attack in 1962, Pakistan has drifted away rapidly. To the Pakistanis [Western arms aid to India] is simply arming their potential enemies and their natural reaction is to look for friends elsewhere, for instance in China, that in particular the West may dislike. But we have, at least, to recognize that Pakistan's 'flirtation' with China has a strictly logical connection with Pakistani pre-occupations about India. . . . If in the process of pursuing their own interests, the Pakistanis irritate the Americans, their feeling is the negative one 'That is just too bad', but not positive pleasure.[68]

The British government was reported to have sent an important message to the Chinese government through President Ayub during his visit to Peking in spring 1965. All in all, London seems to have reacted in a less alarmed way than Washington. Perhaps Britain did not dislike having a source in the Commonwealth through which to communicate with Communist China: a role which had formerly been played by Nehru's government. For Pakistan, it was partly a question of countering India's looming shadow, partly of serving notice on her Western allies who, by arming India, had upset the balance of power in this region to Pakistan's disadvantage. In short, Pakistan's relations with China are a mixture of realism and mutual advantage.

Pakistan's China policy aggravated Indo-Pakistan tensions. Nehru said in the Indian parliament in March 1963 that China was 'interfering in Indo-Pakistan relations'[69]—though in 1955 he had welcomed the Russian 'interference' in Indo-Pakistan relations. The Indian press was conjuring up a non-existent Pakistan-China 'collusion' to 'disturb' India's border, while the Pakistani press continued to point out that the Indian arms build-up, though ostensibly against China, was fundamentally against Pakistan.

Pakistan also made conscious efforts to normalise her relations with the Soviet Union and the other Communist countries. Up to 1961, the Soviet Union had been playing 'a hide-and-seek game of friendship with Pakistan—now threatening the country with rockets, now dangling aid bait'.[70] But thereafter a perceptible change was noticeable. The Soviet Union took note of Pakistan's growing dissatisfaction with the United States; she now offered Pakistan aid as an exercise in 'competitive coexistence'. The process of normalisation in Pakistan-Soviet relations began with the visit of Z. A. Bhutto to Moscow and the conclusion of an oil agreement in February 1961. The oil agreement 'had its own potential prickles for Russia-Pakistan friendship'.[71] Nor was Russia watching the growing Sino-Pakistan ties without concern. She seemed to be growing tired of her unqualified support for and commitment to India. Exploratory overtures between Moscow and Rawalpindi took place in 1963 and 1964. During his visit to India in 1964, the Soviet President, Anastas Mikoyan, 'went so far as to suggest directly to Shastri that it was time for India and Pakistan to seek settlement of their disputes'.[72] The Soviet press also showed the change by not condemning 'reactionary' Pakistan and contrasting it with 'progressive' India. In the 1960s, particularly after 1964, the Soviet Union seemed to have realised that Pakistan was not 'so bad' and India was not 'so good'.

The process of normalising relations culminated in the visit of President Ayub to the Soviet Union in April 1965, when healing was sought for past 'wounds' and new avenues of co-operation were explored. The present author had the opportunity of being a member of President Ayub's entourage to the USSR and could see from close quarters Pakistan's serious bid to normalise her relations with Russia. The effects of Ayub's efforts were revealed in the Soviet Union's impartiality in the Indo-Pakistan armed conflict in the Rann of Kutch in April 1965 and in the Indo-Pakistan war in September of the same year. From taking a palpably partisan attitude, the Soviet Union now seemed to wish to emulate the Western powers' policy of neutrality in Indo-Pakistan relations.

The Indian government is most sensitive to Pakistan's overtures to Moscow. Nothing worries it more than any reported change of attitude on the part of the Soviet Union and in her policies in the subcontinent. 'Indian leaders have built their whole foreign structure on the concept of a geopolitical community of interest between India and the Soviet Union with respect to China.'[73] Hence their great concern and sensitiveness about any improvement of Soviet-Pakistan relations. 'If New Delhi shows signs of wavering on issues affecting major interests, Moscow need only cast a nod in the direction of Rawalpindi, to induce clear thinking.'[74]

It reaffirms the fact that 'containment of Pakistan' is the pivot of Indian foreign policy. Because of their mutual distrust and quarrels, Pakistan and India have followed completely divergent external policies, and fundamental differences in their international outlooks have been a dominating feature. While Pakistan openly concedes that 'India' is the most dominating factor in her foreign policy, India would try to make the world believe that her 'policy of peace' is equally applicable to Pakistan. But the facts belie this and prove 'Pakistan' to be the most important and dominating factor in India's foreign policy. The international outlooks of the two countries will continue to be dominated by their distrust and fears as long as the outstanding disputes are not solved, and as long as Pakistan's right to statehood is not recognised by India without any mental reservations.

9

ARMED CONFLICT, 1965

Before dawn on September 6, 1965, the Indian army attacked Pakistan territory across the international frontier in the Punjab in the direction of Lahore, the second largest city of Pakistan and capital of West Punjab. 'Indian rulers', said President Ayub, 'with their customary hypocrisy have ordered their armies to march into the sacred territory of Pakistan without a formal declaration of war.'[1] According to a message from United Nations sources received by the British Prime Minister, Harold Wilson, the whole of the Indian army, save for four divisions, was attacking in the Punjab. He believed that 'India's aim was the military defeat of Pakistan'.[2] India invaded Pakistan 'in an all-out attempt to break the country's will to fight by seizing Lahore and Sialkot. India threw her armed forces, far larger than Pakistan's, into the invasion. . . '.[3] Her troops launched a three-pronged drive on Lahore, and the assault was preceded by heavy artillery shelling and air bombardment.

Thus began a full-scale war inside the Commonwealth. It was rightly stated that 'few episodes in history are more tragic than this fighting' between two members of the Commonwealth.[4] The British Prime Minister regarded the war between India and Pakistan 'as one of the gravest international developments since the end of the war against Japan', and in a statement on September 6, he said:

I am deeply concerned at the increasingly serious fighting now taking place between India and Pakistan and especially at the news that Indian forces have today attacked Pakistan territory *across the international frontier* in the Punjab. This is a distressing response to the

K

resolution adopted by the Security Council on September 4, calling for a cease-fire. The dangerous situation now created may have the gravest consequences not only for India and Pakistan but also for the peace of the world.[5] (Our italics.)

The British press, true to the national tradition of justice and fair play, also expressed its disapproval of India's aggression against the smaller neighbour. *The Times* stated in its editorial on India's crossing the international boundary of Pakistan:

> If there were any ground for examining India's excuse that the crossing of the frontier was simply a move to forestall Pakistan's plans to do the same, then the grounds were scattered and drowned by the cheering in the Indian parliament yesterday when the Defence Minister reported the attack. . . . If Indians are trying to draw a lesson from their own experience with the Chinese, aiming to deliver one major blow to exact Pakistan's acceptance of Indian rule in Srinagar, they surely mistake all the factors in relations with their neighbour.[6]

The *Guardian* wrote: 'News agencies report from some Indian cities scenes of jubilation recalling those in European cities in the summer of 1914 . . . the Indians have again put themselves in the wrong by crossing the international frontier yesterday. They cannot expect to attract much support from any other country.'[7] 'What must be condemned', declared the *Daily Telegraph*, 'is not merely aggression but also the stupendous folly of it.'[8]

This 'stupendous folly' was the culmination of the tensions, bitterness, hatred and hostility between the two countries that had marked their relations since they gained independence in 1947. Pakistan and India had been on the brink of war on several occasions during the previous eighteen years, and there had been many sharp encounters between their armed forces during that period. On September 26, 1947, little more than a month after independence, no less a person than Gandhi had hinted that 'the Indian government might have to go to war against Pakistan'.[9] The two countries subsequently were involved in a 'limited war' over the mountains of Kashmir which could, at any time, have turned into a full war. Nehru warned Pakistan several times of a full-scale war during 1948. In the 1950s, he threatened 'other methods' and made troop demonstrations on the borders of Pakistan, both East and West, while he was engaged in seizing the state of Kashmir and Jammu. When the Indo-Pakistan war broke out in September 1965, Mehr Chand Mahajan, a former Chief Justice of India, revealed India's plan for war in 1947. After recalling 'the well-known rule of military science that offensive action against an aggressor is the best form of defence', Mahajan said:

> It may interest readers to know that such a decision was taken as early as in 1947 by Sardar Patel, at a meeting held in December of that year in Jammu at General Kulwant Singh's headquarters. This meeting was attended by the Indian Defence Minister, Sardar Balday Singh, General Thimaya, the Maharaja of Patiala, the Jam Sahib of Nawanagar, the late Maharaja Hari Singh . . . [and] a few other high-ranking military officers. General Thimaya was requested to recruit and train guerrillas, and military headquarters were to plan the steps to be taken.[10]

The Indian leaders, as we have seen, could not accept Pakistan without mental reservations. 'Many Hindus were never reconciled to the price of dividing Mother India that had been paid for independence; many wishfully believed that Pakistan would collapse and be reabsorbed.'[11]

The whole military thinking of Indian policy-makers and strategists was governed by their attitude towards Pakistan, and their external policies, as shown in the preceding two chapters, were pursued to isolate and weaken her so that she could either be reabsorbed or at least be reduced to a state of vassalage. Selig S. Harrison pointed out in January 1965:

> The dominant note in the Hindu attitude today is that Hindus have a natural right to rule in modern India as a form of long overdue retribution for the sins of the Mogul overlords. It is not enough that a unified state with a Hindu majority—clearly dominant over a Muslim minority now reduced to 11 per cent—has been established at long last in the Indian subcontinent. The fulfilment of Indian nationalism requires an assertion of Hindu hegemony over the Muslims of the subcontinent in one form or another. Most Hindus would be satisfied with an acquiescent Pakistan within an Indian

sphere of influence, some hope for a confederation and a vocal few would welcome an excuse to annul partition by force.[12]

Such an attitude on the part of Indians is the only adequate explanation of the tragic happenings in the subcontinent in September 1965. 'The Indian rulers', said Ayub, in denouncing the Indian armed attack on September 6, 1965, 'were never reconciled to the establishment of an independent Pakistan where Muslims could build a homeland of their own. All their military preparations during the last eighteen years have been directed against us.'[13]

The fact that, from 1953 to 1962, Indian military adventures against Pakistan were less frequent was due to the partial redressing of Pakistan's serious military imbalance by American arms. But after 1962, when the military balance in the subcontinent was drastically changed in India's favour, thanks to her receiving massive Western arms aid, the threatening posture towards Pakistan became again a prominent feature of Indian policy. In January 1964, when appraising the effects of the military imbalance, Ayub predicted: 'Having built up this enormous war machine, India's leadership would need to justify the great hardships it has imposed on the Indian people in that process. It might also want to regain face which India has lost in the fighting with China. It is possible, therefore, that India might decide to do so— as soon as a suitable opportunity offered itself—by throwing its massive armour against Pakistan.'[14] When the war started in September 1965, he said: 'They exploited the Chinese bogy to secure massive arms assistance from our friends in the West who never understood the mind of the Indian rulers and permitted themselves to be taken in by India's profession that once they were fully armed they would fight the Chinese. We always knew that those arms would be raised against us. Time has proved this so.'[15]

Ayub's analysis of the effects of the military imbalance in the subcontinent was shared by impartial observers. 'India's new supersonic fighters, ground-to-air missiles, modern tanks and submarines would decisively alter the military balance in India's favour', the New Statesman observed. 'With acquisition of the new weapons risks of a showdown with Pakistan grew correspondingly.'[16] When the war broke out in September 1965, the defence correspondent of The Times pointed out: 'There is a real danger that the whole [Indian] army, still smarting at the defeat by the Chinese in 1962, sees the present engagement against Pakistan as a means to expiate that disgrace.'[17] And the same newspaper's New Delhi correspondent made the same point in a report during the war: 'Since the débâcles of the border war with China in 1962, Indian attitudes have presented a bruised and resentful militancy, and since the fighting in the Rann of Kutch in this summer that feeling has been focused on Pakistan.'[18]

By arming India, the big powers had threatened the peace in the subcontinent. India was displaying a sense of militancy as a result of her favourable military imbalance with Pakistan, her traditional foe. Just as the prospect of military help from Japan in 1942 had induced Gandhi, apostle of non-violence, to give up his pacifism and start a violent and ruthless campaign against the British authority in India, which was supposed to be weaker at that moment, so the Indian leaders in 1965 started a full-scale war against a weaker Pakistan in the expectation of a cheap and easy victory. In applying her entire armed might in a bid to conquer Pakistan, India showed no respect for any of the rules and principles which its leaders had preached inside and outside the United Nations. Her sole object was to subjugate a smaller neighbour by sheer physical force. As Harold Wilson rightly pointed out: 'There was no indication from the Indian side of any limitation of its objective, and the acclaim with which the announcement of the extension of the fighting was received in the Lok Sabha suggested that India's aim was the military defeat of Pakistan.'[19] This is the real background of the war of September 1965.

★

We now need to survey briefly the main developments leading to the outbreak of war. Enough has already been said on Kashmir and there is no need to repeat the fact that India had obstructed every constructive move to settle this dispute. Her military reverse at the hands of China in 1962 led many to expect that it might lead to a realistic appraisal of India's attitude and policy towards Pakistan, and that a way might be found to settle the Kashmir dispute. But the Anglo-American initiatives to solve this ruinous dispute came to nothing for there was no change in India's attitude. So the deadlock continued with all its dangerous implications, and peace in the subcontinent continued to be in suspense. Indo-Pakistan relations entered a further bitter phase after the failure of the direct talks on Kashmir in 1963. The tyrannical rule in Indian-held Kashmir continued, the process of oppression was unabated.

The next development in this quarrel was the popular uprising in Kashmir in December 1963, when the whole valley seemed to rise against India's rule. The occasion was the theft of a sacred hair of the Prophet from a shrine six miles from Srinagar. The holy relic had been in Kashmir for over three centuries, and news of its mysterious loss caused widespread and deep unrest in the valley. A mass movement started. In Srinagar on December 27, 1963, hundreds of thousands of wailing men and women came out in processions, carrying the body of one of the dead persons killed by police bullets the previous day. A 'Muslim Action Committee' was formed in Kashmir. The Indian authorities, naturally, tried to present the popular uprising in Kashmir as 'religious frenzy' directed against the local administration. But the accounts given by the foreign press correspondents and observers belied the Indian government's assertion. According to these sources, it was an open rebellion by the people of Kashmir against the Indian rule. In its analysis of the uprising in the 'unhappy valley', *The Economist* said:

> Westerners may have had some difficulty in believing that 100,000 Muslims could be persuaded to demonstrate purely and simply over the theft of a religious relic, even the hair of the Prophet. In fact, they could, but it would be naïve to imagine that was all that lay behind the riots of December which have kept Srinagar, capital of Kashmir, under curfew this week. . . . It must be recognised that 'Kashmir', which means the relationship between Pakistan and India is more explosive than it has been for years.[20]

The Times observed in an editorial: 'Now, less than ever, does it seem possible that the valley can ever be peaceful without some open test of public feeling';[21] and its special correspondent from Srinagar reported: 'The result is that at present the public inclination in the valley is undeniably towards Pakistan and no honest observer there, whatever his own wishes, will deny that in any plebiscite giving a choice between India and Pakistan the valley will now opt for Pakistan.'[22] In another dispatch five weeks later, *The Times* correspondent wrote: 'The political attitudes in the vale of Kashmir which underlay the recent agitation over the theft of the relic of the Prophet Muhammad are now finding more direct expression in demands for a plebiscite.'[23] Similar views were expressed in many other press reports. It was quite clear that the movement was a political one, demanding plebiscite and markedly pro-Pakistan in character. The people in the vale were expressing their feelings more clearly than ever before.

The next development was the release of Sheikh Abdullah on March 31, 1964, after eleven years of imprisonment (with an interval of three months in 1958). The Nehru government regarded his release as a gamble worth taking rather than face the continued uprising for plebiscite. Dr Ralph Bunche, the Under-Secretary of the UN, visited Kashmir in April and said that wherever he went in the state people demanded 'plebiscite and peace'.[24] The Security Council met twice— in February 1964 and then in May—to discuss the issue of Kashmir. India sought to raise the bogy of China in the Security Council to win the sympathy of the Western countries and perhaps also of Russia. Britain's delegate, Sir Patrick Dean, however, called on India and Pakistan to submit their fifteen-years-old dispute over Kashmir to new mediation, possibly with the help of the Secretary-General, U Thant. Britain, Morocco and the Ivory Coast supported Pakistan's contention that the future of the state should be self-determined. But all that the Security Council did was to appeal to India and Pakistan to settle their dispute by direct negotiations and meanwhile to exercise restraint in order to avoid more violence. Not even a resolution reaffirming the previous UN resolutions was passed. Emboldened by the complete inertia of the Security Council, India proceeded to take the final step by integrating the state, abolishing its special status under the Indian constitution.

Before examining this arbitrary act of *force majeure*, we need to see what came of the 'constitutional approach' to the Kashmir issue as made by Nehru before his death through his old friend Abdullah. After his release at the end of March 1964, Abdullah tried to find a formula for Kashmir's independence under the joint protection and control of India and Pakistan. Assuredly no friend of Pakistan, he was nevertheless thoroughly disillusioned and disheartened by his eleven years of imprisonment. Hence he sought to promote Indo-Pakistan understanding so as to settle the Kashmir issue, and in May 1964 he visited Pakistan to discuss the problem with President Ayub. The real nature of Abdullah's mediatory role was disclosed by Nehru who explained his 'constitutional approach'. Nehru was reported to have told Abdullah that he might explore the plan of an 'Indo-Pakistani confederation with Kashmir as a part of India'. If such a confederation could be agreed upon, then the Kashmir valley could gradually grow, in a decade or so, into a semi-autonomous entity within the Indian federation.[25] Pakistan's reaction to such wishful thinking was naturally resentful and critical. President Ayub gave expression to his country-men's feelings when he said: 'The objective of our struggle for Kashmir is to liberate Kashmir and not undo Pakistan.'[26]

Another proposal for the Kashmir issue was an Indo-Pakistan condominium, which was just another device for creating 'constitu-tional links' between India and Pakistan. Behind all these moves lay India's persistent desires and plans to undo the partition of 1947. Hence, the mediatory efforts of Abdullah were not acceptable to Pakistan, nor did they indicate any change of attitude on the part of the Indian government, whose spokesman in the United Nations and ministers at home at the end of 1964 boldly declared Kashmir to be a part of India. After a period of relative relaxation, relations between India and Pakistan again entered a phase of strain and antagonism. All hopes for a peaceful settlement of the Kashmir issue seemed to be doomed for good.

India's new Prime Minister, Lal Bahadur Shastri, after an initial conciliatory posture, presumably to gain control over the situation, proceeded to take the final step in integrating the state and thus shutting the door on negotiation or compromise. On December 4, 1964, the Indian government disclosed that it had moved a step towards the complete absorption of Kashmir. India was attempting to stage a 'back-door coup' to make final her hold over the area of Kashmir on her side of the cease-fire line established under United Nations aegis on January 1, 1949. The Indian government abolished the special status of Kashmir under article 370 of the Indian constitution: a step which even Nehru had not taken during his sixteen-years process of acquiring the state. On December 21, 1964, the Indian President issued a proclamation under which he assumed the powers and functions of both government and legislation in Kashmir. This move belied the hope expressed by the Security Council in May of the same year that both India and Pakistan 'would abstain from any act that might aggravate the situation and that they would take such measures as would reestablish an atmosphere of moderation'.[27] The Indian government's new move was accompanied by a declaration that 'the state's inclusion in the Union was complete, final and irrevocable'.[28]

Pakistan's reactions were naturally bitter. Her government protested and warned that 'the consequences of such attempts to annex Kashmir in repudiation of international obligations and in the face of open and determined opposition of the people of Kashmir will be disastrous'.[29] President Ayub accused India of taking illegal steps towards the integration of disputed Kashmir territory into India. Ayub also regarded it as betrayal because, during his meeting with Shastri on October 12, 1964, he gained the impression that Shastri would go slow on Kashmir. After Nehru's death there was a tacit understanding to let things stand for a while until Shastri found his feet. India's new moves confirmed the suspicion that Pakistan had been tricked.[30]

Reactions inside the Indian-held Kashmir, which had been in a state of unrest ever since the uprising over the theft of the holy relic, were violent and widespread. The Plebiscite Front, the most powerful political group in the state, described the new move as 'undemocratic and anti-people'. It warned that India's action was fraught with grave dangers, and pointed out that 'due to these steps the situation in occupied Kashmir has already worsened to an alarming extent'.[31] On January 15, 1965, a 'protest day' was observed throughout the state which led to police firing in Srinagar. Addressing a huge public meeting on this occasion, Abdullah appealed to the people of Kashmir to 'defeat the purposes of those [sc. Indians] who are trying to tighten the chains of slavery on the Muslims of Kashmir. . . . You cannot achieve freedom by imploring anybody and in view of India's present attitude you have to think how to face her effectively.'[32] Abdullah was arrested in no time and this led to further agitation and popular uprising in the state.

This outbreak of popular discontent in Kashmir was met by a

stronger repressive measure from the government of India. It was the long reign of repression in Indian-held Kashmir, intensified after December 1964, that let loose the forces which culminated in all-out armed conflict between Pakistan and India in the autumn of 1965. Before that, there was another serious encounter between the two armed forces in the Rann of Kutch in April-May of the same year. We now turn from the mountains of Kashmir to the marshy Rann of Kutch.

The conflict in the Rann of Kutch was one more in the long series of hostile clashes between India and Pakistan, but the confrontation in the dismal waterland was the biggest armed clash between the two armies since the Kashmir war of 1948. They battled over a piece of desolate land which Pakistan regards as a lake and India as a swamp, and which is of very little intrinsic value to either. The conflict over the useless Rann of Kutch was yet another symptom of the irreconcilable hostility between Pakistan and India.

The Rann of Kutch has been a disputed territory between India and Pakistan since independence in 1947. The question at issue was not that of demarcating a well-defined border in the area but of agreeing on its precise location. The disputed territory comprises an area of 3,500 square miles, situated roughly north of the 24th Parallel. The dispute pertains to the northern half of the area. On the basis of historical facts and exercise of jurisdiction, Pakistan could lay claim to the whole of the Rann of Kutch over which the former Sind province (now West Pakistan) of British India exercised administrative control. Pakistan, however, contented herself with a claim to the northern half of the Rann. The description of the area as given in the *Imperial Gazette of India*, Volume XI of 1908 (p. 74) seems to substantiate Pakistan's claim. Pakistan also based her claim on the international law applicable to areas which are of the nature of a landlocked sea or a boundary lake. However, at the time of the partition of the subcontinent in 1947, India laid claim to the whole of the Rann of Kutch. As the boundary between the province of Sind and the princely state of Kutch was not clearly defined during the British period, there was scope for claims and counter-claims by the two successor Dominions. The result was that the Rann of Kutch remained a disputed area between the two new states. Recent maps—for example, those in *The*

Times Atlas and the *Oxford Atlas*—also showed the territory as 'disputed area' between India and Pakistan. In fact, India herself admitted that the territory in the northern half of the Rann was a disputed area.

Beyond making a claim, however, India did not take any action to occupy the area, and Pakistan continued to exercise jurisdiction over the disputed area and maintained a police post at Chhad Bet, which is within the northern half of the Rann of Kutch. In 1956, Indian forces, operating under air cover, overwhelmed the Pakistani post and dislodged it from Chhad Bet. The Pakistan government lodged a strong protest against the Indian action, but, in order to avoid an armed clash and in the hope of reaching a peaceful settlement, did not use force to re-establish control of Chhad Bet. Pakistan continued to press for a settlement of the dispute. It was at last discussed in 1960 when President Ayub made determined bids to bring about a rapprochement between Pakistan and India. The latter, however, deferred any settlement. As in Kashmir, the Indian government seemed to rely on the principle of *possession vaut titre*; its whole conduct seemed to be based on 'might is right' and on the belief that Pakistan was unable to recover her territory. This was the attitude which governed India's actions in Junagadh, Hyderabad, Kashmir and in other territorial disputes with her smaller neighbours. Between 1960 and 1965, no progress could be made to settle the Rann of Kutch issue.

By January 1965, it was evident that India, being emboldened by Pakistan's long forbearance over Chhad Bet, was planning further military adventures in the area so as to present her claim to the whole of the Rann of Kutch as a *fait accompli*. Between January and April 1965, Indian military preparations in the Rann were clearly noticeable. The 21st Indian Infantry Brigade was moving from Ahmedabad and deployed in the area. The headquarters of the Indian armed forces in Gujarat state were moved forward to Bhuj to facilitate operational controls, and a large-scale combined operational exercise of military and naval forces was carried out in the area by India in March. Offensive operations began on the night of April 4 and 5, 1965, when Indian forces launched an unsuccessful attack on the post at Ding, within Pakistani territory. Another attack was made on April 8; this attack was also repulsed with heavy losses to the Indians. These particular attacks were the cause of the armed conflict—'a little war'—

which flared up between India and Pakistan in 'the desolate place' on April 9.

Pakistan made a three-point proposal to India, envisaging (i) cease-fire; (ii) restoration of the *status quo*; (iii) negotiations to settle the Rann of Kutch dispute. There was no response from India within five days and military preparations for further attacks were going on. Shastri and other Indian leaders made sabre-rattling speeches in parliament. 'War hysteria' seemed to have developed once again in India. The Home Minister, Nanda, said in the Lok Sabha: 'The question now before us involves the whole of posterity.' The Defence Minister had put the entire Indian army of 800,000 men on the alert, and the Prime Minister declared that 'each of our 450 million people of India is today prepared to make any sacrifice in defence of the motherland'.[33]

Foreign pressmen were, as usual, rebuked for their attitude to India over this dispute. 'Mr Shastri was reported as saying that the foreign press had carried on a mendacious campaign against India, alleging it was she who had committed aggression, that there was war hysteria in India while Pakistan was calm, that India was hindering a peaceful settlement by creating difficulties.'[34] Shastri was surprised that correspondents from democratic countries indulged in 'unhealthy criticism and slanted news'.[35] This is the technique which India usually adopts when the outside world has reason to condemn her actions or policies towards Pakistan. Shastri followed only in Nehru's path. The Indian press described the situation as 'war', 'Pearl Harbor' and so forth.

The real situation was that the Indian forces could not achieve their objectives; in fact, they had military reverses on April 18 when Pakistan launched counter-offensives in the area between Chhad Bet and Biar Bet. 'Indian troops had departed so hastily', wrote Tom Stacey in the *Sunday Times*, 'that they had left behind all sorts of homely things like pyjamas and boots and half-eaten *chappatis*.'[36] Indian troops tried to dislodge Pakistan forces at Biar Bet but were not successful. This made the Indian leaders furious, and hysterical outbursts of anti-Pakistan feelings became the dominant note of the Indian press.

On April 28, 1965, Shastri threatened military action against Pakistan on a battleground of India's own choice. He declared India would decide her strategy and employment of her manpower in the manner she deemed best.[37] In response to this threat, Ayub warned that this would mean 'a general and total war between India and Pakistan'. He added: 'We have been accused of "naked aggression". If we had wanted to commit aggression, we could have chosen a better area than the mudflats of the Rann of Kutch. And there were better occasions—for instance, when the Indian forces were on the run after their defeat at the hands of the Chinese.'[38] The Indian Prime Minister did not remain idle after this warning; the bulk of the Indian forces was moved close to the Pakistan border and there assumed offensive formations. The eve-of-war tension, which had been a regular phenomenon of Indo-Pakistan relations in 1947–52, was revived. The Pakistan government informed the Security Council on May 8 of India's large-scale offensive formations.

The British government played a prominent role in averting this major crisis and in reducing the tensions. Ultimately, Harold Wilson's peace moves triumphed and an agreement was signed on June 30, 1965, between Pakistan and India under a 'one-man peace mission'. The agreement had two aspects: one related to the settlement of the Rann of Kutch dispute, and the other to the disengagement of armies on the Indo-Pakistan borders. The armies of both countries stood in menacing confrontation along the entire border. President Ayub, therefore, felt that an agreement on the disengagement of forces was more important than the settlement of the Rann of Kutch. He described the agreement as a victory, not of Pakistan or India, but of common sense.[39] The Rann of Kutch dispute was to be considered at an India-Pakistan ministerial meeting—a meeting which would never be held because of worsening tensions in the following months. If these negotiations failed, the dispute would be referred to the arbitration of a tribunal consisting of three 'independent persons'. Each government would nominate a member of the tribunal, and the third member, who would be the chairman, would be nominated by the Secretary-General of the United Nations in case of disagreement between the two governments.

Thus, a major armed conflict was averted in the summer of 1965. Before the fighting in the Rann of Kutch in April, the Indian forces in January had occupied Dahagram, an undisputed Pakistani enclave in West Bengal. They withdrew after a few days in the face of Pakistan's firm stand for restoration of the *status quo*. India's military activities in Dahagram and in the Rann of Kutch were manifestations of a revived militant attitude towards Pakistan. As the government of Pakistan pointed out in its letter to the Security Council on April 11, 1965, the constant eruption of trouble along various sectors of the border with India could not be a matter of coincidence.

Fears were expressed that recent conflicts might be the spark that would bring about a major showdown between the two countries—fears which unfortunately proved to be correct in less than four months. What, then, were the causes of India's revived militant attitude towards Pakistan? It has already been stressed that India's attitude was stiffened as a result of her rearmament, which drastically changed the military balance in the subcontinent in favour of India. There were other factors, too. New Delhi might well have calculated that, because of her 'flirtation' with China, Pakistan would get no help or sympathy from the United States in any Indo-Pakistan dispute. Ayub's spectacular trip to China, the development of Sino-Pakistan-Indonesian ties and Pakistan's growing indifference to CENTO and SEATO were greatly resented in Washington. The Indian policy-makers and military strategists seemed to be carefully measuring the widening gap between Washington and Rawalpindi in their plan for a showdown with Pakistan. The Indian government was also greatly concerned at the rapidly rising eminence of Pakistan in the Afro-Asian fold, and was much disturbed by the Soviet Union's declaration in support of 'people who are fighting for the right of self-determination', made in a joint communiqué at the end of President Ayub's visit to the USSR in April 1965. Indian foreign policy came under fire and Shastri's position was becoming untenable. Sheikh Abdullah, who had gone on a pilgrimage, was telling the world about the Kashmiris' bondage under Indian rule. Internally, India's economic conditions were deteriorating fast, and famine was threatening. Under such circumstances, firm actions and a militant attitude against Pakistan 'seemed to a besieged Shastri a handy distraction'.[40] These facts should be kept in mind in analysing the Indo-Pakistan armed conflicts of 1965.

Now let us return to the mountains of Kashmir, whence the fighting spread to the plains of Punjab on September 6, 1965. In May, there were again violent demonstrations throughout the state of Jammu and

Kashmir when Abdullah was rearrested on his return from abroad. The political situation in the state had deteriorated steadily since the popular uprising in December 1964. India's new moves completely to integrate the state; Abdullah's rearrest; repressive measures—all these factors made the Kashmiri people desperate. On this occasion, as they had done before whenever there was any uprising or trouble in Kashmir, the Indian authorities tried to put the blame on Pakistan. That Pakistan gave sympathy and support to the people of Kashmir need not be said; that this support and sympathy were not always confined to mere verbal expressions might also be true. But to put all blame at the door of Pakistan is to ignore the basic fact of the Kashmir issue.

When fresh troubles started in August, Pakistan told the world that the people of Kashmir were in revolt against a tyrannical rule maintained only through the armed might of a foreign power. India, for her part, tried to make the world believe that the people were not involved; it was the 'Pakistani infiltrators' who were responsible for all troubles. The true position, perhaps, lay between the two assertions. The Indian government alleged that about 1,000 to 1,500 'infiltrators' had crossed from Pakistan when trouble started on August 8; subsequently its estimate of the number of alleged 'infiltrators' rose to 7,000.

The cease-fire line in Kashmir is a highly artificial line, with plenty of openings for incidents and controversies. It is not surprising, therefore, if some Kashmiri nationals from Azad Kashmir slipped across the cease-fire line to help their brethren in the struggle against Indian rule. The people of Azad Kashmir are not legally Pakistani nationals; they have a right to go to their homeland. Because of the nature of the terrain, neither the Pakistani nor the Indian forces could prevent them. The government of Pakistan perhaps felt no eagerness to stop it because India had finally closed the door to negotiations and to a peaceful settlement of the Kashmir dispute. It is quite likely that under such circumstances Azad Kashmir people had crossed the cease-fire line. Pakistan's delegate at the Security Council admitted that the Azad Kashmir government had provided arms to its people to join their brethren on the other side of the cease-fire line. That some people of Azad Kashmir who were ex-servicemen had gone from Pakistan's side of the cease-fire line was correct. 'It was natural', said Ayub, 'that their blood relations living on this side of the cease-fire line, mostly war veterans, should get agitated on what was happening to Muslims on the other side of the cease-fire line. They are not infiltrators but sons of the soil having a common stake in the future of their homeland.'[41]

To say that the whole trouble was entirely due to 'infiltrators' is to oversimplify the situation. India maintained about 150,000 troops and police in Kashmir. How could a few hundred, or even a few thousand, 'outsiders' cause such havoc and revolt within forty-eight hours in an area of about 50,000 square miles if the people were not involved? The Indian government alleged that Pakistan had sent 'infiltrators' on August 5, 1965. But on May 15, long before the Pakistani 'infiltrators' had entered Indian-held Kashmir, India occupied three Pakistani posts at Kargail. This was a calculated step to aggravate a situation which was already near explosion point—a resort to the same technique of armed incursion on Pakistani territory as was used in Dahagram and in the Rann of Kutch. It is also significant that, under the agreement over the Rann of Kutch dispute, both governments were supposed to withdraw armed forces from the entire border. Though Pakistan withdrew her troops, India kept her forces along the frontiers of Pakistan. 'India', said Ayub, 'wanted to keep them deployed at such points from where she could pounce upon Pakistan territory.'[42]

Under the pressure of the United Nations, India vacated the Pakistani posts at Kargail but reoccupied them on August 15. Before Pakistani forces intervened in the Kashmir troubles on August 15, Shastri threatened to carry the fight to Azad Kashmir. His Defence Minister announced in parliament that, whenever India had found it necessary to cross the cease-fire line, she had done—and would do so again.[43] On August 23, Indian forces shelled the village of Awan in Pakistani territory, and the next day they again crossed the cease-fire line, seizing two Pakistani posts in the Tithwal sector. A few days later, Indian troops moved in full strength in the Uri-Poonch area and, at the end of August, seized a number of Pakistani posts there. India had thus completely disregarded the cease-fire line. She was planning to seize Azad Kashmir by force. Pakistan's Foreign Minister, Z. A. Bhutto, declared that, since India had bit by bit broken the cease-fire line, she would have no justifiable grounds for complaint if Pakistan also considered it invalid.[44] Thus the cease-fire line, which had been main-tained by UN observers for eighteen years, was completely disregarded and crossed by Indian armed forces.

'These blatant acts of aggression', President Ayub announced, 'cannot and shall not be allowed to go unchallenged'.[45] On September 1, Azad Kashmir forces supported by Pakistan troops crossed the cease-fire line. Units of the Pakistan army moved into the Bhimbar sector and seized Chamb and Deva. The same day, the Indian air force went into action; the conflict was further aggravated. It may be added that Pakistan could have saved the isolated posts that India had seized in the Uri-Poonch sector if she had given the air support which the commanders of these small outposts were clamouring for. Pakistan, however, refused to be the first to add a new dimension to the conflict.

The final dénouement of the plan against Pakistan came before dawn on September 6, when the Indian government implemented its threat to hit Pakistan at a place and time of its own choosing—the threat made by Shastri on April 28, 1965. The desire of extremists in India ever since 1947 was now to be satisfied. Pakistan has always been regarded by many Indians as a 'blot on the map of India that will have to be removed before Indian independence is complete and Indian nationhood real'.[46] The correspondent of the *New York Times* reported from New Delhi on September 6 after the Indian invasion of Lahore: 'Citizens here greeted the news that Indian troops had marched into Pakistan today with an enthusiasm that seemed to ignore the risks of war. People crowded the streets in a jubilant mood: the standard question was "Have we taken Lahore?"'[47]

The Indian military plan seemed to be to occupy Lahore and Sialkot in a blitzkrieg and then dictate 'peace terms'. India's expectations of an easy and cheap victory lay in the comparative military strength of the two countries. When the fighting broke out, India had twenty infantry and mountain divisions, three independent infantry brigade groups, one armoured division and one independent armoured brigade. The armoured division was equipped with British Centurion tanks which each mount a 20-pounder gun. The armoured brigade had upgunned American Sherman tanks, some of which had been modified to carry AMX turrets. Pakistan, on the other hand, had only nine divisions, which included an armoured division equipped with American M48 tanks, and an armoured brigade which had a variety of tanks, including M47s and Shermans.

The imbalance in air strength was even greater. The Indian air force consisted of five Gnat squadrons, five Mystère squadrons, six Hunter VI and three Canberra squadrons, together with three Ouragan and seven Vampire fighter squadrons. Each of these squadrons contained sixteen aircraft. A few Russian MIG-21 supersonic fighters (nine aircraft) were also in service. The number of transport aircraft and helicopters was more than 300. Against this, Pakistan had only nine understrength squadrons. The total strength of her air force was ten F-104 Starfighters, ninety Sabre F-86F, twenty-two B-57 light bombers, and four C-130 transport aircraft.

In naval strength, India had an aircraft carrier, two cruisers, six destroyers and eleven frigates, to Pakistan's single cruiser, five destroyers and three frigates.[48]

It is no wonder that, with such large military balance in her favour, India was tempted to cross the cease-fire line and transform the Kashmir border fighting into a major war. But India's military expectations were not fulfilled because of the gallant resistance by the armed forces of Pakistan. It was noted by foreign observers that 'India has a big numerical strength but the morale of Pakistan is high'.[49] The initial momentum of the Indian attack began to falter very soon.[50] India attacked Lahore on September 6, and by September 8 foreign press correspondents were making such assessments as: 'The war is not going well for India; no bright communiqué about further advances in the Lahore area can disguise the fact.'[51] On September 11, the *Guardian* reported: 'Indian troops have been forced to withdraw on the Kasur sector south-east of Lahore, Mr Chavan, Indian Minister of Defence, announced in Parliament today. Members listened in gloom to Mr Chavan's statement.'[52] Two days later, the *Daily Telegraph* reported: 'Pakistani forces have crossed the border into India and are consolidating their positions at Khem Karan, an important East Punjab town three miles from the frontier on the railway line from Amritsar.'[53]

India had four times the military potential of Pakistan. Moreover, 'in violating the international frontier, she had the advantage of surprise'.[54] The government and army of Pakistan do not claim or pretend that their armed forces performed a miracle. History has many examples of a smaller army, when defending its homeland, repulsing the attacks of more powerful aggressors. In the Indo-Pakistan war, too, Pakistan's armed forces were not engaged in any territorial expansion but were defending their homeland against a powerful aggressor. Herein lay high morale and resolute will.

In the diplomatic field also India sustained a reverse, ruefully discovering that her invasion of Pakistan had little support in the rest of the world. In fact, it had dissipated most of the sympathy India had built up by charges of infiltration in Kashmir by Pakistan. The British Prime Minister's reaction has already been described. For the Commonwealth as a whole, it was a source of great dismay that a general and all-out war had started between two of its members. The Afro-Asian countries were also distressed to find open fighting between two Asian neighbours. Indonesia came out with open support for Pakistan; so also did Iran, Turkey, Jordan and Saudi Arabia.

Turning to the super powers, the Soviet Union and the United States: for the first time since the Suez crisis these two countries seemed to be more or less in agreement on a major international dispute. Washington and Moscow took almost identical stands on the Indo-Pakistan war. Both wanted the fighting to end as quickly as possible and both were most anxious that China should not intervene in it. China had given moral support to Pakistan from the outset, an official statement from Peking on September 7 stating that, 'the Indian Government's armed attack on Pakistan is an act of naked aggression'.[55] When China sent protest notes to India about alleged intrusions across the Sikkim border, many thought that she might open a second front for India on a frontier about which the Indians were nervous. It is doubtful if China would really have intervened, but it seemed highly probable that Chinese threats had deterred India from extending war to the defenceless East Pakistan, where she might have been tempted to score an easy victory after her setbacks in West Pakistan. The Chinese threats also induced a note of special urgency in the big powers' pleas for an end to the fighting. The Soviet Prime Minister, Alexei Kosygin, said in a message to Ayub and Shastri: 'We would not be frank if we did not say that the military conflict in Kashmir also arouses the anxiety of the Soviet Union because it has flared up in a region immediately adjacent to the frontiers of the Soviet Union.'[56] Tass, the Soviet news agency, warned against incendiary statements by nations 'seeking to fan the conflict'.[57] The Tass statement seemed aimed at Peking. The United States Secretary of State, Dean Rusk, also denounced China and praised the Soviet attitude as 'helpful'. The Soviet Union and the United States achieved what was termed a 'coincidence of policy' in the Indo-Pakistan war.

The United States remained cool and indifferent when the frontier of her erstwhile 'principal ally in Asia' was crossed by the Indian armed forces. In complete disregard of the bilateral agreement of mutual defence signed between Pakistan and the United States in 1959, the latter did not even raise a protest as was done by the British Prime Minister. America's attitude seemed to be wholly governed by her anger at Ayub's policy of normalising relations with the Communist countries, more particularly with China. The Indian policy-makers' calculations that Pakistan would get no sympathy from the United States proved correct.

India was, however, perturbed by the Soviet Union's neutrality. Leonid Brezhnev, Secretary of the CPSU, said during the war: 'The bonds of friendship which have already become traditional exist between us and India.' But in the same breath he pointed out: 'We want to develop good neighbourly relations with Pakistan as well. We consider that such relations are in the interest of the peoples of both our countries and we have noted with satisfaction that this effort on our part has met understanding on the part of the Pakistani government.'[58] This reflected Moscow's growing approval of the trends in Pakistan's foreign policy since 1960. Just as the Pakistan-American entente of the Eisenhower-Dulles era had faded, so also the Indian-Soviet harmony of the Khrushchev era seemed to be ended. A decade earlier the Russian view would have been quite different. Then India was seen as a 'non-aligned', 'peace-loving', 'secular' state. Pakistan by contrast was a 'theocracy' and a member of the Western military block. 'But as time went on the Russians came to believe that neither was India so good, nor Pakistan so bad, as they had earlier assumed.'[59] Russia's original interest in India and Pakistan, especially the former, was undoubtedly intended to counter Western influences, to neutralise the effect of Pakistan's military commitments and to maintain India's non-alignment. But during the past few years, the main motive of Russian policy in the subcontinent seemed to be 'containment of China'.[60]

The United States could exert tremendous pressure on both India and Pakistan because of her massive economic aid to them; yet American prestige was low in both countries because of President Johnson's abrupt cancellation of the visits of President Ayub and Prime Minister Shastri to Washington in the spring of 1965. This was likely to weaken the effect of any American diplomatic moves. Moreover, the Soviet Union also wanted the war to end. The State Department, therefore, preferred to work through joint efforts at the United Nations, in which it could also rely on the support of the Commonwealth. The United States had another difficulty: how could she advocate 'peace' in the subcontinent while she was engaged in fighting in another part of Asia? The ineffective role of the United States in the fight between India and Pakistan, who were so much dependent on American aid, indicated the decline of her prestige in Asia.

Meanwhile, the United Nations Secretary-General, U Thant, visited the subcontinent while the fighting and bombing were going on. However, he seemed to be moving at a snail's pace and, unlike his predecessor, he displayed very few dynamic qualities in a crisis involving 600 million people. His mission could achieve very little. But the co-operative efforts of the Soviet Union and the United States at the United Nations brought enough pressure on both parties to end the fighting. After seventeen days of war, a cease-fire was achieved on September 23, 1965. The two armies remained, however, in the various fronts and the explosive situation was by no means eased. The cease-fire was brought about in accordance with a resolution of the Security Council passed unanimously on September 20, 1965, under the joint and co-operative initiatives of the Soviet Union and the United States. Britain had also given full support to the move to effect an immediate cease-fire. The resolution of the Security Council was regarded by the Pakistan government as inadequate and unsatisfactory; it therefore refused to withdraw its armed forces from the battle positions. The two armies continued to face each other with loaded guns and increased bitterness.

Some more dynamic and constructive effort was needed to ease the situation. The Russians seized the initiative and launched a big peace offensive in the subcontinent. In a surprise move on September 4— two days before India crossed the cease-fire line—Kosygin had invited Ayub and Shastri to hold talks on Soviet soil; he had also offered to take part in such a reconciliation meeting 'if both sides wished it'. On September 7, the Soviet government urged India and Pakistan to stop fighting and renewed its offer of 'good offices' if both sides would deem it useful. A Kremlin statement called on the leaders of the two nations to display realism, restraint and understanding of the grave consequences of the development of the armed conflict.[61] Both countries accepted the Russian offer 'in principle' but, as long as the fighting was going on, each government expressed doubts about the fruitfulness of a meeting between Ayub and Shastri. Once the cease-fire was effected, the prospects of the Russian offer became brighter. The United States also exerted heavy pressure to achieve an understanding between the two countries; all American aid to India and Pakistan was suspended until an understanding was reached and troops were withdrawn. This reinforced the Soviet bids for peace in the subcontinent. 'Rarely, if ever, have the two major protagonists in the cold war been working so nearly parallel to cool down a major world hot spot.'[62]

Ultimately, the 'peace talks' began at Tashkent on January 4, 1966, under the guidance and vigilance of the Soviet Prime Minister, who was the chief actor, holding long separate consultations with Ayub and Shastri and simultaneously bringing the two together at the conference table for direct and frank talks. On January 11, an agreement was signed by President Ayub and Prime Minister Shastri which seemed to open a way to the hitherto elusive goal of coexistence between India and Pakistan. The agreement was greeted in many parts of the world as a diplomatic success, applauded by Western and Communist powers alike (with the exception of China): an international consensus unknown since the beginning of the cold war. For Russia it was a big triumph. The Tashkent Conference created an image for Russia as a peacemaker in Asia.

Whether it was a major step towards peace in the subcontinent was, however, not so certain. The Kashmir problem was, of course, far from being resolved at Tashkent. The main achievement there was the agreement for a withdrawal of forces to the previous cease-fire line by a specified early date, February 25, 1966. The two countries declared their 'firm resolve to restore their normal and peaceful relations' and to 'promote understanding and friendly relations between their people'. They stressed the 'vital importance' of neighbourly relations for the welfare of the 600 million of the subcontinent. Since gaining independence, India and Pakistan had made such pious declarations on many occasions—declarations which, in all previous cases, had been nullified by their mutual antagonism.

Pakistan insisted at Tashkent on a reference to Kashmir. This was resolutely opposed by India, who wanted her 'No-War Declaration' accepted. In the final agreement it was stated that the 'interests of the peoples of India and Pakistan were not served by the continuance of tensions between the two countries'. Then was added: 'It was against this background, that Jammu and Kashmir was discussed and each of the sides set forth its respective positions.' President Ayub, when explaining the Tashkent agreement to his people, said: 'We also impressed upon the Indian Prime Minister that peace could not be lasting unless the Kashmir dispute was amicably settled. . . . Pakistan was not prepared to consider Jammu and Kashmir as part of India.'[63] The Indian leaders, on the other hand, emphatically asserted that Kashmir was not negotiable and that India's stand on Kashmir remained unchanged. On balance, it seems that no progress towards a settlement of the Kashmir issue could be made at Tashkent.

In lieu of India's 'No-War Declaration', the agreement provides a 'No-Force Declaration' in accordance with the Charter of the United Nations. Ayub said: 'The Indian Prime Minister wanted us to sign a no-war pact, but we made it clear to him that we would never be a signatory to such a pact unless the Jammu and Kashmir dispute was settled honourably and equitably. We, however, offered to reaffirm our obligation under the UN Charter. This obligation means that nations will not resort to force unless they have explored all avenues of peaceful settlement.'[64] *The Times*, commenting on the 'No-Force Declaration', observed: 'This is far from the no-war declaration that would have assured the Indians that Kashmir was closed to future violence.'[65]

The most substantial part of the agreement was the provision relating to the withdrawal of troops. As neither country had gained complete military victory, both were willing to withdraw forces without loss of prestige. It was provided that 'all armed personnel of the two countries shall be withdrawn not later than February 25, 1965, to the positions they held prior to August 5, 1965, and both sides shall observe the cease-fire terms on the cease-fire line'. Its effect was to return to the situation as it was before the armed conflicts started. By February 5, troops of both countries began moving back on all sectors from the positions they had held. This was preceded by agreement by the two army chiefs under which both sides agreed to dismantle all defences in occupied territory.

The Tashkent agreement further provided that diplomatic missions would return to their posts; war prisoners would be exchanged; refugees would be repatriated where possible. The two countries also agreed to restore economic and trade relations as well as communications. They expressed willingness to continue talks on such mutual problems as the eviction of immigrants and the return of property and assets taken over by either side during the war. Both countries would discourage any propaganda against the other, and would encourage propaganda which would promote friendly relations between them.

The significance of the Tashkent agreement was that it opened a way out of the terrible impasse created by the war in September 1965. It did not solve any outstanding problems of Indo-Pakistan relations, but it paved the way to the restoration of the situation before the armed conflicts. It was no guarantee that the two countries would live in peace as good neighbours, but it certainly eased the explosive situation created by the war.

As noted earlier, the Tashkent agreement was hailed in many parts of the world. The Soviet press was naturally vocal in welcoming it. *Pravda* declared: 'It opens a new chapter in Indo-Pakistan relations, the signing of the declaration is a success for the peace-loving peoples of India, Pakistan, and the Soviet Union who make up almost a quarter of the world population.'[66] The Soviet press, however, did not omit to point out that the 'Tashkent meeting is of great significance today when some Western powers are still trying to settle international problems by the method of *diktat* and by imposing their will on other people . . . the United States is trying to solve the Vietnamese question by means of bloody and criminal aggression.'[67] The American press joined in welcoming the agreement as a step towards peace in the subcontinent, and especially because it was regarded as an effective check on China's influence in the subcontinent.

While the rest of the world welcomed the pact for various reasons, some reactions inside the subcontinent were far from reassuring. In West Pakistan, there were expressions of dismay and frustration. Miss Jinnah, Ayub's opponent in the presidential election of 1965, denounced the outcome of the Tashkent Conference. But when Ayub explained its significance to the nation, the movement against it subsided. The pact was welcomed from the start in East Pakistan. Some of the extremist groups in India were unhappy about it, though the ruling Congress party supported it.

Ayub's acceptance of the Tashkent agreement was based on a realistic appraisal of the military and diplomatic situation prevailing at the moment. There was, however, no change of heart or attitude on either side. With all major problems—including Kashmir—unsolved, it was unrealistic to expect a dramatic change in Indo-Pakistan relations just by one declaration. As has been stressed, the roots of present-day Indo-Pakistan tensions lie in the distant past; they are also coloured by the unhappy experiences of the two new states since they attained independence. The mental images that one has formed of the other are grim and threatening: 'a proven aggressor' and 'a potential enemy'. If the Tashkent spirit is to govern Indo-Pakistan relations, there must be changes in mental outlook. Dynamic and imaginative approaches must be made to overcome the age-old prejudice, hatred, bigotry and fears. It is not an easy task; the outstanding problems, particularly the corrosive quarrel over Kashmir must be solved; then the two countries must sincerely and whole-heartedly apply themselves to change the outlook of the two peoples towards each other.

In the absence of such changes in behaviour patterns and mental outlook, any effort like that made at Tashkent is not likely to 'open a new chapter'. *The Times* correspondent from New Delhi was already reporting in April 1966: 'Most people here and in Pakistan have written it [the Tashkent agreement] off.'[68] On June 3, 1966, Z. A. Bhutto gave the Pakistan National Assembly a list of breaches by India of the Tashkent agreement. Charges made by Bhutto include:

resumption of hostile propaganda and war-like statements by the Indian Prime Minister, Foreign Minister and other leaders against Pakistan; encouragement of secessionist propaganda in East Pakistan; sympathy and help for the 'Pakhtoonistan' movement; violation of the cease-fire line; interference with Pakistan's civil aircraft flying over India; and other similar charges.[69] Earlier, India's new Prime Minister, Indira Gandhi, had informed Moscow of 'Pakistan's breaches of agreement'.[70] The press of the two countries soon reverted from conciliatory words to its customary acrimonious style. Pakistan complained to the Soviet government that its sale of arms to India was against the spirit of the pact. The Russians were reported to have replied that they would consider selling arms to Pakistan on the same terms as they were selling them to India[71]—an assurance which has not yet materialised.

The prospects of peace and stability in the subcontinent do not seem to be bright. Yet, despite the disillusionments of twenty years, we must continue to hope that reason will prevail over prejudice and that these two great Asian peoples will direct their energies and resources to raising their economic conditions rather than to building up armies against each other.

REFERENCES

Full publication details of works cited here will be found in the Select Bibliography.

Introduction

1. See Paul Grimes, *New York Times*, December 2, 1962.
2. Michael Brecher, in Selig S. Harrison (ed.), *India and the United States*, New York 1961, p. 53.
3. Ibid.
4. *The Times*, June 2, 1956.
5. "Indo-Pakistan Relations: Areas of Conflict", *Round Table*, London 1959–60, p. 163.
6. Quincey Wright, in Harrison (ed.), op. cit., p. 55.
7. F. N. Trager, "The United States and Pakistan: A Failure of Diplomacy", ORBIS, Vol. IX, No. 3, 1965.
8. *The Times*, February 23, 1957.

1. Historical Background

1. G. W. Choudhury, "The Impact of Islam in Pakistan", *Current History*, June 1957.
2. See the preamble to the Cabinet Mission Plan of May 1946, in C. H. Philips, *The Evolution of India and Pakistan, 1947–1958*, London 1962, pp. 378–82.
3. *The Economist*, May 17, 1947.
4. Jinnah's Foreword, in "M.R.T.", *Pakistan and Muslim India*, Bombay 1942.
5. I. H. Qureshi, *The Struggle for Pakistan*, Karachi 1965, pp. 10–11.
6. Ahmad Ali, "The Culture of Pakistan", in Richard Symonds (ed.), *The Making of Pakistan*, London 1950.
7. Report of the Indian Statutory Commission, Cmd 3568, HMSO, London 1930, Vol. I, p. 25.

8. Sir Theodore Morrison, "Muhammad Movements", in Sir John Cumming (ed.), *Political India, 1832–1932*, London 1932, pp. 103–4.

9. R. Coupland, *The Indian Problem*, London 1944, p. 72.

10. Ibid., p. 72.

11. Qureshi, op. cit., p. 80.

12. Jinnah, cited in Philips, op. cit.

13. Coupland, op. cit., p. 109.

14. Jinnah, cited in Qureshi, op. cit., p. 88.

15. Abul Kalam Azad, *India Wins Freedom*, London, Bombay and New York 1959, p. 160.

16. Coupland, op. cit., p. 111.

17. Jinnah, cited in Philips, op. cit., p. 347.

18. Coupland, op. cit., p. 178.

19. Abul Kalam Azad, op. cit., p. 161.

20. Sir Percival Griffiths, *The British Impact on India*, London 1952, p. 341.

21. Ibid., p. 341.

22. Cited in Qureshi, op. cit., p. 99.

23. Griffiths, op. cit., p. 341.

24. Sir Maurice Gwyer and A. Appadorai, *Speeches and Documents on the Indian Constitution, 1921–47*, London and New York 1957, Vol. I, p. 411.

25. Coupland, op. cit., p. 186.

26. Qureshi, op. cit., p. 187.

27. Coupland, op. cit., p. 187.

28. Ibid., p. 191.

29. Ibid., p. 191.

30. Qureshi, op. cit., p. 99.

31. Ibid., pp. 105–6.

32. Cited in Philips, op. cit., p. 347.

33. Coupland, op. cit., p. 187.

34. Gwyer and Appadorai, op. cit., p. 417.

35. Philips, op. cit., p. 352.

36. Qureshi, op. cit., p. 113.

37. Ibid., p. 117.

38. Gwyer and Appadorai, op. cit., p. 418.

39. Philips, op. cit., p. 354.

40. Ibid., pp. 353–4.

41. R. G. Casey, *An Australian in India*, London 1947, pp. 74–6.

42. Liaquat Ali Khan, *Pakistan: The Heart of Asia*, Cambridge, Mass. 1950, p. 56.

43. G. W. Choudhury, *Constitutional Development in Pakistan*, London 1959, p. 13.

44. N. W. R. Lumby, *The Transfer of Power in India*, London 1954, p. 78.
45. *Round Table*, March 1946.
46. Lumby, op. cit., p. 89.
47. For the full text of the Cabinet Mission Plan, see Philips, op. cit., pp. 378–82.
48. Griffiths, op. cit., p. 385.
49. Cited in Lumby, op. cit., p. 87.
50. Cited in A. A. Ravoof, *Meet Mr Jinnah*, Lahore 1945, p. 196.
51. Cited in Qureshi, op. cit., p. 283.
52. V. P. Menon, *The Transfer of Power in India*, London and Calcutta 1957; Princeton, N.J., 1959.
53. Lumby, op. cit., p. 100.
54. Ibid., pp. 167–9.
55. Abul Kalam Azad, op. cit., p. 155.
56. Leonard Mosley, *The Last Days of the British Raj*, London 1962, p. 28.
57. Both statements cited in Penderel Moon, *Divide and Quit*, London 1961; Berkeley, Calif. 1961.
58. For the full text of Jinnah's speech, see J. Ahmed, *Speeches and Writings of Jinnah*, Lahore 1952, pp. 419–23.
59. Choudhury, *Constitutional Development . . .* , op. cit., p. 22.
60. Lumby, op. cit., p. 127.
61. Ibid., p. 128.
62. See *Round Table*, March 1947.
63. Ibid.
64. Philips, op. cit., pp. 391–3.

2. INDEPENDENCE: INITIAL DIFFICULTIES AND PROBLEMS

1. Mohammad Ali Jinnah, *Speeches as Governor-General of Pakistan, 1947–1948*, Karachi n.d., p. 12.
2. *The Times*, May 22, 1947.
3. Nicholas Mansergh, *Documents and Speeches on British Commonwealth Affairs*, London 1953, p. 702.
4. Jinnah, *Speeches . . .* , op. cit., p. 30.
5. *The Times*, September 15, 1947.
6. See, for example: Sir Francis Tuker, *While Memory Serves*, London 1950; E. W. R. Lumby, *The Transfer of Power in India*, op. cit.; Ian Stephens, *Pakistan*, London 1962, New York 1963; paperback edn., Harmondsworth 1964.
7. *Dawn*, Karachi, September 15, 1947.
8. *The Times*, August 27 and 30, September 5, 1947.

9. *The Economist*, September 9, 1947.
10. Sir Mohammad Zafrullah Khan, speech at the Security Council, *Security Council Official Records*, Third Year, Nos. 1-1015 (meetings 228-9): hereinafter referred to as SCOR.
11. Stephens, op. cit., p. 231 (Penguin edn. pagination).
12. Lord Ismay, *Memoirs*, London 1690, p. 436.
13. John Connell, *Auchinleck*, London 1956, pp. 920-22.
14. Ibid., p. 927.
15. Stephens, op. cit., p. 221.
16. Jinnah, *Speeches . . .*, p. 31.
17. Ismay, op. cit., p. 431.
18. See: Michael Brecher, *Nehru: A Political Biography*, London and New York 1959; Leonard Mosley, *The Last Days of the British Raj*, op. cit.
19. Connell, op. cit., p. 911.
20. Abul Kalam Azad, op. cit., p. 190.
21. *Pakistan News*, London July 14, 1948.
22. SCOR, op. cit.
23. Stephens, op. cit., p. 208.
24. Mosley, op. cit., p. 216.
25. *The Times*, July 9, 1948.
26. *Pakistan News*, July 9, 1948.
27. Security Council, Document 646, January 15, 1948.
28. *Dawn*, September 22, 1941.
29. *The Times*, September 29, 1947.
30. *Pakistan News*, January 21, 1950.
31. SCOR, op. cit.
32. Connell, op. cit., pp. 220-2.
33. SCOR, op. cit.
34. *The Times*, October 3, 1947.
35. Ibid., September 27, 1947.
36. *Truth*, London, October 3, 1947.
37. *Inquirer*, London, October 4, 1947.
38. *The Economist*, October 4, 1947.
39. SCOR, op. cit.
40. *The Times*, October 1, 1947.
41. Connell, op. cit., pp. 220-2.
42. *Observer*, September 10, 1950.
43. Lord Birdwood, *A Continent Decides*, London 1953, pp. 235-6.
44. *Manchester Guardian*, September 27, 1950.
45. *Pakistan Times*, Lahore, June 22, 23, 24, 1964.

46. Stephens, op. cit., p. 214.
47. Brecher, op. cit., pp. 410–11.
48. Jinnah, *Speeches* . . . , op. cit., p. 32.
49. Sir Percival Griffiths, *Modern India*, London and New York 1957, p. 103.
50. Stephens, op. cit., p. 215.
51. *Dawn*, September 20, 1949.
52. Connell, op. cit., pp. 220–2.
53. *New York Herald Tribune*, January 16, 1948.
54. Connell, op. cit., p. 916.
55. Ibid., pp. 220–2.
56. SCOR, op. cit.
57. *The Times*, August 1, 1951.
58. SCOR, op. cit.
59. Griffiths, *Modern India*, op. cit., p. 106.
60. Ibid., p. 163.
61. Security Council, Document 646, January 15, 1948.
62. *Dawn*, January 9, 1948.
63. *Statesman*, New Delhi, January 13, 1948.
64. *Dawn*, January 9, 1948.
65. *Hindu*, Madras, January 14, 1948.
66. Stephens, op. cit., p. 234.
67. *The Times*, June 20, 1947.
68. Ibid., November 5, 1947.
69. SCOR, Nos. 16–35, 64, 1948.
70. *Dawn*, January 2, 1948.
71. Stephens, op. cit., p. 236.
72. SCOR, Nos. 16–35, 64, 1948.
73. Ibid.
74. Ibid.
75. Ibid.
76. *Daily Telegraph*, October 6, 1947.
77. *The Times*, November 11, 1947.
78. SCOR, No. 64, 1948.
79. *Statesman*, November 13, 1948.
80. SCOR, No. 64, 1948.
81. *New York Times*, October 11, 1948.
82. SCOR, No. 64, 1948.
83. Ibid.
84. SCOR, No. 28, 1949.
85. Ibid.

86. Ibid.
87. *The Times*, April 20, 1948.
88. Ibid., July 31, 1948.
89. Ibid., July 27, 1948.
90. *New York Times*, May 15, 1949.
91. *The Times*, September 15, 1948.
92. Ibid., September 16, 1948.
93. Ibid., September 18, 1948.
94. *Christian Science Monitor*, September 14, 1948.
95. *Dawn*, September 18, 1948.
96. *New York Times*, May 15, 1949.
97. Ibid., September 29, 1948.
98. Ibid., May 15, 1949.
99. SCOR, No. 28, 1949.
100. *Dawn*, October 31, 1948.
101. Nawab Moin Nawaz Jung, *The Situation in Hyderabad*, Karachi n.d.
102. *The Times*, September 18, 1948.
103. Stephens, op. cit., p. 288.
104. *New York Herald Tribune*, January 16, 1948.
105. *Statesman*, August 18, 1947.
106. Ibid., June 16, 1947.
107. Ibid., August 13, 1947.
108. Abul Kalam Azad, op. cit., p. 207.
109. *The Times*, June 5, 1947.
110. *New York Herald Tribune*, June 5, 1947.
111. *The Times*, June 16, 1947.
112. Ibid., June 5, 1947.
113. Ibid., February 26, 1948.
114. Brecher, op. cit., p. 378.
115. Ibid., p. 378.
116. *The Economist*, May 17, 1947.
117. *Dawn*, January 2, 1948.
118. Ibid., July 30, 1948.
119. Quincey Wright, in Harrison (ed.), op. cit., p. 55.
120. *Statesman*, January 8, 1948.
121. *Dawn*, January 20, 1948.
122. *Daily Telegraph*, January 30, 1948.
123. *The Times*, January 19, 1948.
124. *Statesman*, March 22, 1948.
125. *Dawn*, January 2, 1948.

126. Lumby, op. cit., p. 161.
127. "Indian View of the Commonwealth", *Round Table*, September 1950.

3. KASHMIR

1. M. Philips Price, in *Manchester Guardian*, November 11, 1948.
2. Birdwood, op. cit., p. 219.
3. Premnath Bazaz, *The History of Struggle for Freedom in Kashmir*, New Delhi 1954, p. 325.
4. Ian Stephens, *Pakistan*, op. cit., p. 243.
5. SCOR, Nos. 1–15, 1948 (meetings 228–9).
6. Ibid.
7. Ibid.
8. M. Philips Price, loc. cit.
9. Quoted in Sir Zafrullah Khan's speech, SCOR, op. cit.
10. Bazaz, op. cit., p. 322.
11. Ibid., p. 324.
12. Leonard Mosley, op. cit., p. 187.
13. Ibid.
14. Quoted in ibid.
15. Josef Korbel, *Danger in Kashmir*, Princeton, N.J. 1954, p. 57.
16. *Daily Telegraph* and *Daily Mail*, October 7, 1947.
17. *Statesman*, January 5, 1948.
18. Bazaz, op. cit., p. 335.
19. Ian Stephens, *Horned Moon*, London 1953, pp. 109–15.
20. Korbel, op. cit., pp. 79–80.
21. Ibid., pp. 85–6.
22. *Statesman*, January 5, 1948.
23. Bazaz, op. cit., p. 343.
24. Security Council Document 646 of January 15, 1948.
25. *Dawn*, November 17, 1947.
26. *New Commonwealth*, London, January 7, 1957.
27. Security Council Document 628 of January 2, 1948.
28. Security Council Document 646 of January 15, 1948.
29. SCOR, op. cit.
30. Birdwood, Lord, *Two Nations and Kashmir*, London 1956, p. 54.
31. *New York Times*, January 2, 1948.
32. *Observer*, January 4, 1948.
33. *Daily Telegraph*, January 5, 1948.
34. *Manchester Guardian*, March 6, 1948.

L

35. Sir Zafrullah Khan's television interview at Lahore, published in *Dawn*, December 2, 1965.

36. SCOR, 1950 (meeting 464).

37. *Statesman*, September 6, 1948.

38. *Manchester Guardian*, September 13, 1948.

39. See *Report of the UN Commission for India and Pakistan*, Karachi 1948 and 1949.

40. *Annual Register of World Events*, London, 1949, p. 126 (hereinafter referred to as *Annual Register*).

41. *Manchester Guardian*, September 7, 1949.

42. *New York Times*, September 16, 1949.

43. *Daily Telegraph*, December 12, 1949.

44. See *Reports on Kashmir by United Nations Representatives*, Karachi 1962

45. *Annual Register*, 1952, p. 121.

46. *Pakistan News*, July 7, 1951.

47. Korbel, op. cit., p. 222.

48. *New Commonwealth*, January 7, 1951.

49. For this and succeeding quotations in this subsection, see *The Negotiations Between the Prime Ministers of Pakistan and India Regarding the Kashmir Dispute (June 1953–September 1954)*, Karachi n.d.

50. SCOR 1957 (meeting 761).

51. *Dawn*, April 20, 1954.

52. *The Times*, editorial, January 28, 1957.

53. *News Chronicle*, January 28, 1957.

54. Reprinted in *Dawn*, February 1957.

55. *New York Herald Tribune*, January 28, 1957.

56. *Daily Telegraph*, January 26, 1957.

57. SCOR 1957 (meeting 791).

58. General Maxwell Taylor's testimony before the United States Congress, quoted in *Round Table*, 1962–63, p. 289.

59. *New York Times*, November 10, 1962.

60. *Dawn*, December 15, 1962.

61. Ibid., December 17, 1962.

62. *Daily Telegraph*, January 5, 1963.

63. *The Times*, January 16, 1963.

64. *New York Times*, editorial, January 31, 1963.

65. Ibid., January 31, 1963.

66. See "The Clouds Over Kashmir", *New York Times*, May 5, 1957.

67. Based on unpublished papers of the government of Pakistan and personal interview.

68. *Sunday Telegraph*, December 23, 1962.
69. *The Times*, report from New Delhi, reprinted in *Round Table*, 1962–63, p. 290.
70. *Annual Register*, 1963, p. 85.
71. *The Times*, report from New Delhi, reprinted in *Round Table*, 1962–63, p. 290.
72. *New York Times*, February 11, 1963.
73. Ibid., May 4, 1963.
74. *The Times*, May 4, 1963.
75. *Observer* Foreign News Service, December 19, 1962.
76. *Daily Telegraph*, May 16, 1963.
77. *Round Table*, 1962–63, p. 290.
78. *Hindu*, June 16, 1963.
79. *The Times*, February 14, 1964.
80. See "Kashmir Quarrel", *Observer*, September 15, 1957.

4. TRADE AND WATER DISPUTES

1. Douglas Brown, "India and Pakistan: A More Harmonious Phase", *Daily Telegraph*, August 15, 1949.
2. Griffiths, *Modern India*, op. cit., p. 178.
3. Naema Sultan Begam, "Indo-Pakistan Trade Relations", *Pakistan Horizon*, Karachi, September 1950.
4. Griffiths, op. cit., p. 179.
5. *Dawn*, November 14, 1947.
6. B. Barai, "Three Years of Indo-Pakistan Trade: A Review", *Pakistan Economic Journal*, Dacca, December 1950.
7. *The Times*, October 4, 1949.
8. See *The Economist*, October 22, 1949.
9. Griffiths, op. cit., p. 180.
10. *Statesman*, January 5, 1950.
11. *Daily Telegraph*, December 30, 1949.
12. *The Times*, December 28, 1949.
13. See *Christian Science Monitor*, October 20, 1950.
14. *The Economist*, November 12, 1949.
15. Stephens, *Pakistan*, op. cit., (ch. 2, Note 6), p. 274.
16. Cited in, *Pakistan News*, January 21, 1950.
17. *The Times*, April 22, 1950.
18. *Financial Times*, April 27, 1950.
19. *The Times*, April 27, 1950.
20. *Statesman*, September 21, 1950.

21. *The Times*, February 26, 1951.

22. *Manchester Guardian*, February 27, 1951.

23. *The Times*, February 27, 1951.

24. See Press Release No. 650, International Bank for Reconstruction and Development, Washington, D.C., September 1950.

25. Eugene R. Black, "The Indus: A Moral for Nations", *New York Times Magazine*, December 11, 1960.

26. Ibid.

27. Ibid.

28. See "Dividing the Waters", *Round Table*, 1954–55, p. 240.

29. See "Waters of Strife", ibid., 1957–58, p. 364.

30. Ibid.

31. David E. Lilienthal, "Another Korea in the Making", *Colliers*, August 1951.

32. Quoted in *Pakistan News*, September 8, 1951.

33. *Round Table*, 1960–61, p. 72.

34. *Pakistan: The Struggle for Irrigation Water and Existence*, Embassy of Pakistan, Washington, D.C., 1953, p. 17.

35. See F. J. Fowler, "The Indo-Pakistan Water Dispute", *Year Book of World Affairs*, London 1955, p. 101.

36. *No-War Declaration and Canal Water Dispute: Correspondence Between the Prime Ministers of India and Pakistan, January 18–November 24, 1950*, Government of Pakistan, Karachi, 1950.

37. *New York Times*, August 19, 1951.

38. "Waters of Strife", op. cit.

39. Press Release No. 650, International Bank, op. cit.

40. E. R. Black, op. cit.

41. "Dividing the Waters", op. cit.

42. Fowler, op. cit.

43. "Waters of Strife", op. cit.

44. Ibid.

45. Ibid.

46. E. R. Black, op. cit.

47. "Waters of Strife", op. cit.

48. Fowler, op. cit.

49. E. R. Black, op. cit.

50. Press Release No. 650, International Bank, op. cit.

51. Neal Stanford, "Indus Treaty Softens National Antagonism", *Christian Science Monitor*, September 21, 1960.

52. E. R. Black, op. cit.

53. *Dawn*, September 5, 1960.

54. *The Times*, September 15, 1960.

55. *Financial Times*, September 19, 1960.

56. *Guardian* (formerly *Manchester Guardian*), September 20, 1960.

57. *Dawn*, September 5, 1960.

58. *Round Table*, 1960–61, p. 75.

59. Ibid., p. 74.

5. RELIGIOUS MINORITIES

1. Quoted in *Condition of the Indian Muslims*, unpublished document of the Government of Pakistan, 1964.

2. Ibid.

3. *The Times*, August 10, 1964.

4. *Statesman*, April 15, 1964.

5. Quoted in Bazaz, op. cit., p. 346.

6. Ibid., p. 365.

7. *Morning News*, Dacca, August 11, 1964.

8. Ibid., August 20, 1964.

9. *The Times*, August 10, 1964.

10. Stephens, *Pakistan*, op. cit., p. 66.

11. *Dawn*, January 14, 1964.

12. Ibid., January 18, 1964.

13. Ibid., January 21, 1964.

14. *Tribune*, Ambala, March 15, 1964.

15. *Hindustan Times*, New Delhi, March 15, 1964.

16. Ibid., March 27, 1964.

17. Based on unpublished documents of the government of Pakistan.

18. *Report of the Asir Commission*, Dacca 1964.

19. *The Times*, December 6, 1963.

20. *Dawn*, January 14, 1964.

21. *Constituent Assembly of Pakistan Debates: Official Report*, Karachi 1947, Vol. I, pp. 3–6.

22. W. C. Smith, *Pakistan as an Islamic State*, Lahore 1951.

23. *New York Times*, April 11, 1950.

24. *Statesman*, August 2, 1950.

6. 'EDGE OF A PRECIPICE'

1. W. Norman Brown, *The United States and India and Pakistan*, Cambridge Mass. 1963, p. 171.

2. *Annual Register*, 1951, pp. 125–6.

3. *Annual Register*, 1951, p. 119.
4. *Statesman*, January 5, 1950; see also editorials in *Dawn*, February 3–9 and March 15, 1950.
5. *Dawn*, March 25, 1950; and *The Times*, March 30, 1950.
6. *Statesman*, March 28, 1950.
7. *Hindu*, March 18, 1950.
8. *New York Times*, April 7, 1950.
9. *New York Herald Tribune*, March 29, 1950.
10. *Times of India*, New Delhi, February 23, 1950.
11. *The Times*, February 28, 1950.
12. *Statesman*, March 4, 1950.
13. *New York Times*, March 4, 1950.
14. *The Times*, March 25, 1950.
15. Ibid., March 28, 1950.
16. *Pakistan News*, March 18, 1950.
17. *Daily Telegraph*, March 27, 1950.
18. *Dawn*, March 18, 1950.
19. Stephens, *Horned Moon*, op. cit., p. 33.
20. *New York Times*, March 29, 1950.
21. Ibid., April 11, 1950.
22. *New York Herald Tribune*, April 11, 1950.
23. Ibid.
24. *New York Times*, August 8, 1950.
25. *Hindu*, June 25, 1950.
26. *The Economist*, July 22, 1950.
27. *The Times*, October 21, 1950.
28. *Statesman*, August 8, 1950.
29. Ibid., October 10, 1950.
30. *Hindustan Times*, May 5, 1950.
31. *Observer*, January 26, 1964.
32. *Round Table*, 1950–51, p. 78.
33. Ibid., 1951–52, p. 69.
34. *Dawn*, July 16, 1951.
35. *Annual Register*, 1951, p. 124.
36. See *India's Threat to Pakistan: Correspondence Between the Prime Ministers of Pakistan and India, July 15–August 11, 1951*, Karachi n.d. [1951].
37. Ibid.
38. *Dawn*, July 19, 1951.
39. *India's Threat . . .* , op. cit.
40. *Dawn*, July 19, 1951.

41. *India's Threat* . . . , op. cit.
42. *Manchester Guardian*, July 17, 1951.
43. *Daily Express*, July 19, 1951.
44. *The Times*, July 23, 1951.
45. *Manchester Guardian*, July 19, 1951.
46. *Observer*, July 22, 1951.
47. *Daily Telegraph*, July 19, 1951.
48. *New York Herald Tribune*, July 17, 1951.
49. *Daily Telegraph*, July 30, 1951.
50. *Dawn*, August 2, 1951.
51. *Manchester Guardian*, July 24, 1951.
52. *Dawn*, August 3, 1951.
53. *The Times*, August 9, 1951.
54. Ibid., July 21, 1951.
55. *India's Threat* . . . , op. cit.
56. *The Times*, July 28, 1951.
57. *India's Threat* . . . , op. cit.
58. *The Times*, August 1, 1951.
59. *Round Table*, 1951–52, p. 70.
60. *India's War Propaganda Against Pakistan*, Karachi, n.d. [1951].
61. *National Herald Tribune*, Lucknow, July 8, 1951.
62. *India's War Propaganda* . . . , op. cit.
63. Ibid.
64. Ibid.
65. *Dawn*, August 29, 1951.
66. Cited in *India's War Propaganda* . . . , op. cit.
67. R. M. Lohia, *Agla Kadam*, cited in *India's War Propaganda*, op. cit.
68. "Neighbours in Asia", *Round Table*, December 1956.
69. "Indo-Pakistan Relations: Areas of Conflict", *Round Table*, March 1960.
70. *The Times*, November 30, 1950.
71. *No-War Declaration and Canal Water Dispute* . . . , op. cit.
72. Ibid.
73. Ibid.
74. Ibid.
75. Ibid.
76. Ibid.
77. Ibid.
78. Ibid.
79. Ibid.

80. *The Indian Proposal for 'No-War Declaration'*, unpublished document of the Government of Pakistan.

81. Ibid.

82. Z. A. Bhutto, *Foreign Policy of Pakistan*, Karachi 1964, pp. 5–6.

7. DIVERGENT FOREIGN POLICIES: I. 1947–59

1. M. Zafrullah Khan, *Pakistan's Foreign Relations*, Karachi 1951, p. 8.

2. K. Sarwar Hasan, *Pakistan and the United Nations*, New York 1960, pp. 49–50.

3. Liaquat Ali Khan, *Pakistan: The Heart of Asia*, op. cit., p. 11.

4. J. H. Qureshi, "The Foreign Policy of Pakistan", in Joseph E. Black and Kenneth W. Thompson, *Foreign Policies in a World of Change*, New York 1963.

5. *Hindu*, March 8, 1954.

6. *Dawn*, February 23, 1957.

7. Mohammad Ayub Khan, *Speeches and Statements*, Karachi n.d., Vol. I, pp. 119–20.

8. Bhutto, *Foreign Policy of Pakistan*, op. cit., p. 27.

9. Qureshi, op. cit., pp. 453–78.

10. S. Rajan, "India and Pakistan as Factors in Each Other's Foreign Policy and Relations", *International Studies*, 1961–62, p. 349.

11. Ibid.

12. G. F. Hudson, "Soviet Policy in Asia", *Soviet Survey* June–July 1957.

13. Keith Callard, *Pakistan's Foreign Policy: An Interpretation*, New York 1957, p. 11.

14. Ibid., p. 13.

15. Ibid., p. 12.

16. M. Brecher, *India's Foreign Policy: An Interpretation*, New York 1957, p. 19.

17. *Daily Telegraph*, March 26, 1957.

18. *The Times*, June 2, 1956.

19. *New York Times*, February 16, 1955.

20. Wayne A. Wilcox, *India, Pakistan and the Rise of China*, New York 1964, p. 40.

21. Ibid., pp. 38–9.

22. Adda B. Bozeman, "India's Foreign Policy Today", *World Politics*, 1957–58, p. 259.

23. Quoted in *Round Table*, 1962–63, p. 177.

24. Brecher, *India's Foreign Policy . . .*, op. cit., p. 17.

25. Stephens, *Pakistan*, op. cit., p. 267.

26. Jinnah, *Speeches* . . . , op. cit., p. 65.

27. Bhutto, op. cit., p. 17.

28. Donald E. Wilber, *Pakistan*, New Haven, Conn. 1964, p. 303.

29. Bhutto, op. cit., p. 18.

30. *Annual Register*, 1954, p. 108.

31. Sisir Gupta, *India's Relations with Pakistan, 1954–57*, Delhi 1958, mimeograph copy, p. 10.

32. Ibid.

33. See *Annual Register*, 1954, p. 108.

34. *Negotiations . . . Regarding the Kashmir Dispute* . . . , op. cit.

35. Stephens, *Pakistan*, op. cit., p. 268.

36. *Defence and Security in the Indian Ocean Area*, New York 1958, p. *viii*.

37. Cited in Nehru, *India's Foreign Policy*, op. cit.

38. *Defence and Security* . . . , op. cit., p. *iii*.

39. *Statesman*, January 4, 1954.

40. Ibid., January 1 and 4, March 3, 1954.

41. Ibid., March 3, 1954.

42. See S. N. Varma, *Trends in India's Foreign Policy, 1954–57*, Delhi 1957, p. 33.

43. Sir Dashwood Strettle, "Indian Army Before and After 1947", *Journal of the Royal Central Asian Society*, April 7, 1948.

44. Robert Trumbull, in *New York Times*, January 24, 1954.

45. *Round Table*, 1953–54, pp. 192–3.

46. Ibid., p. 196.

47. See *New York Herald Tribune*, February 18, 1954.

48. *Hindu*, March 8, 1954.

49. *Manchester Guardian*, March 2, 1954.

50. *Hindu*, March 11, 1954.

51. Quoted in *Hindu*, March 24, 1954.

52. *Round Table*, 1953–54, p. 78.

53. Hudson, op. cit.

54. Ibid.

55. *Manchester Guardian*, March 19, 1954.

56. Hudson, op. cit.

57. Article, "Islam" in *Soviet Encyclopaedia*, Moscow, 1953 edn, Vol. XVIII, pp. 516–19.

58. *Chronology of International Events and Documents*, November 19–December 2, 1953, London 1954, p. 770.

59. *Annual Register*, 1956, p. 161.

60. Ibid., p. 109.

61. *The Times*, March 12, 1956.
62. "The Bagdad Pact", *Round Table*, 1956–57, p. 221.
63. "Pakistan", ibid., p. 172.
64. Bhutto, op. cit., p. 20.
65. *Round Table*, 1956–57, p. 174.
66. *Defence and Security* . . . , op. cit., p. 83.
67. *The Times*, April 30, 1954.
68. Ibid.
69. Ibid.
70. Ibid., April 29, 1954.
71. Werner Levi, "The Evolution of India's Foreign Policy", *Yearbook of World Affairs*, 1958, p. 122.
72. *The Times*, editorial, May 4, 1954.
73. Ibid., April 23, 1955.
74. Ibid.
75. Ibid.
76. *Annual Register*, 1955, p. 165.
77. "Foreign Policy of Mr Nehru", *Round Table*, 1953–54, p. 367.

8. Divergent Foreign Policies: II. 1959–65

1. See G. W. Choudhury, "Pakistan's Relations with the West", *Eastern World*, London, July 1958.
2. *Annual Register*, 1959, p. 109.
3. Mohammad Ayub Khan, "The Pakistan-American Alliance: Stresses and Strains", *Foreign Affairs*, January 1964.
4. *Dawn*, May 8, 1959.
5. *Daily Telegraph*, October 24, 1959.
6. *Dawn*, May 11, 1959.
7. Based on personal interview with President Ayub and on unpublished documents of the government of Pakistan.
8. *Statesman*, May 5, 1959.
9. Reprinted in *Dawn*, May 8, 1959.
10. Ibid., November 26, 1959.
11. Reprinted in *New York Times*, April 30, 1959.
12. See article by President Ayub's private secretary, *New York Herald Tribune*, European edition, September 12–13, 1959.
13. *Round Table*, 1959–60, p. 81.
14. *Daily Telegraph*, November 27, 1959.
15. Norman Palmer, "India Faces a New Decade", *Current History*, March 1961.

16. *Daily Telegraph*, November 27, 1959.
17. *Round Table*, 1958–59, p. 399.
18. *The Times*, January 12, 1960.
19. Sharokh Sabaval, "India and Pakistan Edge Toward Amity", *Christian Science Monitor*, August 30, 1960.
20. "Lord Louis's Unfinished Business", *Daily Telegraph*, August 15, 1960.
21. C. L. Sulzberger, in *New York Times*, December 24, 1962.
22. John Grigg, "Kashmir and Texas", *Guardian*, December 19, 1965.
23. See *Hindu*, November 16, 1960.
24. Stephen Barber, "Cool West Wind in Pakistan", *Daily Telegraph*, July 11, 1961.
25. Selig S. Harrison, "Troubled India and Her Neighbors", *Foreign Affairs*, January 1965.
26. *Round Table*, 1960–61, p. 409.
27. Ibid., p. 409.
28. Ayub Khan, op. cit.
29. Quoted in *Round Table*, 1960–61, pp. 408–9.
30. Quoted in *Dawn*, editorial "And Now Mr Humphrey", September 15, 1964.
31. Ibid.
32. Barber, op, cit.
33. Ronald Segal, *The Crisis of India*, Harmondsworth 1965, p. 264.
34. Guy Wint, *Communist China's Crusade*, London and New York 1965, p. 100.
35. *Round Table*, 1962–63, p. 183.
36. Based on information in unpublished documents of the government of Pakistan.
37. Ayub Khan, op. cit.
38. Ibid.
39. See Trager, op. cit.
40. For details of India's arms aid, see Ayub Khan, op. cit., and Bhutto, op. cit., p. 105.
41. This account of the Indian arms build-up is based on personal interviews and on unpublished documents of the government of Pakistan. See also Ayub Khan, op. cit., and "Pakistan's Bitterness Inclines Her Towards China", *Observer Foreign News Service*, No. 19427, July 22, 1963.
42. *Dawn*, November 23, 1962.
43. *Christian Science Monitor*, May 8, 1962.
44. *Dawn*, January 7, 1963.
45. *Sunday Times*, October 20, 1963.

46. "Pakistan's Bitterness . . .", op. cit.

47. Ayub Khan, op. cit.

48. Hedrick Smith, *New York Times*, September 8, 1963.

49. *Round Table*, 1963–64, p. 176.

50. Ibid.

51. Harrison, op. cit.

52. Ibid.

53. Ayub Khan, op. cit.

54. Harrison, op. cit.,

55. Ibid.

56. Segal, op. cit., p. 267.

57. *Annual Register*, 1963, p. 88.

58. See "Is Pakistan's Foreign Policy Changing?", *New Commonwealth*, London, July 1962.

59. *Guardian*, May 5, 1962.

60. Ibid.

61. *Dawn*, May 11, 1962.

62. *New York Times*, July 7, 1962.

63. *Dawn*, August 31, 1962.

64. "Pakistan's Bitterness . . .", op. cit.

65. *Dawn*, July 9, 1963.

66. Ibid., July 18, 1963.

67. *Round Table*, 1963–64, p. 88.

68. *The Economist*, August 15, 1964.

69. *Hindu*, March 6, 1963.

70. *Christian Science Monitor*, August 7, 1961.

71. *The Times*, February 14, 1961.

72. Harrison, op. cit.

73. Ibid.

74. Ibid.

9. ARMED CONFLICT, 1965

1. President Ayub's broadcast on September 6, 1965.

2. Harold Wilson's letter to Francis Noel-Baker, published in *Dawn*, January 6, 1966.

3. *The Times*, October 28, 1965.

4. *New Statesman*, September 10, 1965.

5. *The Times*, September 7, 1965.

6. Ibid.

7. *Guardian*, September 7, 1965.

8. *Daily Telegraph*, September 7, 1965.
9. See chapter 2.
10. *Tribune*, Ambala (East Punjab), September 18, 1965.
11. *Sunday Times*, September 18, 1965.
12. Harrison, op. cit.
13. Ayub's broadcast on September 6, 1965.
14. Ayub, op. cit.
15. Ayub's broadcast on September 6, 1965.
16. *New Statesman*, September 10, 1965.
17. *The Times*, September 11, 1965.
18. Ibid., September 13, 1965.
19. Harold Wilson's letter, op. cit.
20. *The Economist*, January 4, 1964.
21. *The Times*, February 14, 1964.
22. Ibid., February 20, 1964.
23. Ibid., March 29, 1964.
24. *Dawn*, April 21, 1964.
25. *Round Table*, 1963–64, p. 388.
26. Ibid.
27. Ibid., 1965–66, p. 76.
28. *The Times*, December 20, 1964.
29. Ibid.
30. Ibid.
31. *Round Table*, 1965–66, p. 76.
32. Ibid.
33. Tom Stacey, "War in the Desolate Place", *Sunday Times*, May 2, 1965.
34. *Observer* Foreign News Service, No. 21422, May 12, 1965.
35. Ibid.
36. Stacey, op. cit.
37. *Statesman*, April 29, 1965.
38. Stacey, op. cit.
39. *Dawn*, July 1, 1965.
40. Stacey, op. cit.
41. *Dawn*, September 16, 1965.
42. Ibid.
43. *Round Table*, 1965–66, p. 77.
44. Ibid.
45. *Dawn*, September 2, 1965.
46. Jacques Nevard, "India versus Pakistan", *New York Times*, May 2, 1965.
47. *New York Times*, September 7, 1965.

48. For details, see: *Sunday Times*, September 12, 1965; *Sunday Telegraph*, September 12, 1965; *Financial Times*, September 7, 1965; *New York Times*, September 7, 1965.
49. *Sunday Telegraph*, September 12, 1965.
50. *The Times*, September 11, 1965.
51. *Guardian*, September 9, 1965.
52. Ibid., September 11, 1965.
53. *Daily Telegraph*, September 13, 1965.
54. *Sunday Telegraph*, September 12, 1965.
55. *Guardian*, September 8, 1965.
56. *Observer*, September 12, 1965.
57. See *New York Herald Tribune*, September 20, 1965.
58. *Soviet News*, London, September 13, 1965.
59. *Financial Times*, September 8, 1965.
60. See *Observer* Foreign News Service, No. 22227, January 12, 1965.
61. *The Times*, September 8, 1965.
62. Anthony Lukas, "India's Shastri: Mission to Tashkent", *New York Times*, December 26, 1965.
63. *Dawn*, January 15, 1966.
64. Ibid.
65. *The Times*, January 11, 1966.
66. Reprinted in *Dawn*, January 21, 1966.
67. *Soviet News*, January 12, 1966.
68. *The Times*, April 20, 1966.
69. *Dawn*, June 4, 1966.
70. *The Times*, April 19, 1966.
71. See *The Times*, June 10, 1966.

SELECT BIBLIOGRAPHY

Including works cited in the text and in References

AHMED, J., *Speeches and Writings of Jinnah*, 2 vols, Ashraf, Lahore 1952.

AHMED, Mushtaq, *The United Nations and Pakistan*, Pakistan Institute of International Affairs, Karachi 1955.

ALBIRUNI, A.H., *Makers of Pakistan and Modern Muslim India*, Ashraf, Lahore 1950.

AMBEDKAR, B. R., *Pakistan and the Partition of India*, Thacker, Bombay 1946.

ATTLEE, C. R., *As It Happened*, Heinemann, London 1954.

AZAD, Abul Kalam, *India Wins Freedom*, Longman, London, Bombay, New York 1959.

AZIZ, K. K., *Britain and Muslim India*, Heinemann, London 1953.

BAZAZ, Premnath, *The History of Struggle for Freedom in Kashmir*, Kashmir Publishing Company, New Delhi 1954.

BERKES, Ross North and BEDI, M. S., *The Diplomacy of India: Indian Foreign Policy in the United Nations*, Stanford University Press, Stanford, Calif. 1958.

BHUTTO, Z. A., *Speeches Before the Security Council, 1964*, Ministry of Foreign Affairs, Government of Pakistan, Karachi n.d.

—— *Foreign Policy of Pakistan*, Pakistan Institute of International Affairs, Karachi 1964.

BIRDWOOD, Lord, *A Continent Decides*, Hale, London 1953; published in USA as *India and Pakistan*, Praeger, New York 1954.

—— *Two Nations and Kashmir*, Hale, London 1956.

BLACK, Joseph E. and THOMPSON, Kenneth W., *Foreign Policies in a World of Change*, Harper, New York 1963—especially the chapters on the foreign policy of India and of Pakistan.

BOLITHO, Hector, *Jinnah: Creator of Pakistan*, Murray, London 1954.

BOWLES, Chester, *Ambassador's Report*, Gollancz, London 1954; Harper, New York, 1954.

BRECHER, Michael, *The Struggle for Kashmir*, Oxford University Press, New York and London, 1952.

—— *India's Foreign Policy: An Interpretation*, Institute of Pacific Relations, New York 1957.

BRECHER, Michael, *Nehru: A Political Biography*, Oxford University Press, London 1959.

BROWN, W. Norman, *The United States and India and Pakistan*, Harvard University Press, Cambridge, Mass. 1963.

CALLARD, Keith, *Pakistan's Foreign Policy: An Interpretation*, Institute of Pacific Relations, New York 1957.

CASEY, R. G., *An Australian in India*, Hollis and Carter, London 1947.

—— *Friends and Neighbours*, Michigan State University Press, East Lansing, Mich. 1958.

CHOUDHURI, Mohammad Ahsen, *Pakistan and the Regional Pacts*, East Publications, Karachi 1958.

CHOUDHURY, G. W. and PARVEZ, Hasan, *Pakistan's External Relations*, Pakistan Institute of International Affairs, Karachi 1958.

CHOUDHURY, G. W., *Constitutional Development in Pakistan*, 1959, rev. edn, Longman, London 1968; Institute of Pacific Relations, New York 1968.

CONNEL, John, *Auchinleck*, Cassell, London 1959.

COUPLAND, R., *The Indian Problem*, Oxford University Press, London and New York 1944.

—— *India: A Statement*, Oxford University Press, London and New York 1945.

CUMMING, Sir John (ed.), *Political India, 1832–1932*, Oxford University Press, London 1932.

CURRAN, J. A., *Militant Hinduism in Indian Politics: A Story of RSSS*, Institute of Pacific Relations, New York 1951.

DAS GUPTA, J. B., *Indo-Pakistan Relations, 1947–55*, Djambatan, Amsterdam 1958.

DESHMUKH, Sir C. H., *The Commonwealth As India Sees It*, Cambridge University Press, Cambridge 1963.

EEKELEN, William F., *Indian Foreign Policy and the Border Dispute with China*, The Hague 1964.

FIFIELD, Russel, *Southeast Asia in US Policy*, Praeger, New York 1963.

FISCHER, Louis, *Russia, America and the World*, Harper, New York 1961.

GREENE, Felix, *The Wall Has Two Sides*, Cape, paperback edn, London 1964.

GRIFFITHS, Sir Percival, *The British Impact on India*, Macdonald, London 1952.

—— *Modern India*, 1957, 4th edn, Benn, London 1965; Praeger, New York 1965.

GUPTA, Sisir, *India's Relations with Pakistan, 1954–57*, Indian Council of World Affairs, New Delhi 1958.

GWYER, Sir Maurice and Appadorai, A., *Speeches and Documents on the Indian Constitution, 1921–47*, Oxford University Press, London and New York 1957.

HARRISON, Selig S., *India: The Most Dangerous Decades*, Princeton University Press, Princeton, N.J. 1960.

―― (ed.), *India and the United States*, Macmillan, New York 1961.

HASAN, K. Sarwar, *Pakistan and the Commonwealth*, Pakistan Institute of International Affairs, Karachi 1950.

―― *The Strategic Interests of Pakistan*, Pakistan Institute of International Affairs, Karachi 1954.

―― *Pakistan and the United Nations*, Manhattan Publishing Co., New York 1960.

Indian Council of World Affairs, *India and the United Nations*, New York 1957.

―― *Defence and Security in the Indian Ocean Area*, New York 1958.

ISMAY, Lord, *Memoirs*, Heinemann, London 1960.

JINNAH, Mohammad Ali, *Speeches as Governor-General of Pakistan, 1947-48*, Pakistan Publications, Karachi n.d.

JUNG, Nawab Moin Nawaz, *The Situation in Hyderabad*, Karachi n.d.

KARUNAKARAN, K. P., *India in World Affairs*, Vol. I, 1947-50, Vol. II, 1950-53, Indian Council of World Affairs, New Delhi 1951. See also Rajan.

KENNEDY, D. E., *The Security of Southern Asia*, Chatto and Windus, London 1965.

KHAN, Abdul Waheed, *India Wins Freedom: The Other Side*, Karachi 1961.

KHAN, Liaquat Ali, *Pakistan: The Heart of Asia*, Harvard University Press, Cambridge, Mass. 1950.

KHAN, Mohammad Ayub, *Speeches and Statements*, 6 vols, Pakistan Publications, Karachi n.d.

KHAN, Sir M. Zafrullah, *Pakistan's Foreign Relations*, Pakistan Institute of International Affairs, Karachi 1951.

KORBEL, Joseph, *Danger in Kashmir*, Princeton University Press, Princeton, N.J. 1954; Oxford University Press, London 1954.

LAHIRY, Ashutosh, *Defence of India*, Alpha-Beta Publications, Calcutta 1965.

LAMB, Alastair, *The China-India Border*, Royal Institute of International Affairs, Oxford University Press, London and New York 1964.

LEVI, Werner, *Free India in Asia*, University of Minnesota Press, Minneapolis 1952.

LUMBY, E. W. R., *The Transfer of Power in India*, Allen and Unwin, London 1954.

"M.R.T.", *Pakistan and Muslim India*, Bombay 1942.

MANSERGH, Nicholas P. N., *Documents and Speeches on British Commonwealth Affairs, 1931-52*, Vol. II., Oxford University Press, London and New York 1953.

MENON, V. P., *The Transfer of Power in India*, Longman, London and Calcutta

1957; Princeton University Press, Princeton, N.J. 1959.

MOON, Penderel, *Divide and Quit*, Chatto and Windus, London 1961; University of California Press, Berkeley, Calif. 1961.

MOSLEY, Leonard, *The Last Days of the British Raj*, Weidenfeld and Nicolson, London 1952.

NEHRU, Jawharlal, *The Unity of India*, Drummond, London 1941.

——— *The Discovery of India*, Signet Press, Calcutta 1946; Day, New York 1946.

——— *India's Foreign Policy: Selected Speeches, September 1946–April 1961*, Government of India, New Delhi 1961.

NOORANI, A. G., *The Kashmir Question*, Manaktalas, Bombay 1964.

PANIKKAR, K. M., *India and the Indian Ocean*, Allen and Unwin, London 1945; Macmillan, New York 1945.

——— *Asia and Western Dominance*, Allen and Unwin, London 1953.

PATTERSON, G. N., *Peking Versus Delhi*, Faber, London 1963; Praeger, New York 1964.

PHILIPS, C. H., *The Evolution of India and Pakistan, 1858–1947*, Oxford University Press, London and New York 1962.

PRASAD, Rajendra, *India Divided*, Hind Kitabs, Bombay 1946.

QURESHI, I. H., *The Muslim Community of the Indo-Pakistan Subcontinent*, The Hague 1962.

——— *The Struggle for Pakistan*, University of Karachi Press, Karachi 1965.

RAJAN, M. S., *India in World Affairs, 1954–56*, Indian Council of World Affairs, New Delhi 1964.

RAVOOF, A. A., *Meet Mr Jinnah*, Lahore 1945.

SEGAL, Ronald, *The Crisis of India*, Penguin, Harmondsworth and Baltimore 1965.

SHERWANI, L. A. et al., *Foreign Policy of Pakistan*, Allies Book Corporation, Karachi 1964.

SIDDIQUI, Aslam, *Pakistan Seeks Security*, Longman, London 1960.

SMITH, W. C., *Pakistan as an Islamic State*, Ashraf, Lahore 1951.

SPEAR, Percival, *India, Pakistan and the West*, 3rd edn, Oxford University Press, London and New York 1958.

——— *India: A Modern History*, London 9; University of Michigan Press, Ann Arbor, Mich. 1961.

STEPHENS, Ian, *Horned Moon*, Chatto and Windus, London 1953.

——— *Pakistan*, 1962, 3rd edn, Benn, London 1967; Praeger, New York 1967.

——— *Monsoon Morning*, Benn, London 1966.

SYMONDS, Richard, *The Making of Pakistan*, Faber, London 1950; Transatlantic Arts, Hollywood, Fla. 1950.

TINKER, Hugh, *India and Pakistan: A Political Analysis*, 1962; rev. edn, Pall

Mall, London 1967; Praeger, New York 1968.

TUKER, Sir Francis, *While Memory Serves*, Cassell, London 1950.

VARMA, S. N., *Trends in India's Foreign Policy, 1954–57*, Indian Council of World Affairs, New Delhi 1957.

WILBER, Donald E., *Pakistan*, Yale University Press, New Haven, Conn. 1964.

WILCOX, Wayne A., *India, Pakistan and the Rise of China*, Walker, New York 1964.

WINT, Guy, *Communist China's Crusade*, Pall Mall, London 1965; Praeger, New York 1965.

——— (ed.), *Asia: A Handbook*, Blond, London 1966; Praeger, New York 1966.

ARTICLES

"Foreign Policy of Mr Nehru", *Round Table*, September 1954.

"Is Pakistan's Foreign Policy Changing?", *New Commonwealth*, July 1961.

"India: After Chinese Aggression", *Round Table*, March 1962.

"India: Non-Alignment and the Great Rift", *Round Table*, September 1963.

"India and Her Neighbours", *Round Table*, September 1956.

"India and Pakistan", *Round Table*, June 1964.

"Indo-Pakistan Relations: Areas of Conflict", *Round Table*, March 1960.

"Neighbours in Asia", *Round Table*, December 1956.

"Pakistan: A Flexible Foreign Policy", *Round Table*, December 1963.

"Pakistan: A Step-Child of the West", *Round Table*, September 1963.

"Pakistan: A Turning-Point for Asia", *Round Table*, March 1963.

"Pakistan: America in the Indian Ocean", *Round Table*, March 1964.

"Pakistan: Conflicting Views on Foreign Policy", *Round Table*, June 1958.

"Pakistan: Foreign Policy Under Review", *Round Table*, March 1962.

"Pakistan and Her Neighbours", *Round Table*, June 1956.

"Pakistan's Bitterness Inclines Her Towards China", *Observer* Foreign News Service, No. 19427, July 12, 1963.

"Pakistan's Relations with the People's Republic of China", *Pakistan Horizon*, 3rd quarter 1961.

BARAI, B., "Three Years of Indo-Pakistan Trade: A Review", *Pakistan Economic Journal*, Dacca, December 1950.

BLACK, Eugene R., "The Indus: A Moral For Nation ", *New York Times Magazine*, December 11, 1960.

BOZEMAN, A. B., "India's Foreign Policy Today", *World Politics*, 1957–58.

CHOUDHURI, Mohammad Ahsen, "Pakistan and the Regional Pacts", *Pakistan Horizon*, Karachi, June 1956.

CHOUDHURY, G. W., "The Impact of Islam in Pakistan", *Current History*, June 1957.

────── "Pakistan's Relations with the West", *Eastern World*, July 1958.

────── "Pakistan-India Relations", *Pakistan Horizon*, July 1958.

────── "Pakistan Under General Ayub", *Current History*, March 1961.

FOWLER, F. J., "Indo-Pakistan Water Dispute", *Year Book of World Affairs*, 1955.

GRIFFITHS, Sir Percival, "India and Pakistan", *Journal of the Royal Central Asian Society*, Vol. XLVIII, 1961.

HARRISON, Selig S., "Troubled India and Her Neighbors", *Foreign Affairs*, January 1965.

HUDSON, G. F., "Soviet Policy in Asia", *Soviet Survey*, 1957.

KHAN, Mohammad Ayub, "The Pakistan-American Alliance: Stresses and Strains", *Foreign Affairs*, January 1964.

KRIPALANI, J. B., "For Principled Neutrality", *Foreign Affairs*, October 1959.

LEVI, Werner, "Evolution of India's Foreign Policy", *Year Book of World Affairs*, 1958.

NAEMA, Sultan Begam, "Indo-Pakistan Trade Relations", *Pakistan Horizon*, September 1950.

PALMER, Norman, "India's Outlook on Foreign Affairs", *Current History*, 1956.

────── "The United States and Pakistan", *Current History*, March 1958.

────── "India Faces A New Decade", *Current History*, March 1961.

PANDIT, Vivaya Lakshmi, "India's Foreign Policy", *Foreign Affairs*, April 1956.

RAJAN, M. S., "India and Pakistan as Factors in Each Other's Foreign Policy and Relations", *International Relations*, April 1962.

RASTOGI, B. C., "Alignment and Non-Alignment in Pakistan's Foreign Policy, 1947–60", *International Studies*, October 1961.

TRAGER, Frank N., "The United States and Pakistan: A Failure of Diplomacy", *Orbis*, Vol. IX, No. 3, 1965.

OFFICIAL PUBLICATIONS AND DOCUMENTS

I. UNITED NATIONS

India's formal complaint to the United Nations: s/628, January 2, 1948.

Pakistan's counter-complaint to the United Nations: s/646, January 15, 1948.

First Interim Report of the United Nations Commission for India and Pakistan (UNCIP): s/1000, November 22, 1948.

Second Interim Report of UNCIP: s/1196, January 10, 1949.

Third Interim Report of UNCIP: s/1430, December 9, 1949.

Debates on Kashmir in the Security Council: There have been lengthy debates on Kashmir since 1948, but the principal arguments advanced by India and Pakistan may be found in the Security Council Official Records for 1948, especially No. 1, 15, April 19; No. 6, 74, May 26; supplement for November.

Debates on Junagadh: see Security Council Official Records for 1948, No. 64.

Debates on Hyderabad: see Security Council Official Records for 1949, No. 28.

For UN representatives' reports on Kashmir, see under Pakistan below.

2. INDIA

India States, Government of India, New Delhi 1950.

Indo-Pakistan Trade Relations, August 15–December 31, 1949, Government of India, New Delhi 1950.

Pakistan's War Propaganda Against India, September 1950–June 1951, Government of India, New Delhi 1951.

White Paper on Jammu and Kashmir, Government of India, New Delhi 1948.

All-India Congress Committee Resolutions on Foreign Policy, 1947–57, All-India Congress Committee, New Delhi 1957.

Background of India's Foreign Policy, The, All-India Congress Committee, New Delhi 1952.

3. PAKISTAN

Cease-fire and After, Pakistan Publications, Karachi 1965.

Constituent Assembly of Pakistan Debates: Official Reports, Government of Pakistan, Karachi 1947.

India Sets the Subcontinent Alight, Pakistan Publications, Nos. 1 and 2, Karachi 1965.

India-Pakistan Question, The, Permanent Mission of Pakistan to the United Nations, New York 1962.

India's Threat to Pakistan: Correspondence between the Prime Ministers of Pakistan and India, July 15–August 11, 1951, Ministry of Foreign Affairs, Karachi n.d.

India's War Propaganda Against Pakistan, Ministry of Information, Karachi n.d.

Indus Waters Treaty, The, Government of Pakistan, Karachi 1960.

Inside Kashmir, Government of West Punjab, Lahore 1948.

Kashmir and the People's Voice, Pakistan Publications, Karachi 1964.

Liaquat-Nehru Agreement, The, Ministry of Foreign Affairs, Karachi 1950.

Negotiations Between the Prime Ministers of Pakistan and India Regarding the Kashmir Dispute, June 1953–September 1954, Government of Pakistan, Karachi n.d.

No-War Declaration and Canal Water Dispute: Correspondence Between the Prime

Ministers of Pakistan and India, January 18–November 24, 1950, Government of Pakistan, Karachi 1950.

Pakistan: The Struggle for Irrigation Water and Existence, Embassy of Pakistan, Washington, D.C. 1953.

President Ayub on the Crisis Over Kashmir, Pakistan Publications, Karachi 1965.

President Ayub's Offer of Friendship to India, Pakistan Publications, Karachi 1964.

Report of the Asir Commission on the Eviction of Indian Muslims in Assam, Government of East Pakistan, Dacca 1964.

Reports of the United Nations Commission for India and Pakistan, Government of Pakistan, Karachi 1948 and 1949.

Reports on Kashmir by United Nations Representatives, Government of Pakistan, Karachi 1962.

4. UNITED STATES

Kashmir: A Chronology, 1947–65, Bureau of Intelligence and Research, Research Memorandum RNA 55, Washington, D.C. 1965.

Pakistan Faith Builds a New Force in Asia, Department of State, Washington, D.C., March 1953.

Report of the Special Study Mission to the Middle East, South and South-East Asia and the Pacific, Senate Committee on Foreign Relations, Washington, D.C. 1956.

Report on India by Ambassador George V. Allen, Senate Committee on Foreign Relations, Washington, D.C. 1954.

INDEX

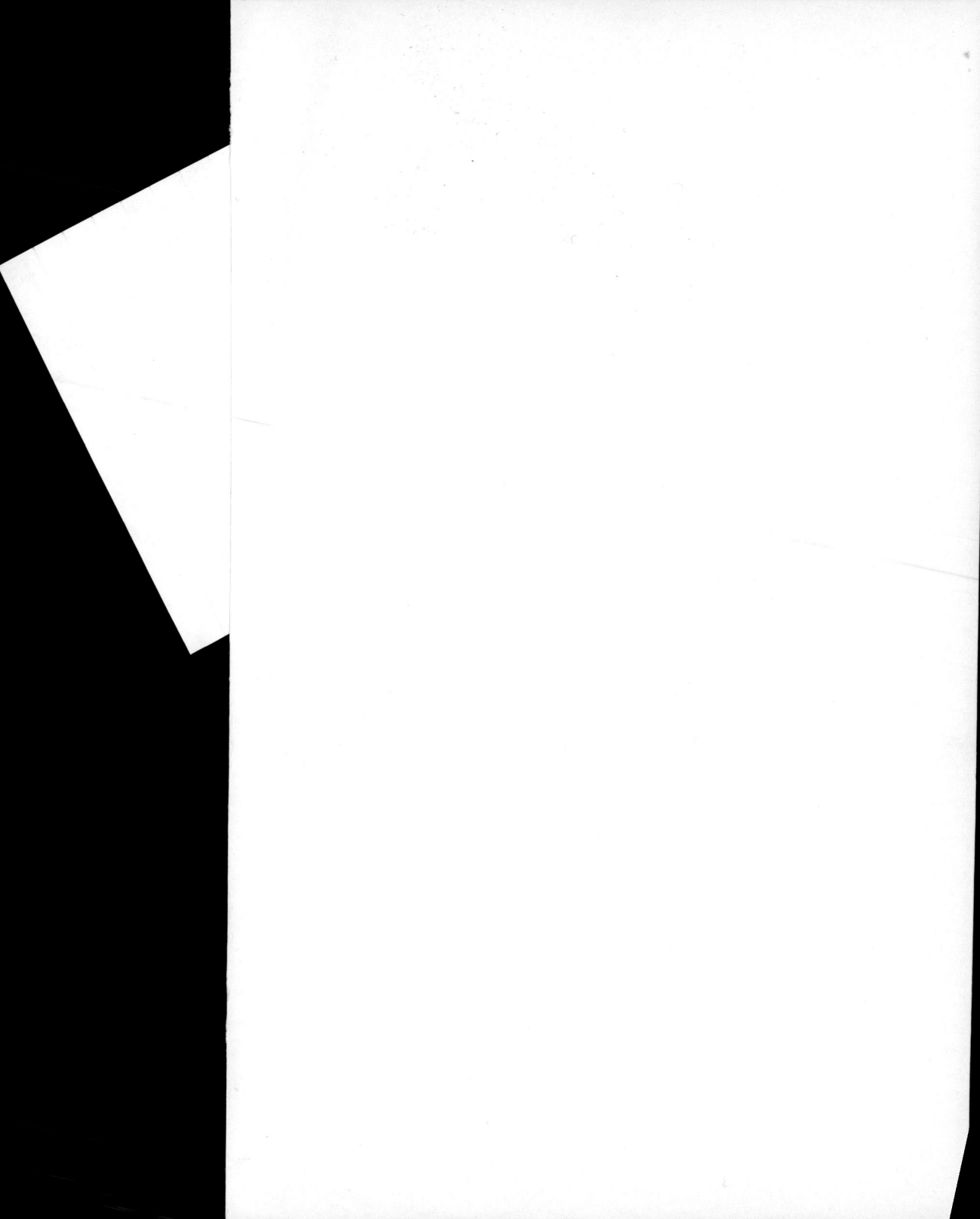